POLITICAL AND ECONOMIC FORMS
OF MODERNITY

UNDERSTANDING MODERN SOCIETIES: AN INTRODUCTION

Series editor: Stuart Hall

Book 1   *Formations of Modernity*
edited by Stuart Hall and Bram Gieben

Book 2   *Political and Economic Forms of Modernity*
edited by John Allen, Peter Braham and Paul Lewis

Book 3   *Social and Cultural Forms of Modernity*
edited by Robert Bocock and Kenneth Thompson

Book 4   *Modernity and its Futures*
edited by Stuart Hall, David Held and Anthony McGrew

For general availability of all the books in the series, please contact your regular supplier or, in case of difficulty, Polity Press.

This book forms part of the Open University course D213 *Understanding Modern Societies*. Details of this and other Open University courses can be obtained from the Central Enquiry Service, The Open University, P.O. Box 200, Milton Keynes, MK7 2YZ; Tel: 0908 653078.

Cover illustration: John Tandy *Abstract composition* (*c.* 1930) Private Collection, London. Reproduced by courtesy of the Redfern Gallery, London, and by kind permission of Mrs Suzanne Tandy.
Photo: A.C. Cooper.

POLITICAL AND ECONOMIC FORMS OF MODERNITY

EDITED BY JOHN ALLEN
PETER BRAHAM AND PAUL LEWIS

POLITY PRESS IN ASSOCIATION WITH THE OPEN UNIVERSITY

Copyright © The Open University 1992

First published 1992 by Polity Press in association with Blackwell Publishers Ltd
and The Open University
Reprinted 1993, 1995

Editorial office:
Polity Press
65 Bridge Street,
Cambridge CB2 1UR, UK

Marketing and production:
Blackwell Publishers Ltd
108 Cowley Road,
Oxford OX4 1JF, UK

ISBN 0 7456 0961 9
ISBN 0 7456 0962 7 (pbk)

A CIP catalogue record for this book is available from the British Library.

Edited, designed and typeset by The Open University

Printed in Great Britain by Redwood Books, Trowbridge

CONTENTS

Understanding Modern Societies Course Team

Stuart Hall	Professor of Sociology and Course Team Chair
Maureen Adams	Secretary
John Allen	Senior Lecturer in Economic Geography
Margaret Allott	Discipline Secretary, Sociology
Robert Bocock	Senior Lecturer in Sociology
David Boswell	Senior Lecturer in Sociology
Peter Braham	Lecturer in Sociology
Vivienne Brown	Lecturer in Economics
Dianne Cook	Secretary
Robert Cookson	Senior Editor, Social Sciences
Helen Crowley	Lecturer in Women's Studies, North London Polytechnic
James Donald	Senior Lecturer in Cultural and Community Studies, University of Sussex
Paul du Gay	Post-graduate student, Sociology
Molly Freeman	Discipline Secretary, Sociology
Bram Gieben	Staff Tutor, Social Sciences
Peter Hamilton	Lecturer in Sociology
David Held	Professor in Politics and Sociology
Paul Lewis	Senior Lecturer in Politics
Vic Lockwood	Senior Producer, BBC
Anthony McGrew	Senior Lecturer in Politics
Gregor McLennan	Professor of Sociology, Massey University, NZ
David Scott-Macnab	Editor, Social Sciences
Graeme Salaman	Senior Lecturer in Sociology
Jane Sheppard	Graphic Designer
Paul Smith	Media Librarian
Keith Stribley	Course Manager
Kenneth Thompson	Professor in Sociology
Alison Tucker	Producer, BBC
Pauline Turner	Secretary
Diane Watson	Staff Tutor, Social Sciences
David Wilson	Editor, Book Trade
Chris Wooldridge	Editor, Social Sciences

Consultants

Harriet Bradley	Senior Lecturer, Sunderland Polytechnic
Tom Burden	Tutor Panel
Tony Darkes	Tutor Panel
Celia Lury	Lecturer in Sociology, University of Lancaster
Denise Riley	Researcher in political philosophy
Alan Scott	Lecturer in Politics, University of East Anglia
Jeffrey Weeks	Professor in Social Relations, Bristol Polytechnic
Geoffrey Whitty	Professor of Sociology of Education, Institute of Education, University of London
Steven Yearley	Professor of Sociology, University of Ulster

External Assessor

Bryan Turner	Professor of Sociology, University of Essex

PREFACE

Political and Economic Forms of Modernity is the second book in a new series of sociology textbooks which aims to provide a comprehensive, innovative and stimulating introduction to sociology. The four books in the series, which is entitled *Understanding Modern Societies: An Introduction*, are listed on page ii. They have been written to suit students and readers who have no prior knowledge of sociology and are designed to be used on a variety of social science courses in universities and colleges. Although part of a series, each book is self-contained to facilitate use with students studying different aspects of the history, sociology and ideas of modern society and its international context.

The four books form the central part of an Open University course, also called *Understanding Modern Societies*. Open University courses are produced by an extensive course team consisting of academic authors and consultants, a panel of experienced tutors, an external academic assessor, editors and designers, BBC producers, academic administrators and secretaries. (The full course team responsible for this course is listed on the opposite page.) Every chapter has been subjected to wide-ranging discussion and improvement at each of several draft stages. The result is a unique series of textbooks which draw on the cumulative academic research and teaching experience of the Open University and the wider academic community.

All four books have three distinctive features. First, each chapter provides not only a descriptive, historical account of the key social processes which shaped modern industrial societies, and which are now, once again, rapidly transforming them, but also analysis of the key concepts, issues and current debates in the related academic literature. Secondly, each chapter includes a number of extracts from classic and contemporary books and articles, all of them pertinent to the chapter. These are printed conveniently at the end of the chapter in which they are discussed. They can be distinguished from the main text (and can thus be found easily) by the continuous line down the left-hand margin. The third important feature of the text is that it is *interactive*: every chapter contains specially designed exercises, questions and activities to help readers understand, reflect upon and retain the main teaching points at issue. From the long experience of Open University course writing, we have found that all readers will benefit from such a package of materials carefully designed for students working with a fair degree of independence.

While each book is free-standing, there are some cross-references to the other books in the series to aid readers using all the books. These take the following form: 'see Book 1 (Hall and Gieben, 1992), Chapter 4'. For further information on a writer or concept, the reader is sometimes referred to the *Penguin Dictionary of Sociology*. Full bibliographic details of this dictionary are provided where relevant at the end of each chapter, together with other references which suggest further reading which can be undertaken in each area.

In the long collaborative process by which Open University materials are made, the editors of such a volume are only the most obvious of those who have helped to shape its chapters. There are many others with responsibilities for the detailed and painstaking work of bringing a book with so many parts to completion. Our external assessor, Professor Bryan Turner, provided invaluable intellectual guidance, comment, advice, stimulus and encouragement at every stage of the production of these books. Our course manager, Keith Stribley, has done an excellent job of helping us all to keep to schedules, maintaining high standards of editorial consistency, and liaising between course team academics, editors and production. We owe special thanks to Molly Freeman, Maureen Adams, Pauline Turner, Dianne Cook and Margaret Allott for really marvellous secretarial support. Rarely in the history of word-processing can so many drafts have been produced so swiftly by so few. Our Open University editors, Chris Wooldridge, David Scott-Macnab, David Wilson and Robert Cookson, have improved each chapter with their insight and professionalism, usually under quite unreasonable pressures of time, and with unfailing good nature. Thanks also to Paul Smith, our media librarian, for his creative work in finding so many of the illustrations. Debbie Seymour, of Polity Press, has been a constant source of encouragement and good sense.

Finally, the chapter authors have borne stoically our innumerable criticisms and suggestions, and have managed to preserve the essence of their original creations through successive rounds of amendments and cuts. Their scholarship and commitment have made this book what it is.

John Allen, Peter Braham and Paul Lewis

INTRODUCTION

John Allen and Paul Lewis

Political and Economic Forms of Modernity continues the story about the formation of modern societies explored in the first book of this series. It builds upon some of the modern developments that were in place, though not yet fully formed, at the start of the nineteenth century. Modernity, as conceived here, coincides with the beginnings of a fully industrialized, capitalist economy and the development of the nation-state system. For this reason, our focus is selective, concentrating upon modern political and economic processes and institutions in western, advanced societies, although moving beyond such a focus where appropriate to include the global network of relations that marks out modernity from its earlier tentative forms (discussed in the previous volume, *Formations of Modernity*).

Some of the issues and processes that we are concerned with span the whole of the modern period, whereas others take shape only in particular eras. Citizenship, for example, has a long and diverse history, whereas the welfare state is of more recent origin. Similarly, industrialism has been a marked characteristic of modern life, yet arguably only reached its zenith in the form of mass production in the second half of the twentieth century. Indeed, this also points to another way in which we have been selective. Although our enquiry into political and economic forms of modernity ranges across different time periods, taking in developments over the last three centuries or so, the principle focus of this book is the twentieth century, and especially the period after 1945. This volume explores modern political and economic forms in a period which many take to be the peak of their development. This is therefore not a straightforward chronological approach, but rather one which identifies certain moments within the modern period as key to our understanding of modern political and economic developments. It is in such moments that the dynamism of these developments is likely to be most apparent.

The first half of this book is organized around modern states and their political forms, especially those of liberal democracy and citizenship. It confronts a number of critical questions about the nature of modern politics, engaging in particular with the idea that there is a distinctive modern political culture and examining how far this is expressed in new forms of social movement. The second half of the book is organized around the nature of modern industry, with particular attention paid to the forms of manufacturing and service work within a modern economy. An explicit attempt is made to identify the dynamic characteristics of modern industry; that is, those parts of an economy which shape and influence the direction of economic change and workplace experience.

As in every kind of social enquiry, however, the question of which political and economic features are representative of the dominant character of modern societies is the subject of much debate. For example, the extent and the influence of Henry Ford's mass production techniques within modern economies is contested, as is the significance and role of mass democracy in modern political life. One of the aims of this book is to open up these kinds of issues which, in different ways, reveal something about the heartlands of modern political and economic life and its institutions. This book does not, therefore, attempt to convey an exhaustive account of the political and economic dimensions of modern society. Rather, its aims are to introduce some of the key political and economic forms which make up the modern order, and to examine the various ways in which they have been debated and interpreted. We stop short, however, of considering whether this order may now be coming to an end and whether we are perhaps witnessing a series of changes that are taking us beyond modernity into a new era. This topic is the subject-matter of Book 4, *Modernity and its Futures*, the final volume in this series.

Political and Economic Forms of Modernity comprises eight chapters. The book opens with an analysis of the idea and limits of modern democracy. In Chapter 1, 'Democracy in modern societies', Paul Lewis examines the origins of democracy and the form it has taken in modern societies. Political democracy and the democratic ideal have their roots in the ancient world, but it is in modern societies that democracy and democratic forms have become most widespread. The chapter looks at the processes that contributed to this outcome and the developments within democracy itself that have made it currently the most widely-approved and dynamic of modern political forms. It is important, though, to point out at this early stage that this view emerges from the perspective of the early 1990s, and that democracy has by no means been universally acclaimed as the most appropriate form of political modernity even in relatively recent times. Prior to the Second World War, dictatorship was also widely recognized as a suitable form of rule in modern societies, and Hitler and Mussolini had their admirers well beyond the borders of Germany and Italy. Even later, one-party rule was frequently seen as a solution to the problems of backwardness in post-colonial societies and the most appropriate vehicle for economic development.

By the 1980s, however, dictatorship found few apologists and liberal-democratic forms were extending their influence throughout the world. Indications of democratic development were growing stronger across the globe, from Asia to Latin America. Socialist democracy, as practised in the Soviet Union and Eastern Europe, was increasingly showing its shortcomings and attracting criticisms from within its own societies as well as from more established competitors. But democracy, as a concept that has been applied from ancient Greece to many areas of the late twentieth-century world, and which is capable of developing variants as diverse as those of liberal democracy and socialist democracy, spanning societies as different as those of advanced capitalism and others experiencing socialist industrialization, is clearly open to alternative interpretations and has been used to describe a wide range of institutions and political practices.

The contrasts between direct democracy and representative, or liberal, democracy have been at the heart of many of the critical political conflicts of the modern world and have entered into some of its most significant ideological battles. In general, the Marxist political tradition has been identified with notions that are antithetical to the ideas and practice of representative democracy and liberalism. This conflict emerged as the dominant ideological contrast of the twentieth century after the Russian revolution of 1917. Only recently has the fierceness of this competition begun to abate as the political, economic and social shortcomings of socialist democracy in the Soviet Union became increasingly evident, and as the countries of East-Central Europe removed themselves from its sphere of influence.

But liberal democracy has by no means been free of its own problems and these are explored in Chapter 1 in association with a reading by Norberto Bobbio, who identifies three major obstacles to the development of political democracy under the conditions of modern society. According to Bobbio, the complexity and level of technological development which is part of modernity, the bureaucratization of modern societies, and the increased problems faced by democratic systems in satisfying the demands made of them, all produce serious obstacles to the implementation of the democratic ideal. These factors, it is not difficult to recognize, are closely related to the conditions of modern statehood: its characteristically high levels of technocracy and bureaucracy, and the apparent tendency of state power to be exercised in its own interests rather than those of the democratic society with which it coexists.

Chapter 2, 'The state in advanced capitalist societies', moves on to consider the nature of the advanced capitalist state and the relations it has developed with modern society. Modern democracy did not emerge in its full form until the twentieth century, and has been subject to considerable change during recent decades. Over the same period the state has grown enormously in size and influence, directing many of its activities to the diverse functions of welfare provision and the accumulation and exercise of military power. In this chapter, Anthony McGrew sets out to identify common patterns within the diversity of the advanced capitalist world in terms of the development, characteristics, activities and functions of the state. While highly developed states with extensive powers seem, like democracies, to be one of the dominant political forms of modernity, they also show considerable diversity and have significant differences within their broad similarities. Nevertheless, the development of the potential to wage industrialized warfare since the end of the nineteenth century and the establishment of the extensive welfare systems, particularly since 1945, have been powerful factors conditioning the emergence of a particular kind of advanced capitalist state.

What underlies this enormous growth of the state in modern societies, and in whose interests does it act? Has it expanded in response to social pressure and society's demands for state functions, or is it in some way autonomous, having gained the capacity for self-generating growth? Again, McGrew suggests, a differentiated answer might be the most plausible one because advanced capitalist states are themselves diverse and seem to differ considerably in their structure, strength and degree of autonomy from society. Further elements of uncertainty and pluralism enter into the picture when account is taken of globalization processes and the international context of contemporary state activity, which may serve to limit sovereignty and state autonomy while at the same time enhancing its ability to pursue wider, external objectives.

Chapter 3, 'Political culture and social movements', is concerned with political culture and social movements and raises further questions about the social context of state action, the influence of social values and the articulation of social interests within political life. As in Chapters 1 and 2, discussion here involves consideration of the role and influence of civil society in relation to the state and centres of political power. Social movements, argues Alan Scott, are a product of modernity and have developed under similar conditions to those which gave rise to nation-states, industrial production and modern forms of political representation. Like modern liberal democracy and the advanced capitalist state, social movements constitute a further — though less structured — form of political modernity. The focus on this area also directs attention to new social movements. These date mostly from the 1960s (although early black civil rights movements in the United States may also be included under this heading) and have been based on race, gender and youth consciousness rather than older social movements with a clear class-based affiliation. The 'new' social movements address such issues as peace, ecological and environmental questions, feminism and sexual preference. The parallel rise of pro-democracy movements in Eastern Europe returns our attention to the east-European focus introduced in Chapter 1 and the idea of anti-politics as a distinctive orientation within modern societies.

There are also links between the post-totalitarian objectives which characterize movements identified in Chapter 1 and the post-industrial base of the new social movements discussed by Alan Scott in Chapter 3. These links suggest, according to some conceptions, a fundamental shift in the character of collective action within modern societies and a move away from established forms of political action towards less organized and more culturally-oriented activity. The 'new' social movements are less a response to social conditions or a reflection of social relations than one element in a more complex pattern in which collective action and its institutional context interact to sustain social movements and influence the course of their development. Such perspectives link further with themes like the relationship between capitalism and democracy introduced in Chapter 1, and the processes of incorporation (exemplified by the position of the workers' movement and socialism within parliamentary democracies) in the advanced capitalist state discussed in Chapter 2.

Chapter 4, 'Citizenship and the welfare state', moves down from the broad structures of the advanced capitalist state and liberal democracy, and away from the social movements that carry the momentum of collective action, to focus on the implications of political modernity for the individual and the development of modern conceptions of citizenship. What, asks Denise Riley, does this everyday term ('citizenship') now mean with respect to life in modern societies? An instant answer is likely to refer to membership of a nation-state; but the autonomy of states — certainly those in western Europe and those of a smaller size — seems to be declining and non-Western cultures have not generally provided favourable conditions for nation-state development at all. Modern citizenship, as the chapter makes clear, is a rather more diffuse and differentiated concept than we are often likely to think. Its development, not surprisingly, has been closely associated with the rise of modern democracy and the extension of suffrage. Citizens, accordingly, are people who are members of nation-states who are entitled to vote.

This implies that citizenship, like democracy, has been as much about criteria of exclusion as of inclusion. Electoral rights and citizenship were initially linked to property, and only later extended to unpropertied men and women. The universalization of citizenship, moreover, has occurred under conditions which also enshrine principles of inequality and this also affects the nature and implications of the status of citizenship. Capitalism and citizenship, as the sociologist T.H. Marshall has argued, were at war, and, despite its undoubted virtues and the claims made on its behalf, the welfare state could not resolve all the tensions that arose from this situation — in particular, those concerning the position of women. Furthermore, Britain's patchy record of post-war economic achievement and the growing role of supranational forces and global economic pressures have also set limits on the conception of a national, welfare-based citizenship. Modern citizenship in Britain is also placed in a new light by such developments as the drawing up of the Social Charter by the European Community and the growing perception of rights set within a framework broader than that of the nation-state.

Continuing the discussion presented in Book 1, *Formations of Modernity*, the nation-state thus appears as the dominant political form of modernity, but one which is nevertheless unable to resolve the conflicting tendencies and demands that modern societies have given, and continue to give rise to.

With Chapter 5, 'Fordism and modern industry', the focus of the book shifts from the political to the economic. The move, however, is not absolute, for part of the vision of modern society that is conjured up by the concept of Fordism is that of national governments devising macro-economic policies to sustain the long post-1945 economic boom. In Chapter 5, John Allen explores the central characteristics of Fordism: mass production based upon assembly line techniques, large factories turning out standardized goods, the creation of the mass worker and the role of the state in the formation of mass markets. For many, this powerful, Fordist vision of production represents the culmination of modern industrial development. It is this moment which puts the modern into industry and which captures the dynamism of modernist progress. For some, Fordism is a metaphor for modern capitalism as such: a means of talking about not just a set of mass industries or mass technologies but about a society in which a new way of life was being shaped and formed. Gramsci, in his *Prison Notebooks* written in the early 1930s, was one of the first writers to use the term 'Fordism' to refer to cultural values that took their meaning from the 'American label'. Others find the term rather pretentious for claiming, as it does, to explain the pattern of post-war growth across all the advanced capitalist economies. It is this claim in particular that is examined in Chapter 5.

The first part of the chapter is concerned with the assertion that the Fordist industries took some kind of lead role in shaping the post-war industrial economies. It traces the emergence of mass production techniques in the American system of manufacture and describes the social and technical innovations of Henry Ford in the early part of this century which led to the wider dissemination of mass production methods. It was not until after the Second World War, however, when mass production was coupled with mass purchasing power, that the notion of Fordism as an industrial era took hold. Its tenacity as a metaphor relies heavily upon its imaginative vision rather than upon any systematic analysis of the dominance of mass manufacturing industries in modern economies.

In the latter part of the chapter, a critical distance from the concept of a Fordist mode of growth is obtained through a discussion of what we mean by the notion of 'a modern manufacturing economy'. In particular, the concept of industry is opened up to reveal implicit assumptions about what we take to be the 'engine' or 'motor' of growth within a national economy. This section reminds us that the concepts with which we choose to describe and explain the workings of the modern economy, including that of Fordism, are not as innocent as they may appear. The chapter concludes by outlining some of the social and economic consequences of post-war economic discourse.

Chapter 6, 'The divisions of labour and occupational change', then directs our attention away from the nature of modern industry towards the pattern of post-war changes in occupations and jobs. A central consideration of the author, Peter Braham, is to show how complex divisions of labour are a key characteristic of modern economies. Industry in the modern sense is based upon divisions between skills, tasks, qualifications and experience, with various forms of segmentation in the labour market reflecting such differences. None of these differences, however, can be fully understood in the absence of an analysis of how jobs and tasks become gendered and also racialized. Braham draws our attention to the fact that in the post-war period, in particular, throughout the industrial economies, labour markets were (and are) characterized by gender and ethnic segregation. The rapid increase of women in industrial labour forces, and their channelling into the expanding service occupations, often on pay and conditions below those of their male counterparts in manufacturing, is one of the prominent characteristics of a modern, late twentieth-century economy.

Another characteristic is the migration of labour from the less developed countries to those with modern advanced economies. If the formation of the modern economy was bound up with, and in many ways dependent upon, the colonization of 'other' peoples in pre-modern economies, the post-1945 era represented the movement of the margins to the core economies. Obviously the pattern and flow of labour varies considerably from economy to economy, not only in terms of numbers but also in terms of the historical ties between countries. Nonetheless, what is important in broad terms is the global impact on the modern nations that such a development represents. This theme is taken further in Books 3 and 4 and points forward to cultural questions of social and national identity.

The attention paid to the international migration of labour also alerts us to another form of globalization — namely, the rise of a new international division of labour. Since the Second World War there has clearly been a widening of the global division of labour, orchestrated by multinational firms and encouraged by the governments of some of the less-developed nations. The form and scope of this development is the subject of much debate, yet the phenomenon itself raises a number of interesting questions about the future of manufacturing in the 'old' modern economies such as the UK. One such question is whether the margins are now beginning to 'hollow out' the modern industrial core by displacing manufacturing jobs from the centre, or whether the modern economies are shifting to a new form of industrial work and organization, perhaps one beyond Fordism. Again, this points towards issues considered more fully in Book 4, *Modernity and its Futures*.

Chapter 7, 'Work design and corporate strategies', by Graeme Salaman, provides a detailed account of the nature and formation of modern factory work. The narrative of this chapter is organized around the emergence of the large-scale bureaucratic workplace which grew out of the concentration of production and the advantages to the employer of a more detailed division of labour. Once gathered together in factories, the large workforces gave rise to the new activity of management which sought to achieve a measure of control and discipline over the labour force and the organization of work. The rise of modern management is located in this moment, but its dynamic expression is reached with the development of Taylorist and Fordist work regimes.

Taylorism arose out of the scientific management movement in the USA at the end of the nineteenth century and it marks off modern work organizations from the craft system and sub-contract relationships. Based upon a managerialist view of labour and a set of practices which sought to intensify the application of the division of labour to work tasks, the nub of Taylorism can be found in the bureaucratization of the structures of control over the workforce. Tightly-drawn job boundaries, increased job fragmentation and the rigid separation of mental from manual tasks provided a particular conception of work design. Salaman goes on, however, to show how the rationalization of the work process took a different form under a Fordist regime as technology, rather than the reorganization of labour, imposed a work discipline based on the assembly line.

Charlie Chaplin's 1936 film, 'Modern Times' caught this new work regime and its destruction of commitment in vivid outline. Indeed, Chaplin's film, even allowing for its exaggerated scenes of the social impact of line technology, did isolate the paradox of modern work design: that management's attempts to wrest control of the work process from labour clashes with management's need to obtain commitment to, and identification with, the job. The remainder of Chapter 7 is concerned with this paradox and the strategies adopted by management in their attempts to resolve it. Salaman identifies two distinct approaches, one based on control of the workforce and the other based on achieving and maintaining its consent, and he argues that much of modern management involves an oscillation between these two poles as the limits of each one are reached in turn. Success, as Salaman puts it, breeds its own failure, either in excessive control over the workforce or in lost control. This is a classic modernist dilemma.

Finally, Chapter 8, 'Power, conflict and control at work', by Diane Watson, opens up the question of control at work to include, among others, the strategies used by employees to gain control over their own work process. A central theme here is that even in the most constrained of work situations — say that of assembly-line production — there is still a 'space' for resistance and the power to exert some degree of control over the work situation. More than this, the chapter reminds us that power and conflict in the modern economy do not just shape the relations between capital and labour or between manager and managed; strategies of control are many and varied and take place between worker and customer, and between men and women at the workplace. Our attention is drawn to the different sites of power within the modern economy and the different sets of relations in which power may be exercised with effect. This view of a plurality of powers represents a shift in thinking away from the notion that there is only one site of power and one set of relations within the modern capitalist economy — namely, the confrontation between capital and labour within the large-scale factory.

On this basis, and drawing links with an earlier discussion of the sexual division of labour (Chapter 6), Watson sets out to show how occupational roles in the medical profession are 'gendered' through techniques of male power and through resistance to those techniques by women. Patriarchal power exercised at the workplace has effectively secured the best of work and rewards within the medical profession, although not without meeting resistance from women.

This chapter focuses intentionally on individual experience, and on the importance of images of self that are both managed and contested. The modern self, as Daniel Bell (1976) and others have observed, finds expression in the search for self-fulfilment and the denial of imposed limits to experience. At the workplace, however, the principles of organization are, as we have seen, based upon steep hierarchies, vertical chains of control and the bureaucratization of work experience. There is a dislocation between these two areas of modern life which conveys something of the contradictory experience that is distinctively modern. It is to the double-sided character of modernity that we now briefly turn.

Chaplin's film 'Modern Times' once again provides a sense of the two sides of modern progress. The magnitude of technical change, as symbolized by the oppressive size of the new mass technology, conveys a sense of both the scale of modern progress and of the powerlessness of the 'little' worker. There is, on the one side, the sheer mastery of modern technology — a force capable of transforming the physical world of natural resources into material progress — and, on the other side, the prospect of work experience characterized by the discipline of repetitive, meaningless tasks.

Both Marx and Weber understood the double-sided character of modernity, yet they differed over how the modern era would develop and what would follow. Where Marx emphasized the possibility of the struggle between the two classes — capital and labour — leading to the emergence of a new kind of society based upon less degrading social relationships, Weber stressed the negative characteristics of bureaucracy, in particular the imposition of impersonal rules which limit prospects for individual self-fulfilment and spontaneity. Looking back, we can see that if Marx erred on the optimistic side of what the modern 'project' would finally deliver, Weber's view of bureaucracy is perhaps too pessimistic in its denial of creativity and autonomy within modern organizations. Neither Marx nor Weber, however, could have fully anticipated that the development of modern industry would lead to a distinct trade-off between mass consumption and mass production, where the material advantages offered by the former would be gained only in exchange for dull, mindless work in the latter. Of course, the majority of workers in the post-war industrial economies had only a small part to play in this trade-off, but if any industrial era can lay claim to the mass worker, it is what has become known as the Fordist era.

Nor is it just the economic domain of modernity that is characterized by the two sides of progress. In the political domain, while essential attributes like the powerful attachment to military force and issues of security were well established in the early modern period, the nature and functions of the state have been transformed over the past century. The form and scale of activities undertaken by the contemporary state are vastly different from those seen in the nation-states of the early modern period. State responsibility for the welfare and material security of its citizens has mushroomed in the twentieth century alongside the pursuit of traditional goals like the maintenance of security and order. The combination of the two functions within the state — welfare and warfare, especially since the rise of 'industrialized warfare' — provides yet further illustration of the contradictory character of the developed modern world.

Modernity, therefore, should not be conceived as a unified whole, but rather as an era composed of different interlocking social processes, each with its own distinctive history and mode of expression. We need to say a little more about this conception. The first point to note is one that was stressed in Book 1 — namely, our concern to avoid the impression that there is only one path of modern development along which all societies will eventually proceed. This view of development clearly has a certain persuasive force when you consider the equation of modern progress with industrialism and the idea that a Fordist 'stage' of mass production is part of the normal route. When people talk about twentieth-century industry or bureaucracy, or government or even architecture, in terms of mass scale, standardization, universality, and the like, we need to remind ourselves of the uneven character of modern development, the plurality of modern economies and states, and the contingent quality that brings together a particular constellation of processes and institutional forms in one place at one time.

The stress here upon 'multi-causal' explanations of modern development should not be read as: the more diverse the social elements identified and the more contingent the quality of their interactions, the better the explanation. Effective accounts are not necessarily those that simply include layer after layer of detail, as if in itself the more complex an account, the more powerful is its ability to explain. It depends upon what it is precisely that we wish to explain. In this book, what we wish to explain are the political and economic forms of modernity, and thus historical and geographical contingency are part of that story, if not the whole story.

Drawing attention to the contingent quality of modern development is not, however, the same as saying that history and its outcomes amount to a series of social and geographical accidents. When Giddens talks about the diffusion of industrialism as having created 'one world' (1990, pp.76–7), he is referring to a globalization of industrial development which has distributed the benefits of economic growth unevenly, affected the day-to-day lives of people across the world in diverse ways, and also, interestingly, raised the prospect of harmful ecological change on a global scale. Similarly, political influence reinforced with the international use of military force has been a determining factor in the strengthening of democratization processes in various parts of the world and there are strong global connections between liberal democracy and capitalism. The external influence is even more apparent in the case of the contemporary state itself and the form it takes under conditions of advanced capitalism. There are few political issues that can now be defined as purely domestic or international. Indeed, the modern state may be seen as much as a point of contact and linkage between diverse forms of local, regional and global pressure as a territorial entity in its own right. In both cases, it is the interconnections between places and peoples, and the nature of those connections, that we need to unravel if we wish to understand why modern life takes different forms in different places. But this is to run ahead of ourselves.

The final aspect of this volume that you should note is that the processes and topics chosen, as well as the historical periods examined, reflect what the authors consider to be relevant or important. Such choices are open to debate, as are the interpretations that authors offer of the different aspects of modern society. This recognition is part of what Stuart Hall referred to in the Introduction to Book 1 (*Formations of Modernity*) as the 'greater reflexivity ... the attention to language and the plural character of "meanings"' which is beginning to characterize much social science writing.

A greater sensitivity to the plurality of meaning is also evident in the actual processes and institutions discussed. This is reflected in the discourse of modern phenomena such as 'citizenship', 'democracy', 'the Keynesian state', or indeed 'Fordism'. The latter, for example, as we have seen, has been regarded as a metaphor for the whole of capitalist society in the post-war period, as well as just one kind of job design. Yet whatever meaning we wish to invest in the concept of Fordism, we cannot escape from the meanings that others attribute to it. Much the same can be said for the concept of modernity. This volume and Book 3, *Social and Cultural Forms of Modernity*, may both be characterized as explorations of the diverse forms of modernity and their ambiguous meaning.

References

Bell, D. (1976) *The Cultural Contradictions of Capitalism,* Basic Books, New York.

Giddens, A. (1990) *The Consequences of Modernity,* Polity Press, Cambridge.

CHAPTER 1   DEMOCRACY IN MODERN SOCIETIES

Paul G. Lewis

CONTENTS

1   INTRODUCTION

Democracy as a social value and form of political organization can be traced back to the ancient world, but its career as a dominant principle of political life has been restricted to modern societies, and its greatest success in underpinning processes of general democratization and the achievement of mass democracy has been of even more recent date. Democracy as such was not a major feature of political thought during the Enlightenment, although the criticisms of absolutism and advocacy of natural rights, social equality and political reform evident at that time (as outlined in Chapter 1 of *Formations of Modernity*, Hall and Gieben, 1992), made an important contribution to the strengthening current of democratic thought in the modern world. Democratic ideas gained greater prominence towards the end of the eighteenth century with the outbreak of the French Revolution. But it was only towards the close of the following century that the idea of mass democracy, a democratic process in which virtually all adult members of society participated in some way or another, gained general acceptance and became a pre-eminent value in modern political life.

It has been a more recent development, concentrated in the period following the Second World War and in even later years, that democracy has become a common form of political organization and, increasingly, a major characteristic of modern societies. While the idea and practice of democracy extends back to classical Greece, then, it is only much more recently that it became a general principle of social life and democratization gained impetus as a central process of modern society. This career raises a number of questions which will be explored in this chapter about the place of the democratic idea in modern social life and the relationship of democratization to other constitutive processes of modern societies. These include:

1   What has democracy meant in history? Why were democratic principles disregarded for much of the period of recorded history and why did they then gain favour towards the end of the eighteenth century?

2   How does the modern idea of mass democracy differ from earlier conceptions and what was the social context in which processes of mass democratization emerged in the late nineteenth and twentieth centuries?

3   What is the relationship between democracy and the operation of developed capitalist society and how far can a contradiction be detected between the two principles of social organization?

4   How far is democratization a dominant constitutive process of modern societies?

Initial questions about the meaning and historical development of democracy will be discussed briefly and answered before progressing to consider issues surrounding the rise of mass democracy. Processes of democratization in modern society will be examined more closely and central issues pursued in the context of recent developments and the demise of communist dictatorship in East-Central Europe.

2   THE IDEA OF DEMOCRACY

Democracy refers to 'rule' and the 'people' (rule by, of and for the people, for example) and comes to us directly from the ancient Greek terms which had broadly the same meaning. The idea of 'the people' did not necessarily have the positive connotations it came to acquire in more recent times and often carried implications of the masses or mob, democracy then referring to an undesirable state of mob-rule — an idea still by no means alien to some contemporary conceptions. Democracy was a popular form of rule in which the people did have power and actually wielded it. This did not mean that it was viewed positively. As Raymond Williams pointed out in his discussion of major components in the vocabulary of modern society,

> the fact is that, with only occasional exceptions, democracy, in the records that we have, was until the nineteenth century a strongly unfavourable term, and it is only since the late nineteenth and early twentieth century that a majority of political parties and tendencies have united in declaring their belief in it. This is the most striking historical fact.
> (Williams, 1976, p.83)

ACTIVITY 1   Turn to *The Penguin Dictionary of Sociology* and read the entry on DEMOCRACY. What definition of democracy can you derive from it and what do you understand to be the major concerns of sociology with modern democracy?

The *Dictionary* directs attention to parliamentary democracy (the form of democracy operating in Britain, for example), and key aspects of it, such as the election of leaders by a system based on competing political parties for which all citizens have a vote (universal franchise). Sociological accounts of democracy have been concerned with features of modern society such as the consequences of mass participation in the formal political process, the relation of democracy to components of social development and the way in which its objectives have been pursued in organizational form. We shall pay attention to these questions later in the unit. It is worth noting here that the *Dictionary* definition focuses on parliamentary democracy, which is a specific political form and by no means covers all aspects of the idea of democracy. While parliamentary practices have had a lengthy history in some countries, they generally involved the extension of political participation to a relatively narrow social group and by no means implied the same arrangements as a modern, mass democracy. In some societies prior to the nineteenth century notable individuals were given the right to assemble and express their opinion (and thus to speak their mind in a 'parlement'), but this was very different from ideas of mass democracy and popular power.

PARLIAMENT
of EDWARD I.

Parliament of Edward I

Early notions of democracy (which, therefore, by no means necessarily carried a favourable connotation) meant direct rule by the mass of the population. Rule by elected representatives, and early forms of what we have come to understand as representative democracy, could thus be regarded as non–democratic in the seventeenth century (Williams, 1976, p.84). During the discussion that attended the American Revolution (independence being declared in 1776) and the preparation of the American Constitution (issued in 1787), however, Alexander Hamilton expounded the principles of *representative* democracy and argued its virtues, this now being the conception that has come to prevail in modern western democracies. While Britain provided the model of constitutional rule for early political reformers and the *philosophes* of the Enlightenment, the principles of representative government were elaborated and implemented more vigorously in America and France in the wake of their respective revolutions (see *Formations of Modernity,* Hall and Gieben, 1992, Chapter 2). The elaboration of the principle of representation (first advocated during the English Civil War, 1642–48, by the Levellers) was soon regarded as placing the possibility of democracy in contemporary societies in a wholly new light. By combining the democratic idea of rule by the people with that of representation and rule by elected representatives (a notion certainly alien to classical democracy), the achievement of democracy within the new form of the modern nation-state became a viable option, promising a revolutionary political transformation as well as preserving constitutionality and the gains of liberal forces (Dahl, 1989, pp.28–30). These developments had further implications for the evolution of the democratic idea.

Alexander Hamilton

When the essence of democracy became associated with the process of representation, the nature of the people represented and its implications for the political order tended to become correspondingly less important. The process of representation and the means by which it was achieved came to attract more attention. The idea of 'the people' was, in any case, also subject to considerable variation. Women and slaves were not citizens and did not form part of the Greek *polis,* or political community, and some restrictions on the ability of members of the human community to participate in political processes always exist in modern democracies. Children and the mentally insane, for example, do not have the vote today. The parameters of exclusion, however, have been steadily narrowed over the centuries. The period immediately following the Enlightenment was again a watershed in this sense. It was during the French Revolution (which began in 1789) that the idea of popular power — in the sense of the political order embracing a large part of the people, receiving their approbation and providing the people with the possibility of the direct exercise of their rights — gained momentum and became central to a significant political movement.

But this revolutionary eruption, and challenge to one of the major established European state forms, reinforced sentiments elsewhere against democracy and against those urging its practice in the sense of the direct exercise of popular power. It strengthened the distinction between procedural definitions of democracy and conceptions that associated it with popular power, this now becoming the basis of a major political division as well as reflecting a conceptual difference:

> Democracy was still a revolutionary or at least a radical term to the mid-nineteenth century, and the specialized development of representative democracy was at least in part a conscious reaction to this, over and above the practical reasons of extent and continuity. It is from this point in the argument that two modern meanings of democracy can be seen to diverge. In the socialist tradition, democracy continued to mean *popular power*, a state in which the interests of the majority of the people were paramount and in which these interests were practically exercised and controlled by the majority. In the liberal tradition, democracy meant open election of representatives and certain conditions (democratic rights, such as free speech) which maintained the openness of election and political argument. These conceptions, in their extreme forms, now confront each other as enemies. (Williams, 1976, p.85)

It was, therefore, against the background of the French Revolution and its aftermath that the two modern meanings of democracy can be identified — one associated with the liberal tradition and placing prime emphasis on the free election of political representatives and the maintenance of conditions for their effective operation, and a second which promoted the idea of a popular power capable of furthering the interests of the majority of the people, involving the mass of the population in the pursuit of those interests and developing under modern conditions with the socialist movement.

The latter conception was considerably different from the paths of social improvement envisaged during the Enlightenment by John Locke (1632–1704) and the Baron de Montesquieu (1689–1755), who advocated limited government and the separation of powers (let alone from those who placed their hopes in the actions of enlightened

despots). But it was close to the ideas of direct democracy elaborated by
Jean-Jacques Rousseau (1712–78). The ideas of Locke and Rousseau
diverged significantly in relation to theories of the state, and
conceptions of sovereignty and constitutional order (see Book 1 (Hall
and Gieben, 1992), Chapter 2). These ideas also involved significantly
different approaches to democracy and the means for its
implementation in modern societies. These different meanings, as we
shall see, took on further significance as ideas of mass democracy
developed with the growth of modern industrial societies during the
nineteenth century. The institutional expression of representation and
the conditions and form of its organization became of critical
importance as the masses claimed the right of entry into formal political
life and participation in legislative processes.

John Locke

Ideas of popular power which emerged with the growing socialist
movement gained new significance with the rise of an industrial
working class which came to occupy a central position in modern
societies based on new forms of economic and technological
development but which in its early stages was excluded from effective
political participation. As the idea of democracy moved further to the
front of political debate and its interpretation became increasingly
identified with the interests and aspirations of different social groups,
its meaning also became more frequently contested and the object of
conflicting claims. In the late twentieth century virtually everyone has
wanted to be regarded as a democrat (at least with a small 'd') and few
contemporary politicians would be happy to be identified as anti-
democratic. But it is clear that different traditions of democratic thought

and practice have developed, although the origins and nature of these differences have also been subject to a range of conflicting interpretations. Williams pointed to the liberal and socialist interpretations, and associated these with the contrasting emphases, on the one hand, on representation and its associated electoral practices and conditions and, on the other, on the idea of popular power and the pursuit and control of popular interests.

American sociologist Robert Nisbet also makes a broad distinction between two schools of democratic thought, but on a different basis. Whereas in his view liberalism is about immunity from power, democracy is concerned with the theory and structure of political power (note the link with Williams' characterization of the liberal tradition of democracy, which is primarily concerned with representation and the distancing of the popular source of democratic power from the procedures and objects of its exercise). Specific to democracy is the idea that the legitimacy of power derives from the consent of the people in the exercise of that power through government. Much, then, depends on who 'the people' are and what conception of them is adopted:

> We may regard the people as simply a numerical aggregate of individuals regarded for political administrative purposes as discrete and socially separated, an aggregate given form and meaning only by the nature of the State and its laws. Or, alternatively, we may regard the people as indistinguishable from a culture, its members inseparable from families, unions, churches, professions, and traditions that actually compose a culture. The difference between the two ways of considering the people is vast, and it is decisive in any political theory of democracy. The 'will' of the people is one thing, substantively, when it is conceived in purely political terms as arising from a vast aggregate of socially separated, politically integrated individuals. It is something very different when it is conceived in terms of the social unities and cultural traditions in which political, like all other, judgements are actually formed and reinforced.
> (Nisbet, 1962, p.249)

The question, it should noted, is not one of how direct the participation of the people in key political processes should be. Neither is the issue the same as deciding which members of society and how many of 'the people' should be entitled to act as citizens and be fully empowered with democratic rights: such as the right of political participation and voting, for example.

What Nisbet is concerned with is more the sociological question of whether the people are more appropriately regarded as an aggregate of individuals or as members of society embedded in and, in any meaningful terms, inseparable from their cultural affiliation and membership of social groups — although it will soon be clear that the distinction also has more practical political implications. The view of the people as an aggregate of individuals leads directly to an emphasis on the state as an agency of social and political integration and provides it with a leading role among other forms of social association. It underwrites a unitary view of democracy, whose origins can be traced directly to major thinkers of the Enlightenment and the French rationalists. Not surprisingly, a major impetus to its development came with the French Revolution and its extension to neighbouring areas on the European continent like Germany. It was this development of the French revolution that marked its turn into a new phase and brought it into direct conflict with the established European monarchies and absolutist states.

The state-centred conception of democracy has, however, been increasingly influential in the modern world and has provided an attractive model for developing countries in the twentieth century. In the alternative view, the state is one of a multiplicity of social associations, and participation in a plurality of groups is seen as characteristic of a people's participation in political life and a precondition of democratic development. This, again, accords with the liberal conception of democracy and ideas of limited government and has strongly influenced the development of model democracies like England, the United States and Scandinavia. It is not difficult to decide which of the two conceptions of democracy Nisbet favours. As he notes, democracy has made great progress since the middle of the nineteenth century in terms of increasing the collective power of the people — but the means that have accompanied or been used to achieve this have brought greater social uniformity and reduced diversity and pluralism, themselves preconditions for the development of the non-unitary principle of democracy. This he clearly deplores, and he equates the spread of unitary democracy with greater bureaucratic centralization (Nisbet, 1962, p.254).

Factors linked with this development include: the importance of mass warfare for modern societies (a factor which was also given prominence in the account of the rise of the modern state in Chapter 2 of Hall and Gieben,1992; see also the following chapter), a prevalent intellectual stress on unity and continuing faith in historical necessity. Here, too, the legacy of the Enlightenment and the *philosophes* is clearly evident. Nisbet's view, further, is that major features of modern society have disproportionately favoured the development of unitary democracy following the realization that state power could be enhanced rather than diminished by embracing the democratic principle and expanding its popular base. Conditions for the development of liberal democracy can, therefore, be seen to require considerably more than adherence to the principle of popular sovereignty. The problematic consequences of the rise of mass democracy for popular power, civil autonomy and the pursuit of public interests are indeed a major aspect of the spread of democratization and the development of political life under modern social conditions which will be pursued further later in this chapter. But, before that, we shall review the progress made up to now in this section.

Cast your mind back over the different variants and interpretations of democracy you have already encountered in this section. Try to list (1) the main distinctions that have been made, and (2) their implications for the nature of democracy in modern societies.

You have already been acquainted with a number of important distinctions:

1   between direct and representative democracy, the latter forming the basis of political democracy in modern times.

2   between the two modern meanings of democracy identified by Williams (1976): that of popular power, the original principle of democracy later embodied in the developing socialist traditions, and liberal interpretations which stress processes of representation and the conditions of their effective operation.

3   between contrasting conceptions of 'the people', whose consent to government underlies the very idea of democracy and who may be understood to be formed either as an aggregate of individuals or as a socially and culturally structured entity with discernible features of institutionalized pluralism. This difference is associated by Nisbet with (respectively) unitary, state-centred notions of democracy and the liberal democracy more characteristic of Anglo-Saxon countries.

This provides us with the conceptual basis with which to examine the process of democratization and its relation to other processes which have played a major part in the development of modern societies. We shall turn to examine why democracy has become such a powerful principle in modern societies and why the process of democratization has been such a major feature of their development.

3   THE DEMOCRATIZATION OF MODERN SOCIETIES

The onset of mass democracy in Britain (involving the acceptance of the democratic principle by the majority of the political establishment) and — at the same time — the progressive installation of a framework restrictive of the more radical emanations of popular power can be located during a period that began around the middle of the nineteenth century. There had long been a suspicion, and rejection, of democracy for carrying the threat of mob-rule, the degradation of the educated and cultured elite and the dictatorship of the least favoured members of society. With the growth of an industrial working class and recurrent signs of its discontent, there was a natural fear that mass democracy would lead to seizure of the wealth and property of the privileged classes as well as the end of their political dominance. John Stuart Mill, too, argued for a 'rational democracy' whose premise was 'not that the people themselves govern, but that they have security for good government', the best government being necessarily 'the government of the wisest, and these must always be few'. He was, however, less fearful of the form of government than of the dominance of an undifferentiated and mediocre public opinion and of the threat posed by democracy to individual liberty (Arblaster, 1987, pp.48–9). With this view Mill remains a prime spokesman for modern liberal democracy. Anxieties about the implications of mass democracy persisted and warnings were heard during the debate that preceded the 1867 Reform Act (which extended the franchise to most householders).

3.1   THE EMERGENCE OF MODERN DEMOCRACIES

But, while reservations about some consequences of mass democracy have persisted (as seen in the views of Nisbet, for example), the worst fears soon proved to be illusory and a rapid change in public attitudes to political democracy became apparent. The emergence of mass democracy did not prove to be such a threat to the dominant classes as had once been thought. Why was this so? What entered into the change in public attitudes to the issue of democracy and the extension of the franchise? The reasons for the change in public opinion were several and, as is often the case when an ill-defined threat is at issue, the situation turned out to be more complex than originally thought. The working-class vote was, as Arblaster (1987, p.50) points out, divided between the existing (Liberal and Conservative) parties (the development of modern, broader-based parties had begun some time earlier) and it took a considerable time and much effort for socialist parties to emerge from the working class itself.

The working class was far less homogeneous than it appeared to those who felt themselves threatened by it, and there were significant divisions within it in terms of skills, wealth, security and organizational experience (there were, equally, very significant economic and political differences between the dominant classes as Moore, 1967, took pains to make clear). Neither was the progressive extension of the franchise (invariably amongst the male population in the nineteenth century) the same thing as the crystallization of a democratic society or political order. Indeed, it was precisely the non-revolutionary outcome of the extension of the vote towards the end of the nineteenth century that made the more thorough-going democratization of British society generally acceptable at a later date, as it became apparent that democracy would not mean the end of civilization or, more practically, the removal of all privileges and material advantages from those who enjoyed them.

The final step towards the acceptance of mass democracy, suggests Arblaster (1987, p.50), was taken in the wake of the First World War and in response to the enormous toll taken of all social groups in the name of universal social values. Such sacrifices, as President Wilson put it, 'could be demanded in the name of democracy which could not be expected for mere patriotism for the social order as it was'. Soon after the end of the First World War, then, the democratic principle had gained acceptance in a number of the more developed Western countries and the consolidation of mass democracy, according to contemporary conceptions, could be said to have been achieved by 1928 in Britain with the extension of the franchise to the whole female population. By this stage, political democracy was also firmly established in Scandinavia, to a large extent in the dominions of the British Empire (New Zealand, Australia, Canada) and, of course, the United States — although major groups, particularly blacks, were in practice excluded from the political community in large areas of the country. Literacy and poll tax requirements barred many from the voting booth in the southern states and it was only around 1970 that the Fifteenth Amendment was enforced and black adults were routinely given the vote.

Alabama, 1965: blacks attempt to protest against being prevented to register for the vote

Democracy was introduced after the war in Weimar Germany but was, of course, succeeded by the Nazi rule of Adolf Hitler. Other developed Western countries (France, Switzerland) still denied the vote to women during the inter-war period. As war and militarism were shown in Chapter 2 of Hall and Gieben,1992, to be major factors in the formation of modern states, so the consequences of warfare were highly significant for the emergence of modern democracies. The defeat of the Axis powers in 1945 meant the end of the fascist capitalist dictatorships and split the conservative coalition of the bourgeoisie and entrenched traditional interests in Germany and Japan which, as Moore (1967) has described, had earlier blocked the path of democratic development. Democratization was also advanced in victorious nations as mobilization and issues of national unity came to the fore in a war effort. The truism of class differences being transcended by the drive for national unity certainly played a part in the process of democratization in Britain.

It was, as we have seen, sentiments of national unity and shared sacrifice in Britain during World War I that finally overcame lingering resistance to democracy, brought about full male suffrage in 1918 and facilitated the inclusion of women in the electorate ten years later. The two world wars contributed to democratization by helping to extend democracy in its early locations, like Britain, and breaking the dictatorial mould of competing capitalist nations like Germany and Japan. It was, then, primarily the forces set in motion by industrial capitalism and global warfare that were responsible for the establishment of mass democracy, its consolidation in the countries that had been the pioneers of democratization and extension to those whose path of capitalist development had been followed by the development of fascism rather than the consolidation of parliamentary democracy. Mass democracy thus came into its own after the Second World War, its victory expressed in the establishment of universal (or near-universal) adult suffrage throughout much of the developed capitalist world.

Significant exceptions were not lacking — female disenfranchisement in Switzerland and the effective exclusion of blacks in the American South — but it was clearly more solidly established than ever before. As had been the case in nineteenth-century Britain, economic conditions were uniquely advantageous for the support of the democratic order and the exercise of the rights it promised — although in this case these conditions held throughout much of the developed world for a quarter-century after the end of the war. These also provided some opportunity for the satisfaction of further democratic demands. In Britain, for example (as during World War I), the experience of national mobilization in pursuit of shared war aims created a basis in 1945 for the crystallization and pursuit of a more extensive range of democratic objectives, which this time went further than the establishment of formal democracy and a fully representative system of government.

Generally, however, democratization and the spread of mass democracy in the modern (predominantly developed, capitalist) world concerned the establishment of the practices and institutions of representative government and of the liberal variant of democracy. In the conception of Therborn (1977), this referred to states with representative governments chosen by an electorate made up in principle of the whole adult population whose votes carry equal weight and who are permitted to vote in line with their political preference without fear of state intimidation. Dahl (1989, pp.212–20) spells this out in more detail and argues, further, that the change of scale reflected in the establishment of modern democracy in the nation-state, and its particular consequences, have helped bring about the development of a set of political institutions that distinguish modern representative democracy from all other political systems. This outcome he defines as **polyarchy**, which is distinguished by two broad characteristics: citizenship is extended to a relatively high proportion of adults, and the rights of citizenship include the opportunity to oppose and vote out the highest officials in the government.

These general features of polyarchy Dahl (1989, p.221) associated with the presence of seven institutions which give form and substance to the underlying democratic principles:

1   Elected officials in whom control over government decisions is constitutionally vested.

2   Free and fair elections, during which officials are chosen with reasonable frequency in the presence of no or relatively little coercion.

3   Inclusive suffrage, which involves practically all adults in the election of officials.

4   The right to run for office and the openness of elective offices in the government to most adults.

5   Freedom of expression and the right of citizens to express themselves on political matters without danger of punishment.

6   Alternative information and the right of citizens to have access to knowledge and information not subject to government control.

7   Associational autonomy, which helps citizens achieve their rights by forming relatively independent organizations — including political parties and interest groups.

These features should, of course, be embedded in practice and not just appear as nominal rights of political window-dressing. They reflect the form actually taken by democracy in modern societies and are not just part of a theoretical vision.

ACTIVITY 3   Think back over what you have learnt from this section and list the main factors that have entered into the emergence of modern democracies. Check back and see if there is anything you have missed.

3.2   CAPITALISM AND DEMOCRACY

The establishment of political democracy has occurred predominantly in modern societies at a relatively advanced level of capitalist development, and democratization has appeared to progress together with capitalist modernization, meaning in broad terms the achievement of modernity in terms of the formation of urban industrial societies under the auspices of the private ownership of productive resources and the dominance of the profit motive. To some extent, this association is not difficult to understand. Effective democracy requires a literate, informed public with sufficient social skills to make their political participation meaningful — which in turn implies a developed and relatively modern social order. Capitalism has been associated with the development of market relations and the absence of imposed regulative mechanisms, the development of a liberal order with minimum state interference. This, too, can be understood to accord with the extension of civic rights, and the development of social autonomy. But in other ways the relationship between capitalism and democracy can be seen as more problematic. As many of the socially privileged noted before (and, indeed, after) the general acceptance of democratic principles, the extension of political equality to include the labouring and unpropertied masses appeared to pose a major threat to the advantages of those who gained from the processes that perpetuated and extended existing structures of inequality.

In fact, though, as noted previously, the extension of the franchise at least did not seem to challenge the *modus operandi* of capitalism or the economy of modern capitalism but rather helped to stabilize the socio-political conditions under which it operated. This was soon recognized by leading socialists like Engels and Lenin, but general arguments and explanatory hypotheses in this area are, as Therborn (1977, p.32) has suggested, not adequate to pin down the dynamics of a relationship that has developed in a range of societies over several centuries and has by no means followed the same path of development. It is misleading to read in too direct a correspondence between capitalism and bourgeois (or liberal, parliamentary) democracy. But there does seem to be a underlying relationship between capitalist development and the progress of democratization, capitalism containing a number of tendencies that are conducive to the process. The prime relationship of relevance here, it has been suggested by Therborn, is one related to the characteristic feature of bourgeois democracy involving a 'competitive division within a basic framework of unity'. Precisely what this means is outlined in the extract from Therborn, to which you should turn now.

ACTIVITY 4   Now read **Reading A, 'The rule of capital and the rise of democracy'**, by Goran Therborn, which you will find at the end of this chapter. List the inherent tendencies within capitalism identified by Therborn (they are numbered by him) that have influenced the development of central features of bourgeois democracy. What is the nature of the 'division within unity' that underlay the development of this form of democracy?

Six inherent tendencies of capitalism can be identified that Therborn associates with the development of democracy, while in terms of concrete historical development the new framework of unity appeared in the form of the modern nation-state (see the discussion in Chapter 2 of Hall and Gieben,1992, which relates to this). The emerging freedom of trade and industry created a network of 'divisive competitive relationships which ran through the new ruling class of the unified and sovereign states ... it was in this unity-division of national state and market that the process of democratization originated'. Democracy was thus typically introduced (as in Britain) for the upper layers of the bourgeoisie and commercialized landowners and then extended to other sections of the bourgeoisie, less elevated middle-class groups and others with a minor stake in the system — like householders. This appeared to be a general tendency — but there was nothing inevitable about its progress. As Moore outlined in his *Social Origins of Dictatorship and Democracy* (1967), particular social conditions and a specific historical heritage played an important part, although the process was not inevitable and change could also result in an exclusive compromise between the bourgeoisie and established land-owners, thus blocking the path towards democracy.

The progress towards mass democracy occurred within a framework combining unity and division— sections of the working class benefiting from the drive of the bourgeoisie for greater political representation and forming part of an alliance in the move towards greater democratization. There was, however, concerted resistance to democratization as a general process and to the legislation of universal rights. The defeat of the British Chartists in the 1840s was thus a notable reverse to the process of progressive democratization, although most of their demands were later granted gradually, on a piecemeal basis. While working-class agitation was often an indispensable part of the bourgeois movement towards democracy, it was notable that the political advance of the working class was dependent on the patronage of the bourgeoisie and was 'nowhere capable of achieving democracy by its own unaided resources' (Reading A, p.56). The fate of the Russian revolution of 1917, the most renowned example of an historic political victory in the name of the working class, can be seen as a practical confirmation of this view.

Democratization, while extending the range of political rights within a society, has therefore also meant the confirmation of working-class subalternity and a practical inferiority which affirms the conditional nature of its social and political rights. Przeworski (1986, p.63) stresses this point and notes that 'the democratic system was solidified in Belgium, Sweden, France and Great Britain only after organized workers were badly defeated in mass strikes and adopted a docile posture as a result'. Nevertheless, the progress of democracy was generally consistent and in some countries quite rapid, largely because capitalist

Chartist demonstration

development was also dynamic and far more intensive than the early
bourgeoisie had ever imagined. It was this intensive economic
development that made the political advance of the working class more
acceptable than it had originally been. The class war turned out to be
much less of a zero-sum affair (in that it did not involve the decisive
defeat of one of the contestants) than many had believed, and the
underlying principles of capitalism and democracy by no means proved
to be contradictory, although this did not mean that the progress of
democracy was unqualified or that the advance of previously excluded
groups took place on their own terms.

3.3   SOCIALIST DEMOCRACY AND DETOTALITARIANIZATION

The spread of democracy has not only proved to be compatible with the
development of capitalism but has, in the twentieth century, been
mainly concentrated in those areas dominated by capitalist production.
Democratization was certainly more limited in the communist world.
Russia experienced what was described as a proletarian revolution in
1917, but the objectives that underlay the social and political upheaval
were mixed and its implications for the establishment of democracy
very qualified. The key background conditions for what happened in
Russia during 1917 were provided by the weakening of the Russian
Empire in the face of the unsustainable costs of modern industrialized
warfare for a semi-developed power and the dissolution of its social
fabric after more than two years of appalling war losses. Warfare may

well be, as outlined in Chapter 2 of Hall and Gieben (1992), a major constitutive element of the modern state. It has also undermined the foundations of semi-traditional, partially modernized empires. Following a desperate offensive in June 1917 launched, under a socialist prime minister, by the post-Tsarist Provisional Government, the army crumbled as its largely peasant constituents turned their back on war in the search for peace and food and set out to assert their claims on land in the increasingly restive countryside.

Workers, aristocrats, bourgeois and intellectuals were also active, though far from unified in terms of organization or political objectives. The Bolsheviks, a hard-line minority of the Russian social-democrats (or Marxist socialists), had considerable success in mobilizing the relatively small industrial working class, a clear perspective on the need to seize political power and considerable confidence in their capacity to do so. These mixed elements underlay their victory in the October revolution. Cast in terms of Marxian socialism, the Bolshevik vision resolutely rejected all thought of liberal democracy or representative government and looked forward instead to forms of direct democracy premised on the full development of society's productive resources and the progression of world society through a process of concerted development. Elements of representative democracy or spontaneously arising forms of direct democracy were in practice soon expunged in the communist party-state (the Bolsheviks began calling their party 'communist' in 1918) and its apparatus was increasingly dedicated to the imposition of political discipline under Stalin's leadership and, particularly after the forced collectivization of agriculture in 1929–31, the co-ordination and administration of economic processes.

In accordance with its line of descent from Marxian socialism and the evolving Russian variant of Marxism-Leninism, the Soviet form of political dictatorship and bureaucratic state domination was termed 'socialist democracy'. Having virtually nothing to do with any understanding of democracy and, more arguably, little association with socialism either, Soviet practice gave rise to an influential form of one-party rule that nevertheless made some appeal to democratic principles. This was not based on competitive elections, the open choice of representatives and free circulation of information and opinion that enters into the operation of mass western democracies. A major part of the Soviet claim rested on criticism of the shortcomings of liberal democracy and assertion of the superiority of collectivist values and mass action over individualism (you may recall here the contrasts identified by Williams and Nisbet which can be related to these issues). The lack of liberal democracy and absence of representative government was, it was often argued, compensated for, or even transcended by, an indigenous version of popular power reflected in social mobilization and high levels of involvement in official organizations and in the operation of a communist version of welfarism.

This was summed up in the official conception of socialist democracy as developed by Soviet theorists and defined in the following terms:

The fundamental difference of socialist democracy lies in the fact that for the first time in history it spelled government by the toiling majority, the multi-million masses. And this is real government by the people, and not just a declared one, for it is based on social ownership of the means and instruments of production. The innovative character of socialist democracy lies in the fact that it not only proclaims a wide range of socio-economic, political and personal rights and freedoms but also guarantees them. Public ownership of the means and instruments of production is the chief way of doing this, the main guarantee. Abolition of the exploitation of man by man resulted in the transition from formal to genuine equality.

Soviet democracy guaranteed by the Constitution of the USSR means equality of rights of all citizens of the country in every sphere of economic, political, social and cultural life.

Relationships between the state and individuals are totally different under socialism. While guaranteeing the citizens' rights the state bears responsibility for the implementation of these rights.

Yes, we do call Soviet socialist democracy genuine democracy. For we judge it by the extent to which the masses take part in the running of production, the state and public affairs. Such an opportunity extends to every Soviet citizen.
Socialism: Theory and Practice (1981), pp.31–2.

While there was certainly some basis for Soviet criticism of the practice of liberal democracy and of the nature of 'actually existing democracy' in Western countries (more on this in Section 4), there was little evidence to support their claims of superior democratic practice. Soviet citizens did take part in administration and public affairs on a mass basis but their influence on decision making, and their participation in the selection of those placed in positions of authority, was, to say the least, minimal. Many did participate in the political process but the participation took place along firmly regimented lines and was hardly voluntary or self-motivated. Continuing debate over these issues was curtailed by the acceleration of Soviet *perestroika* in the late 1980s, the political implosion of most of the European communist states at the end of the decade and the progressive collapse of many sectors of the economy in Eastern Europe and the Soviet Union, developments which had a critical political and economic impact on the distant dependencies and satellites of the Soviet Union. Political change in these areas had not, of course, been absent throughout the post-war period — but developments like the replacement of mass terror by selective repression during the post-Stalin era was a step towards constitutionalism and democracy taken from a very low level. Attempts at political democratization had not been absent and examples occurred during 1956 in Hungary, 1968 in Czechoslovakia and through 1980 and 1981 in Poland. Each time, the attempts were reversed by military means and a stronger dictatorship reimposed. The foundations of totalitarianism persisted in the sense that single-party rule was reinforced, Marxism-Leninism reaffirmed as the sole public orthodoxy and political stability maintained by extensive coercion.

But democratization in modern societies is not restricted to the formal steps taken towards political democracy. Under the fossilized political shell of the communist party-state, the official forms of 'socialist democracy' and its totalitarian practice, social changes occurred which fostered alternative forms of democratization whose development exerted increasing pressure on the communist dictatorship and went some way to explaining why the East European regimes collapsed so rapidly and completely at the end of the 1980s. As well as universalism and representation, Arato (1985) argues, modern democracy implies pluralism and greater political diversity, which has meant that the limitations placed on political democratization and the restriction of political democracy *per se* in Eastern Europe could be to some extent sidestepped and compensated for by alternative forms of popular action.

These forms of action were of critical significance to developments in Eastern Europe and played an important part in the collapse of the communist dictatorships. They might encompass a range of small-scale actions like the achievement of confessional freedom, the establishment of an independent peace group or, alternatively, a free trade union and the organization of a workers' council. This could mean the extension of popular action to areas otherwise exempt from democratic control. At the same time, such actions stopped short of attempts to establish parliamentary democracy and left untouched the political underpinnings of dictatorship. But the association of political dictatorship with signs of growing civil democracy did point to emerging patterns of democratization and the possibility of new forms of political development in modern societies.

Indications of the historical relationship between democracy and totalitarianism have been made earlier in the discussion, the democratization of some states (Germany, Japan) being achieved only at the cost of a world war and the military defeat of fascist regimes. The collapse of East European communism in 1989 suggested a further way in which democracy might emerge from totalitarianism. Whereas massive external force was needed to crush the fascist regimes and install democracy in Germany and Italy, totalitarianism in Eastern Europe seemed to collapse from within, a process in which internal social forces played a major part. The external burdens of superpower rivalry and the costs of military competition, onerous for the Western powers but economically overwhelming for the Soviet Union and the socialist economic system of the Warsaw Pact countries, also played a part here, draining funds from consumer sectors and maintaining the militaristic ethos of state-centred socialism. The process of democratization was, moreover, in countries like Hungary and Poland, essentially peaceful — although the experience of violent repression in earlier years (1956, 1970, 1976, 1981–2) influenced later developments.

Romanian revolutionaries, Christmas 1989

Detotalitarianization in Romania and Albania had more violent aspects
and was not absent from the German Democratic Republic and
Czechoslovakia. But generally, it has been argued, the collapse of
communist dictatorship in Eastern Europe was greatly facilitated, if not
caused directly, by a gradual process of social change, the growing
alienation of the mass of society from virtually all aspects of formal
political life, and the crystallization of new ideas of democracy rooted
in the experience of everyday life. The increasing evidence of the
economic failure of the command economy, linked with the military
burden mentioned earlier, and the disappointed hopes of Eastern
consumerism (encouraged by socialist governments previously to take
people's minds off politics) reinforced these sentiments.
Democratization, many argued, was also fed by the strong social
commitment to its values that had developed under communism and its
gradual extension helped create the conditions for the swift collapse of
the dictatorial state. Further light on the nature of the social processes is
shed by the extract from Konrad, in which he outlines the
understanding of democracy that increasingly undermined the practice
of communist dictatorship.

ACTIVITY 5   Now read **Reading B, 'Anti-politics'**, by George Konrad.

What kind of democracy does Konrad identify in Eastern Europe after
the elimination of Solidarity from Polish public life in 1981? What
encouraged its development and what form did it take?

George Konrad, a Hungarian writer and sociologist, identifies the 'spontaneous cohesion' of society that underlay the democratic movement of Solidarity and sketches in a number of features of the East European social context that encouraged the formation of informal groupings, the development of a specific form of civil society and tendencies of spontaneous democratization in the areas of communist domination. These included the persistent demand for self-government, free communication within society, and continuing attachment to non-materialist values that fed the development of social autonomy and supported tendencies towards democratic self-government. It was such factors which encouraged the collapse of totalitarian dictatorship in Eastern Europe despite its capacity for centralized control and the power of its state apparatus. In this view, the turning-point of 1989 reflected the growing tension that had developed between democratic society and a dictatorial state in Eastern Europe — a civil society with increasing capacity for autonomous action and committed to self-government, and a communist state with declining authority and minimal capacity to manage processes of social and economic change, but with strong residual powers of repression and coercive self-defence.

These developments confirmed other judgements on the social underpinnings of modern democracy and the view that a process of questioning was implicit in social practice (without the actors necessarily being aware of it) and that 'the work of ideology, which is always dedicated to the task of restoring certainty, cannot put an end to this practice' (Lefort, 1988, p.19). Democracy, in distinction to totalitarianism, remains an historical society which preserves and welcomes indeterminacy, while the process of democratization is one of institutionalizing uncertainty, of 'subjecting all interests to uncertainty' (Lefort, 1988, p.16; Przeworski, 1986, p.58). Totalitarianism, many would argue, was based primarily on the rigidity of its ideological vision and expressed itself less in the capacity to maximize state power over society than in the desire to do so. But, even in the absence of a formalized, dogmatic ideology, the conditions of modern society themselves produce tendencies that encourage the regimentation and control of society, foster the routinization of political processes and enhancement of their predictability, and consequently discourage indeterminacy and minimize uncertainty. Having looked at the processes that have facilitated the rise of modern democracy and the spread of democratization, we now turn to examine some of the limits and problems they encounter in modern societies.

4   THE LIMITS AND PROBLEMS OF MODERN DEMOCRACY

The position of democracy was thus consolidated and strengthened in the countries of developed capitalism following World War II, and democratizing tendencies rapidly gained momentum in developed communist countries at the end of the 1980s following a tendency that had already become established elsewhere. In 1985 it was estimated that 16 states had moved towards democracy during the previous 10 years, while only six had moved in the reverse direction (*The Economist*, 8 June 1985). The global trajectory of democratization has been presented in various ways. Huntington (1990, pp.36–7) identified a first wave lasting from 1820 to the post-World War I years, a second wave after World War II involving the decolonialization process and lasting until about 1960, and a third wave which began in 1974 with the end of the Portuguese and Greek dictatorships and lasted throughout the 1980s. Accordingly, 26 countries could be described as democratic in 1922, 39 in 1962 and 50 in 1989. Dahl (1989, pp.234–9) points to three slightly different periods for the growth of 'polyarchy': 1776–1930, 1950–59 and the 1980s.

On this basis, 18 full polyarchies (to use Dahl's expression introduced in the last section) and three male polyarchies (i.e nominal democracies with an exclusively male franchise) were identified in 1930, between 36 and 40 countries for the 30-year period after 1945 and around 50 (not quite a third of the 168 nominally independent countries then in existence) by the middle of the 1980s. The extension of representative government and the acceptance of democracy as a general principle of political life, first in a few and then in a greater number of countries, reflected the extension of the principle of political equality and the provision of greater opportunities for greater electoral participation. But the acceptance of the democratic principle and the establishment of mass democracy in a number of countries has not necessarily been the same thing as the democratization of society or its political order. Conditions for the exercise of political rights were by no means distributed equally. Democracy in the sense of popular power being accepted and exercised as a dominant political form has certainly not been a prevalent feature of public life even in modern societies.

4.1   DEMOCRATIZATION IN MODERN SOCIETIES

Democratization generally meant the acceptance of liberal, representative democracy and its grafting on to existing systems of more elitist rule but, at least up to the post-World War II period, even in the more restrictive of the modern meanings it had evolved, democracy was only partially implemented in the great majority of the more developed societies. The establishment just of the liberal variant of democracy had, too, been accompanied by a considerable extension of the role and powers of the state which, in some conceptions (Nisbet, 1962), itself represented a threat to the democratic principle and undermined conditions for the development of a fuller conception of democracy. It could be argued, further, that democratic principles themselves were only partly accepted within many societies. There was, clearly, considerable open resistance to the idea of popular power and its implications (generally identified as socialist under contemporary conditions) and the unitary conception of democracy was held by others to be an unacceptable deviation from basic principles.

The increasing public acceptance of democratic principles has, therefore, been accompanied by a growing emphasis on just one of the possible variants of democracy, while there has been a tendency for direct opposition to the democratic ideal to be replaced by technical and empirically grounded doubts concerning its viability under the conditions of modern society. The complexity of modern societies and the technical expertise involved in the decision-making processes of contemporary government, for example, has been claimed to be incompatible with mass politics and extensive popular participation. The advance of democracy in a general sense can therefore be described as partial and by no means necessarily based on universally accepted values. It has been doubted by some whether there really was any global movement in the direction of democracy or popular power after World War II (Arblaster, 1987, p.56), although the collapse of dictatorships in Southern Europe and, more recently, in Latin America and Eastern Europe may provide grounds for reviewing this judgment.

Democratization has, therefore, firmly established itself on the political agenda of modern societies but often remains restricted in its social reach. Contradictions between such interrelated aspects in the development of modern societies are not difficult to identify. While war had the effect of consolidating political democracy and extending representative government in Britain after 1918, World War II raised the social expectations of British combatants and stimulated demands for the satisfaction of more extensive democratic rights. The British electorate in 1945 promptly voted out the victorious Conservative leader, Winston Churchill, and installed a Labour government committed to the introduction of a welfare state. Underlying these aspirations was a conception of democracy which drew closer to the idea of popular power and went considerably beyond more formal institutional notions of representative democracy. The transformation of Britain into a fully representative democracy after the First World War had provided little satisfaction for those who experienced defeat as trade unionists in the General Strike of 1926 or others in the older industrial areas who suffered long-term unemployment during the Depression.

Formal democratic rights were not felt to be sufficient; greater economic security and personal autonomy were also coming to be perceived as critical features of a fully democratic society; the idea of substantive democracy was coming to supplement or replace that of formal democracy — involving reference to a regime characterized 'by certain

Hunger march of the unemployed, 1932

ends and values towards whose realization a certain political group
aims and works. Behind these ends and values, which are used to
distinguish a democratic from an undemocratic regime not just formally
but substantially, lies the principle of equality' (Bobbio, 1989, p.157).
This principle referred not just to the legal equality provided for by
liberal constitutions but also to a social form which contained major
elements of economic equality. Formal democracy, concerned primarily
with the form of government, is thus distinguished from a substantive
democracy more concerned with its content. This conception of
democracy was certainly more strongly articulated by the Labour
government of 1945–50 than it had been by any previous government in
Britain and, in pushing democratization beyond the liberal form of mass
representation, was seen as a radical form of political change.

To those strongly imbued with the principles of representative
democracy, like most American observers, it could appear as a socialist
revolution — albeit one achieved by consent (Brinton, 1965, p.4). The
welfare state saw the introduction of a national health service, the
extension of the state education system following the 1944 Act and the
introduction of mechanisms of enhanced income support which
affirmed principles of social democracy and the promise of increased
equality. In such processes, ideas of modern citizenship received more
concrete definition. Moreover, although economic conditions were
tough in the immediate post-war years, gradual recovery from war-time
devastation and austerity, and the inception of a process of steady
growth, provided a context in which such rights could be established in
practical terms and their implementation reaffirmed as a major element

of the post-war social order. Post-war recovery and economic growth within a context of international stability also meant that, as had been the case after the 1867 Reform Act nearly a century earlier, working-class conditions could be improved without threatening the incomes or economic base of middle-class groups.

The commitment to the welfare state soon came to be shared by the Conservative Party and such principles of 'social democracy' were largely removed from the arena of party political conflict for several decades (it was significant that such aspects of substantive democracy came under critical scrutiny and attack in the 1980s, after the process of steady economic growth came to an end and the economic interests of different groups came into greater conflict). The development of ideas of modern citizenship (which is the subject of Chapter 4 of this book) involved consideration of the pluralization of power (the empowerment of groups which had tended to be marginalized and the provision of greater access to the decision-making procedures of larger scale, hierarchical organizations) and the democratization of spheres other than the political and beyond the formal remit of representative government. The transformation of power relations in the workplace and the establishment of industrial democracy (see the entry in *The Penguin Dictionary of Sociology*) were seen as increasingly important, although clearly raised further questions about the relationship of democracy to capitalism. The model of welfarism developed in Britain and Scandanavia was eventually adopted and replicated, at least in part in most advanced capitalist democracies — including Western Europe and the United States. But a gap between democratic ideals and, as Italian political theorist Norberto Bobbio (1987, p.26) put it, 'actually existing democracy' was clearly detectable and full realization of the democratic ideal remained a distant prospect. Six 'transformations' of democracy have been identified by the same writer which account for the discrepancy — susceptible to interpretation by the right, as the onset of semi-anarchy threatening the disintegration of the state or, by the left, as parliamentary democracy becoming an autocratic regime. We now turn to examine the nature of these transformations.

4.2   THE CONDITIONS OF ACTUALLY EXISTING DEMOCRACY

The first transformation refers to the original idea of modern democracy — based on an individualistic conception of society distinct from the classical conception, envisaging a state lacking the divisions produced by feudal estates or by the intermediary bodies of a corporatist society which assign individuals a defined though limited role in the social order through membership of a specialized group. Instead, the individual in a modern democracy seems to have had decreasing influence, while the different views and interests characteristic of a pluralist democracy have instead been those originating from and reflecting those of a multiplicity of large organizations, special associations, professional bodies and trade unions, and diverse political parties. Secondly, the form of political representation characteristic of modern representative democracy — one barring the imposition of a binding mandate on the individual representative — has been consistently violated and subverted by the unceasing pursuit of particular interests and the influence exerted over individual representatives and decision-making centres by pressure groups. Modern democracy, thirdly, has proved incapable of counteracting or eliminating oligarchical power (power exercised jointly by a privileged few), which has flourished in the activities of the numerous elites of contemporary societies and with the replacement of ideas of individual autonomy and the practice of liberty by procedures of representative democracy.

A fourth limitation on democratization has been been its failure to extend into other areas of social life adjacent to the political, and the weak penetration of democracy into big business and bureaucracy. This development reflects the weakness of contemporary democracy as a social democracy: not defined by the number of those who have the right to participate in making decisions that concern them but rather by the number of contexts or places where they can exercise that right. Fifth, the persistence of 'invisible power' — in the form of security complexes, secret states, informal mafias and other organized means for the avoidance of public accountability — reduces the capacity of citizens to control those in power. Finally, a sixth 'transformation' has been the replacement of the educative process of political activity and participation by growing political apathy and an increasing tendency amongst those empowered with political rights not to use them (Bobbio, 1987, pp.26–36). These transformations are also interpreted as 'broken promises' of a lofty democratic ideal, whose implementation takes the form of 'brute facts' which fall far short of the aspirations which originally accompanied their appearance. The basis of these transformations are outlined in the extract from Bobbio, which you should turn to now.

ACTIVITY 6   Now read **Reading C, 'The future of democracy',** by Norberto Bobbio.

What are the three root causes of the broken promises identified by Bobbio? Briefly outline the restrictions they place on the practice of democracy.

The broken promises of contemporary democracy Bobbio traces to the importance of technical expertise in modern society and the antithetical relationship of technocracy with democracy, the progressive bureaucratization of modern society and the multiple relations that have developed (not least because of the rise of welfarism) between the democratic state and the bureaucratic state, and to the rapid growth of demands on democracies in terms of their provision of increasing goods, rights and services. In this, he seems to echo the doubts of theorists, like Schumpeter (1965) with his reformulation of modern democracy in terms of 'competitive elitism', who have found classic doctrines of democracy unrealizable within the context of modern society and largely inappropriate to the objectives and inclinations of the modern citizen (see entries on ELITE and POLITICAL PARTIES in *The Penguin Dictionary of Sociology*, and also Held, 1987, Chapter 5). There is, as Arblaster (1987) has noted, a not inconsiderable current of sociological thought that has emphasized in empirical terms the obstacles to democratic practice in modern society and has presented theoretical doubts about the feasibility of putting democratic principles into practice.

Dahl (1989, pp.266–8) identifies a number of thinkers (including Marx, Lenin, Mosca, Pareto, Michels and Gramsci) with the view that democracy is little more than another guise for minority domination, and associates with their judgment the common-sense conclusions that many derive from practical experience of social life. This practical view he introduces in this way:

> Can anyone who is active in organizational life fail to notice how often, even in ostensibly democratic organizations, it is the few who make the decisions and the many who do little more than go along? If majorities really are governed by minorities, we might ask, why is this so? Although the writers above give special emphasis to different factors, I think they would all agree on the crucial importance of the relatively enduring (though ultimately impermanent) structures and institutions — social, economic, political — that strongly shape choices and opportunities for large numbers of people over a comparatively long time. To take an extreme case, in a country ruled by the military, no matter how meritocratic or egalitarian recruitment and promotions may be, only a few can enter into the ruling group. The top of a pyramid has only a limited space; and by definition all theories of minority domination interpret the world as made up of structures of power in which the top is considerably smaller than the bottom. Probably all the writers mentioned would also agree that in the last two centuries the structures and institutions of capitalism, markets, and bourgeois society have been enormously important in determining patterns of domination. It is structures like these that also influence the specific composition of the ruling class: what sorts of persons are likely to enter into it, what sorts are not. For it is *within* these structures, and in considerable measure because of them, that individuals and aggregates of individuals — classes — achieve their domination.
> (Dahl,1989, p.266)

The writers mentioned by Dahl represent a variety of different, and contradictory, ideologies and contrasting ideas of minority rule and the bases of their power.

They all, however, do more than point out the obvious fact that there are significant inequalities in society and have in common, according to

Dahl (1989, p.272), the belief either that a satisfactory approximation of democracy is impossible or that it is only possible under conditions which have never yet existed or are likely to be impossible in the conceivable future. They tend to regard the very idea of democracy as illusory and essentially inappropriate to modern life. But these writers also have in common, in Dahl's view, a theoretical orientation pitched at a high level of generality as well as a certain vagueness, and they do not argue through their position to establish the chain of control their theories imply or provide the evidence that would be necessary to demonstrate that such dominance exists. In short, they suggest the existence of a prior commitment to proof of the impossibility of democracy. Whether marked by a pessimistic fatalism about modern societies or holding hopes of utopian revolutionary solutions, they show little confidence in their contemporary democratic capacities. These views are clearly related to Bobbio's discussion of the 'broken promises' of the democratic ideal (particularly in relation to technocracy and bureaucracy), but there are also differences. Unlike elite theorists, Bobbio is less inclined to reject notions of popular sovereignty or to doubt the process of representative government, arguing rather for the extension of social democracy and the democratization of society.

But if the conditions for democratization have not been wholly advantageous in modern societies and the progress of democracy limited under advanced capitalism, developments elsewhere were by no means more impressive. The wave of decolonization that gathered pace some years after 1945 and led to the dismemberment of all the West European empires saw the creation of many new independent states in the Third World and the establishment of a more extensive international base for national sovereignty. The carefully crafted parliamentary systems rarely showed much capacity for survival, though, and the socio-economic preconditions of democracy again revealed their importance — this time by demonstrating the fragility of democratic forms and the vulnerability of democratic processes in an environment dominated by the imperatives of development. By the 1980s, Dahl (1989, p.239) was able to identify Botswana, with a population of 1.26 million, as the sole polyarchy on the whole African continent.

The absence of national unity or an integrated cultural identity, in association with the perceived needs of rapid economic development, defence (or aggression) and social mobilization, favoured the replacement of formal democracy by dictatorship — though this did not necessarily create better conditions for socio-economic development. The tenacious adherence to parliamentary democratic forms, as in the case of India, also effectively came under criticism for forming part of a social complex of backwardness and blocking further socio-economic development (Moore, 1967). But, as we have seen, the process of democratization on a global scale again gathered strength in the 1970s, having particular effect in Southern Europe, Latin America, South-East Asia and, finally Eastern Europe. Barrington Moore's work, published in the late 1960s, was written when there was little evidence of international progress towards democracy and hopes of post-colonial political development were being disappointed in many parts of the globe. This may explain some of the pessimism he showed concerning the frustrated economic development of the country known as the world's largest democracy (India), and his identification of fascism and communism as 'routes to the modern world' comparable to that of the liberal democracy that was established in the countries of advanced capitalism.

The disappointment of hopes of democracy was particularly marked in the case of Africa, where problems of poverty and economic development have been particularly evident and various forms of dictatorship have remained entrenched. It was notable also that tentative moves towards democracy were made in some of the Asian countries (Taiwan, South Korea) where the extent and rate of economic development had been particularly impressive. The link between democratization and economic development, particularly in the form of capitalist growth, again appeared to be strengthened by more recent developments. Barrington Moore's influential work was concerned, as we have noted, not just with the social origins of dictatorship and democracy but also with the nature of contrasting routes to the modern world. As he emphasized, the contrasting routes to the modern world presented themselves at different stages of historical development and were clearly marked by the date of their appearance. Their stability and long-term viability showed significant differences. After the defeat of the Axis powers and throughout the second half of the twentieth century, developed capitalist states, as should be well established by now, have taken a predominantly democratic political form. The fascist 'revolution from above' can no longer be seen as a viable contemporary form of modernization.

More recently, the third route marked out to the modern world, communist revolution from below (distinct both from the bourgeois democratic path and that of fascist dictatorship), has also come into question not just for its actual and potential political nature but also for its status as a viable vehicle of modernization (Lewis, 1990, pp.253–4). Contemporary experience seems both to confirm the earlier proposal that political democracy does have an intimate relationship with the development of modern societies and advanced capitalism, and to suggest that sustained and effective modernization has been more successfully achieved within some democratic framework (although there is certainly no deterministic mechanism involved). While the third —communist — route to the modern world, characterized by left-wing dictatorship established through peasant revolution (Moore, 1967, p.xii), emerged stronger from World War II (the Soviet Union gaining a satellite empire in Eastern Europe and finding new allies in China, North Korea and, later, North Vietnam), the viability of communism as a variant of modernization also later proved to be dubious. If there have been clear limits to the acceptance of democratic principles and their practice in developed capitalist societies, alternative routes to the modern world have certainly not provided a better basis for democratization or stable patterns of social development.

4.3   THE DEMOCRATIZATION OF POST-TOTALITARIAN SOCIETIES

The strengthening of a global tendency of democratization in the 1970s and 1980s, in association with growing pressures for global economic integration on a capitalist basis, provide a specific context for the transition to democracy of the post-totalitarian societies of Eastern Europe. These societies confront less the limits to democracy seen in the countries of developed capitalism than problems of democratic transition, which combine tensions found in many contemporary societies with the inheritance of a problematic pattern of political and social development.

While the problems of sustaining and extending democracy there are different from those under the conditions of developed capitalism, they nevertheless reflect some of the organizational dilemmas common to most modern societies, as well as the particular consequences of their own path of historical development. The legacy of communist rule, as part of what we may now recognize to be a failed strategy of modernization including a specific programme of political development, has significant consequences for the democratization of Eastern Europe. One notable condition was provided by a reaction against the former communist parties' domination of the public, and even parts of the private, sphere as well as the general politicization of social life. Eastern Europe has not been alone in experiencing such a response to the decline of the totalitarian left. Writing before the overt crisis of the communist party-state that emerged in 1989, French theorist Claude Lefort (1988, p.4) also noted that the collapse of the myth of Soviet or Chinese socialism and the declining popularity of Marxism (evident in France since the early 1970s) had not led to a rehabilitation of the notion of the political. East European communism, not surprisingly, also produced wide-spread contempt and distaste for official political activity, and it was as Lefort had noted, 'as though the condemnation of totalitarianism implied the condemnation of the political as such'.

This dislike of politics and suspicion of all politicians certainly gained strength in Eastern Europe (although it is by no means restricted to Europe and post-communist societies) and contributed to the growing self-awareness of a civil society. For Konrad (1984, p.92) 'antipolitics', as presented in the essay which —significantly — provides the title for his book, strives 'to put politics in its place' and presents itself as the 'ethos of civil society'. Those Europeans who had lived through most of the post-World War II period under communist rule had had enough of centrally-organized political activity, the dominance of the party over social life and the ubiquity of the leadership's propaganda and political slogans. The monopolization of public life by the single party had the effect of separating the notion of the political from any idea of authentic self-rule or autonomous activity. It was this experience that led Romanians during their revolution to cry that they were demonstrating for 'democracy, not politics' (see Jorgensen, 1992). It is an outcome that recalls Nisbet's critical presentation (Section 2) of the consequences of unitary democracy and dangers of the unrestricted growth of state activity.

But this also had implications for the establishment of political democracy and the development of what Dahl calls polyarchy, the institutions and form of political system that make a democratic society possible. The resilience of civil society under communist dictatorship, and the growing drive for democratization, by no means resolved all problems surrounding the establishment and operation of a democratic order, either on the practical or theoretical level. Soon after the collapse of communism in Poland, such features as the care taken to avoid public manifestations of political conflict, popular responses to political leadership that were emotive rather than reasoned, more intense criticism of politicians, and public reluctance to accept the validity of new political institutions all suggested that East European distaste for the political had not diminished at all. Similar responses in terms of public disillusionment and signs of major organizational confusion could be detected in Hungary and post-communist East Germany (Lewis 1990, pp.260–1). Arato's earlier insight (1985, p.323) that a critical element in East European democratization related to the democratization of its political culture remained highly relevant.

The speed and comprehensiveness of the collapse of the communist order in Eastern Europe meant that the prospect of democracy was opened up with startling rapidity in the absence of any firm indications as to whether the social conditions for its establishment and consolidation yet existed. It should be evident by now, however, that the democratization of modern societies (at least in the case of the older and more established democracies) has been a lengthy and contentious process which involved extensive conflict. The emergence of democracy in Britain as a political process can be clearly traced back at least as far as the Civil War and the subsequent Glorious Revolution (1688), which acted as a foundation for the establishment of a constitutional state, providing a framework for the resolution of religious conflicts and subsequent toleration, a major contribution to the establishment of democracy and pluralist development. In America and France, the process of political democratization can be dated from the end of the eighteenth century. In all three cases, the emergence of mass democracy was not complete until well into the twentieth century, and many would say that the process remains in many important respects still uncompleted.

In terms of the general record of modern democracies the time-scale is shorter but still, from the point of view of the post-communist societies, quite daunting. Dahl (1989, p.315) provides some empirical guidance with his statement that 'in countries where the institutions of polyarchy have existed for as long as twenty years or more, the breakdown of democracy and its replacement by an authoritarian regime is extraordinarily rare'. Huntington (1990, p.42) has proposed a 'two-turnover' test and suggests that democracy has been institutionalized

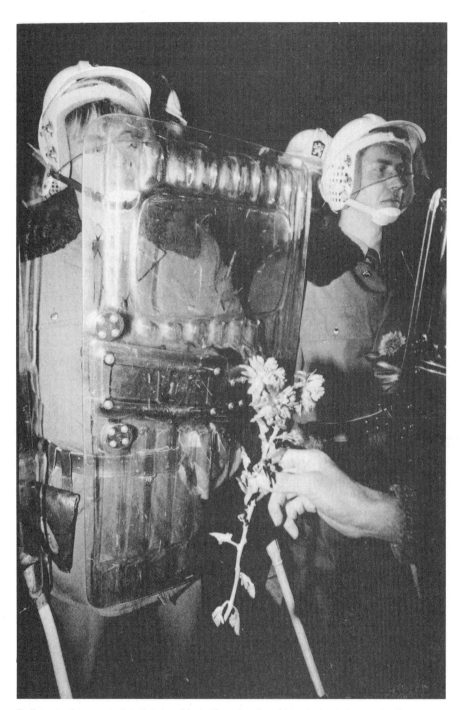

Collapse of communist dictatorship in Czechoslovakia: student demonstration
November 1989

'when one duly elected party or coalition turns over power to a duly
elected successor party or coalition and this second elected government
then also voluntarily gives up power after losing an election'. The
length of time this could take was, of course, less certain, although by

1990 only one of the relatively new democracies (Portugal) had passed the test. Democracies, it was at least clear, were not only historical societies but also the result of a substantial historical process.

In terms of the limits and problems of modern democracy, the most that could be done in the wake of the collapse of communism in Eastern Europe to further analysis and prediction was to list the factors most likely to be significant in the process of democratization. American political scientist and analyst of political development Samuel Huntington (1990, pp.42–3) identified six factors and made some specific observations:

1   The extent of the country's previous experience with democracy. In Eastern Europe, Czechoslovakia is in the lead with Romania and Bulgaria at the other extreme.

2   The level of social and economic development of the country. Czechoslovakia and East Germany have the advantage here.

3   The success of the authoritarian regime. Peoples who make a success of authoritarianism appear to be more likely to make a success of democracy. No East European country rates high here, but East Germany and Hungary are probably in the lead.

4   The extent, depth and strength of independent social and political organizations. Poland is uniquely advantaged with respect to this factor.

5   The ability of the government to take and implement tough decisions dealing with economic reform. No new regime has scored here, but Poland is taking the lead in attempting to do so.

6   The extent of polarization between social classes, regions and ethnic groups. In most countries highly antagonistic groups are beginning to develop political consciousness and to mobilize for political purposes. The degree to which these cleavages will be destabilizing is unclear.

With respect to the democratization of post-communist societies, one immediate problem resided in the fact that the apparent victory of civil society over communist dictatorship might lead not to political democracy but to populism. This refers to direct political dominance by 'the people' with little regard to constitutional arrangements, the institutional mediation of power relations or any protection of minority rights. The desires and aspirations of a greater fraction of society might be better satisfied by the political arrangements of the post-communist order, but this was not necessarily the same thing as the establishment of political democracy. Post-communist Eastern Europe was in fact experiencing similar dilemmas and sharing problems related to those faced by Western nations in the early modern period during analagous stages of their political development. The problems of post-totalitarian development merged with those seen in the West during earlier phases of political development. Civil society, as Keane (1988, p.22) points out with clear echoes of Thomas Hobbes, 'can also degenerate into a battlefield' and, for several reasons, sovereign state power is an indispensable condition for the democratization of civil society. By itself, civil society by no means secures the weak from the power of the strong, or provides a central point for social coordination and mechanisms of relatively low-cost conflict resolution. There were certainly major differences in historical context and in the role played by a whole range of factors (social, economic, international, cultural). But some of the critical choices, and the range of solutions to the problems placed on the agenda by the growth of demands for more extensive and effective participation in government and for control over the mechanisms of social development, recalled the historic conflicts we have examined earlier. One of these problems was outlined in the Polish press by Wojciech Sadurski (1990) a year after the formation of a non-communist government, and you should read this now.

ACTIVITY 7   Now read **Reading D, 'Populism and the constitution'**, by Wojciech Sadurski.

What was the nature of the political predicament identified by Sadurski and faced by those seeking to find democratic solutions to the problems of Polish society. What solutions were proposed?

The predicament identified by Sadurski was similar to that which emerged during earlier periods in the West and which fuelled the fears of those who were anxious about the consequences of mass democracy: namely, that the demands of the majority would be likely to ride roughshod over minority rights. While historic Western fears were class-based, those identified in modern Poland were largely cultural, moral and religious. Yet they both referred to driving forces within a democratization movement, the aspirations of a new and increasingly powerful working class in eighteenth and nineteenth century Western Europe and the convictions of a civil society in the East frequently sustained by religious faith and supported organizationally by a strong Church (it is hardly accidental that this conflict first emerged in Poland, where the Catholic Church retained its greatest social influence). Mill's fears of the tyranny of the majority (referred to at the beginning of Section 3) have also been echoed in Polish views recorded in the press that 'a state in which morality forms the law is a totalitarian state' (*Polityka*, 29 September 1990).

The solutions proposed also showed similarities and pointed to the institutions and procedures of liberal democracy. The historic Western response to the problem was the development of representative institutions and an emphasis on limited government. Sadurski directs attention to the importance of constitutional provisions, the defence of civil rights and the preservation of freedom for minorities. The resolution of such conflicts has invariably involved a lengthy period of debate and antagonism, the evolution of group relations being a matter of considerable complexity which carried little hope of rapid

Walesa and Pope John Paul II

conciliation. If democracies are, in distinction to totalitarian systems, historical societies (Lefort,1988, p.16), democratization is also an historical process involving major changes in established relations between social groups and the evolution of specific conceptions of democracy. Both these factors emerge in the problematic course of democratization accelerated by the collapse of the East European communist dictatorship in 1989.

The situation outlined above suggests that the social dynamic of East European democratization neither diminishes the contemporary importance of established democratic procedures and issues of representation (in fact, it rather highlights their role) nor points to the imminent removal of the obstacles to 'social democracy' seen in the West (Bobbio, 1987, p.55). The key Western process of democratization, he argues, concerns not the transition from representative to direct democracy but the extension of democratic powers, previously restricted to national political processes, to the various spheres of civil society. This is the sense of contemporary democratization, in which political democracy develops into social democracy. In terms of post-communist Eastern Europe, however, it implies that the foundations of political democracy need to be firmly laid in a society and the institutions of a democratic state established in their own right, rather than majority preference and the sentiments of civil society translated directly into government policy. As the failed attempt to practice direct democracy in the form of its Soviet variant suggested, principles of constitutionalism and representation seem to be indispensible components of modern democracy if it is to be achieved within the confines of the nation-state.

5   CONCLUSION

This brief survey of some of the limits of modern democracy and problems of democratization in the West and East does not claim to offer any judgement on the condition of contemporary democracy or predictions about its future development. Nevertheless, the account of its emergence and examination of the social conditions under which it has developed does tell us something about the nature of modern democracy and provide some insight into the dynamics of contemporary variants. Let us review the major points made in this chapter.

Mass democracy as a contemporary political phenomenon emerged and progressed with the development of modern society in its industrial and urban form. Its origins can be traced back to the eighteenth century, although its characteristic variants developed gradually in specific places throughout the nineteenth century and gained a wider presence only in more recent times. It has invariably taken the form of representative democracy — which was virtually inevitable in view of the contemporary prevalence of the nation-state — which stands in some contrast to classical models of democracy and has attracted the criticism of those who adhere to ideas of direct democracy. It has, further, developed in close association with processes of capitalist modernization, while the close relationship between capitalist development and liberal democracy has been confirmed more recently by developments in Southern Europe, Latin America and Eastern Europe.

The spread of democratization in the late twentieth century, though, has been accompanied by a growing awareness of the weak social underpinnings of formal democratic procedures, the restriction of its social reach and certain conditions of modern social life that constrain its effectiveness. This survey has thus suggested the partial achievement and relative fragility of democratic values and procedures even in countries which, in Barrington Moore's phrase, took a parliamentary democratic route to the modern world and where some of the roots of democracy were established at the same time as the foundations of modern society. Its instability is likely to be that much greater in countries like those in Eastern Europe and parts of South-East Asia which have become involved in recent processes of global democratization or where — like others in Latin America — democratic forms and aspirations have an established history but an already patchy record of democratic implementation and achievement.

Different factors are likely to enter into the differing situations. In Eastern Europe it may well prove to be social and political as well as the more obvious economic factors that are important for the process of democratization. This is because of the anti-political legacy left by communist dictatorship, and the ambiguous implications of the elements of a civil society which played a part in the collapse of communism and are likely to determine the nature of the democratic transition they have embarked on. While it is the weakness of 'social democracy' and limitations on the achievements of a strongly-rooted representative democracy that seem to pose the greatest problems in established Western polities, in areas like Eastern Europe it is the weakness and ill-defined character of formal democratic institutions and the machinery of representation that seem to be the area of greatest uncertainty in the early stages of democratic transition.

The implications for democracy of the civil societies that have been identified there also remain ambiguous, since they tend to reinforce the anti-political legacy of communist rule, merge with continuing elements of a non-democratic political culture and encourage populist rather than constitutional solutions to the problems and conflicts of post-communist transition. This comment, however, is not meant to offer a negative appraisal or forecast of democratic prospects but a reasoned view of the complex relations between the various factors involved. Democracies are not just the product of historical, and sometimes very lengthy, processes of development but also embody elements of indeterminacy and unpredictability. It was, after all, the failure of totalitarianism to cope with such elements of uncertainty that helped bring about its downfall and unveil the prospect of democracy.

REFERENCES

Abercrombie, N., Hill, S. and Turner, B.S. (eds) (1988) *The Penguin Dictionary of Sociology*, 2nd edn, Harmondsworth, Penguin.

Arato, A. (1985) 'Some perspectives of democratization in East Central Europe', *Journal of International Affairs* vol.38, 2.

Arblaster, A. (1987) *Democracy,* Milton Keynes, Open University Press.

Bobbio, N. (1987) *The Future of Democracy,* Cambridge, Polity Press.

Bobbio, N. (1989) *Democracy and Dictatorship*, Cambridge, Polity Press.

Brinton, C. (1965) *The Anatomy of Revolution*, New York, Vintage Books.

Dahl, R.A. (1989) *Democracy and its Critics,* New Haven, Yale University Press.

The Economist, 8 June 1985, London.

Hall, S. and Gieben, B. (eds) (1992) *Formations of Modernity*, Cambridge, Polity Press.

Held, D. (1987) *Models of Democracy,* Cambridge, Polity Press.

Huntington, S.P. (1990) 'Democratization and security in Eastern Europe', in Volten, P. (ed.) *Uncertain Futures: Eastern Europe and Democracy*, New York, Institute for East-West Security Studies.

Jorgensen, K.E. (1992) 'The end of anti-politics in central Europe', in Lewis, P.G. (ed.) *Democracy and Civil Society in Eastern Europe,* London, Macmillan.

Keane, J. (1988) *Democracy and Civil Society*, London, Verso.

Konrad, G. (1984) *Antipolitics*, London, Quartet Books.

Lefort, C. (1988) *Democracy and Political Theory*, Cambridge, Polity Press.

Lewis, P.G. (1990) 'Democratization in Eastern Europe', *Coexistence*, vol.27, 2.

Moore, B. (1967) *Social Origins of Dictatorship and Democracy*, London, Allen Lane.

Nisbet, R.A. (1962) *Community and Power*, New York, Galaxy Books.

Polityka, Warsaw.

Penguin Dictionary of Sociology: see Abercrombie *et al.* (1988).

Przeworski, A. (1986) 'Some problems in the study of the transition to democracy', in O'Donnell, G., Schmitter, P.C., and Whitehead, L. (eds), *Transitions from Authoritarian Rule,* Baltimore, John Hopkins.

Sadurski, W. (1990) 'Populism and the Constitution', *Polityka*, 8 September.

Schumpeter, J.A. (1965) *Capitalism, Socialism and Democracy*, London, Unwin Books.

Socialism: Theory and Practice (1981), October, pp.31-2, Moscow, Novosti Press reprint journal.

Therborn, G. (1977) 'The rule of capital and the rise of democracy', *New Left Review,* 103.

Williams, R. (1976) *Keywords*, London, Fontana Books.

THE RULE OF CAPITAL AND THE RISE OF DEMOCRACY

Goran Therborn

Capitalism and democracy: inherent tendencies

Bourgeois democracy has been attained by such diverse and tortuous routes that any straightforward derivation from the basic characteristics of capitalism would be impossible, or at least seriously misleading. Nevertheless, the facts that democracy ... did not appear anywhere prior to capitalism; that some capitalist countries have experienced a purely internal development of democracy; and that all major advanced bourgeois states are today democracies — these naturally call for some elucidation of the tendencies inherent within capitalism. These may provisionally be grouped according to their effect upon two central features of bourgeois democracy: (a) inclusions of the masses in *part* of the political process, (b) under conditions of representative government and electoral competition.

1   Bourgeois democracy has always succeeded mass struggles of varying degrees of violence and protractedness. The first inherent tendency, then, will be found in *the conditions favouring popular struggle*. Legal emancipation of labour and the creation of a free labour market, industrialization, concentration of capital are all intrinsic tendencies which simultaneously lay the basis for a working-class movement of a strength and stability inachievable by the exploited classes of pre-capitalist modes of production. In accordance with Marx's analysis of the growing contradictions of capitalism, the working class is, *ceteris paribus*, strengthened by the advance and development of capitalism. This explains the traditional sociological correlations of democracy with wealth, literacy and urbanization — factors which bear upon the relationship of forces in the class struggle. And, as we have already seen, the labour movement has itself played a vital role in the struggle for democracy.

2   However, we also remarked that in general the working class has not won a share in the political process in the heat of battle. On the contrary, it has been more common for the bourgeoisie to make concessions after a period of successful resistance to reform. Apparently, working-class participation must in some sense be to the bourgeoisie's advantage. Although in Germany and Austria in 1918 and 1945 (possibly also in Belgium and Sweden in 1918) and in Italy in 1945 the alternative to bourgeois democracy was an attempted socialist revolution, actual defence against proletarian revolution does not seem to have been a directly determining factor. In all these cases, it was not the insurrectionary proletariat but foreign armies that overthrew the existing regimes, whereupon the old internal democratic forces at last got the upper hand. Of greater importance was the specifically capitalist art of industrialized warfare. The First World War was fought both with massive conscript armies and with whole civilian

Source: Therborn, G. (1977) 'The rule of capital and the rise of democracy' *New Left Review*, 103, pp.28–34.

populations mobilized for military production. For this effort even the Wilhelmine Reich admitted the Social Democrats into the governmental machinery; against this background, too, the suffrage was extended in Belgium, Canada, Britain and the United States.

3   National unification and liberation have everywhere been seen by the bourgeoisie as a strategic necessity for the development and protection of trade and industry and the breaking of feudal dynastic power. And for these aims it has often found it invaluable to enlist popular support. The extension of suffrage in Denmark, Germany, Norway, Finland and Italy (for the imperialist Libyan expedition) formed part of a process of national unification.

4   Feverish development of the productive forces is another feature peculiar to the capitalist mode of exploitation. One of the main reasons why nineteenth and early twentieth-century liberals could deny the compatibility of democracy with private property was their dread that popular legislatures and municipal bodies would greatly increase taxation. However, they were disregarding the elasticity and expansive capacity of capitalism. Higher levels of taxation have liquidated neither private property nor capital accumulation. Rises in productivity make possible a simultaneous increase of both rates of exploitation and real incomes of the exploited masses. This is, of course, not in itself conducive to democracy. But it is relevant in so far as it provides the bourgeoisie with an unprecedentedly wide room for manoeuvre in dealing with the exploited majority.

5   So far we have deliberately talked in very general terms of popular mobilization and incorporation of the working class into the political process. But such mobilization need not be democratic. In their very different ways, wartime Wilhelmine Germany, Fascism and third world 'populism' all testify to that. What makes capitalist democracy at all possible is a characteristic unique among known modes of production. Capitalism is an impersonal mode of exploitation, involving the rule of capital rather than personal domination of the bourgeoisie. It certainly does not function in the manner of an automatic machine, but it does operate as production for ever greater profit under conditions of impersonal market competition. The rule of capital requires a state — for both internal and external support and protection — but as long as it upholds the separate realm of capitalist 'civil society', this state does not have to be managed personally by bourgeois. And in the long history of democratization, bourgeois politicians have learnt the many mechanisms at their disposal to keep the state in harmony with the needs of capital.

6   ... And we have seen that the fight of the working class for universal suffrage and freely elected government was never by itself sufficient to enforce the introduction of bourgeois democracy. This raises the question whether there are other internal tendencies of capitalism, which, under certain conditions, may generate forces of democratization apart from working-class struggle. One such tendency may be immediately identified. Capitalist relations of production tend to create an *internally competing, peacefully disunited ruling class*. In its development, capital is

divided into several fractions: mercantile, banking, industrial, agrarian, small and big. Except in a situation of grave crisis or acute threat from an enemy (whether feudal, proletarian or a rival national state) bourgeois class relations contain no unifying element comparable to the dynastic kingship legitimacy and fixed hierarchy of feudalism. Furthermore, the development of capitalism has usually stimulated the expansion of petty commodity production, before tending to destroy it. Thus, the commercialization of agriculture transformed a self-subsistent peasantry into an agrarian petty bourgeoisie with distinct interests of its own.

In the absence of a single centre, some kind of elective, deliberative and representative political machinery became necessary. Therefore, propertied republics or parliamentary monarchies developed at an early stage in the formation of capitalist states — for example, the Italian, German and Swiss city republics, the United Provinces of the Low Countries, Britain, the United States, France and Belgium (the latter after 1830). As regards freedom of the press, the material basis of its appearance was the launching of newspapers as capitalist enterprises like any other. This was still a democracy for the bourgeoisie only, and fractionalization of capital has only contributed to a democracy including the rest of the population in conjunction with the other tendencies referred to above. Thus, the decisive role in a number of instances of contingent military defeat shows that capitalism does not necessarily develop forces of sufficient strength to extend the basis of democracy to the masses. ...

Democratization and class struggle

In the last few decades, despite striking *prima facie* evidence to the contrary — European Fascism, third-world military dictatorships, etc. — functionalist and/or evolutionist conceptions of a 'normal' relationship of correspondence between the rule of capital and bourgeois democracy have quite often informed the analyses of both Marxist and non-Marxist writers. Our historical examination of the political constellations in which democracy was established in the major and most advanced capitalist countries has revealed the inadequacy of such general arguments and explanatory hypotheses.

Nevertheless, bourgeois democracy is no mere accident of history, and capitalism does contain a number of tendencies which are conducive to processes of democratization. Thus, it has frequently, and correctly, been observed that bourgeois democracy entails a competitive division within a basic framework of unity — even if this statement is interpreted in a naively idealistic way, by reference to ideology and varieties of 'political culture'. But the concrete economic and political dynamic of the rise of capitalism does involve the struggle for and development of a new divided unity. This appears as the nation state, freed of the barriers and boundaries of dynastic legitimacy, feudal enfiefment and provincial tradition. The establishment of national sovereignty and unity resulted from struggles against royal absolutism, foreign dynasties and provincial separatism. These were the stakes of the Dutch wars against Spain in the sixteenth and seventeenth centuries; the seventeenth-century English revolution and civil war; the US Declaration of Independence; the French Revolution of 1789; the 1830 August revolution in Belgium; the unification of Switzerland, Italy, Germany, and of the Canadian, Australian and New Zealand colonies; the Meiji Restoration in Japan; the establishment of the constitutional Eider state in Denmark; the emancipation of Norway and Finland; and even the constitutional struggles within the Habsburg empire. Only in Sweden, with its long-standing national unity and peculiar mixture of estates and parliament dating from the eighteenth century, were anti-dynastic and anti-parochial national struggles not a central component of the nascent process of democratization. ...

Freedom of trade and industry created a network of divisive competitive relationships which ran through the new ruling class of the unified and sovereign states. The market replaced the hierarchical pyramid of medieval and Absolutist feudalism. And it was in this unity-division of national state and market that the process of democratization originated. This happened fundamentally in one of two different ways. In certain cases, democracy was first introduced for upper layers of the bourgeoisie (including commercialized landowners) who alone had the right to vote and form parliamentary or republican governments. Other sections of the bourgeoisie and petty bourgeoisie were subsequently included in this structure, according to widely varying tempos and modalities. However, where the bourgeois revolution stopped half way, democratization began as a constitutional compromise between the old landowning ruling class — including its apex, the dynasty — and the bourgeoisie. This system then developed either into a propertied democracy, as in Scandinavia, the Netherlands and Belgium, or into a still largely non-democratic form of government based on an extended franchise, as in Austria, Germany and Japan.

These are, of course, only the principal routes followed by the process, and specific detours such as the Jacobin regime of 1793 also have to be taken into account. But if these routes accurately express the general pattern, as I believe they do, then we may conclude that bourgeois democracy, in the same way as its Athenian predecessor, first arose as a democracy for male members of the ruling class alone. Only after protracted struggle were these rights extended to the ruled and exploited classes as well. ...

Leaving aside Switzerland, where armed male artisans and peasants won democratic rights in a series of violent struggles in the 1830s, 40s and 50s, neither of the two main processes of this first stage led to the establishment of democracy for all adult men, not to speak of the whole adult population. With this one particular exception, then, competitive capitalism has nowhere led to bourgeois democracy as a result of its own positive tendencies. A Marxist analysis of capitalism, however, must take up centrally the contradictions of the system. And it has been the development of the basic contradiction between capital and labour that has carried democracy beyond the boundaries of the ruling class and its props. Thus, the second stage in the struggle for democracy was largely shaped by the emergence of the working class and the labour movement. We have already seen how the capitalist mode of production gives birth to an exploited class with capacities of organized opposition far superior to those of any previous one. In fact, the labour movement fought almost everywhere not only for higher wages and better working conditions, but also for political democracy — either as an end in itself (the British Chartists or the Australian and New Zealand trade-union movement) or as an integral part of the struggle for socialism (the parties of the Second International).

However, the working-class movement was nowhere capable of achieving democracy by its own unaided resources and this tells much of the strength of bourgeois rule. From the Chartists in the 1840s to the Belgian Social Democrats just prior to, and the Japanese workers just after, the First World War such attempts always resulted in defeat. Only in conjunction with external allies were the non-propertied masses able to gain democratic rights; and it was above all the propertied minorities who in the end answered the critical questions of timing and form — of when and how democracy was to be introduced. Thus, the process of democratization unfolded within the framework of the capitalist state, congealing in the form of bourgeois democracy rather than opening the road to popular revolution and socialist transformation. ...

READING B ANTI-POLITICS

George Konrad

The democracy we have — among ourselves

It was no accident that Eastern Europe's most significant democratic movement chose the name Solidarity — a reference to society's spontaneous cohesion, independent of the state, organizing from below, easily driven underground, but ineradicable from the soil.

Our part of the world is looking for its own authentic movement, one that will grow out of the contemporary reality of Central and Eastern Europe. So long as we are unable to reach agreement on who and what we are, we will of necessity imitate others. We are trying to delineate the consciousness of Central Europe, feeling our way, trying to avoid both Eastern and Western models. We could never really approximate the Western ones, even if we wanted to.

The efforts of our Polish friends have now — on the surface — suffered defeat; but the demand for communal self-governance was not a passing tactical gesture, and it will not disappear from the agenda. Where there is no self-government, society falls into a state of passive dependency; it is unable to do anything without directions, and when it gets directions it drags its feet about carrying them out. If there is no self-government, our neglected state economies will stagger to the brink of crisis. The demand for self-government is the organizing focus of the new Central European ideology.

Source: Konrad, G. (1984) *Antipolitics,* Quartet Books, pp.195–202.

The various communities in solidarity are not so much interested in governmental power as in communication within the broad society and between similarly situated groups. So long as the basis of sovereignty in our countries is not self-government but the 'democratic' centralism of the Communist Party, the censorship will maintain the jerry-built structure of power.

Centralized Party rule and censorship are inseparable. Hence the democratic movement is fundamentally anti-censorship. Expanded consumption cannot substitute for freedom of thought, and anyway there's not much chance of getting it; censorship and the shortage economy are also inseparable. Living standards are higher in Hungary than in other communist countries to the same extent that our censorship is milder. ...

We are anything but collectivists, we don't place the values of the community above the value of individuals. Instead of the community, we speak of circles of friends in which the free and equal relations of autonomous individuals are more valuable than the alleged effectiveness of the organs of power.

In theory it is easier to socialize a communist state than a capitalist society. If the dictatorship relaxes, if there is no fear that the tanks will roll, self-government will spring up of its own accord wherever thinking people work and live together. There is self-government even under a police state, but only in the sphere of private life.

Opinions forced out of the public arena are transferred to the medium of conversation, from the mass media to personal ones. It is this intimate, living verbal tradition that gives our society its original stamp. The assertions and complaints of official propaganda are greeted by the public with instant suspicion, since there can be no legal counter-assertions and countercomplaints. Every means of directing opinion is in the hands of the state, yet this gigantic machine, if not altogether powerless, nevertheless has a very limited effect.

Amid this uncontrollable sea of private conversations, our own system of values is beginning to take shape. It is not identical with the state's value system or with that of capitalism. Respect for money and property have not undermined the other values in the moral consciousness of the young intellectuals who set the tone for society's thinking. A kind of undifferentiated goodwill takes first place for them and makes itself felt more widely than in the circumscribed circle of the bourgeois family organized around consumption. ...

Autonomy's slow revolution does not culminate in new people sitting down in the paneled offices of authority. I cultivate in myself the illusion that the people who are working for autonomy in Eastern Europe have no desire to lounge in velvet chairs of ministers, in front of microphones and cameras. I could be wrong: people are capable of strange reactions when an opportunity presents itself. Anyway I still say, let those remain in the government who have a weakness for power. My hope is that, since the dictatorship has already lost its revolutionary sheen, governments in Eastern Europe will learn to wield power more graciously. ...

We seek freedom mainly in the areas where we are already freer and can hope to be even more so — where we are our own bosses because we have no superiors, and where we are left most to our own devices: in the area of our free time. The eight hours that we spend at the workplace are not entirely our own. There, if we are lucky and clever, we can do something that we enjoy and that we ourselves consider worthwhile, but there is no guarantee of that; it doesn't depend on us alone. At work we have in effect sold ourselves; we are not our own men and women, but the employer's. Anyone who defines himself by the eight hours he spends earning his bread has given a profound inner affirmation of his dependence. A description of the institutions of the world of work is an extremely impoverished description of a society. Autonomy, if it means anything, means that I am not identical with my status. I sidle away from it. I step into it as into a costume. ...

The Hungarians have best shown their acumen, perhaps, in their ability to go forward where it was easier to do so: in the parallel economy and culture — that is, in the sphere of free time. Small business, independent seminars, agricultural societies, and *samizdat* publications are organized in private homes. Official premises belong to the state, homes to 'society'. Home and free time: these are the spatial and temporal dimensions of civil independence.

Seeking the line of least resistance is more a resourceful way of struggling than a timid one. We are not trying primarily to conquer institutions and shape them in our image but to expand the bounds of private existence. People spend their forty-two hours a week working inside formal organizations, but if the remaining one hundred and twenty six are their own, then one cannot help noting — and it is odd that our sociologists have not done so — that considerable scope is available for the development of civil society. The evening and the weekend are yours, you can do with them whatever you wish. At work there is censorship, at home there is none. Just imagine if interesting conversations were going on in a million homes; if someone didn't like it, what could they do about it?

In our society, democratic criticism more often raises objections to the institutional organization of working time, but is that really the most important thing? Those forty-two hours are not the most important part of our human reality, and we even make over some of that time for our own private purposes. Here in Eastern Europe, at least, I don't know anyone who wouldn't try to turn paid working time into private time through a little friendly conversation with a fellow worker, if nothing more. As for the rest, the other one hundred and twenty-six hours, that is a good deal more — even if we are long sleepers, for no one can deny that our dreams are our own. Spreading out our lives before us in the plane of time, we get the surprising and illuminating impression that we spend the greater part of our time, even here in Budapest, in a democracy. The working day is theirs, the free time is ours. ...

READING C THE FUTURE OF DEMOCRACY

Norberto Bobbio

... the project of political democracy was conceived for a society much less complex than the one that exists today. The promises were not kept because of obstacles which had not been foreseen or which cropped up unexpectedly as a result of 'transformations' (in this case I believe the term 'transformations' to be appropriate) in the nature of civil society. I will point out three of them.

First, as societies gradually change from a family economy to a market economy, from a market economy to an economy which is protected, regulated and planned, there is an increase in the number of political problems whose solution requires technical expertise. Technical problems require experts, an expanding team of specialized personnel. This had already been noticed over a century ago by Saint-Simon, who had predicted the substitution of the government of jurists by the government of scientists. With the progress of statistical techniques, which outstrip anything which Saint-Simon could have remotely imagined and which only experts are able to use, the need for the so-called 'rule of the technicians' has increased out of all proportion.

Technocracy and democracy are antithetical: if the expert plays a leading role in industrial society he cannot be considered as just any citizen. The hypothesis which underlies democracy is that all are in a position to make decisions about everything. The technocracy claims, on the contrary, that the only ones called on to make decisions are the few who have the relevant expertise. In the time of absolute states, as I have already said, the common people had to be kept at bay from the *arcana imperii* because they were considered too ignorant. Now the common people are certainly less ignorant. But are not the problems to be resolved, problems like the struggle against inflation, securing full employment, ensuring the fair distribution of incomes, becoming increasingly complicated? Do not these problems, by their very nature, require scientific and technical knowledge which are no less arcane for the man or woman in the street (no matter how well educated)?

The growth of the bureaucratic apparatus

The second unforeseen obstacle to emerge is the continued increase in the scale of bureaucracy, i.e. of a power apparatus arranged hierarchically from top to bottom, and hence diametrically opposed to the system of democratic power. Assuming that grades of power exist in any society, a political system can be visualized as a pyramid; but whereas in a democratic society power is transmitted from the base upwards, in a bureaucratic society power descends from the top.

The democratic state and the bureaucratic state have historically been much more interconnected than might be thought from contrasting them

Source: Bobbio, N. (1987) *The Future of Democracy*, Polity Press, pp.37–9.

so starkly. All states which have become more democratic have simultaneously become more bureaucratic, because the process of bureaucratization is to a great extent the consequence of the process of democratization. Proof of this is the fact that today the dismantling of the Welfare State, which had necessitated an unprecedented bureaucratic apparatus, conceals the proposal, if not to dismantle democratic power, then certainly to reduce it to within clearly circumscribed limits. The reasons why democratization should have gone hand in hand with bureacratization, which is after all something Max Weber clearly envisaged, are generally understood. When those who had the right to vote were just property owners, it was natural that they should ask the public authority to perform a single basic function: the protection of private property. This gave rise both to the doctrine of the limited state, the night-watchman state, or, as it is known now, the minimal state, and to the constitution of the state as an association of property owners for the defence of that natural right which was for Locke precisely the right to property. From the moment the vote was extended to the illiterate it was inevitable that they would ask the state to set up free schools, and so take on board a responsibility unknown to the states of traditional oligarchies and of the first bourgeois oligarchy. When the right to vote was also extended to non-property owners, to the have-nots, to those whose only property was their labour, it resulted in them asking the state for protection from unemployment, and in due course for state insurance schemes against illness and old age, for maternity benefits, for subsidized housing etc. So it was that the Welfare State came about, like it or not, as the response to demands emanating from below, demands which were, in the fullest sense of the word, democratic.

The inability to satisfy demand

The third obstacle is intimately bound up with the question of the overall ability of a democratic system to 'deliver the goods': a problem that in the last few years has provoked debate over the so-called 'ungovernability' of democracy. In essence the central issue is this: first the liberal state, and then by extension the democratic state, have contributed to the emancipation of civil society from the political system. This process of emancipation has created a situation where civil society has increasingly become an inexhaustible source of demands on government, which in order to carry out its functions properly must make adequate responses. But how can government respond if the demands generated by a free society are increasingly numerous, pressing and onerous? As I have said, the necessary precondition for any democratic government is the guarantee of civil liberties: well, freedom of the press, freedom of assembly and association are all channels via which the citizen can appeal to those in government to ask for advantages, benefits, special terms, a more equal distribution of resources. The quantity and rapid turnover of these demands are such that no political system, however efficient, is able to cope with them. This results in the so-called 'over-loading' of government and the necessity for the political system to make drastic choices. But one choice excludes another, and not making certain choices produces dissatisfaction.

It does not stop there. The speed with which demands are made of government by citizens is in marked contrast to the slowness with which the
complex procedures of a democratic political system allow the political
elite to make adequate decisions. As a result the mechanism for inserting
demands into the system and the one for extracting responses are increasingly out of phase, the first working at an ever faster rate while the second
slows down more and more. This is precisely the opposite of what happens in an autocratic system, which is capable of controlling demand,
having previously stifled the autonomy of civil society, and is in practice
quicker to make appropriate decisions since it is freed from the obligation
to observe complex decision-making procedures like those peculiar to a
parliamentary system. In short, democracy is good at generating demands
and bad at satisfying them.

READING D   POPULISM AND THE CONSTITUTION

Wojciech Sadurski

What is the truly democratic solution when the majority of society wants
religion in state schools and a minority regards this as an infringement of
its right to religious freedom and judges that religious instruction in
schools, even if voluntary, constitutes a form of pressure incompatible
with free choice in matters of conscience? What is the democratic solution
when the majority oppose the possibility of abortion and a minority wish
to preserve the right to such an operation? What should be done in a
democracy when the majority thinks that indecent publications and films
should be banned on moral grounds and a minority wishes to have the
right to decide about its own reading matter and entertainment?

Some have no doubt as to the answers to these questions. In a democracy,
they say, the will of the majority should prevail. When all the arguments
have been put, it simply remains to count the votes. Thus it turns out that
in the context of current controversies a statistically determined public
opinion seems to support those who wish to reinforce traditional moral
and religious norms with state compulsion. In this manner, too, *conservatives eagerly make use of democratic arguments.* Vigorous defenders of
plain folk criticize 'the left' (imagined or real) for their elitism, lack of faith
in the healthy reason of society, their undemocratic treatment of the
majority of society. ... The other side is frequently helpless in this argument: it knows what it does not want, but finds it difficult to express
positively its elements of protest against the conservative currents. The
argument of democracy emerges as a verdict against which there is no
appeal.

It does not have to be like this: the argument between conservatives and
defenders of individual freedom is not a conflict between 'democrats' and
'elitists'. Democracy is a complex concept involving more than just the
realization of the will of today's majority. No contemporary Western
democracy takes the form of a populist system in which a majority of 51

Source: *Polityka*, 8 Sept 1990, Warsaw

percent (or even 91 percent) of voters can do as they wish. That much we know. It remains to review the arguments used to justify such restrictions of the will of the majority which, at the same time, do not destroy democracy ... In the history of Western political thought we can identify two traditional ways of conceptualizing democracy. According to one, democracy is that form of government under which the true values of society can best be discovered. In the second conception, democracy is a method of reaching compromises between competing interests and social preferences. ...

It is natural that, almost by definition, all democratic currents assign a special, privileged role to the social *majority*. But the role of that majority is different in the two traditions. According to the first tradition, which we call 'populist', the majority rules because it is 'right'. The special status of the majority emerges from the fact that it is in some way closer to the identification of the true ideals and goals of society ... In the second tradition, which we may describe as 'liberal', the majority rules not because it is closer to the discovery of 'the truth' — such a goal has no place in political life in general. The will of the majority must prevail because the interests and preferences of all citizens should have equal weight in shaping laws and policies and, in the case of conflict between competing interests and preferences, the assignment of equal weight to the interests of each individual means that the preference of the majority receives priority.

What is more important, the status of the *minority* is different in both these currents. In the populist current the minority is just wrong, it is mistaken: *the fact that you have found yourself in a minority means that you were wrong.* The simple identification of democracy with the unrestricted realization of the will of the majority finds full theoretical justification in (Rousseau's) doctrine... It is different according to the liberal conception. As the real aim of politics is the coordination of interests, priority for the interests of the majority must not inevitably mean that the interests and the preferences of the minority are ignored. On the contrary: *the test of liberal democracy is respect for the rights and interests of those who are in the minority.* This we all know: democracy is the power of the majority which respects the rights of the minority. ...

But a dilemma still exists, as in concrete conflicts of interest it also happens that it is not possible to reconcile the interests of all interested parties. The nature of the conflict sometimes means that it has a 'zero-sum' character, that the victory of one side means the defeat of the other. There is either religion in schools or there is not; it is either permitted to terminate pregnancies or it is not. 'Compromise' solutions (e.g. religious instruction — but only on a voluntary basis; permission for the termination of pregnancies — but hedged around with rigorous limitations) in such cases are often an illusion since, as we know, *in practice the conflict is about principles and one side will regard this form of compromise as a defeat.*

No ideal solution exists therefore. But this does not mean that there are not good solutions, in the sense of those which can at least reduce the awareness of defeat on the part of those involved in the conflict of interests. Here we must invoke institutional and legal solutions. For liberal democracy, and — we repeat — all contemporary Western democracies are to a far greater extent liberal than populist democracies, appeals to institutions and procedures in response to the fundamental dilemma outlined above. This is based on the deeper wisdom which suggests that procedural justice is often an appropriate substitute for a solution substantively satisfying all parties, if the latter cannot be reached. ...

I have in mind a complicated process in which the limits of political decisions (including legal norms) are set in a principled way by general rules, permanent and known in advance, which define not only the procedures for taking political and legal decisions (and also the structure and powers of leading organs) but also the unchallengeable rights of the individual... The important thing is that the political system creates a framework for continuous solution of the fundamental conflict that develops between democracy in the sense of the will of the majority and constitutionalism as a principled restriction of it ... The function of constitutionalism as a method of restraining representative democracy is therefore the defence of the rights and freedom of those whose interests the representative organs are not inclined or obliged to represent. ...

The moral thus emerges that democracy is not synonymous with populism, the power of the majority does not mean omnipotence with regard to the minority. The rights of individuals and minorities should not be decided by plebiscite, and the Constitution should defend minorities from the passions, anxieties and dislikes of the majority. This is, moreover, not just the outcome of philosophical reflection but also a strategy dictated by simple caution. Today them, but tomorrow ... ? It is worth remembering that.

CHAPTER 2 THE STATE IN ADVANCED CAPITALIST SOCIETIES

Anthony McGrew

CONTENTS

1   INTRODUCTION

In all advanced capitalist societies the state has come to acquire immense influence over its citizens. Its activities permeate almost every single aspect of daily existence such that few of us may claim that our lives are entirely 'untouched' by the state. Thus, studying any university course immediately draws us into indirect contact with the state through its funding of higher education and granting of university charters. Similarly, as citizens, members of households, consumers, recipients of welfare, employees or employers we cannot escape the more direct interventions of the modern state through its powers to tax, pass laws, coerce, enforce and to re-distribute resources and life-chances. As Mann has observed:

> The state can assess and tax our income and wealth at source, without our consent or that of our neighbours or kin; it can enforce its will within the day almost anywhere in its domains; its influence on the overall economy is enormous; it even directly provides the subsistence of most of us (in state employment, in pensions, in family allowance etc.). The state penetrates everyday life more than did any historical state.
> (Mann, 1988, p.7)

Undoubtedly, social historians in the late nineteenth century made very similar comments on the expanding role of the state in the era of liberal capitalism. Yet simply in terms of the size and complexity of the state apparatus, let alone the proportion of national income controlled by government, the advanced capitalist state (ACS) bears little direct resemblance to its nineteenth-century progenitor. Mann is therefore surely correct to assert the historically unique character of the ACS, particularly in relation to its pervasive influence within modern society. So central has it become to modern existence that the role of the state has emerged as a dominant theme in political, as well as intellectual, debates concerning the future development of advanced capitalist countries. On the one hand the 'new right' advocate curtailing its power whilst the left, and social democratic forces, continue to promote a vital role for the state in reforming advanced capitalist society. Yet despite the actual attempts (throughout the 1980s) of Conservative administrations in Britain and the US to reduce the level of government intervention in social life, the state in both societies has not contracted significantly although its activities have been re-directed. 'Big government', as Rose characterizes it, appears to be a permanent feature of advanced capitalist nations: 'Big government is here to stay ... Whatever political perspective is adopted, within the immediately foreseeable future the size of government can change only marginally. This is true whether the margin for change involves growth or cutting back' (Rose, 1984, p.215).

Understanding the nature of modern societies demands an understanding of the modern state. Certainly there exists a symbiotic relationship between the two: the state is embedded in social life, whilst social processes influence the form and activities of the state itself. In many respects ' ... states are central to our understanding of what a society is' (Mann, 1988, p.19). Understanding the ACS involves exploring both its more 'benign' activities — welfare — as well as its 'darker' side — warfare and coercion. Without an appreciation of both these dimensions, any discussion of the ACS would be deficient. This is because the ACS is at one and the same time both a 'welfare state' and a 'warfare state'.

Moreover, in making sense of the ACS, it is essential from the outset to recognize the incredible diversity of state forms amongst those nations which make up the advanced capitalist world: the West as opposed to the 'Rest'. Within the OECD — (Organization for Economic Co-operation and Development) which is essentially a 'club' for Western capitalist states — state forms vary dramatically in terms of institutional structures and modes of welfare provision. To make one obvious comparison, the US has a federal and Presidential system of government combined with minimal public provision of welfare and minimal state intervention in the economy, whilst Sweden has a unitary and parliamentary system of government combined with extensive welfare programmes and intervention in the economy. Developing a sophisticated understanding of the modern capitalist state requires acknowledging this diversity. However, in concentrating upon the ACS it is important not to forget the existence of quite different state forms in other industrial societies, such as the former command economies of Eastern Europe, and the newly industrializing nations of Latin America and South-East Asia. This chapter deals only with the ACS.

The fundamental aim of this chapter is to discover whether, in the light of this incredible diversity, it is possible to construct any meaningful general observations about the nature, functions and role of the state within advanced capitalist societies. Without prejudging subsequent discussion the answer would appear to be a qualified 'yes'; acknowledging that a robust understanding of the modern capitalist state cannot be constructed from the purely particular but must embrace a 'universalizing comparison' (Tilly, 1984, Chapter 6). Such comparison contextualizes the diversity of state forms by bringing into focus the common features, structures and processes which define the advanced capitalist state. Relying upon a comparative approach, the discussion in this chapter centres upon three key questions:

> First, given the diversity of state forms within the advanced capitalist world is it possible to identify common patterns in respect of the development, characteristics, activities and functions of the state?

> Second, how are we to make sense of the role and actions of the state in governing advanced societies, and in whose interests does it 'rule'?

> Third, in what ways do international or global forces condition the activities of the modern capitalist state?

These questions define the intellectual boundaries of our enquiry whilst the substantive focus is advanced capitalist states. By the concluding section you should be in a position to develop your own responses to these three questions and to analyse critically the responses of others, including those of the author.

2   THE ADVANCED CAPITALIST STATE: DIVERSITY AND UNIFORMITY

Within the diplomatic world the state is generally taken to be co-terminous with society and the nation. When the UK Ambassador to the United Nations delivers a speech to the Security Council, this is as a representative of the British state, the 'official' voice of the nation and British society. From the outside the state therefore appears to be indistinguishable from 'society'. Not surprisingly, it is fairly common to find the terms frequently used interchangeably. But, from the 'domestic' perspective, the state is commonly understood as simply 'the government', the institutions of political rule: an entity separate from or even above society. These popular but conflicting understandings of the term 'the state' suggest the need for a more rigorous conceptualization.

An obvious starting point is to view the state in terms of the 'idea' of rule; a set of *public institutions* — government, parliament, armed forces, judiciary, administration; and a set of *public functions* — law-making, maintaining order and security. As the earlier discussion in Chapter 2 of Book 1 (Hall and Gieben, 1992) indicated, the state is the locus of supreme authority within a delimited territory; authority which is reinforced by a monopoly of physical coercion. Mann offers a (neo-Weberian) definition of the state as:

1   a differentiated set of institutions and personnel embodying
2   centrality in the sense that political relations radiate outwards from a centre to cover
3   a territorially demarcated area, over which it exercises
4   a monopoly of authoritatively binding rule-making, backed up by a monopoly of the means of physical violence.

(Mann, 1988, p.4)

Three important points flow from this definition. First, it emphasizes that the generic notion of the state embraces much more than the popular notion of 'government' — e.g. the Thatcher government, the Major government, or the Bush administration etc. — since it refers to the whole apparatus of rule within society e.g. government, police, army, judiciary, nationalized industries etc. Second, and closely associated with the first point, is the idea that the state defines the realm of supreme authority within society. The essence of the state is therefore to be distinguished from the specific agencies or institutions (the police, courts, social security etc.) which give effect to that supreme authority. In simple terms the state as the realm of *public power* is to be differentiated from the agencies of rule within society. Third, as the embodiment of supreme authority, the state is thereby the primary law-making body within a defined territory. Through its institutions of rule the state formulates, implements and adjudicates the laws and legal framework which govern civil society. Mention of 'civil society' in this context demands a further conceptual clarification.

'Civil society', as indicated in Chapter 2 of Book 1 (Hall and Gieben, 1992), refers to those agencies, institutions, movements, cultural forces and social relationships which are both privately or voluntarily organized and which are not directly controlled by the state. This includes households, religious groups, trade unions, private companies, political parties, humanitarian organizations, environmental groups, the women's movement, Parent-Teacher Associations and so on. In simple terms, 'civil society' refers to the realm of *private power* and private organizations whereas the state is the realm of public power and public organizations. Of course, this is by no means a fixed or finely calibrated distinction since the public and the private can never be so readily differentiated. Feminists, for instance, would argue that power relations in the household are significantly structured by the welfare and regulatory activities of the state and so are not constituted solely in the private sphere. Through its powers to make law as well as its spending, taxing, employment, education, health and social security policies, the state is deeply enmeshed in the institutions and processes of civil society. In effect, through its actions or inactions, the state effectively establishes the contours and constructs the framework of civil society. It is therefore possible to argue that the state constitutes civil society because of its power to define and redefine the legal and political boundaries between the public and private spheres. A clear illustration of this is the relatively recent recognition by the British courts of the offence of rape within marriage; an offence which was never previously subject to legal redress. A rather different illustration concerns the privatization of publicly owned corporations, such as BT or British Gas, which has involved redrawing the boundaries between the public and the private spheres in the economic domain. Both these examples underline the dynamic character of the state-civil society relationship. As Mitchell observes: 'The distinction must be taken not as the boundary between two discrete entities, but as a line drawn internally within the network of institutional mechanisms through which a social and political order is maintained' (Mitchell, 1991, p.78).

ACTIVITY 1   To make some sense of Mitchell's observation, examine Figure 2.1 (overleaf), which offers a typology of the major organizations and institutions within society.

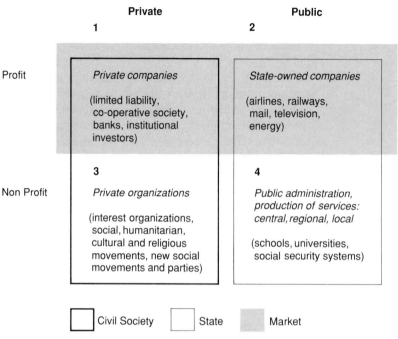

Figure 2.1   Types of societal organizations
Source: Adapted from Bertramsen *et al.*, 1991, p.121

From the figure you will observe that quadrants 2 and 4 embrace those organizations generally understood as the state; quadrants 1 and 3 refer to those organizations constituting civil society; and quadrants 1 and 2 the realm of the market. But notice the overlap between these categories.

Before continuing try and identify a specific example of each of these types of organizations.

2.1   THE ACS: A COMPARATIVE PERSPECTIVE

Whilst it is possible to define the state in abstract terms, the actual institutional forms of the contemporary state vary enormously amongst the advanced capitalist nations of the West. Constitutional arrangements, political structures, social formations, national wealth and productive power, differ considerably. Although all claim the democratic mantle, they differ, as Lijphart has shown, between federal (US, Germany) and unitary (UK, France, Japan) state structures as well as between parliamentary (UK, Japan) and presidential (US, Finland) systems of government (Lijphart, 1984). Militarily and economically, too, there is enormous diversity. To give one startling comparison: the US defence budget in 1990 was equal to almost twice the GDP of Belgium and approaching half that of the UK. These states also differ significantly in terms of the nature of their welfare state provision. Some countries, like Sweden, have a comprehensive welfare regime whilst others like the US have limited state provision of welfare. This diversity, along with its implications for how we progress beyond the particular to a more general understanding of the ACS, is analysed in the first reading for this chapter.

ACTIVITY 2   Reading A provides an overview of the emergence of the modern welfare state and indicates the diversity of welfare state regimes which have arisen in response to distinctive national historical, cultural and political conditions. When reading it you should take notes upon the following themes:

1   the typology of welfare state regimes: residual vs institutional; austerity vs expansion;

2   the periodization used in accounting for the emergence of the welfare state;

3   the crisis of the 1970s and the distinctive sets of national policy responses.

Now read **Reading A, 'Continuities and changes in the idea of the welfare state'**, by Jens Alber, which you will find at the end of this chapter.

Alber's approach to his subject matter is extremely instructive. Having alerted the reader to the substantial diversity of welfare regimes amongst advanced capitalist states, he nonetheless identifies common features and common patterns of development. Furthermore, he utilizes these common features in constructing broad typologies of states — Scandinavian and Continental versions of the welfare state; the austerity countries and the expansion countries — as an initial step in comparing different welfare state regimes. Building upon this approach he suggests the feasibility of constructing general theoretical explanations which can account for the nature of different types of welfare state regimes or different types of national policy response to the crisis of the 1970s and 1980s. Thus it is both the *substantive content* as well as the *method* used by Alber in his study which is valuable here, since it confirms the value of comparison as a technique in sociological enquiry. Moreover, it indicates the feasibility of constructing general accounts of the state despite the obvious diversity of state forms within capitalist societies. Whilst remaining sensitive to the differences between the OECD states which constitute the advanced capitalist world, we can now draw upon this comparative approach in the search for common features and general patterns in respect of the size, growth and role of the state in advanced capitalist societies.

Since the turn of the century, one of the most striking features of all advanced societies has been the enormous expansion of the apparatus of government. Rose (in Table 2.1 overleaf) details the massive growth in central government departments in all Western nations indicating the extensive bureaucratization of the state.

Table 2.1   The growth in central government departments 1849–1982

	1849	1982 (number of ministries)
France	10	42
Canada	8	36
Italy	11	28
United Kingdom	12	22
Denmark	8	20
New Zealand	19	19
Sweden	7	18
Germany	12	17
Norway	7	17
Belgium	6	15
Finland	11	15
Ireland	11	15
Australia	7	14
Austria	9	14
Netherlands	9	14
USA	6	13
Switzerland	7	7
Average	9.4	19.2

Source: Rose, 1984, p.157

Similarly the growth of public expenditure in Western nations over the last one hundred years represents further evidence of the enormous expansion of state activity.

ACTIVITY 3   Examine Table 2.2 and answer the following questions:

1   which states had the highest rates of public expenditure in 1980?

2   does the evidence confirm Alber's typology of austerity and expansion states?

3   how well do Alber's (post-1880) phases of welfare state development map on to the data here?

Commenting upon similar public expenditure figures, Pierson observes that a state which controls 11 per cent of GDP (near the average for the turn of the century) is a fundamentally different entity than one which controls three times that figure (the average for the contemporary Western state) (Pierson 1991, Ch.2).

Besides disbursing significant resources, the state in most advanced societies is also a major, if not the largest, single employer.

ACTIVITY 4   What do Tables 2.3 and 2.4 on page 74 suggest about the major trends in state employment in the post-war period?

Table 2.2   Public expenditure in fifteen OECD countries as % of GDP

Year	Belgium	Denmark	W.Germany	Finland	France	UK	Ireland	Italy	Canada	Netherlands	Norway	Austria	Sweden	Switzerland	USA
1850						11.1									
1855		8.4													
1860		9.4				10.7									
1865		11.2									5.8				
1870		9.2	13.3		11.0	8.7					5.9				
1875		8.3													
1880		8.9	9.9		15.4	9.1					6.8			16.5	
1885		10.0													
1890		10.6	12.9		15.0	9.2					7.4			15.0	7.1
1895		10.3				10.4									
1900		10.8	14.2		15.2	14.9				8.9	9.9			11.1	7.9
1905		10.0	15.1		14.6	12.4				8.8					
1910		12.3			14.4	12.7				8.8	9.3				
1915		11.5	17.0			12.7				9.1			11.2	14.0	8.5
1920		15.3			34.2	27.4				18.5	12.8		10.9		12.6
1925		13.4	22.4		21.9	23.6	21.5			14.9			14.1	17.0	11.7
1930		13.5	29.4		22.1	24.7	20.8			15.2	17.4		14.0	17.4	21.3
1935		17.5	29.8		35.4	23.7	27.8			18.0	18.1		17.1	23.7	
1940		19.2	36.9		29.2	33.4	26.8			18.3	19.1		17.7	23.9	22.2
1945		20.0			37.2	45.5	22.6				29.3		19.3	29.3	
1950	22.6	19.4	30.8		28.4	30.4	27.4			27.0	25.5	25.0	23.5	19.8	23.0
1955	24.7	23.6	30.0		32.2	30.2	27.5	27.8	27.1	28.5	26.8	27.5	26.4	17.4	24.9
1960	30.3	24.8	32.0	26.7	34.6	32.6	28.0	30.1	28.9	33.7	29.9	32.1	31.1	17.2	27.8
1965	32.3	29.9	36.3	31.3	38.4	36.4	33.1	34.3	29.1	38.7	34.2	37.9	36.0	19.7	28.0
1970	36.5	40.2	37.6	31.3	38.9	39.3	39.6	34.2	35.7	45.5	41.0	39.2	43.7	21.3	32.2
1975	44.5	48.2	47.1	37.1	43.5	46.9	47.5	43.2	40.8	55.9	46.6	46.1	49.0	28.7	35.4
1980	51.7	56.0	46.9	38.2	46.2	44.6	48.9	45.6	40.7	62.5	49.4	48.5	65.7	29.7	33.2

Source: Berger, 1990, p.117

Table 2.3   Public employment as a percentage of national employment, 1951–80

| | Public employment | | |
	1951	1980	Change
	%	%	%
Sweden	15.2	38.2	+23.0
Britain	26.6	31.7	+5.1
Germany	14.4	25.8	+11.4
Italy	11.4	24.3	+12.9
USA	17.0	18.8	+1.8

Source: Rose, 1984, p.132

Table 2.4   Changes in employment in major functional programmes, 1951–80

	Britain (% increase in numbers since 1951)	Germany	Italy	Sweden	USA
Social programmes					
Education	161	225	298	123	270
Health	167	217	289	628	209
All social programmes	163	182	283	455	244
Nationalized industries					
Post Office	31	79	105	130	27
Transportation	-48	-27	50	-27	660
All nationalized industries	-13	65	120	76	134
Defence	-54	n.a.	-19	-10	-39
Total change, all programmes	22	111	123	217	72

Source: Rose, 1984, p.136

Clearly the scale and changing patterns of public employment have important ramifications for national labour markets and the nature of work as well as social divisions and domestic political alignments. For example, the biggest growth in public employment has been in those sectors, such as health, education and personal social services which have tended increasingly to recruit women. In 1981, ' ... 65-75 per cent of college educated women in Germany, Sweden and the US were employed in the social welfare industries' (Pierson, 1991, p.135).

But it is not simply the scale of public expenditure and employment which distinguishes the ACS from earlier historical states, it is also the nature of its activities. In comparison with traditional state forms, the balance between the welfare and warfare activities of the state has shifted decidedly in favour of the former.

ACTIVITY 5   In Chapter 2 of Book 1 (Hall and Gieben, 1992) figures were given concerning the relative balance between civil and military spending by the early modern state. In this formative period military spending dominated state budgets. But what does the evidence in Tables 2.5, 2.6 and 2.7 suggest (see pp.75–6)?

The historical evidence appears to confirm that the transformation from a warfare-dominated to a welfare-dominated state has been particularly marked across all advanced capitalist nations in the post-second-world-war era. In terms of the post-war changes in the composition of state budgets (Table 2.5), the changing pattern of major state activities (see Table 2.6) and the expansion of non-military-expenditure (Table 2.7), the ACS has become increasingly welfare-oriented.

Both Tilly and Therborn refer to this remarkable transformation as a process of 'civilianization' of the modern state (Tilly, 1990; Therborn, 1989). But it would be more accurate to conceive the state in the majority of advanced nations as both a welfare and a warfare state: a characterization which will be justified in a subsequent section.

It would appear reasonable, on the basis of this broad overview, to offer four general observations about the state in advanced capitalist countries. First, in terms of both the nature and scale of its activities, the contemporary state bears only mild resemblance to its historical counterparts depicted in earlier chapters. Whilst there are obvious

Table 2.5   Military expenditure as a percentage of state budgets 1850–1975

Year[a]	Austria	France	UK	Netherlands	Denmark	Germany
1850		27.4				
1875		23.2			37.8	34.0
1900		37.7	74.2	26.4	28.9	22.9
1925	7.7	27.8	19.1	15.1	14.2	4.0
1950		20.7	24.0	18.3	15.6	13.5
1975	4.9	17.9	14.7	11.3	7.4	6.4

[a]Dates are very approximate
Source: Tilly, 1990, p.124

Table 2.6   Changes in the scale of major public programmes in the UK

	Public expenditure (change % share GNP 1954–80)	Public employment (change % labour force 1951–80)
	%	%
1 *Big increase in money and employment*		
Health	200	243
Education	82	162
2 *Big increase in money*		
Income maintenance	105	(n.a.)
Debt interest	94	(trivial)
3 *Little change in money and employment*		
Economic infrastructure	16	(n.a.)
Public enterprises	(n.a.)	18
4 *Big fall in money and employment*		
Defence	-49	-35

Source: Rose, 1984, p.193

Table 2.7   State (Non-military) expenditures as a percentage of GNP

Year	Britain	France	United States	Japan
1780	5.7			
1790	7.0			
1820	11.0			
1830	8.8			
1840	7.1			
1850	7.6			
1860	6.4			
1870	4.5			
1880	4.0			
1890	3.8	9.6	1.9	6.3
1900	3.5	8.5	1.8	7.4
1913	4.0	6.1	1.0	8.3
1920	14.5	15.0	4.5	5.4
1930	14.7	11.2	2.7	8.1
1938			6.5	17.3
1950	19.2	21.9	10.4	16.0
1960	17.5	18.1	9.6	10.8
1970	22.7	23.5	11.9	10.3
1980	28.5	27.2	17.2	17.6

Source: Adapted from Rasler and Thompson, 1989, p.152

continuities, such as the powerful attachment to military force and military security, the nature and functions of the state have been transformed over the last century. Second, its functional responsibilities have expanded considerably to embrace the welfare and material security of its citizens alongside the traditional goals of maintaining security and order. Third, given its sheer size and complexity, it would appear over-simplistic to treat the ACS as some kind of monolithic entity which operates in a unified manner. Rather, the state is a highly fragmented and in some respects de-centred apparatus of rule. Fourth, despite the tremendous variation amongst ACSs in terms of political structures, state forms and welfare provision, they also exhibit many common features and similar evolutionary patterns. In view of this fact, it does not seem entirely fanciful to engage in generalizations about, or to construct general theoretical accounts of such a heterogeneous set of states. On the contrary, an intriguing question arises: how do we account for these common features and broad similarities amongst such a diverse collection of states?

3 THE FORMATION OF THE ACS

In his overview of the formation of the modern nation-state in Chapter 2 of Book 1 (Hall and Gieben, 1992), David Held focused upon the role of war and the role of capitalism. The modern state, it was argued, was forged by the intersection of external and internal forces. Although much of the traditional literature on the evolution of the state tends to give primacy to the latter, more recent scholarship has combined this with an emphasis upon the profound significance of war and modern warfare in accounting for the nature of the advanced capitalist state (Mann, 1986). Such an emphasis is to be welcomed since ' ... who, living in the twentieth century, could for a moment deny the massive impact which military power, preparation for war, and war itself, have had upon the social world?' (Giddens, 1985, p.22). Accordingly, the approach adopted here will extend the analytical framework deployed in Chapter 2 of Book 1 to examine the underlying forces which have determined both the nature and the development of the state in advanced capitalist societies.

3.1 THE LOGICS OF MILITARISM

Tilly (as noted earlier) identifies one of the distinctive features of contemporary Western states as the 'civilianization' of government (Tilly, 1990, p.122). In comparison with early modern states, the ACS is entirely in civilian hands. Paradoxically, this civilianization of government has been accompanied by the 'militarization' of society in the wake of the industrialization of warfare. National security in the modern age is no longer a matter of ensuring that the barracks are constantly manned. Rather, it demands state intervention to organize society and industry so as to ensure that, should war occur, military requirements can be rapidly met. Modern warfare has become incredibly capital intensive such that a sophisticated and well resourced industrial and technological infrastructure, organized by the state, is essential to national defence. As a consequence: 'Preparation for war ... is a continuous activity, reaching into all aspects of society and eroding, even nullifying, conventional distinctions about the 'civil' and the 'military' spheres of life' (Pearton, 1982, p.11).

One of the distinctive features of all advanced industrial societies is the interlocking nature of the civil and military domains. At one level, it finds expression in the technologies and infra-structure which are very much part of everyday existence. Advanced telecommunications, the miniaturized electronics found in many household appliances, satellite TV, jet aircraft, and nuclear power, not to mention modern management techniques, such as operational research, government statistics, and sophisticated satellite cartography, all have their origins or stimulus in the military sector or military requirements. Equally, many civil technologies or facilities have direct military uses. During the 1991 Gulf War, American military commanders were able to use portable telephones linked through private sector satellites, such as those of the American Telephone and Telegraph Company, to communicate directly with their home bases; and in Britain, National Health Service hospitals were temporarily 'mobilized' to deal with military casualties. But this erosion of the civil-military distinction is not solely expressed in the dual use which can be made of most modern technologies or facilities. Rather more significant is the fact that the traditional distinction between war-time and peace-time has been steadily eroded by the industrialization of warfare. Whilst there are obvious political and international legal distinctions between the two conditions, in practice defence in the modern era totally depends upon the constant preparation for war. This was demonstrated unambiguously in 1990 by the incredible swiftness with which the allied nations were able to deploy unprecedented military force to the Middle East in order to liberate Kuwait from Iraqi occupation.

Even with the passing of the Cold War, continuous preparation for war remains a perfectly 'normal' feature of advanced societies. To ensure national security in an age of technological warfare the state must organize the industrial, technological, and economic resources of society in order to produce the sophisticated weapons systems required and to sustain a highly professional military machine. Militarism is therefore deeply embedded in all modern industrial societies.

Whilst 'embedded militarism' may be a normal feature of advanced societies, it is not accompanied, as in previous historical epochs, by military rule or a strong propensity for military aggression. On the contrary, modern militarism articulates '... an attitude or a set of institutions which regard war and the preparation for war as a normal and desirable social activity' rather than the military domination of society *per se* (Mann, 1988, p.127). A cursory examination of most Western societies would confirm that, despite the demise of the Cold War, defence remains a central preoccupation of all ACSs. In the US, Britain, France, Germany and Japan, military or security-related functions may no longer account for the largest slice of state expenditure, yet national security and military requirements permeate the whole of society. This is simply because, in order to produce advanced weapons systems and to maintain a military technological edge, the state is implicated in a 'military-industrial-bureaucratic-techno-complex' (MIBT) (Thee, 1987).

According to Thee, the MIBT is a self-sustaining structure, representing a fusion of the state and agencies within civil society, whose sole purpose is to prepare for war. It embraces the common interests and symbiotic relationships between the military, the defence-related segments of the state bureaucracy, politicians whose constituencies receive military contracts, industries which rely on defence work, unions which seek to protect their members' jobs, and producers of knowledge (universities, research establishments etc.) all of which depend upon the maintenance or expansion of defence spending. Moreover, it is a structure which has become internationalized, through the operation of alliance organizations like NATO (the North Atlantic Treaty Organization) and the increasing globalization of defence production.

With the decline of the Cold War, the deeply rooted nature of militarism within advanced capitalist societies has become more 'visible'. Successive attempts to reap a significant 'peace dividend', through the contraction of the military machine, have met with powerful resistance from those sectors and communities likely to lose out. In the US and the UK (where the military are the largest single consumers of goods and services in their respective national economies), the defence effort so permeates society that attempts to reduce it threaten to undermine the technological competitiveness of the most advanced sectors of industry and the prosperity of those regions, such as the Sun-belt states or the South East respectively, which have benefited from high levels of defence spending (Lovering, 1990; Gummett and Reppy, 1991).

Accounts of the MIBT vary in their interpretations of its causal dynamic. Many neo-Marxists locate its dynamic in the nature of capitalism, either in terms of the drive for profit on the part of capital or the state's use of military spending to regulate the capitalist economy. Power elite theorists, such as C. Wright Mills, account for it in terms of the confluence of interests between military, political and economic elites within capitalist societies (Mills, 1956). Others explain it as a product of coalition building amongst bureaucratic, political, military and industrial agents and groups who have essentially common interests in sustaining military innovation and capabilities (MacKenzie, 1990). A rather different approach is advocated by Mann and Giddens. They consider militarism within advanced societies, as expressed most visibly in the MIBT, to be a consequence of the industrialization of war in the context of a global states system in which 'might is right' (Mann, 1988; Giddens, 1985). This particular argument, which combines insights from historical sociology and international relations, locates modern militarism in a comparative and global context. It explores why militarism has become 'embedded' in the very fabric of advanced societies as well as how, together with the actual experience of two world wars, it has contributed to the transformation of the state within Western nations since the turn of the century. Put simply, the argument is that in a global system of sovereign nation-states each state is the only guarantor of its own security. But, because each state arms to defend itself, this immediately generates insecurity in surrounding states. Insecurity is therefore a permanent structural feature of the global states system. Accordingly states must constantly prepare for the eventuality of war if they are to feel secure. Combine this with the industrialization of war, which requires the state to organize society in such a way that facilitates this permanent preparation for war, and the consequence is an 'embedded militarism', to varying degrees, within all advanced societies.

In a magisterial study of the impact of modern warfare on society, Pearton argues that, since the close of the last century, the industrialization of war has played a primary role in transforming the relationship between state, society and the economy in Western countries (Pearton, 1982).

A machine shop for making gun carriage parts, 1892

Industrialization required the state to forge direct links with private industry in order to secure the supply of modern military hardware. New technologies which had significant military implications, like the railway and the telegraph, were nurtured or supervised by the state. In Germany, for instance, railway construction was directed and controlled by the military, as was the development of the chemical industry (McNeill, 1983). State intervention in industry to strengthen the nation's military capability was driven by the fear that to lag behind a potential rival would be to court defeat should war occur. Competition between states, generated by the endemic insecurity of the inter-state system, combined with the industrialization of warfare rapidly eroded the traditional *laissez-faire* approach to the economy. By 1913, for instance, one-sixth of the entire British workforce was dependent solely on navy contracts. As Pearton comments 'The state, in all countries, began to undermine the liberal economy in regard to its military requirements, even before the [First World] War broke out' (Pearton, 1982, p.49).

When it came, industrial war brought with it destruction and human suffering on a scale never before witnessed in western civilization. Unlike war in the seventeenth or eighteenth centuries, the First World war was a total war. It involved the mobilization of entire national populations and economies.

> WHAT CAN I DO?
> How the Civilian May Help in this Crisis
> Be cheerful.
>
> ...
>
> Write encouragingly to friends at the front.
>
> ...
>
> Don't repeat foolish gossip.
> Don't listen to idle rumours.
> Don't think you know better than Haig.

In Britain, France, Germany, Russia and the United States the state was forced to engage in direct regulation of the economy, controlling those sectors considered vital to the war effort. The concept of the 'home front' entered common parlance as the 'real' battleground — the Western front — placed increasing demands upon society and the economy (see Table 2.8).

Table 2.8   War expenditure and total mobilized forces, 1914–19

	War expenditure at 1913 prices (billions of dollars)	Total mobilized forces (millions)
British Empire	23.0	9.5
France	9.3	8.2
Russia	5.4	13.0
Italy	3.2	5.6
United States	17.1	3.8
Other Allies*	-0.3	2.6
Total Allies	*57.7*	*40.7*
Germany	19.9	13.25
Austria-Hungary	4.7	9.00
Bulgaria, Turkey	0.1	2.85
Total Central Powers	*24.7*	*25.10*

*Belgium, Romania, Portugal, Greece, Serbia
Source: Kennedy, 1987, p.274

Industrialists and trade unionists were co-opted into the state machine to manage the 'home front'. Scientific knowledge and technological innovation were also harnessed to military requirements. During this period the state discovered a capacity to 'manage' society and the economy; a realization which was to have important consequences for post-war reconstruction. As Beveridge, the 'founder' of the British welfare state, remarked in 1920, 'We have ... under the stress of war, made practical discoveries in the art of government almost comparable to the immense discoveries made at the same time in the art of flying' (quoted in Smith, 1986, p.61).

Beyond the destruction — the human toll was appalling with over 7.7 million combatants killed — the unintended and unforeseen consequences of the war were far reaching. Pearton notes that ' ... industrialized war enabled the state to tighten its grip on society and

Central London recruiting depot

make industry responsible to its demands' (Pearton, 1982, p.174). In the political domain the need to mobilize entire populations accelerated, as Paul Lewis observed in the previous chapter, processes of democratization.

It also, according to Pierson, helped lay the ideological foundations of both the 'welfare state' as well as expanded notions of citizenship (Pierson, 1991). In the economic domain new industries, such as aircraft manufacture, grew rapidly whilst the traditional industries were modernized. The world of work changed too. Widespread diffusion of 'Fordist' techniques of mass production were encouraged by wartime demands and state initiatives. In addition, the war also triggered a massive surge in trade unionism. Nor did the household escape change with the temporary expansion of the female labour market and the decline of domestic service. According to McNeill, the extent of these changes added up to a 'social metamorphosis' (McNeill, 1983, p.317).

If the 'Great War' marked a ' ... discontinuity in our culture' (Pearton, 1982, p.49) the Second World war underwrote a further phase in the re-structuring of state–society relations in all Western societies. By comparison with 1914 the war effort demanded state intervention in the economy and society on an unprecedented scale. For example, allied armaments production in 1943 alone equalled that for the entire period 1914–18 (see Table 2.9 overleaf).

Along with the mobilization of industry and science, the mobilization of the entire civil populations transformed the relationship between the state and its citizens.

Salute from Hoover

Table 2.9   Armaments production of the powers, 1940–3 (billions of 1944 dollars)

	1940	1941	1943
Britain	3.5	6.5	11.1
USSR	(5.0)	8.5	13.9
United States	(1.5)	4.5	37.5
Total of Allied combatants	*3.5*	*19.5*	*62.5*
Germany	6.0	6.0	13.8
Japan	(1.0)	2.0	4.5
Italy	0.75	1.0	-
Total of Axis combatants	*6.75*	*9.0*	*18.3*

Source: Kennedy, 1987, p.355

In addition, some 13 million battle deaths and at least as many civilian deaths, combined with the unimaginable scale of the destruction and dislocation wreaked across Europe and the East, reinforced demands for extensive state intervention in the process of post-war reconstruction. In Britain, reconstruction witnessed the birth of the 'welfare state', whilst in Germany and Japan reconstruction brought a complete social and political transformation as the 'victors' imposed their own vision of liberal-capitalist democracy. Within all Western countries the unforeseen legacy of war involved both an expanded role for the state as well as a deepening of citizenship rights and democracy (see for instance the previous chapter and Chapter 4 of this book).

According to Milward, the war experience contributed to a decisive change in the role of the state within Western capitalist nations:

> The hope that the economy could be managed, and the political will that it should be managed, were greatly reinforced by the knowledge of the more detailed workings of business and industry which central governments were forced to acquire between 1939 and 1945. That is perhaps the most immediately obvious historical consequence of the changes in the direction of the economy in the second world war. Capitalist economies had been made to function in a very different way and it is easy to see in the plans for reconstruction that their economic shibboleths had been much altered by the war experience. Governments were persuaded that their economic powers were much more extensive and their economic duties more compelling.
> (Milward, 1987, p.128)

The war crystallized social and political forces around 'managed capitalism' — state intervention in and management of the economy to ensure full employment combined with the provision of welfare services. Titmus, a leading sociologist of the period, attributed this in Britain to the fact that the war ' ... spread and quickened a trend towards social altruism and crystallized within the nation demands for social justice' (quoted in Fox, 1986, p.36). Yet, in many other respects the war, but particularly the holocaust, stood as a clear indictment of

the central ideals of European civilization — the attachment to
inevitable social progress, instrumental rationality, and Western cultural
supremacy — which had been fixed in the Western imagination since
the age of the Enlightenment *philosophes*. In this sense, the war had a
dramatic impact upon the West marking a new discontinuity in western
culture and its collective consciousness.

A further discontinuity between the pre-war and the post-war worlds
arose with the bombing of Hiroshima and Nagasaki in August 1945. The
advent of nuclear weapons, which epitomized the harnessing of science
and technology for military purposes, transformed modern warfare.
With the development of the Cold War, two nuclear armed camps
confronted each other for over 40 years in the knowledge that 'hot' war
would extinguish humanity. In this context defense became
synonymous with deterrence. But for deterrence to be credible required
permanent preparation for war on a scale which demanded extensive
state activity in organizing society's economic, industrial, technological
and human resources to ensure production of the most advanced
military hardware and to the highest possible technical standards. The
result was a post-war remilitarization of societies in both the East and
the West anchored into position by global alliance structures. President
Eisenhower, in his famous speech warning of the dangers posed by the
'military-industrial complex', feared this remilitarization would
undermine Western societies through its corrosion of democratic
practices and its distortion of the capitalist economy. Paradoxically, the
military burden was more severely felt in the Eastern bloc where, as
Paul Lewis noted in the previous chapter, it helped along the decline of
state socialism.

'Embedded militarism', despite the demise of a bipolar world, remains a
distinctive feature of all advanced societies. Of course within the West
there exists significant diversity with respect to both the scale of
national military efforts and the particular dynamics of militarism. Yet,
for all the major Western states, embedded militarism retains its
common roots in the industrialization of warfare and the workings of a
global states system in which security is measured solely in units of
military-industrial capabilities. Thus, as Giddens and others have
argued, the logics of militarism together with the actual experience of
war in the twentieth century have been key processes in the formation
of the ACS (Giddens, 1985). However, the story so far remains
essentially one-dimensional.

3.2   THE LOGICS OF CAPITAL

> The welfare state ... is a major aspect of politics, policy, and states
> of our time. Alongside liberal democracy, it may be said to be the
> most pervasive feature of the everyday politics of western
> countries. Health and social care, education, and income
> maintenance constitute today the predominant everyday activities
> and pecuniary efforts of the states of advanced capitalism.
> (Therborn, 1989, p.62)

The universal nature of the modern welfare state, to which Therborn refers, has been attributed to the dynamics of industrial capitalism. But the primacy now attached to welfare provision in all advanced capitalist societies is a recent and somewhat surprising development. No account of this development can ignore the complex interplay between endogenous factors, such as class conflict, and exogenous factors, such as war or international economic crises (Gourevitch, 1986).

In the post-war period, 'managed capitalism' — through which, to varying degrees, the state in western societies accepted some responsibility for ensuring full employment, providing welfare services and a modicum of social justice — emerged as the dominant 'framework' for organizing the continued reproduction of advanced capitalism. 'Managed capitalism', it has been argued, was based upon a historic class compromise between capital and labour in which the state played a critical mediating role. Through a combination of Keynesian and interventionist economic policies, the state sought to sustain economic growth and full employment whilst simultaneously, through its welfare programmes, it attempted to redress some of the inequalities inherent in capitalism. Corporate capital and organized labour accepted in return the need to look beyond their own sectional interests to the furtherance of the collective interests of the nation. In Britain, 'managed capitalism' was associated with the institutionalization of the welfare state — i.e. the establishment of the NHS, the extension of educational provision, the implementation of the Beveridge report — and an attachment to consensus politics. But in some respects the UK was atypical, in so far as the post-war commitment to managed capitalism in other countries, for example Sweden and the US, largely reflected the consolidation of a 'historic compromise' between corporate capital, organized labour and the state which had been arrived at in response to the trauma of the Great Depression.

Although the US and Sweden are viewed as polar opposites in respect of welfare state provision — with the US considered a 'welfare laggard' in comparison to Sweden's comprehensive welfare provision — both nonetheless have much in common in so far as they experimented with a kind of 'welfare state project' as part of a social democratic/reformist response to the economic crisis of the 1930s. Underlying this reformist response was a coalition of agricultural, labour and corporate interests which in partnership with the state forged a successful accommodation of interests around progressive policies of 'managed capitalism'. In the case of the US this was articulated in Roosevelt's New Deal, whilst in Sweden it took the form of the Saltsjobaden Accord and the entrenchment of social democratic rule (Gourevitch, 1986, Chapter 4). However, in the UK social reformism took hold in the process of post-war reconstruction, rather than in the context of international economic crisis. Despite the diverse trajectories of national developments, there can be no disputing the fact that the post-war period witnessed a universal expansion of the welfare state (coupled with an explicit attachment to Keynesian strategies of economic management) within the western capitalist world.

ACTIVITY 6   The short extract below summarizes the key elements of the social democratic/reformist account and vision of the welfare state. In reading it you should:

1   take notes on the nature of Keynesianism,

2   and identify some of the reasons behind the centrality of Keynesianism to the eventual form of the welfare state in most capitalist societies.

Now read **Reading B, 'Social democracy and the coming of the "Keynesian welfare state"'**, by Christopher Pierson.

Within the last decade the social democratic account of the welfare state has drawn substantial criticism in relation both to its historical accuracy and its intellectual coherence. Historically, the social democratic 'story' tends to play down the continued significance of deep social and class divisions within capitalist societies, with its stress on the social and political consensus surrounding the welfare state. Yet it is clear that in the majority of advanced capitalist nations the post-war consensus on bounded or 'managed capitalism' has not survived the global economic crisis of the 1970s and the subsequent national economic re-structuring. In the UK, for instance, the emergence of 'Thatcherism' in the 1980s is often taken to define the end of 'consensus politics'. Similar, though not as dramatic political changes in Germany, the US, Sweden and other western states in the 1980s underline the fragile and historically contingent character of 'managed capitalism'. Furthermore, this account fails to acknowledge that many of the original and more radical welfare state measures were introduced, not by social democratic or socialist regimes, but by liberal or conservative governments (Pierson, 1991).

Recent scholarship on the origins of the welfare state tends to place greater stress on the role of organized working class interests as well as on the fragile nature of the coalitions which nurtured its formation (Esping-Andersen, 1985; 1990). Moreover, it seems simplistic, as do so many social democratic accounts, to assume that governments promoting social reform merely responded to societal pressures. Quite clearly, as much of the historical evidence confirms, the development of welfare programmes was sometimes driven by the state's own requirements ' ... not least in the securing of a citizenry fit and able to staff its armies' (Pierson, 1991, p.35). As Giddens observes, state managers had a political interest in developing welfare programmes since they afforded an expanded scope for official 'surveillance' and created new mechanisms of social control (Giddens, 1985). Nor should it be forgotten that, whilst much of the visible activity of the welfare state involves responding to the failings of the market, welfare programmes and state intervention also function to support and sustain, rather than supplant, the market system (Therborn, 1987).

In comparison with the 'social democratic paradigm', the Marxist tradition stresses the functional role of the welfare state in sustaining capitalism. Of course, within this broad tradition there is considerable theoretical diversity. Despite this diversity, two distinctive approaches can be discerned: the first locates the origins of the welfare state and 'managed capitalism' in the class struggles of capitalist society; the second considers it a mechanism for 'regulating' (but in no sense resolving) the contradictions within capitalist society. In both cases the emphasis is upon the welfare state as a *capitalist* state.

The class struggle approach considers managed capitalism primarily as a regime for ensuring the continued reproduction and maintenance of an essentially exploitative capitalist socio-economic order.

The capitalist hierarchy

Unlike the social democratic paradigm, which considers the welfare state as a 'real' class compromise, this approach conceives it as an apparatus of social control:

> From the capitalist point of view state welfare has contributed to the continual struggle to accumulate capital by materially assisting in bringing labour and capital together profitably and containing the inevitable resistance and revolutionary potential of the working class ...
>
> ... the social security system is concerned with reproducing a reserve army of labour, the patriarchal family and the disciplining of the labour force. Only secondarily and contingently does it function as a means of mitigating poverty ...
> (Ginsburg, 1979, p.2)

Gough echoes this critique in suggesting that 'managed capitalism' has never been based upon a real accommodation of class interests but rather reflected the '... ability of the capitalist state to formulate and implement policies to secure the long-term reproduction of capitalist social relations' (Gough, 1979, p.64). The development of the welfare state in the UK, Germany, Sweden and the US are often quoted to validate this argument. Piven and Cloward, for instance, argue that in the case of the US the New Deal reforms were essentially a response to '... the rising surge of political unrest that accompanied this [Great Depression] economic catastrophe' (Piven and Cloward, 1971, p.45). However, this 'social control' perspective is not entirely convincing. On the one hand, according to Pierson ' ... it is difficult to sustain the argument that the growth of the welfare state was exclusively or even preponderantly in the interests of the capitalist class' (Pierson, 1991, p.54). On the other hand it adopts an uncomplicated view of the state as an extension of the ruling class with limited autonomy and no independent sources of power.

A second approach locates the origins of the welfare state in the contradictions of capitalist society, and more specifically in the dynamic tension between democracy and capitalism. A major exponent of this 'neo-Marxist' position is Claus Offe. His analysis concentrates upon the welfare state as a form of 'crisis management' whose primary purpose is to regulate the contradictions between liberal democracy and market capitalism (Offe, 1984): contradictions which Paul Lewis alluded to in the previous chapter (Chapter 1 of this book). Offe's argument is that the welfare state emerged as an apparatus to 'reconcile' the demands of citizens, expressed through the democratic process, for a more secure standard of living with the requirements of a crisis-prone capitalist economy in which accumulation — continuous acquisition of capital — 'rules'. Because democracy and private accumulation can never be successfully reconciled, the welfare state functions as a form of 'crisis manager', constantly attempting to secure both 'continued accumulation' and 'continued legitimation' (Pierson, 1991, p.58).

Offe's approach provides a complex appreciation of the origins of the welfare state without denying the significance of the political struggles and class compromises — 'managed capitalism'. As he notes, underlying the development of the welfare state:

> ... is a politically constituted class compromise or accord ... It is easy to see why and how the existence of this accord has contributed to the compatibility of capitalism and democracy ... each class has to take the interests of the other class into consideration: the workers must acknowledge the importance of profitability, because only a sufficient level of profits and investment will secure future employment and income increases; and the capitalists must accept the need for wages and welfare state expenditures, because these will secure effective demand and a healthy, well-trained, well-housed and happy working class. (Offe, 1984, pp.193-4)

This analysis emphasises the 'autonomous' character of the welfare state — i.e. actively reconciling contradictions — in comparison with other theories which stress its essentially class based or social democratic character. Moreover, unlike the social democratic/reformist account, it considers this reconciliation is neither stable nor permanent but rather is subject to continuous negotiation and adaptation. In effect, the state is trapped in a cycle of crisis management. In Offe's view, the welfare state and 'managed capitalism' are thus historically contingent; they have no fixed institutional or political form; and neither are necessarily permanent features of the political terrain of advanced capitalism. However, critics have pointed to the strong functionalist logic which underpins Offe's analysis: that is, the needs of capitalism seem to predetermine the action and responses of the state. As a consequence, the state is projected as a kind of 'black box' rather than an arena within which socio-political struggles are played out.

If the logic of capitalism has shaped the formation of all modern welfare states, it has nonetheless been mediated by distinctive national social and political formations which have culminated in very different types of welfare regimes. Therborn attempts to impose some order on this diversity by creating a typology of welfare state regimes (Therborn, 1987). Welfare states are classified along two dimensions: whether the commitment to full employment is relatively strong or relatively weak; and whether entitlements to social benefits are extensive or restrictive. This, as Table 2.10 shows, produces a four-fold categorization of welfare states from the strong-interventionist type, the Scandinavian model, to the market-oriented type, such as the US and the UK. You may notice too, that the two highest defence spenders in the West (the UK and the US) also have in common minimal welfare state provision.

Table 2.10 A typology of welfare states

		Social entitlements	
		High	**Low**
Commitment to full employment	**High**	Strong interventionist welfare states	Full employment-oriented small welfare states
	Low	Soft, compensatory welfare states	Market-oriented welfare states

Thus, as Pierson notes, we can identify the following four categories:

Strong interventionist welfare states (extensive social policy, strong commitment to full employment)

Sweden, Norway, Austria, (Finland)

Soft compensatory welfare states (generous social entitlements, low commitment to full employment)

Belgium, Denmark, Netherlands, (France, Germany, Ireland, Italy)

Full employment-oriented, small welfare states (low social entitlements, but institutional commitment to full employment)

Switzerland, Japan

Market-oriented welfare states (limited social rights, low commitment to full employment)

Australia, Canada, USA, UK, New Zealand.

(Pierson, 1991, p.186)

Capitalism has been a central force in the formation of the contemporary state. As this section has argued, both social democracy and neo-Marxism have much to say about the relationship between capitalism and the nature of the ACS. Whilst these traditions have particular strengths and limitations both share one common failing: a tendency to underplay the significance of international or exogenous forces of socio-political change. As Gourevitch's study of the impact of international economic crisis on Western capitalist states demonstrates, the emergence of 'managed capitalism' and the welfare state had a powerful external stimulus in the global depression of the 1930s:

Out of the traumas of the depression of the 1930s and of World War II the countries of Western Europe and North America had forged a 'historic compromise'. Bitter enemies had worked out a truce built around a mixed economy, a kind of bounded capitalism, where private enterprise remained the dynamo but operated within a system of rules that provided stability, both economic and political.
(Gourevitch, 1986, p.18)

International economic crises are in many respects the equivalent of war in the sense that they may disrupt established frameworks of national economic management as well as the political and social coalitions which sustain them. No account of the ACS can therefore afford to ignore the ways in which global economic forces intrude upon the processes of state formation. Alber, in Reading A, observes how the global economic recession of the 1980s disturbed the social and political basis of 'managed capitalism' and promoted a restructuring, if not a retrenchment, of welfare provision in all western states. Whether this spells the end of organized or 'managed capitalism', as some would argue, or whether it merely represents a temporary deviation from established practice remains a vigorously debated topic. What is incontestable, however, is the increasing significance of global conditions in defining the types of welfare regimes which can realistically survive in a more economically inter-connected world system. As Gourevitch observes in the contemporary era ' ... pressure has built up to curtail state spending and interventions. Whatever the differences in partisan outcomes, all governments have been pressed in the same direction' (Gourevitch, 1986, p.33). The implication is that exogenous forces of change have a strategic role in accounting for the form of the ACS.

ACTIVITY 7   At this point you should review Sections 3.1 and 3.2 in respect of

1   the different theories which have figured in accounts of the formation of the ACS;

2   whether such theories stress endogenous or exogenous factors;

3   the limitations of these theoretical positions.

Make notes on each of these headings before proceeding to the section summary.

3.3   THE WELFARE-WARFARE STATE: A REVIEW

Mann argues that ' ... capitalism and militarism are both core features of our society but they are only contingently connected' (Mann, 1988, p.127). The discussion in the preceding pages would appear to confirm his position. Taking the question of the welfare state, for instance, there can be little dispute that it is a product of both the dynamics of capitalism and the unintended consequences of war. Yet there is little common agreement upon precisely how the intersection of these causal forces culminated in the institutionalization of the modern welfare state. Given such uncertainty, a reasoned conclusion might be that, whilst the ACS has been, and continues to be, fashioned by both militarism and capitalism, the intellectual temptation to give causal primacy to one over the other has to be resisted in favour of a more eclectic approach which recognizes the complex intersection of these forces (see Figure 2.2).

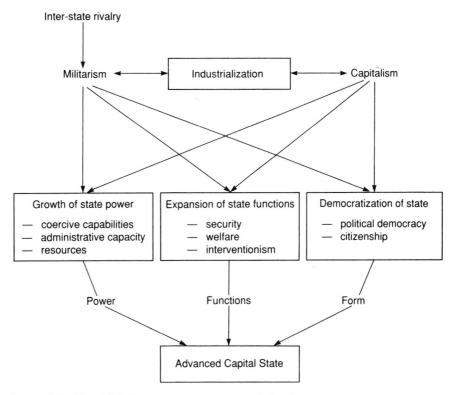

Figure 2.2   The ACS: Formative processes and structures

Such eclecticism reflects the reality that the ACS has always faced both inwards and outwards; inwards towards society and outwards towards a system of states. Accordingly the ACS continues to be defined by the complex interplay between endogenous and exogenous processes of change: the domestic realm of socio-economic conflict and the external realm of inter-state rivalry respectively.

4   PUTTING THE ADVANCED CAPITALIST STATE IN PERSPECTIVE

The discussion so far has concentrated on the dynamic processes of formation: an overview of the development of the ACS but in 'fast-forward' mode. In this section we shift from 'fast-forward' mode, continuing the video metaphor, to a 'freeze frame' or synoptic mode in an attempt to understand the functions and the power of the state in advanced capitalist nations. As the previous discussion has demonstrated, the post-war period witnessed a massive expansion of the state apparatus and state activity in all Western societies. This raises a series of intriguing questions: Does this expansion represent an accretion of power by the state in capitalist societies? Or is it a sign of a weak state unable to resist societal demands? In whose interests does the ACS 'rule'? Is the state best conceived as a 'capitalist' state or an 'autonomous' state? These are somewhat intimidating questions. Perhaps by engaging with some of the existing literature which has analysed these issues we can begin to sketch in the outlines of some 'answers'. Not only will this involve confronting different theoretical approaches to the state but also focusing upon '... the state's authoritative actions and inactions, the public policies that are and are not adopted' (Nordlinger, 1981, p.2): what the state does or fails to do.

As the Alber reading highlighted, the global economic crisis which began in the 1970s and continued into the early 1980s corroded the domestic social and political foundations of 'managed capitalism', with the consequence that the role of the state has come under increasing scrutiny in all ACSs. Even in Sweden, social democratic governments have been forced to re-think the state's role in response to domestic political crises and international economic conditions. And in France a socialist government was forced to embrace aspects of the 'new right' agenda. By the 1990s, given the collapse of 'state socialism' in Eastern Europe (explored in the previous chapter), the proper extent of state intervention in civil society and the legitimate boundaries of state power remain issues which continue to occupy a strategic position (if at times somewhat camouflaged) on the domestic political agenda within the majority of ACSs.

Political controversy within society over the proper role of the ACS has had the effect of rejuvenating the study of the state within sociology and associated disciplines. A 'state debate' has emerged delivering some new insights into the ACS. Within this debate, two distinct approaches can be identified to the key questions of state power and the relationship between state and civil society. 'Society-centred' approaches, which embrace a variety of theoretical traditions, view the ACS as tightly constrained by the structure of power within society and heavily reliant, for the most part, upon the political support and economic resources generated by powerful private actors. In effect, the tendency is for state action or inaction to reflect the interests of the dominant groups within society, whether dominant classes or elites. Thus Nordlinger writes that the ACS in such approaches '... is commonly seen as a permeable, vulnerable, and malleable entity, not necessarily in the hands of most individuals and groups, but in those of the most powerful' (Nordlinger, 1981, p.3). In comparison 'state-centred approaches' stress the power of the ACS in relation to societal forces and its ability to act '... contrary to the demands of the politically best endowed private actors, whether these are voters, well organized 'special interest' groups, the managers of huge corporations, or any other set of societal actor' (Nordlinger, 1981, p.2). Within each of these two general approaches can be located a heterogeneous grouping of theoretical accounts of the ACS. These are given more exposure in the two subsequent sections.

4.1   SOCIETY-CENTRED APPROACHES

Paul Lewis in Chapter 1 of this book has identified the emergence of
liberal democracy with both the extension of the franchise and the
consolidation of social and political pluralism. Representative
government in all ACSs is supplemented by the existence of a universe
of diverse social and political groupings within civil society. In addition
to the 'vote', citizens thus have the ability to channel their demands on
the state through those social groups, organizations, or movements with
which they are associated. Accordingly, liberal democracy, as the
previous chapter implied, is commonly equated with polyarchy: a
system in which power and political resources are largely fragmented.
Within this classical pluralist tradition, the state's role is primarily
conceived as processing political issues and securing a societal
consensus by delivering policy outcomes that do not diverge
substantially from the status quo and which reflect the demands of the
public. Such a conception implies an essentially neutral or broker
model of the state, and a correspondingly wide dispersion of power
throughout society such that no one group or set of interests
systematically dominates the political process.

Few political scientists or sociologists would accept that classical
pluralism offers even a remotely accurate account of the state or policy
making in ACSs. Even its original proponents, Robert Dahl and Charles
Lindblom, no longer argue that it provides a fair representation of
American liberal democracy at work, let alone democracy in other ACSs
(Dahl, 1985, Lindblom, 1977). Coming to terms with the structural
changes in capitalist societies in the 1960s and 1970s, particularly the
growth of state bureaucracy and state interventionism within the
economy, has forced advocates of classical pluralism to review their
assumptions and adapt their account accordingly. In virtually all
capitalist societies, the growth of corporate power and state bureaucracy
has 'distorted' the political process. Nordlinger even refers to the ACS
as the 'distorted liberal state' (Nordlinger, 1981, p.157). Moreover, the
increasing specialization, technical nature and overwhelming volume of
policy issues has encouraged the formation of functionally
differentiated 'policy communities' e.g., health, social security, energy,
defence, education etc. Within these 'policy communities' officials and
experts from the responsible state agencies concerned, together with
representatives of the most influential or knowledgeable private
organized interests, formulate public policy often with only very limited
participation by elected politicians.

Health policy in most ACSs is formulated in this manner. In the UK, for
instance, Department of Health officials, representatives of the
professional medical associations (BMA etc.) and other major interests
(i.e. pharmaceutical companies) jointly determine much health policy.
Moreover, in most key policy sectors such consultative machinery or
policy networks are institutionalized through formal or informal
committee structures. Japan is a principal example of such

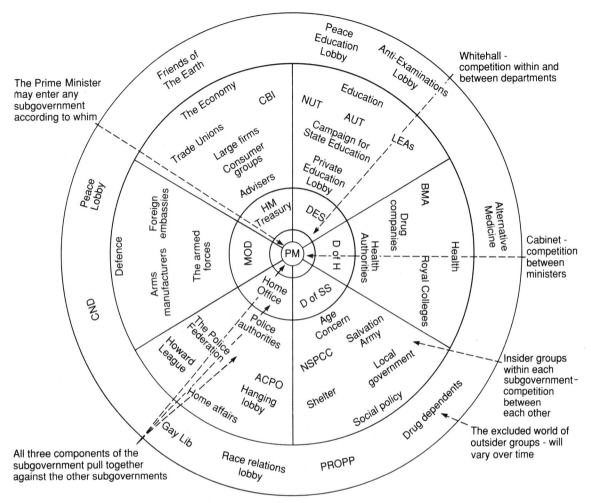

Figure 2.3   Pressure groups and policy communities
Source: Kingdom, 1991, p.421

institutionalization, since in almost every policy sector government departments have spawned considerable numbers of consultative committees through which the major organized interests and experts are co-opted into the policy formulation process (Eccleston, 1989). This 'privileging' of the most powerful organized interests within the policy process limits effective democratic participation, since it excludes the less influential and specifically those critical of the status quo who become relegated to 'outsiders'. It also reinforces executive domination of the policy process since Parliaments or legislatures are substantially by-passed. Accordingly, neo-pluralists paint a picture of the democratic process in most ACSs as one of unequal and restricted group competition in which there exists a 'privileging' within the policy process of the more powerful organized interests within civil society. In the case of business and corporate interests, neo-pluralists argue that such 'privileging' is a structural necessity rather than a consciously articulated choice made by state managers or politicians. For, as Lindblom acknowledges: 'Because public functions in the market system rest in the hands of business, it follows that jobs, prices, production, growth, the standard of living, and the economic security of everyone all rest in their hands. Consequently government officials cannot be indifferent to how well business performs its functions' (Lindblom, 1977, p.122). The consequence of this is that:

> It becomes a major task of government to design and maintain an inducement system for businessmen, to be solicitous of business interests, and to grant them, for its value as an incentive, intimacy of participation in government itself. In all these respects the relation between government and business is unlike the relation between government and any other interest group in society. (Dahl and Lindblom, 1976, p.xxxvii)

Neo-pluralism delivers an account of the ACS that is significantly removed from that of classical pluralism. Power in capitalist societies is argued to be highly concentrated whilst corporate interests and economic issues dominate the political agenda. The existence of such inequalities in the distribution of power resources and in access to government decision makers undermines the classical pluralist notion of a highly competitive political process which no single set of interests can systematically dominate. Furthermore, since the state in a capitalist society has to be constantly attentive to the needs of corporate capital, the pluralist fiction of a neutral arbiter between competing interests is replaced with the notion of a 'distorted liberal state'.

Evidence of a further kind of 'distortion' of the liberal democratic state is to be found in the numerous studies of social and political 'elites' which some argue exercise extensive power within capitalist society (Mills, 1956). Elite theories stress the natural tendency for power within all social institutions and organizations to become centralized within the hands of a dominant group or *elite*. This is particularly the case in capitalist societies where mass politics, the centrality of huge organizations in social life, the growth of bureaucracy, reliance upon expertise etc., encourage the formation of elites. Several recent studies of British and American society point to the domination of key social institutions, such as the military, civil service, church, business, finance, the press, the judiciary and so on, by elites whose members share similar social backgrounds and often similar political outlooks (Scott, 1991, Domhoff, 1978). In Britain the key elites are remarkable in the degree to which they share common social origins. Corresponding studies of Japanese society suggest equivalent conclusions (Eccleston, 1989). Some elite theorists therefore argue that, because elites tend to be recruited from the same social strata, they function as a socially cohesive political group. Many decades ago, C. Wright Mills argued that American society was ruled by a power elite and this remains a 'popularized' explanation of the American political process (Mills, 1956). As Lukes acknowledges, political influence rarely has to be exerted openly but rather operates more 'informally' within elite networks. Accordingly, it is through their ability to shape the political agenda, so avoiding open confrontation where their interests may be under threat, linked with a societal attachment to consensus decision making, that enables elites to 'control' the political process. But the existence of elites, however defined, does not convincingly demonstrate that the political process is directed or even considerably influenced by their activities. Elitist accounts share in common a view of the ACS as permeated at key levels by dominant social elites such that the state apparatus is perceived as functioning substantially in the interests of a (powerful) minority of its citizens.

If elite theorists point to the existence of a 'ruling elite' within ACSs, Marxism, at least its classical brands, points to a 'ruling class' (Scott, 1991). This distinction is critical, for within traditional Marxist accounts it is the class nature of capitalist society and the consequent class nature of the state itself that is fundamental to an understanding of power and the state in western societies. A classical Marxist account of the state is to be found in Ralph Miliband's *The State in Capitalist Society* (Miliband, 1969). Miliband argued that power within capitalist society resides within a fairly cohesive capitalist class. In effect, the state substantially expresses and acts to secure 'bourgeois' dominance within capitalist society. This is achieved because, within Britain, the US, France and other capitalist societies, state managers, those in senior positions in business, the military, the judiciary and so on are largely recruited from the ranks of the dominant capitalist class. In addition, the 'ruling class' can exploit its social networks to gain access to the key decision making sites within state and civil society. The state is also constrained by the need to ensure continued capital accumulation. Taken together Miliband therefore constructed what is broadly regarded as an 'instrumentalist' account — in the sense that the state is conceived as an instrument of capital — of the ACS (Held, 1987, p.207-8).

This account attracted considerable criticism, mostly from within Marxist or *marxisant* circles. Poulantzas argued that an 'instrumentalist' account was insensitive to the structural factors which conditioned state action, namely its need to secure the conditions for the continued reproduction of capitalist society even when the necessary action conflicted with the short-term interests of the capitalist class . For Poulantzas, the ACS often acted 'relatively autonomously' from the capitalist class where such action was functional to the long term stability of the capitalist order. Evidence for this, Poulantzas argued, was to be found in the institutionalization of the welfare state which appeared to conflict with the core interests of the capitalist class. These two polarized positions of 'instrumentalism' and 'structuralism' have shaped an on-going debate within neo-Marxism on the role of the state in advanced capitalist societies.

ACTIVITY 8   You should now read **Reading C, 'Class and power in contemporary capitalism'**, by Ralph Miliband. You should take notes on the following topics:

1   the relationship between state power and corporate power;

2   the autonomy of the capitalist state;

3   the cohesiveness of the capitalist class.

What differences of emphasis do you detect in Miliband's position from his earlier views outlined above?

Try to identify the similarities and differences between Miliband's account and the neo-pluralist account discussed earlier.

Despite their origins in rather different theoretical traditions, the various accounts of the ACS which have been elaborated in the last few pages all share a common preoccupation with the societal constraints upon and the social basis of state power. They represent the central core of 'society-based approaches' to the ACS. For they consider that the autonomous power of the ACS is severely compromised by its dependence upon dominant socio-economic groups for the political and economic resources essential to its continued survival. Whether exaggerated or not, this claim requires critical scrutiny.

4.2   STATE-CENTRED APPROACHES

When President Truman initiated the Marshall Aid Plan to provide direct financial assistance for the post-war reconstruction of Europe, he did so in the knowledge that powerful corporate, labour, and political elites at home openly opposed the policy.

Despite overwhelming opposition from industrialists, labour unions, and a significant section of its own party, the first Thatcher government in Britain pursued a severely deflationary economic strategy at the peak of an economic recession in which unemployment had reached well over 3 million. Japanese rice farmers face the 1990s with the gloomy prospect of mass bankruptcies following their government's decision to liberalize the rice trade — so allowing imports of cheaper US rice to flood the domestic market — even though farmers remain a powerful force within the governing LDP party. What each of these vignettes appears to illustrate is the autonomous power of the state; its ability to articulate and pursue actions and policies which can run counter to the interests of the most dominant or powerful groups (classes) in society.

Nordlinger, in his extensive study of the autonomy of the liberal democratic state, delivers a powerful critique of 'society-centred approaches' to the ACS precisely because they ' … strenuously [deny] the possibility of the state translating its preferences into authoritative actions when opposed by societal actors who control the weightiest

President Truman announces the Marshall Plan

political resources' (Nordlinger, 1981, p.3). Attempts to understand the autonomous power of the state have generated a range of 'state-centred approaches' to the study of the ACS.

A very influential strand of theorizing has been that of the 'New Right' which, as noted earlier, launched a sustained attack on the welfare state in the 1980s. Underlying 'new right' accounts of the ACS is an unusual juxtaposition of neo-conservative and neo-liberal political philosophies. The result is an interesting diversity of theoretical interpretations. Yet within this broad 'school' there is a shared set of assumptions that the state is not subordinate to societal forces but can and does act quite autonomously. Focusing upon the massive post-war expansion of the welfare state in capitalist societies, 'new right' accounts lay stress on the internal political and bureaucratic imperatives of the state rather than on a massive upsurge in societal demand for welfare provision. Governments and politicians are conceived as having a rational, institutionally based interest in expanding state welfare programmes and expenditure since this helps win votes and consolidates their own power bases. Moreover, competition between parties for political office encourages politicians to '... create unrealizable citizen expectations of what the government can deliver ...' (Dunleavy and O'Leary, 1987, p.102), and so to increase citizen demands upon the state. State bureaucracy also has a rational incentive to expand since this enhances the budgets, career prospects and bureaucratic power of state managers. Since welfare programmes are labour-intensive, there are additional pressures from public-sector unions to sustain or increase spending levels. This suggests the conclusion that: 'Under liberal democratic and adversarial political arrangements, and without some sort of constitutional constraint upon the action (and spending) of governments, politicians, bureaucrats and voters acting rationally will tend to generate welfare state policies which are ... in the long run unsustainable' (Pierson, 1991, p.47). As the Alber reading highlighted, during the late 1970s and throughout the 1980s, this analysis of the state captured the political imagination of many conservative politicians throughout the industrialized world since it appeared to offer a convincing account of the 'crisis of the welfare state'. Both in Britain and the US it strongly informed the political agenda of radical conservative administrations which sought to 'roll back the state'.

Central to 'new right' thinking is a conception of the ACS as a powerful and 'despotic' bureaucratic apparatus which has its own institutional momentum. Rather than the highly responsive and responsible state envisaged in pluralism, many 'new right' accounts proffer an image of the ACS as a quasi-autonomous set of governing institutions with enormous resources and administrative power at its disposal.

This portrait of an extremely powerful state apparatus would not be rejected totally by all state theorists. Indeed, throughout the 1970s and 1980s there was a general awareness that, within all capitalist societies, the state had acquired a more directive role with respect to the economy and civil society. This was predicated on studies of the policy-making process which demonstrated a growing tendency towards the 'institutionalization' of powerful organized interests — e.g. trade unions, professional associations, employers' organizations, corporate capital — within the state decision making apparatus (Schmitter, 1974). Since trade unions and business interests could potentially disrupt or undermine state policy, the obvious solution was to 'incorporate' them into the policy-making arena. In the environment of economic crisis which pervaded the 1970s, this appeared a highly effective political strategy for governments to adopt since it provided a formal framework within which the state could attempt to hold together the post-war consensus on 'managed capitalism': a consensus increasingly threatened by rising unemployment and surging inflation. Accordingly, the 1970s witnessed an intensification of this process of incorporation as well as its regularization through formal institutional mechanisms. In Britain, the CBI and TUC participated in many 'tripartite' structures whilst in Sweden and other Scandinavian democracies such forums played a critical role in the formulation of national economic strategy. But in return for institutionalized access to government, so providing these groups with a privileged position in the policy process, the state acquired expanded control over these 'private' associations. As a result, rather than limiting its scope for autonomous action such 'corporatist' strategies enhanced the autonomous power of the state (Nordlinger, 1981, p.171). Thus, in the mid-1970s the TUC and CBI in Britain found themselves locked into a 'social contract' arrangement with the state in which, for few immediate tangible benefits, both agreed to contain national wage demands and price rises respectively. Despite the 'social contract' operating against the direct material interests of their own members, both these associations 'policed' its operation on behalf of the state.

'Corporatism' (which describes this process of incorporation) is much more than a state strategy for dealing with the inherent crisis tendencies within advanced capitalist societies. Several writers have suggested that it is a novel institutional form of the ACS — a particular kind of state structure — which is evident to varying degrees in Sweden, Norway, Austria, Finland and the Netherlands (Schmitter, 1974). Panitch, for instance, considers corporatism as '... a political structure within advanced capitalism which integrates organized socio-economic producer groups through a system of representation and co-operative mutual interaction at the leadership level and mobilization and social control at the mass level' (Panitch, 1980, p.173). Others have pointed to a more limited conception of corporatism as a mode of public policy making, restricted to a delimited set of policy sectors in almost all ACSs. This is often referred to as *sectoral corporatism*. In this regard Japan is particularly interesting since the incorporation of the major organized interests into government is distinguished by its sectoral nature and by the exclusion of labour interests (Eccleston, 1989). Whilst it is no longer as evident in the UK, Schmitter argues that corporatism nonetheless remains a visible feature of the political economy of most European nations (Schmitter, 1989) (see Table 2.11).

Table 2.11   A cumulative scale of corporatism

1	Pluralism United States, Canada, Australia, New Zealand;
2	Weak corporatism United Kingdom, Italy;
3	Medium corporatism Ireland, Belgium, West Germany, Denmark, Finland, Switzerland (borderline case);
4	Strong corporatism Austria, Sweden, Norway, the Netherlands;

Not covered by the scale are cases of

5	'Concertation without labour' Japan, France.

Source: Lehmbruch, 1984, p.66

Corporatist theoreticians accept that although corporatism may no longer reflect the political reality in all capitalist societies, nevertheless where they do exist corporatist modes or forms of policy making articulate the autonomous power of the state. This is so because:

> State officials have the greatest agenda setting capacity ... since they decide who is to participate in consultations and invariably they chair the relevant committees. Hence their policy influence seems bound to be considerable. Administrative elites in the Scandinavian countries are disproportionately represented on all

the commissions and boards and committees engaged in
corporatist policy making. If the policy making area is technical
and complex, public officials have a decided advantage. ... Finally
if the relevant interests in the corporatist process are conflicting
and balanced, then the opportunities for state elites to act
autonomously are immensely enhanced.
(Dunleavy and O'Leary, 1987, p.195-6)

Contemporary neo-Marxist accounts of the ACS share some of the same
conceptual terrain with corporatist and 'new right' theorizing. One
significant area of overlap is in the primacy given to politics and the
corresponding emphasis upon the state as '... an actor in its own right
pursuing particular interests ... different from those of societal agents'
(Bertramsen *et al.,* 1991, p.98). There is also a shared recognition that
there can be no effective differentiation between the state and civil
society. However, what distinguishes recent neo-Marxist accounts is a
concentration upon the 'capitalist' nature of the contemporary Western
state. According to such accounts, the state in advanced societies is
essentially 'capitalist' not because it acts in the interests of a dominant
capitalist class, nor because it is constrained to do so by structural
forces which prevent the prosecution of alternative anti-capitalist
policies. Rather it is a 'capitalist state' because, in the process of
sustaining and reproducing its own programmes, state managers must
sustain and create the conditions for private capital accumulation. Since
the state itself is heavily dependent upon the revenues derived from the
taxation of profits and wages to maintain its programmes, failure to
facilitate capital accumulation is likely to have politically destabilizing
consequences (Carnoy, 1984, pp.133-4). How state managers formulate
strategies for encouraging private accumulation, and precisely what
policies are followed, remain complex and indeterminate processes
suffused by politics since '... there can be no single, unambiguous
reference point for state managers how the state should serve the needs
and interests of capital' (Jessop, 1990, p.357). In this respect the state in
advanced capitalist societies is accorded extensive autonomy from
capital, yet still remains essentially a 'capitalist state'. This is
underwritten too by the state's need to secure the legitimacy of its
actions within the context of a liberal-democratic polity.

ACTIVITY 9   You should now read **Reading D, 'The welfare state as "the crisis of
crisis management"'**, by Christopher Pierson.

Offe points to the apparent contradiction between the state's need to
sustain its legitimacy and the need to sustain the conditions for private
accumulation. By contradiction Offe is referring to the fact that both are
essential to the survival of the state but each can pull it in opposing
directions. Since the state's power derives in part from the legitimacy
accorded it through the political process, it cannot afford to be
perceived as acting partially, by systematically privileging corporate

capital, without endangering its political support. Yet, to sustain mass support, it requires substantial revenues to finance welfare and other programmes. However, revenues derive largely from the taxes on profits and wages so that the state is obliged to assist the process of capital accumulation and thus act partially. As a consequence, the state in advanced capitalist society is caught between the contradictory imperatives of accumulation and legitimation, i.e. between 'capitalism' and 'democracy'. Reconciling this contradiction prises open a political space for the state to formulate and pursue strategies and policies which reflect '... the institutional self-interest of the actors in the state apparatus' (Offe, 1976, p.6). This 'autonomy' is enhanced further by the fact that there are diverse and conflicting interests between different sectors of capital, e.g. industrial, financial, national as against international etc., and within civil society more generally. Accordingly, the precise strategies and policies adopted by the state to reconcile the conflicting demands of capitalist accumulation and legitimation are a product of political negotiation and the outcome of a rather indeterminate political process within which '...the personnel of the state try to ensure their own jobs and hence ensure the continued existence of the State apparatuses' (Carnoy, 1984, p.136).

Alber, in Reading A, emphasized the diverse responses amongst advanced states to the economic crises of the late 1970s and 1980s. In the UK and the US, this was the era of 'Thatcherism' and 'Reaganomics' respectively. Both articulated strategies for rejuvenating and re-structuring the domestic economy to make it more competitive with new centres of economic power such as Japan and Germany. 'Thatcherism', in particular, articulated a break with post-war orthodoxy by pursuing an economic strategy, involving 'rolling back the state', encouraging competition, privatization, and reforming the welfare state. This was accompanied by a distinctively 'populist' political strategy designed to sustain essential support for and legitimation of these radical policy initiatives. Even so, many 'unpopular' policy measures were adopted and implemented against the back drop of considerable resistance. In other advanced countries, rather different, although equally unpopular and resisted, economic and political strategies were adopted to deal with the crisis. In France, a socialist government abandoned nationalization and in Sweden the social democratic government jettisoned the long standing commitment to full employment (Gourevitch, 1986).

Recent scholarship has focused upon the critical role of the state in organizing the appropriate political and economic conditions for the successful accumulation of capital. Jessop, in his analysis of the 'Thatcher era' in the UK, suggests that the state adopted a highly proactive role throughout the 1980s (Jessop et al., 1988). Rather than simply reacting to the economic crisis, it sought to pursue a determined transformation of the British economy and society through a radical agenda of reform, marketization, industrial restructuring and economic rationalization. Through the active assertion of an ideological programme — 'Thatcherism' — the state sought '... the mobilization and reproduction of active consent through the exercise of political, intellectual and moral leadership' (Jessop quoted in Bertramsen *et al.,* 1991, p.110). This was achieved by the state consciously building, manipulating and consolidating its own 'power base': a dynamic coalition of quite different social groups and political actors e.g. the skilled working class, the City, 'new right' groups, moral crusaders etc., as well as appealing to more 'populist' sentiments within British society (Jessop *et al.,* 1988). In this regard the state is conceived more as a kind of 'power broker' constructing and sustaining the political coalitions vital to the success of its strategy for enhancing corporate profitability whilst simultaneously marginalizing societal resistance to its policies. There exists here a trace of, what some would identify as 'Marxist–pluralism'.

4.3   STATE AUTONOMY AND STATE POWER

This short excursion into theories of the ACS has offered a variety of accounts concerning the functions of the state in advanced capitalist societies (see Table 2.12) and the issue of in whose interests the state 'rules'. But equally it appears it has left us with a nagging question: which of these two sets of approaches to the ACS — the society-centred or the state-centred — is the more convincing?

Table 2.12   Theoretical accounts of the ACS

	neo-Marxist	Weberian/pluralist
Society-centred	structural and instrumental accounts (Miliband, Poulantz)	elitist (Mills) neo-pluralism (Lindblom, Dahl)
State-centred	post-Marxist (Offe, Jessop)	(neo-) corporatism (Lehmbruch) new right (neo-institutionalism)

One way in which these two distinctive approaches can be reconciled is by acknowledging the significant differences between ACSs in terms of the resources (administrative, political, coercive, financial, ideological, knowledge), capacities and instruments of state power. Mann refers to these resources and capacities as embodying the 'infrastructural power' of the state by which he means the ability '... to penetrate civil society and implement decisions throughout the realm' (Mann, 1988, p.4). Some ACSs have considerable 'infrastructural power' and others relatively less so. The greater the infrastructural power of the state, the greater is its influence over civil society. Accordingly it is possible to differentiate, as do both Krasner and Skocpol, between 'strong' states and 'weak' states (Krasner, 1978; Skocpol, 1985). A 'strong state' is one which is able to implement its decisions against societal resistance and/or can resist societal demands from even the most powerful private groups (Nordlinger, 1981, p.22). By comparison a 'weak state' can do neither of these things '... owing to societal resistance and lack of resources' (Bertramsen *et al.,* 1991, p.99). Studies which have exploited this typology tend to classify ACSs such as Japan and France as 'strong states' whilst the US and Canada are classified as 'weak states' (Atkinson and Coleman, 1990).

One logical implication of this typology is the conclusion that state-centred approaches might best explain the power and policies of 'strong states', whilst society-centred approaches are better at accounting for the actions and policies of 'weak states' (Betramsen *et al.*, 1991, p.100). Furthermore, the distinction can be utilized to account for the very different styles of policy making which occur in different policy sectors within the same state. Thus, in some policy sectors the state may be considered strong whilst in other policy sectors it is considered weak (Atkinson and Coleman, 1990). In this case, both society-centred and state-centred approaches provide equally helpful insights into state action (see Goldthorpe, 1984). In addition, the infrastructural power of any state varies over time with the result that states historically can be conceived as becoming stronger or weaker. Recognizing this underlines the relevance of both state-centred and society-centred approaches to the ACS.

It would appear that the notion of choosing between state-centred and society-centred approaches is somewhat spurious. As McLennan observes, 'statism', or state-centred accounts, may be '... designed to complement rather than replace society-centredness' (McLennan, 1989, p.233). The upshot of this is that in attempting to explain the power and actions of the ACS a 'modest theoretical eclecticism' has to be embraced even if it is intellectually uncomfortable.

5   PUTTING THE ADVANCED CAPITALIST STATE IN ITS PLACE

No contemporary analysis of the ACS can afford to ignore the stresses to which it is subject because of its strategic location at the intersection of international and domestic processes. As the earlier discussion has made clear, both the formation and the nature of the ACS can only be properly understood by reference to both endogenous and exogenous forces of social change. Moreover, as patterns of global interconnectedness appear to be intensifying, the distinctions between the internal and the external, the foreign and the domestic, seem increasingly anachronistic. A moment's reflection on some of the critical social issues which confront the ACS, such as drug abuse or the environment, would confirm that each has a global or transnational dimension. Few issues can now be defined as purely 'domestic' or specifically 'international'. On the contrary, it is more accurate to view states as confronted by 'intermestic' problems. However we choose to recognize the erosion of this traditional distinction, the central point is that all ACSs are increasingly subject to globalizing forces which impose powerful constraints on state sovereignty and press heavily upon the everyday lives of its citizens.

5.1 GLOBALIZATION AND THE ACS

Globalization '... should be understood as the re-ordering of time and distance in our lives. Our lives, in other words, are increasingly influenced by activities and events happening well away from the social context in which we carry on our day-to-day activities' (Giddens, 1989, p.520). To talk of globalization is to recognize that there are dynamic processes at work constructing and weaving networks of interaction and interconnectedness across the states and societies which make up the modern world system. Globalization has two distinct dimensions: scope (or stretching) and intensity (or deepening). On the one hand it defines a process or set of processes which embrace most of the globe or which operate worldwide: the concept therefore has a spatial connotation. Politics and other social activities are becoming 'stretched' across the globe. On the other hand it also implies an intensification in the levels of interaction, interconnectedness, or interdependence between the states and societies which constitute the world community. Accordingly alongside the 'stretching' goes a 'deepening' of the impact of global processes on national and local communities.

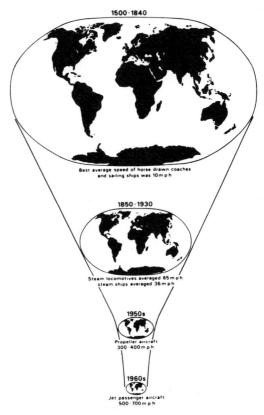

The shrinking world

Far from being an abstract concept, globalization articulates one of the more familiar features of modern existence. A single moment's reflection on the contents of our own kitchen cupboards or fridges would underline the fact that, simply as passive consumers, we are very much part of a global network of production and exchange.

In his analysis of the welfare state, Alber in Reading A stresses the significance of global forces — the economic crisis of the 1970s and early 1980s — in stimulating a restructuring of welfare provision within all capitalist societies. A combination of factors made it increasingly difficult for governments, of whatever political persuasion, to sustain the growth in welfare programmes which had occurred in the 1960s or to protect workers from the consequences of growing international competition. The kind of 'managed capitalism' which had emerged in the post-war period no longer meshed with an increasingly globally integrated economic and financial system. Full employment or extensive welfare provision which require high levels of taxation, are difficult to sustain when capital is so readily mobile and foreign competition so intense. Underlying this erosion of 'managed capitalism' in the 1980s has been an acceleration in processes of economic globalization and the consequent break-up of the post-war global order.

As Keohane observed, 'the European welfare state was built on foundations provided by American hegemony' (Keohane, 1984, p.22). 'Managed capitalism' did not simply reflect a domestic political settlement but rather was constructed upon the post-war global settlement of a liberal (free trade) world economic order underwritten by US military and economic power. Within this world order, structures of global economic management, such as the International Monetary Fund (IMF) and General Agreement on Tariffs and Trade (GATT), nurtured the economic conditions which helped sustain the rapid post-war growth of Western economies and enabled the massive expansion of welfare provision. Both 'managed capitalism' and a regulated world economy were mutually reinforcing. However, by the mid-1980s the combined effects of economic recession, the resultant global economic restructuring, the intensification of the financial and economic integration of Western economies, and the emergence of new centres of economic power such as Japan and Germany, had seriously undermined the post-war global capitalist order. As the 1990s dawned, the conditions essential to the survival of the welfare state in its conventional form had been transformed:

> ... the reconstruction of the international political economy has definitively altered the circumstances in which welfare states have to operate. Exposing national economies and national corporatist arrangements to the unregulated world economy has transformed the circumstances under which any government might seek, for example, to pursue a policy of full employment ...

The deregulation of international markets and of financial institutions, in particular, have tended to weaken the capacities of

the interventionist state, to render all economies more open and to
make national capital and more especially national labour
movements much more subject to the terms and conditions of
international competition.
(Pierson, 1991, pp.177, 188)

For some, this process of 'reconstruction' signals an even more
profound shift in the nature of global capitalism. Lash and Urry, for
instance, argue that organized or 'managed capitalism' is giving way to a
form of 'disorganized capitalism' in which national economies are
becoming increasingly beyond the control of national governments,
partly as a consequence of the accelerating globalization of production
and exchange (Lash and Urry, 1987, p.308; Offe, 1984). But it is not
simply the capacity of the capitalist state to control its own economy
that is at issue.

Writing in the early 1970s, Morse pointed to the ways in which the
global movement of goods, money, ideas, images, knowledge,
technology, etc., challenged the ability of the ACS to govern effectively
within its own territory (Morse, 1976). Morse argued that growing
international interdependence diminished the effectiveness of national
governments and thereby encouraged a corresponding attachment to
international forms of regulation or co-operation. Over the last three
decades there has been a startling expansion in levels of international
co-operation . Through a myriad of international institutions, such as
the IMF, GATT, International Civil Aviation Organization, International
Telecommunications Union, Organization of Economic Cooperation and
Development etc., informal arrangements such as the G7, and
international networks of key policy makers, advanced capitalist states
have created a vast array of *international regimes*: sets of international
rules, norms, procedures, modes of decision making and organizations.
These embrace those issue-areas in which states have become
increasingly interdependent or where transnational activities create
common problems. Such regimes seek to regulate high policy domains,
such as defence and global finance, as well as welfare policy domains
such as the trade in narcotics, environmental issues and AIDS.

International regimes, in effect, express the growing internationalization
of the advanced capitalist state and the internationalization of state
elites. Within Europe, this internationalization has culminated in the
evolution of the European Communities from a common market into a
quasi-supranational political structure which can take decisions binding
upon member governments: a contemporary illustration of this
legislative power being the implementation across the EC of the Social
Charter. Advanced capitalist states are enmeshed in an extensive array
of formal and informal international regimes which make them
simultaneously both the determinants as well as the objects of an
expanding field of international regulatory practices. In some domains,
the sovereignty of the ACS is severely compromised by its participation
in these regimes whilst in others it is sometimes enhanced. Clearly

President Gorbachev and leaders of the G7 leading Western states meet to discuss global issues, London, July 1991.

ACSs have always operated under external constraints of all kinds. However, it is frequently argued that international co-operation restricts the exercise of state autonomy — the capacity to act independently, within circumscribed parameters, in the articulation and pursuit of domestic and international policy objectives — across a range of policy domains. Yet, in a more interconnected world, international co-operation has become increasingly vital to the achievement of a host of domestic policy objectives. For instance dealing with drug addiction requires international co-operation to combat the global trade in narcotics, whilst domestic economic management demands co-operation on interest rates and currency fluctuations. The ACS thus confronts a major dilemma as it attempts to balance effectiveness against a potential loss of autonomy.

For some, such a choice merely reinforces growing evidence of the decline of the nation-state and calls into question its continued viability. However, for now that particular argument is left in abeyance to be explored in Book 4, *Modernity and Its Futures* (Hall *et al.*, 1992).

6   THE ACS: A REVIEW

This chapter set out to examine three questions:

First, given the diversity of state forms within the advanced capitalist world is it possible to identify common patterns in respect of the development, characteristics, nature and functions of the state?

Second, how are we to make sense of the role and actions of the state in governing advanced societies and in whose interests does it 'rule'? and

Third, in what ways do international or global forces condition the activities of the modern capitalist state?

In Section 2 we adopted a broad comparative approach in order to isolate the common features and diverse forms of the ACS. This analysis was extended further in Section 3 through a comparative historical examination of how the twin processes of militarism and capitalism have contributed to the formation of the ACS. In Section 4 a rather more synoptic approach was adopted in exploring both society-centred and state-centred accounts of the role and functions of the state in advanced capitalist societies. Finally in Section 5 we dealt with the consequences of globalization for the nature of the contemporary ACS and its capacity to ensure the welfare of its citizens.

Throughout this chapter great stress has been placed upon the diverse forms as well as the common features of the state in advanced capitalist societies. Tremendous diversity is apparent in respect of institutional structures and welfare regimes. Yet commonalities do exist in so far as these states share broadly similar patterns of development, have acquired comparable roles and functions, and share a common experience in attempting to reconcile the often competing demands of private accumulation with liberal democracy. Moreover, as the chapter has argued, the traditional distinctions and boundaries between the public (the state) and the private (civil society), the civil and the military, and the foreign and the domestic have become increasingly blurred by the forces of modernity. As a result the state in all advanced capitalist societies may be entering a new 'era' in which the very architecture of politics itself is experiencing a profound transformation (Cerny, 1990). Making sense of the ACS therefore demands a refreshing theoretical eclecticism in which the dynamic interplay between capitalism and militarism, as well as between national and international processes and conditions, is explicitly acknowledged (Giddens, 1985; 1990).

REFERENCES

Abercrombie, N., Hill, S. and Turner, B.S. (eds) (1988) *The Penguin Dictionary of Sociology*, 2nd edn, Harmondsworth, Penguin.

Alber, J. (1988) 'Continuities and changes in the idea of the welfare state', *Politics and Society* , vol.16, no.4, pp.451–68.

Atkinson, M.M. and Coleman, W.D. (1990) 'Strong states and weak states; sectoral policy networks in advanced capitalist economies', *British Journal of Political Science*, vol.19, pp.47–67.

Berger, J. (1990) 'Market and state in advanced capitalist societies', in Martinelli, A. and Smelser, N. *Economy and Society*, London, Sage.

Bertramsen, R.B., Thomsen, J.P.F., and Torfing, J. (1991) *State, Economy and Society*, London, Unwin Hyman.

Carnoy, M. (1984) *The State and Political Theory*, Princeton NJ, Princeton University Press.

Cerny, P. (1990) *The Changing Architecture of Politics*, London, Sage.

Dahl, R.A. (1985) *A Preface to Economic Democracy*, Cambridge, Polity Press.

Dahl, R.A. and Lindblom, C. (1976) *Politics, Economics and Welfare*, 2nd Edition, Chicago, Chicago University Press.

Domhoff, G. (1978) *Who Really Rules?*, Santa Monica, Calif., Goodyear Publishing.

Dunleavy, P. and O'Leary, B. (1987) *Theories of the State : the Politics of Liberal Democracy*, London, Macmillan.

Eccleston, B. (1989) *State and Society in Post-War Japan*, Cambridge, Polity Press.

Esping-Andersen, G. (1985) *Politics against Markets*, Princeton NJ, Princeton University Press.

Esping-Andersen, G. (1990) *The Three Worlds of Welfare Capitalism*, Cambridge, Polity Press.

Fox, D.M. (1986) 'The NHS and the Second World War', in Smith, H.L. (ed.) *War and Social Change*, Manchester, Manchester University Press.

Giddens, A. (1985) *The Nation-State and Violence*, Cambridge, Polity Press.

Giddens, A. (1989) *Sociology*, Cambridge, Polity Press.

Giddens, A. (1990) *The Consequences of Modernity*, Cambridge, Polity Press.

Ginsburg, N. (1979) *Class, Capital and Social Policy*, London, Macmillan.

Goldthorp, J. (ed.) (1984) *Order and Conflict in Contemporary Capitalism*, Oxford, Clarendon Press.

Gough, I. (1979) *The Political Economy of the Welfare State*, London, Macmillan.

Gourevitch, P. (1986) *Politics in Hard Times*, Ithaca, Cornell University Press.

Gummett, P. and Reppy, J. (1991) 'Military industrial networks and technical change in the new strategic environment', *Government and Opposition,* vol.25, no.3, pp.287–304.

Hall, S. and Gieben, B. (eds) (1992) *Formations of Modernity*, Cambridge, Polity Press.

Hall, S., Held, D. and McGrew, A. (eds) (1992) *Modernity and Its Futures*, Cambridge, Polity Press.

Held, D. (1987) *Models of Democracy*, Polity Press, Cambridge.

Held D. (1992) 'The development of the modern state', in Hall, S. and Gieben, B. (eds) (1992).

Jessop, B. (1990) *State Theory,* Cambridge, Polity Press.

Jessop, B., Bonnett, K., Bromley, S. and Ling, T. (1988) *Thatcherism,* Cambridge, Polity Press.

Kennedy, P. (1987) *The Rise and Fall of the Great Powers,* London, Unwin Hyman.

Keohane, R.O. (1984) 'The world political economy and the crisis of embedded liberalism', in Goldthorpe, J. (ed.) *Order and Conflict in Contemporary Capitalism,* Oxford, Clarendon Press.

Kingdom, P. (1991) *Government and Politics in the UK*, Polity Press, Cambridge.

Krasner, S. (1978) *Defending the National Interest*, Princeton NJ, Princeton University Press.

Lash, S. and Urry, J. (1987) *The End of Organized Capitalism,* Cambridge, Polity Press.

Lehmbruch, G. (1984) 'Consertation and the structure of corporatist networks', in Goldthorpe, J., (ed.) (1984).

Lijphart, A. (1984) *Democracies,* New Haven, Yale University Press.

Lindblom, C. (1977) *Politics and Markets,* New York, Basic Books.

Lovering, J. (1990) 'Military expenditure and the restructuring of capitalism', *Cambridge Journal of Economics*, vol.14, pp.453–67.

MacKenzie, G. (1990) *Inventing Accuracy: A Historical Sociology of Missile Guidance*, Boston, Mass., MIT Press.

McNeill, W. (1983) *The Pursuit of Power,* Oxford, Basil Blackwell.

McLennan, G. (1989) *Marxism, Pluralism and Beyond,* Cambridge, Polity Press.

Mann, M. (1986) *The Sources of Social Power,* vol.1, Cambridge, Cambridge University Press.

Mann, M. (1988) *States, War and Capitalism,* Oxford, Basil Blackwell.

Miliband, R. (1969) *The State in Capitalist Society*, London, Quartet Books.

Mills, C. Wright (1956) *The Power Elite,* Oxford, Oxford University Press.

Milward, A. (1987) *War, Economy and Society 1939–1945,* London, Pelican.

Mitchell, T. (1991) 'The Limits of the State', *American Political Science Review*, vol.85, no.1, March, pp.77–96.

Morse, E. (1976) *Modernization and the Transformation of International Relations*, New York, Free Press.

Nordlinger, E. (1981) *On the Autonomy of the Democratic State*, Harvard, Mass., Harvard University Press.

Offe, C. (1976) 'Laws of motion of reformist state policies', mimeo.

Offe, C. (1984) *Contradictions of the Welfare State,* London, Hutchinson.

Panitch, L. (1980) 'Recent theorizations on corporatism', *British Journal of Sociology,* vol.31, no.2, pp.159–87.

Pearton, M. (1982) *The Knowledgeable State*, London, Burnett.

Penguin Dictionary of Sociology: see Abercrombie *et al.* (1988).

Pierson, C. (1991) *Beyond the Welfare State?*, Cambridge, Polity Press.

Piven, F. and Cloward, R. (1971) *Regulating the Poor*, New York, Pantheon Books.

Rasler, K. and Thompson, W.R. (1989) *War and State Making*, Boston, Unwin Hyman.

Rose, R. (1984) *Big Government*, London, Sage.

Schmitter, P. (1974) 'Still the century of corporatism?', *Review of Politics,* vol.36, pt.1, pp.85–131.

Schmitter, P. (1989) 'Corporatism is dead! Long live corporatism', *Government and Opposition,* vol.24, no.1, pp.54–73.

Scott, J. (1991) *Who Rules Britain?,* Cambridge, Polity Press.

Skocpol, T. (1985) 'Bringing the state back in', in Evans, P.R., Rueschemeyer, D. and Skocpol, T. (eds) *Bringing the State Back In*, Cambridge, Cambridge University Press.

Smith, H.L. (ed.) (1986) *War and Social Change*, Manchester, Manchester University Press.

Thee, M. (1987) *Military Technology, Military Strategy and the Arms Race*, London, Croom Helm.

Therborn, G. (1987) 'Welfare state and capitalist markets', *Acta Sociologica*, vol.30, no.3, pp.237–54.

Therborn, G. (1989) 'States, populations and productivity: towards a political theory of welfare states', in Lassman, P. (ed.) *Politics and Social Theory*, London, Routledge.

Tilly, C. (1984) *Big Structures, Large Processes, Huge Comparisons*, London, Sage.

Tilly, C. (1990) *Coercion, Capital and European States*, Oxford, Basil Blackwell.

READING A   CONTINUITIES AND CHANGES IN THE IDEA OF
            THE WELFARE STATE

Jens Alber

'Welfare State' or 'Welfare States': Cross-National Variations

... It would be extremely misleading to venture generalizations on the nature of the welfare state in Western countries from the experience of one or two countries. Rather, we should try to arrive at an empirically substantiated typology of Western welfare states based on a careful mapping of cross-sectional variations. In Western Europe, we can distinguish between a *Scandinavian and Anglo-Saxon version* of the welfare state (Denmark, Finland, Norway, Sweden, United Kingdom, Ireland) and a *Continental version* (Belgium, Netherlands, France, Italy, Austria, West Germany, Switzerland). The former emphasizes social services rather than social transfers, the transfer schemes have universal coverage with a focus on the provision of minima, and financing is heavily based on general revenues. The latter emphasizes earnings-related and status-preserving social transfer payments, places more limits on coverage, and relies to a lesser degree on general revenue financing. A second — and empirically more problematic — typology distinguishes 'institutional' and 'residual' welfare state models in the Western world. In the residual model, welfare state schemes are selectively targeted on the poorer strata with guaranteed minima and only a mildly progressive tax system, whereas in the institutional model the schemes have a more universal coverage and rather generous benefits financed with the help of a highly progressive system of taxation. ...

Variations in welfare state profiles must be related to differences in organizational and institutional contexts as well as to national policy traditions dating back to the prehistory of the modern welfare state. Besides the national variations, however, we can also detect common features in the historical extension of welfare state boundaries.

Common Boundaries of the Welfare State

In a historical perspective, we can distinguish five general phases of welfare state development in Western Europe that to some extent cut across the national divergences (see Table 1). First, in the *prehistory* of the modern welfare state, national poor laws were developed. The policy choices in this period structured subsequent welfare state developments. This period extended roughly to the late nineteenth century. Poverty was perceived as an individual shortcoming, and support was given only in combination with tight controls. Public policy centered on the maintenance of collective order rather than on individual well-being.

Towards the end of the nineteenth century, the policy conception changed radically. As social insurance programs were adopted, the collective causes of misery were highlighted and individual well-being became a recognized policy goal, firmly established in individual legal entitle-

Source: Alber, J. (1988) *Politics and Society*, vol.16, no.4, pp.451-68.

ments. However, the scope of welfare schemes was still targeted selectively on the working class. The concern with public order was still central, the major objective being to integrate the workers into the capitalist economy and the national state. Public efforts centered on income maintenance for workers, and the range of state services in health, housing, and education remained limited. Prior to World War 1, the ratio of welfare spending to GDP remained below 5 percent throughout all Western European countries. However, as contemporary research on the impact of program age on current spending levels has shown, an important institutional basis for welfare provisions had been laid. This phase may therefore be considered the *takeoff* period of the modern welfare state.

Table 1   Phases of Welfare State Development in Western Europe

Phases	Time	Core welfare state concept
Prehistory	1600-1880	Policing the poor
Takeoff	1880-1914	Social insurance to integrate workers
Expansion	1918-1960	Social services as an element of citizenship
Acceleration	1960-1975	Promotion of quality of life
Slowdown	1975-	New mix of state, associational, and private responsibilities?

After World War I, a long period of *expansion* began in which the scope and the range of welfare state activities was successively widened. The coverage of social insurance schemes was extended to white-collar strata and independent categories, health and education facilities were expanded, and public housing programs were adopted. Welfare services came to be perceived as a fundamental element of citizenship rights. National variations remained great, but in all countries the welfare expenditure ratio grew. The expansionary trend was spurred after World War II, which had strengthened national unity. In the leading country (Germany), the ratio of welfare spending to GDP had exceeded 20 percent during the interwar period. The Western European average climbed to 15 percent by 1960.

During the 1960s, welfare state expansion accelerated considerably. From 1960 to 1975, the average welfare expenditure ratio in Western Europe jumped from 15 to 27 percent. Income maintenance schemes now attained universal or nearly universal coverage, and benefit levels were repeatedly improved. Sizable resources were channeled into the health and housing sectors, and participation ratios in institutions of higher learning multiplied. The traditional idea of state provision of minima gave way to the new notion of state responsibility for optima. In several countries flat-rate minimum benefits were combined with earnings-related supplements. In institutional terms, the Western European welfare states came to resemble one another, as even the few remaining associational provisions were superseded by public schemes. In order to evaluate the effectiveness of public policy, several countries developed social indicator systems designed to measure the quality of life, for which the state now assumed a public responsibility. This was also part of a larger effort to move from a merely reactive social and economic policy to a more active engineering of societal development based on scientific analysis and forecasts. Thus, several countries set up national economic advisory councils to mobilize professional expertise (for example, the United Kingdom in 1961, West Germany in 1963).

With the recession of the mid-1970s these high-flying projects came to a sudden end. If we use the welfare expenditure ratio as the chief indicator, the speed of welfare state expansion was considerably curbed (see Figure 1 below). Some countries even witnessed a *standstill* or slight decrease in welfare spending relative to GDP. However, the wide variety of policy responses to the economic crisis seems to have led to an increase in national divergences (scrutinized in more detail below). ...

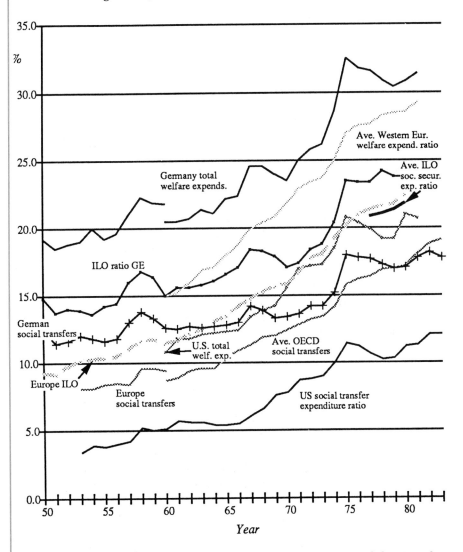

Figure 1   Postwar social expenditure ratios in Western Europe and the United States

Policy responses to the economic crisis since the mid-1970s

A sound analysis of recent policy developments would, of course, require a systematic look at recent changes in welfare legislation, which is far beyond the scope of this contribution. Here, I can call only on information on the development of various social expenditure ratios, which may be regarded as a crude (and not fully valid) indicator of welfare state efforts. Relying on three different statistical definitions and sources, Figure 1 depicts the postwar development of the average Western European expenditure ratios as well as the developments in Germany and the United States.

Expressed in terms of social spending, the welfare state grew moderately in the 1950s, at an accelerated speed from 1960 to 1975 with particularly steep increases during the first half of the 1970s, and at a markedly decelerated pace since 1975. Judging from the Western European average, the expansionary trend of the welfare state has been curbed but not stopped in the most recent crisis period. Only in Germany and the United States do we find a sharp rupture with past growth patterns. The social expenditure ratios of these countries have remained stagnant or even declined slightly since 1975. This illustrates once more the diversity of international developments and the pitfalls of general conclusions based on the rather atypical German or U.S. cases.

A closer look at national expenditure profiles shows two, rather discrepant patterns of development in the most recent period (see Table 2). On the one hand, in *austerity* countries welfare state expansion has more or less come to a halt. These include the Continental countries Germany and Switzerland and the Scandinavian countries Norway and Finland, as well as the United States. On the other hand, in *expansion* countries the expenditure ratios continued to grow, reaching a peak only in the most recent year covered in the statistics. These include the Scandinavian countries Sweden and Denmark, and the Catholic countries Belgium and France on the Continent and Ireland, as well as Austria and Italy, where the growth was more modest and interrupted by marked phases of stagnation. In Britain, expenditure growth was sharply curbed from 1976 to 1979, but then increased again to new peaks in the early 1980s. The Netherlands witnessed steady expansion except for a short and sharp decline from 1976 to 1977. In a comparative perspective, Britain ranks closer to the austerity countries, and the Netherlands closer to the expansion countries. The empirical patterns are not fully consistent for all definitions of social expenditure, and even the expansion countries had at least short interludes of interrupted growth during the late 1970s. In summary, however, we can say that the welfare state has continued to grow in most Western European countries even throughout the most recent period of austerity. Only in four countries have the expansionary trends come to a visible halt. Nowhere, however, did the expenditure ratios fall below the record levels reached in the early 1970s. This suggests an interpretation of the recent period as a phase of consolidation rather than of welfare state dismantling.

Table 2   The Development of Social Expenditure Ratios in Western Europe
Since 1975

	ILO social security expenditures, 1980	OECD total welfare expenditures, 1981	OECD social transfer expenditures, 1983
Peak reached in most recent year covered by statistics	Belgium, Denmark, France, Ireland, (Italy), Netherlands, Sweden, U.K.	Austria, (Belgium), (Denmark), France, Ireland, Italy, Sweden, U.K.	Austria, Belgium, Finland, France, (Ireland), Italy, Netherlands, Switzerland
Peak reached earlier (year)	Austria (1978), Norway (1979), Finland (1978), Germany (1978), Switzerland (1977)	Finland (1977), Germany (1975), Netherlands (1975), Norway (1978), Switzerland (1976)	Denmark (1982), Germany (1982), Norway (1979), Sweden (1982), U.K. (1982)
Stagnation or shrinkage (years)	Germany (1976–77), Finland (1978–80), Switzerland (1978–79)	Finland (1977–81), Norway 1979–81), Netherlands (1976–77), Germany (1976–77), Switzerland (1977–78)	Germany (1976–77), Norway (1979–80), Switzerland (1977–81), Finland (1978–82)
Moderate growth with interruption (years of interruption)	Ireland (1976–78), Italy (1976–77), Norway (1978–80), U.K. (1976–78), Austria (1976–80)	Austria (1978–80), Denmark (1976), Italy (1976–77), U.K. (1976–80)	Austria (1979–80), Ireland (1976–79), Italy (1975–80), U.K. (1978–79, 1982–83)
Expansion (years with interruption)	Belgium (1978), Denmark (1977), France (1979), Netherlands (1978), Sweden (1978–79)	Belgium (-), France (-), Ireland (1976–78), Sweden (-)	Belgium (1979–81), Denmark (1976–77, 1983), France (-), Netherlands (-), Sweden (1981–83)

NOTE: Parentheses around the name of a country indicate countries that are difficult to classify; a (-) indicates no years when expansion was interrupted.

The marked national variations in policy responses require an explanation. If we look at party control of government as one potential determinant, the striking fact is that the rupture with expansionary trends in the austerity countries occurred under social-democratic governments (West Germany, 1975-1982; Finland, 1976-1982; Norway, 1975-1981; Switzerland, 1977-1981). Even in the United Kingdom, the most visible rupture with past trends occurred while the Labour party was in office. The continuous expansion in Belgium and Denmark took place under center-left coalitions, whereas the growth in France and Sweden largely occurred while center-right governments were in office. This suggests once more that we must understand the welfare state as a product of manifold political forces.

To arrive at a satisfactory explanation of the differences in policy responses, we must combine the analysis of socio-structural factors with a closer look at the recent crisis constellation. Following Walter Korpi's argument about the potential for welfare backlash [protest against welfare cuts] in residual and institutional welfare states, I would assume that severe austerity measures are most easily pursued in countries with less developed welfare states where only a minor proportion of the electorate depends on welfare state schemes and where benefits are not generous enough to make the white-collar strata an ally of the welfare state. Even though Korpi's distinction of the two types is empirically problematic, it is noteworthy that the four least developed Western European welfare states, Switzerland, Britain, Finland and Norway, are all found among the austerity countries. West Germany, the only remaining country with marked stagnation, occupies a middle place in the rank order of European welfare states.

So far, however, the changes in political rhetoric have been more marked than the changes in policy. Even in the austerity countries curtailments remain limited. Up to the present the political modifications of the welfare state may be characterized as piecemeal adjustments and a "muddling through" rather than as a fundamental departure to new policy horizons.

However, the recent period of austerity also spurred fresh conceptual thinking about welfare state issues in intellectual and political circles.

READING B SOCIAL DEMOCRACY AND THE COMING OF THE 'KEYNESIAN WELFARE STATE'

Christopher Pierson

... Early social democrats were distinguished from their more radical socialist opponents not by rejection of the final *aim* of socialization, of the economy, (which formally, at least, they endorsed), but by their differing (gradualist or evolutionary) *method* for achieving such an end. Neo-classical economics insisted that capitalism required the free-play of untrammelled market forces. It seemed that for its socialist (including social democratic) opponents, socialism must by contrast be premised upon some form of centralized and directive planning and investment. However, the social, political and economic costs of transition to such a socialized/planned economy were great, perhaps insurmountable, for social democrats pledged to the introduction of socialism through the medium of liberal parliamentary democracy. The 'solution' to this social democratic dilemma was to be found in the development of Keynesian economic policy in association with the promotion of an expanded welfare state — the so-called *Keynesian Welfare State*. It is in this way that the welfare state comes to assume its familiar centrality in social democratic thinking.

For social democracy, the vital importance of Keynesianism resided in its status as 'a system of political control over economic life' (Skidelsky, 1979, p.55). Its great strategic beauty lay in its promise of effective political control of economic life without the dreadful social, economic and political costs that social democrats feared 'expropriation of the expropriators' would bring. Though Keynes was not a socialist, he was an opponent of the belief that capitalism was a self-regulating economic system. Above all, it was the neo-classical belief in a self-regulating market mechanism securing full employment that Keynes sought to subvert, indeed to invert.

Source: Pierson, C. (1991), *Beyond the Welfare State*, Cambridge, Polity Press, pp.26–8.

... It was the duty of governments to intervene within the market to generate an enhanced level of 'effective demand', promoting both the propensity to consume and to invest, so as to ensure sufficient economic activity to utilize all available labour and thus to secure equilibrium at full employment. To achieve this, a whole range of indirect measures — including taxation policy, public works, monetary policy and the manipulation of interest rates — were available to the interventionist government.

Keynes' advocacy of a 'managed capitalism' offered a neat solution to the social democratic dilemma of how to furnish reforms for its extended constituency and maintain its long-term commitment to socialism without challenging the hegemony of private capital. ...

Economic *control* could be exercised through the manipulation of major economic variables in the hands of the government. The owners of capital could be *induced* to act in ways which would promote the interests of social democracy's wide constituency. At the same time, social democratic governments could shape the propensity to consume, through taxation and monetary policy, as well as through adjusting the level of public spending. They could also rectify the disutilities of the continuing play of market forces through the income transfers and social services that came to be identified with the welfare state. Happily, the raising of workers' wages and income transfers to the poor, a 'vice' in classical economics, suddenly became, given the tendency of lower income groups to consume the greater part of their incomes, a Keynesian 'virtue'. Social democracy was thus able simultaneously to secure the 'national interest' and to service its own constituency.

For traditional social democrats, then, the development of the welfare state institutionalized the successes of social democratic politics. The Keynesian revolution made possible the transition from the (zero-sum) politics of production to what, under conditions of economic growth, were the (positive-sum) politics of (re-)distribution. As Berthil Ohlin described it in the 1930s, 'the tendency is in the direction of a "nationalization of consumption" as opposed to the nationalization of the "means of production" of Marxian socialism' (Ohlin, 1938, p.5). It was a two-fold strategy built upon active government intervention through 1) the macro-management of the economy to ensure economic growth under conditions of full employment and 2) a range of social policies dealing with 'the redistribution of the fruits of economic growth, the management of its human effects, and the compensation of those who suffered from them' (Donnison, 1979, pp.146-50).

References

Donnison, D. (1979) 'Social policy since Titmus', *Journal of Social Policy*, vol.8, no.2, pp.145–56.

Ohlin, B. (1938) 'Economic progress in Sweden', *The Annals of the American Academy of Political and Social Science*, vol.197, pp.1–6.

Skidelsky, R. (1979) 'The decline of Keynesian Politics', in Crouch, C. (ed.) *State and Economy in Contemporary Capitalism*, London, Croom Helm.

READING C CLASS AND POWER IN CONTEMPORARY CAPITALISM

Ralph Miliband

... State power is controlled by the people who occupy the command posts of the state system — presidents, prime ministers, and their immediate ministerial and other colleagues and advisers; top civil servants; senior officers in the armed forces, the police, and the surveillance and intelligence agencies; senior judges; and the people in charge of state enterprises, regulatory commissions, and similar agencies. In some political systems (such as that of the United States), the list would also include senior members of the legislative branch. In some strong federal systems (such as the Canadian), provincial prime ministers and their colleagues and advisers might also be taken to be part of the state elite. Generally speaking, however, the senior people in weak federal systems, and in local or regional government everywhere, would not qualify for inclusion as members of that elite. Their power, in many instances, may not be negligible; but it is not of the same kind as the power exercised by the controls of state power at the centre of affairs.

I noted earlier that different parts of the state system are often at odds with each other; and this is certainly the case in regard to the dealings which government, legislators, judges, and regulatory agencies have with this or that capitalist interest. It is not uncommon, for instance, for legislatures to pass laws relating to one aspect or other of business, only to find them invalidated by the courts. Even so, the state system does, in this as in other respects, usually function with a reasonable degree of coherence (which is not the same as competence); and we may therefore leave aside for the moment the constant frictions which attend the relationship between different parts of the system.

What, then, is the relationship between state power and corporate power?

... the corporate elite and the state elite stand on a par with each other: both dwell on the same level of the commanding heights of the social order.

This is not how capital and the state are viewed in the traditional Marxist perspective. In that perspective, the state, however great its importance and power, is taken to be ultimately subordinate to the capitalist class, or to the impersonal but inexorably compelling power and logic of capital, or to a combination of both. The 'relative autonomy of the state' may be invoked to qualify this subordinate position, but does not negate it: the power of capital and capitalists, in Marxist terms, is ultimately decisive in regard to what the state does, and also, which is scarcely less important, in what it does not do.

Source: Miliband, R. (1989) *Divided Societies*, Oxford, Oxford University Press, pp.30–36.

It is right to stress that the state is indeed located in a given economic context which is decisively shaped by the capitalist mode of production; and that what the state does or does not do is crucially affected by the imperative requirements of capital and by the power of those who own and control capital.

However, the danger which this emphasis presents is that it tends to devalue the power of the state, and the fact that its power has often been used for purposes and policies which were not only pursued without reference to the capitalist class, but also at times against the wishes of many parts of that class, or even the whole of it. It is because the state has had, and still has, this power that it has been able to make itself the architect of the reforms which have been such a conspicuous part of the history of capitalism in the last hundred and fifty years or so.

It may well be said that this reforming activity of the state has never gone so far as to create a root and branch challenge to the interests of capital; and that even in its most reforming guise, the state remains the protector of the social order, not a means of weakening it. But however this may be (and the impact of reform is rather more complex than this), the implication is that unless the state actually engineers revolutionary change, it has to be seen as subordinate to capital. This is too restrictive, in so far as it focuses on the extreme ends of a spectrum, whereas the state usually operates within the spectrum.

The point is of importance in relation to class struggle. The state does not, normally and of its own volition, intervene in class struggle on the side of labour. But this does not mean that it is necessarily subservient to the purposes and strategies of capital. It is in fact often compelled, by virtue of its concern for the defence and stability of the social order, to seek some intermediate position, and to act upon it, however much that position may differ from the position of capital.

Nothing of this must be taken to mean that the state is not the ultimate protector of a capitalist-dominated social order. But it is to suggest that the state provides such protection as those who control it think fit, and, in many different spheres, with a high degree of independence — even at times with complete independence, though always, of course, within a determinate economic, social, political and cultural context. ...

It is to take account of the independence and power of the state that I have advanced the notion of a *partnership* between corporate power and state power — a partnership between 'two different, separate forces, linked to each other by many threads, yet each having its own separate sphere of concerns'.

The terms of this partnership are not firmly fixed; and the relations between the partners, though close, are far from smooth. There are in fact many bones of contention between them, and a good deal of suspicion and even contempt. This arises from the fact that each partner does have its own sphere of concerns, and that this tends to produce tension and conflict between them. 'The true meaning of freedom for the American bourgeoisie', it has been said — but the point does not only apply to the American bourgeoisie — 'is the ability of those who own or control economic resources to allocate or appropriate them as they see fit — without interference from labour unions or government officials'; and capital does indeed have an extraordinary degree of freedom from 'interference', even though the decisions which flow from its exercise have direct and major consequences for workers, towns, regions and countries. But there are nevertheless *some* constraints upon that freedom, most of them imposed by the state; and imposed, it may be added, for the sake of the health and stability of the capitalist social order itself.

The state's interventionist propensities and its imposition of constraints on business are particularly marked in periods of crisis and unrest. It is notable, for instance, that even in the United States, where the capitalist class is more powerful than its equivalent in any other advanced capitalist country, 'between 1965 and 1975, more than twenty-five major pieces of federal regulatory legislation in the area of consumer and environmental protection, occupational health and safety and personnel policy were enacted by the Federal Government'. Those were of course years of great turmoil in the United States; and some of the measures in question, it may also be noted, were taken by the Nixon Administration, which no one could suspect of radical tendencies. It is also relevant, however, to note that many of the same measures were grievously undermined by the Reagan Administration after 1981, in a period of political stagnation and conservatism. Similar instances of constraint upon business by way of state intervention, and of the erosion of such constraints, are to be found in all advanced capitalist countries.

These differences, tensions, and conflicts between corporate power and state power are real and important; but they do not for the most part greatly impair the underlying cohesion which binds capital and the state. It is in this respect a perverse and obfuscating methodology which postulates that, because the power elite and the rest of the dominant class are not perfectly united in regard to the policies to be pursued, they cannot be said to be cohesive at all.

The cohesion which is to be found in power elites and dominant classes is based on a number of distinct but related factors. The most important of these, it seems reasonable to assume, is the very basic material set of interests which the members of these classes have in common, in terms of property, privilege, position, and power. Here, by definition, are the people who have done very well out of the existing social order and who, quite naturally, have every intention of continuing to do very well out of it, for themselves and their offspring.

Nor is this simply a matter of mere cynical self-interest. On the contrary, there is also the very strong conviction that the system in which these people have themselves done very well is also the best possible for others who have not been so fortunate. Ideological dispositions, in other words, constitute a crucial bond between members of power elites and dominant classes in general.

At the very heart of these dispositions, there is the profound belief that 'free enterprise' is the essential foundation of prosperity, progress, freedom, democracy, and so forth, and that it is also therefore synonymous with the 'national interest'. People who take this view may admit that 'free enterprise' occasionally produces unwelcome results; but these, they also believe, must be taken to be blemishes which do not in the least bring the system itself into question. Viewed in this way, the notion that capitalism (or whatever else it may be called) is not the best possible system in an imperfect world is readily taken to be an absurd aberration, concocted by dreamers and propagated by agitators and demagogues.

The ideological differences which do nevertheless exist among the people in question in regard to capitalism are mostly concerned with the degree of state intervention and regulation which it requires. Also, there are of course innumerable differences and disputes over specific items of policy and strategy which arise between members of dominant classes. But however sharp these may be, they do not seriously impair an underlying consensus about the essential goodness and validity of the system itself.

… Mention should also be made here of another factor of cohesion, closely related to the previous ones: this is the common patterns of life shared by members of the dominant class, either by virtue of social provenance, or by absorption. This also produces networks of kinship and friendship, old school associations, intermarriage, club membership, business and political ties, common pastimes and leisure pursuits, rituals of enjoyment and formal celebrations, all of which are based on and reinforce a common view of the world, of what is right and, even more important, of what is wrong. …

READING D THE WELFARE STATE AS 'THE CRISIS OF CRISIS MANAGEMENT': OFFE

Christopher Pierson

Perhaps the most developed account of the welfare state as the contradictory and contested product of continuing capitalist development within the neo-Marxist or, more properly, 'post-Marxist' literature is that developed by Claus Offe. Offe follows classical Marxism in arguing that 'the "privately regulated" capitalist economy' is innately crisis-prone. However, this is not best understood as a predominantly *economic* crisis. In fact, the welfare state emerges as an institutional/administrative form which seeks to 'harmonize the "privately regulated' capitalist economy with the [contradictory] processes of socialization this economy triggers' (Offe, 1984, p.51). The welfare state is that set of political arrangements which seeks to compromise or 'save from crisis' what classical Marxism had identified as the central contradiction of capitalism — that between social forces and private relations of production. The welfare state arises then as a form of systemic crisis management.

Source: Pierson, C. (1991) *Beyond the Welfare State?*, Cambridge, Polity Press, pp.58–9.

For Offe, the structure of welfare capitalism can be characterized in terms of three sub-systems as below:

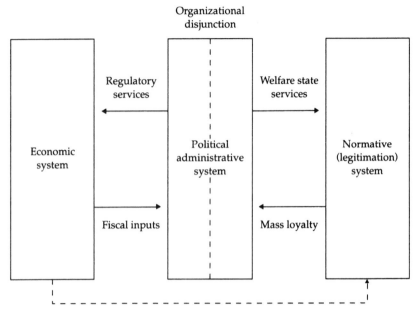

Three subsystems and their interrelationship
Source: Offe, 1984, p.52

According to Offe, the economic sub-system of capitalism is not self-regulating and has dysfunctional consequences for the legitimation sub-system. The state has to intervene in and mediate between the other two sub-systems to secure on the one hand, continued accumulation, and on the other, continued legitimation. Correspondingly the state under welfare capitalism is to be seen as a form of crisis management — and for twenty five years following the Second World War a remarkably successful one.

References

Offe, C. (1984) *Contradictions of the Welfare State*, London, Hutchinson.

CHAPTER 3 POLITICAL CULTURE AND SOCIAL MOVEMENTS

Alan Scott

CONTENTS

1   INTRODUCTION

States are not free-floating. They exist within societies with particular values and traditions, and this fact both constrains and facilitates their actions. While the importance of the relationship between a state and its social environment has been recognized, research and analysis have tended to focus on the demands placed upon the state by interest groups (in pluralism) or on the state as an instrument of class rule (in Marxism), or on the state as a regulator of class relations (e.g. in the literature on 'neo-corporatism' — see Chapter 2). The role of what has been called 'political culture' has received less attention. 'Political culture' has generally been taken to refer to the national traditions within which a state operates. Such a usage is very broad, says little about where these 'traditions' originate, and is perhaps in some danger of degenerating into national stereotyping.

'Culture', on the other hand, has a multiplicity of meanings, both in everyday and social scientific usage (see the earlier discussion in Chapter 5 of Book 1 (Hall and Gieben, 1992)). Here I shall use the term to refer to two related phenomena: (i) those *value orientations and conventions* which are implicit in social action; (ii) *imagined communities* of shared experience, life-style, and knowledge. In this chapter I shall try to show that 'culture' in the above sense is relevant to politics in two ways:

1   it facilitates forms of 'collective action' upon which proto-political organizations (eg. moral crusades, protest movements, etc.) are dependent;

2   in turn, the values generated through these forms of collective action constitute part of both the external and internal environment within which politics operates.

By 'collective action' we mean cooperative action taken by a number of individuals acting in concert and with common goals. The term is wider than 'social movement', as it includes activities within voluntary associations, etc. 'Social movements' are generally defined in terms of their goals (bringing about or preventing social change), their reliance on 'mobilizing' individuals into collective action (demonstrations, occupations, etc.), and their organizational characteristics. (See, for example, Scott, 1990, p.6.)

In this discussion, culture will be linked to politics through the concept 'social movement' rather than 'national tradition'. This is not because I believe that social movements are the sole source of political values (though some commentators have been inclined to argue this), but because they form rather visible points at which culture and politics meet.

This chapter will discuss the relevance of social movements not only for understanding political culture but also for understanding processes of class formation, the relationship between state and civil society, and the nature of collective action. Section 2 will discuss the meaning and significance of social movements, and introduce the major types of social scientific approach to them. Section 3 will illustrate some aspects of the relationship between politics and culture. The next two sections will examine structuralist and social action approaches to understanding social movements. These approaches are interested in different aspects of social movements and this will be reflected in the topics of these sections. Section 4 will focus on broad social changes in explaining social movements, and on the distinction between 'old' and 'new' movements. Section 5 will examine problems of social movement organization and the interaction between movements and their institutional environment.

2 SOCIAL MOVEMENTS: THEIR NATURE AND SIGNIFICANCE

2.1 THE NATURE AND SIGNIFICANCE OF SOCIAL MOVEMENTS

What general images are evoked by the term 'social movement'? Demonstrations, marches, banners, speeches. Or perhaps more specific examples come to mind: Bertrand Russell leading the Aldermaston marches in the 1950s and early 1960s; suffragettes chained to Whitehall railings; candle-lit demonstrations in Prague or Leipzig. Some of these images are probably very specific indeed — namely, individual paintings, photographs, films or television programmes.

Perhaps we are accustomed to thinking of social movements in these terms; as striking but essentially fleeting moments. We are aware of their impact on extraordinary events such as those in Eastern Europe in 1989, but it is less common to think of them when reflecting upon everyday life. This may be a mistake. With a few examples we can illustrate the historical role of social movements in shaping social institutions and the intellectual climate.

Most commentators agree that social movements are the historical product of industrialization, and many would identify the workers' movements as the first modern social movement:

> People have, to be sure, banded together more or less self-consciously for the pursuit of common ends since the beginning of history. The nineteenth century, however, saw the rise of the social movement in the sense of a set of people who voluntarily and deliberately committed themselves to a shared identity, a unifying belief, a common programme, and a collective struggle to realize that programme.
> (Tilly, 1984, p.303)

Charles Tilly, whose work on historical social movements has shaped much of the current debate, goes on to identify the peculiarities of industrial society which brought these movements into being. Among the factors he mentions are: 'an emphatic nationalization of politics, a greatly increased role of special-purpose associations, a decline in the importance of communities as the loci of shared interests, a growing importance of organized capital and organized labour as participants in power struggle' (ibid., p.309). In other words, the preconditions for the rise of social movements are also those for the nation-state, industrial production, modern forms of political representation such as political parties, and ideologies such as liberalism and socialism. Indeed, for Tilly, these developments are linked. Social movements then are a product of 'modernity'.

The impact of workers' movements on the institutions of contemporary capitalist societies can hardly be overstated, even if they did not, or could not, secure the ends imputed to them by orthodox Marxists. Modern social democratic parties stem from nineteenth-century worker's movements, while the welfare state has, in part at least, likewise been moulded by them. This fact is recognized in the arguments of theorists of the welfare state for whom contemporary forms of citizenship (see Chapter 4) stem from 'working-class mobilization'. For Esping-Andersen, for example, the success (or failure) of workers' movements in wringing concessions from employers and the state to protect themselves from the effects of unchecked market forces has shaped modern 'welfare regimes' within different national contexts:

> ... it is defensible to examine the working-class mobilization thesis in terms of a process of social democratization of the welfare state. By this we mean the capacity to substitute for the characteristics dominant in either a liberal or conservative regime, a comprehensive, universalistic, 'de-commodifying', full employment welfare state.
> (Esping-Andersen, 1990, p.110)

It is also interesting to note for the sake of later discussion (in Section 5.2), that Esping-Andersen views this as a two-way process in which the institutions of the welfare state affect the subsequent development of working-class mobilization: 'social policy helps define the relevant boundaries of collective identity because, for workers, it constitutes such a vital element in their livelihood' (ibid., p.109). For example, unemployment insurance can, at least under certain circumstances, lower risks involved in working-class collective action, and thus strengthen the workers' power base.

A further stimulus to recent social scientific interest in social movements has been the rise of so-called 'new social movements' since the 1960s, and particularly around the events of 1968. These movements, which were in many respects prefigured in black civil rights movements in the USA from the 1940s, appeared different from the workers' movements in a number of respects. They were not, for example, class-based, at least in many of their demands and the social identities to which they appealed: race, gender, youth, etc. Much of the recent interest in social movements is clearly a reaction to developments in the 1960s and the reappearance of forms of mass collective action within both capitalist and state socialist societies.

Two more recent developments have reinforced this trend. Firstly, the 1970s and early 1980s saw the rise of ecology movements in Western Europe. The ecological movement has provided the major source for the founding of new political parties in western democracies. Since support for these new parties comes disproportionately from the centre-left (see Müller-Rommel, 1990), they have presented social democratic parties in particular with a threat or opportunity which influenced the direction of these larger parties in countries where the Green Movement has been strongest (e.g. West Germany, as was). Secondly, social movements organized around cultural or human rights activities, the church, etc., were a factor in shaping the form of collapse of East European socialist regimes.

In classical social theory we occasionally find even broader claims being made for social movements than these. Max Weber's *The Protestant Ethic and the Spirit of Capitalism* (discussed at length in Chapter 5 of Book 1 (Hall and Gieben, 1992)) provides one renowned example:

> In order that a manner of life so well adapted to the peculiarities of capitalism could be selected at all, i.e. should come to dominate others, it had to originate somewhere, and not in isolated individuals alone, but as a way of life common to whole groups of men.
> (Weber, 1930, p.55)

Weber, you will recall, identified minority religious movements (puritanical forms of Protestantism, particularly Calvinism) as the original bearer of this revolutionary form of life. This movement created the ethical basis of modern capitalism: the 'spirit of capitalism'. The spirit of capitalism is linked to capitalist society through the activities of the entrepreneur, and it was these activities which had to be grounded in a specific conception of the moral universe; a conception characterized by Weber as 'inner-worldly asceticism'. In Weber's analysis, value changes are accredited a central role in bringing about fundamental social change, and these value changes are said to have their origin in social (in this case religious) movements. As we shall see, this form of explanation is still used in social movement analysis. In relation to more recent debates, it is also interesting to note that Weber ascribes to Calvinism effects and consequences which went far beyond the bounds of the movement itself: 'The Puritan wanted to work in a calling; we are forced to do so' (ibid., p.181).

An adequate social scientific definition of social movements must differentiate them from a number of related phenomena: spontaneous acts of protest such as riots, terror campaigns, organized interest groups such as trade unions, political organizations such as parties, and wholly cultural movements such as some religious sects. It is probably futile, as some social scientists have done, to attempt to find a single unifying characteristic which performs all these tasks simultaneously.

While recognizing the special nature of social movements, it is also necessary to be historically sensitive and aware of the dynamic nature of movements and the fluidity of their boundaries with the related social phenomena listed above. For example, a social movement, or parts of it, can be transformed into a terrorist organization. The Baader-Meinhof group in West Germany in the 1970s was one development from the peace and student movements of the 1960s, although I would argue that this relationship was not one determined by the nature of the movement; it was historical and contingent, rather than necessary and logical. Alternatively, a social movement can develop into a political party, as with several recent Green Parties in Western Europe. As later discussion will suggest, these boundaries are inherently unstable.

Most attempts to define social movements make some reference to the following features:

1   at least occasional mass mobilization;

2   tendency towards a loose organizational structure;

3   spasmodic activity;

4   working at least in part outside established institutional frameworks;

5   bringing about social change (or perhaps preserving aspects of the social order) as a central aim.

We can see these considerations in the arguments of Joachim Raschke, a leading contemporary German theorist of social movements.

ACTIVITY 1   You should now read **Reading A, 'On the concept 'social movement'**, by Joachim Raschke, which you will find at the end of this chapter.

How does Raschke attempt to distinguish social movements from (i) spontaneous acts of protest; and (ii) forms of collective action such as voluntary associations? How successful is he in this?

Raschke's 'definition' in fact contains a number of substantive empirical claims and hypotheses. It assumes, for example, that the motivation of actors engaged in political action cannot be reduced to the calculation of individual self-interest. Although I find this plausible, it is by no means an uncontested claim.

2.2 CONTRASTING APPROACHES

There are two contrasting traditions of explanation for collective action. The first stems from Le Bon's analysis of crowd psychology (1947), and treats collective action as essentially irrational; as a spontaneous outburst, or even as hysterical behaviour. In a milder form this tradition lived on into the work of the functionalist sociologist Neil Smelser who, in his *Theory of Collective Behaviour* (1962), still viewed collective action as a generalized reaction to social strain. Even in this modified form, a variety of quite distinct episodes — 'hostile outbursts', 'panic', etc. — are reduced to the common denominator of collective behaviour. Mancur Olson's *The Logic of Collective Action* (1965) is the source of the second tradition. According to Olson's 'economic decision-making' (or 'rational choice') model, collective action is merely a means through which the rational instrumental actor can pursue self-interest: I will act as part of a collective where this appears to me to be the most efficient way of pursuing my interests.

Although these models are quite distinct, they produce a common problem: they make it difficult to see why collective action should occur at all. On the collective behaviour model, such action is simply irrational and reactive. On the economic decision-making model it is difficult to explain why collective action occurs because the conditions under which I can best pursue my interest through collective action may be highly exceptional. The issue here is the so-called 'free-rider problem'. Olson argues that it will not normally be in my interests to join in collective action because the effort will normally be greater than the reward. If I am a member of a trade union which is on strike for higher pay, I can hope to receive the benefit of an increased wage whether or not I participate in the strike. Since my participation costs me as an individual (e.g. in forgone wages), and since the reward of higher pay is impersonal (i.e. a 'public good' received by all), it is rational for me to free-ride; that is, to accept the rewards but not make the sacrifice.

These models have in common a highly reductionist view of collective action as *either* irrational *or* rational but instrumental. Subsequent developments in the study of collective action and social movements which we shall consider in Sections 4 and 5 have attempted to enrich the model of social action, and thus make the occurrence of such action less mysterious. Before we examine these later accounts, I wish to consider the cultural character of social movements as a way of enriching our understanding of their workings.

3   THE CULTURE OF POLITICS

One of the central insights of the Italian Marxist, Antonio Gramsci, was that political parties are cultural as well as political phenomena. Gramsci's concern was with the emergence of a progressive 'national-popular' movement embodied in the Communist Party (the 'modern Prince' — a euphemism which Gramsci used to circumvent the prison censor). Such a force could only emerge through economic *and* moral reform, and on the basis of cultural resources within the working class which the political party could cultivate:

> The modern Prince must be and cannot but be the proclaimer and organizer of an intellectual and moral reform, which also means creating the terrain for a subsequent development of the national-popular collective will towards the realization of a superior, total form of modern civilization.

> These two basic points — the formation of a national-popular collective will, of which the modern Prince is at one and the same time the organizer and the active, operative expression; and intellectual and moral reform — should structure the entire work. (Gramsci, 1971, pp.132–3)

But what does this mean in practice? In *Workers' Culture in Weimer Germany,* W.L. Guttsman describes the cultural practices associated with the German workers' movement prior to the Nazi seizure of power, and the arguments which sustained those practices. The latter were in

The illustrations in this chapter exhibit aspects of social movement repertoires. Otto Griebel's *Die Internationale* (1928–30) portrays the revolutionary workers' movement as a multinational and invincible force.

In Curt Querner's *Demonstration* (1930) the imagery is more overtly
militaristic. The demonstrators appear to be marching in step, fists clenched.
The total, or near total, absence of women in both paintings underlines the
conception of social movement as army.

many respects similar to Gramsci's views. For the SPD (Social
Democrats) and the KPD (Communist Party), as for Gramsci, the cultural
activities of the Party played a central role in building upon the cultural
resources of the working class while at the same time educating it.
Workers' culture was promoted by the SPD and the KPD in order to
secure a sense of collective identity among workers and resist what
Gramsci called the 'hegemony' (ideological domination) of church,
state, and capital. Guttsman describes, for example, the promotion of a
'festival culture' (*Festkultur*):

> The new *Festkultur* sought to give a tangible expression to the new ideals about the role of culture within the working class and to the techniques which ought to be employed to create new forms of community and to provide new foci of enthusiasm and loyalty for the working masses.
> (Guttsman, 1990, p.234)

This festival culture consisted in the substitution of unofficial days of celebration (e.g. in commemoration of the Parish Commune or of the murders of Rosa Luxemburg and Karl Liebknecht, leaders of the abortive revolution of 1918) for official national celebrations, and the organization of artistic and sporting events, fêtes, etc., for those occasions.

Guttsman interprets these events as conscious attempts to secure a sense of working-class identity and solidarity through ritual:

> May Day celebrations had always combined elements of demonstration and agitation, and, ideally, an apotheosis of the ideal of working-class solidarity, combined with elements of abandon and razzmatazz.
> (ibid., p.240)

This would support Eric Hobsbawm's (1983) contention that 'invented traditions' around May Day were attempts to rival the officially promoted traditions and rituals which proliferated from the late nineteenth century onwards. In order to secure class identity against an officially supported 'national identity', the SPD and KPD also supported worker's cultural organizations (e.g. choirs, literary societies, etc.). It was hoped that an anti-bourgeoisie morality could be developed through such artistic and sporting activities.

We should note, however, that Guttsman speculates that this emphasis upon worker's culture and festivals may have been counterproductive for the workers' movement in the long run: 'it sought to enrich the personal life of the participants; and it may thus have contributed to the relative quiescence of sections of the German working class in the face of threats to the fabric on which this culture was built' (ibid., p.253).

What is the general significance of such activity for the social scientific understanding of the political role of culture in the formation of collective action? In the first place it suggests that 'community', in the sense of a 'solidarity' ethic, may be a precondition of effective and sustained collective action. But such a sense of community does not spring organically from the soil of common experience and life-chance alone. The 'community' of the workers' movement was actively fostered. It borrowed from bourgeois culture (Guttsman gives the example of nudism), trying to give that culture a new meaning, it 'invented traditions', and so on. Benedict Anderson in his analysis of nationalism (1983) speaks of the nation as an 'imagined community' (see also Book 4 (Hall *et al.,* 1992), Chapters 5 and 6), but this notion is helpful in analysing social movements too. It gets us away from the Romantic notion deeply embedded in much sociological thought of 'organic', and usually 'lost', communities; whether they be pre-industrial (Tönnies' *Gemeinschaft*) or proletarian cultures. The culture of the workers' movement, Guttsman's analysis suggests, was a social achievement brought about by conscious intellectual and practical effort; it was an attainment rather that a pre-existing condition of the early trade union movement.

The recognition of the significance of culture in the sense of sustained networks of interpersonal association plus ritual, etc. has been developed further in the work of the contemporary Italian theorist of social movements, Alberto Melucci.

ACTIVITY 2   You should now read **Reading B, 'Nomads of the Present'**, Alberto Melucci's analysis of social movement 'networks', and of the 'latent' and 'visible' stages of social movement activity. Are social movement areas 'cultural laboratories' for new values and life-styles, as Melucci suggests in the book from which Reading B is taken? If so, can this also be said of older social movements such as the worker's movement? Bear in mind the above discussion of the culture of the workers' movement.

Melucci is concerned to demonstrate that contemporary movements are not primarily political, nor are they to be reduced to their visible or organizational manifestations. He stresses the diversity of contemporary social movements and argues that the cultural networks which give rise to them are more enduring and significant than more 'visible' but shorter-lived incidents of political protest. While political protest and collective action may make social movement demands clear, those demands are grounded in alternative values and life-styles in the community. It is in this sense that Melucci considers networks to be 'cultural laboratories' for new and innovative social relations:

> In the 1980s collective action came to be based on 'movement areas' … These take the form of networks composed of a multiplicity of groups that are dispersed, fragmented and submerged in everyday life, and which act as cultural laboratories. They require individual investments in the experimentation and practice of new cultural models, forms of relationships and alternative perceptions and meanings in the world.
> (Melucci, 1989, p.89)

This analysis is highly suggestive. It raises the following questions, and suggests affirmative answers to each of them:

Prague, 19 November 1989: memorial for those beaten by police at a demonstration two days earlier. Prior to 1989, the Church — as the central remaining institution of 'civil society' in Eastern Europe — was a major focus of oppositional activity and debate. It was at the centre of what Melucci refers to as 'social movement networks'. Consequently, much of the symbolism of protest in Eastern Europe in 1989 was explicitly religious.

1   Is the character of collective action changing?

2   Specifically, is it moving away from organized and political action towards dissipated and largely cultural activity?

3   Are social movements increasingly achieving their effect through the creation of alternative life-styles, values, and behaviour patterns rather than through integration into existing political institutions?

These are the questions to be considered in the following section where we examine the related issues of class and social change.

4   STRUCTURAL APPROACHES: SOCIAL MOVEMENTS AS RESPONSES TO SOCIAL CHANGE

4.1   PREAMBLE: STRUCTURAL VERSUS ACTION APPROACHES TO THE INTERPRETATION OF SOCIAL MOVEMENTS

> 'What *is* the answer? ... In that case, what is the question?'
> (Gertrude Stein's reported last words)

One of the attractions and frustrations of social science is that different perspectives frequently disagree not only on the answers, but also on what exactly the relevant questions are. This makes it difficult to assess competing views because they appear to be concerned with different issues and focus on distinct aspects of social reality.

In the study of social movements, what I shall call 'structural' approaches address two questions:

1   What broad social changes do social movements reflect?

2   What broad changes might they bring about?

Behind these questions is a view of social movements as *responses to and agents of fundamental social change*. The focus of attention is on the nature of their response (especially the movements' 'ideologies') and possible outcomes (the 'stakes' involved).

In contrast, 'social action approaches' address the following questions:

1   What are the reasons for and barriers to our involvement in collective action?

2   What must a social movement do to secure that involvement and pursue its aims?

In answering these questions the focus of attention has been on the organizational nature of social movements and on the responses of other social groups and institutions to their activities.

It is not surprising that these differences in formulating the question also produce differences of interpretation. Structural approaches tend to focus on the differences between 'old' social movements (those central to 'industrial society') and 'new' social movements; (those said to be now emerging within 'post-industrial' society). Social action approaches make relatively little of this distinction between new and old movements, but rather view social movements as special types of organization with specific aims, a developing organizational form, and a career or life cycle.

Similarly, while both approaches offer an explanation of possible success or failure of a social movement, they have different criteria of what that success or failure amounts to. On a structuralist account, 'success' equals bringing about fundamental social change, while 'failure' consists in being absorbed into the mainstream political process or other social institutions. In social action approaches the absorption of a social movement's demands tends to be viewed as a criterion of its success in pursuing its aims, even if it results in the transformation or decline of the movement itself. In the former case, the survival and expansion of the movement has priority; while in the latter case the pursuit of instrumental aims is thought more important than the survival of the movement.

It is important to bear the above in mind in the following discussion. In this section, I shall discuss the question of old versus new social movements which is central to the structuralist interpretation. In Section 5 we shall look at social movements as organizations requiring resources, pursuing ends, and following a career pattern.

In Table 3.1 I have tried to sum up some of these differences of approach.

Table 3.1   Structural versus social action approaches to social movements

	Structural	Social action
Main object of analysis	Movement's ideology and the 'stakes' involved	Social movement organization and institutional environment
Causes of social movement's activity	Response to structural social change	Response to exclusion of groups (e.g. from the polity)
Nature of aims	Non-negotiable	Potentially negotiable
Nature of action	Anti-institutional	Potentially institutional
Movement location	Civil society	State/civil society boundary
Criteria of success	Creation of new values, form of life (i.e. transcendence of current social relations)	Integration/institutionalization of movement and its aims (particularly into the polity)
Determinant of success	Attaining the movement's 'highest level of meaning'	Tackling organizational problems of collective action plus institutional response

4.2 'OLD' VERSUS 'NEW' SOCIAL MOVEMENTS

Within the structural approach, we can identify two broad perspectives on the relationship between social movements and social class, the nature of contemporary society, and the sources of social change:

1 *Orthodox Marxist thesis*: social movements are ultimately class-based. Where, as in the case with feminism or ecology, they do not explicitly have class as their theme, they form either a distraction from the central (class) conflict within capitalist societies, and/or they can potentially form a (subordinate) part of the opposition towards capitalism.

2 *Post-industrial society thesis*: class has been displaced as the central focus of conflict and change in post-industrial societies, in which consumption rather than production is the key activity, and knowledge the central means of production. Post-industrial society theorists seek new foci and locations of conflict, and new social actors. The workers' movement is no longer taken as the central social movement within contemporary society.

This typology is something of an oversimplification. The orthodox Marxist position, as described, is very orthodox indeed. Most writers in this tradition do in fact recognize the multiplicity of conflicts, even if they tend to assume that those around class are in some sense 'more fundamental'. There are also intermediate positions, and differences of view within them.

Structural accounts focus on the relationship between social movements and the type of social circumstances in which they can be found, and are concerned with the ways in which movements attempt to change those circumstances. Underlying these concerns is the assumption that the character of social movements is *determined* by external social conditions. Alain Touraine makes this explicit when he writes: 'there is only one social movement for each class in each type of society' (1983, p.4). This sets the research programme as the search for that central social movement.

Touraine distinguishes two types of society in which social movements play a central part: the industrial and the post-industrial (or 'programmed') society. Industrial societies are distinguished from post-industrial ones primarily in terms of their organization of production: as manufacture- or knowledge-based respectively. Their difference in production has implications for the potential sources of contention, the agents of potential social change, and the role of state power. It may be helpful to set out these alleged differences in the form of a table (see Table 3.2).

Table 3.2   Industrial and post-industrial society

	Industrial society	Post-industrial society
Organization of production	Manufacture-based	Knowledge-based
Source of domination/ potential conflict	Control over the organization of work is the focus of class domination	'Class domination consists [more] in managing the production of the data-processing apparatus' (Touraine, 1982, p.6)
Principle of social stability/ change	Balance	Constant transformation of patterns of social production
Power	Concentration of state power	Diffusion of state power: 'power ... is less unified in these societies than anywhere else, and the state is no longer the all-powerful god' (Touraine, 1982, p.6)

Source: based on Touraine, 1982

To these two social types are said to correspond two qualitatively different forms of social movement: the workers' movement and so-called 'new social movements' respectively. In industrial society, where the main focus of social conflict is the workplace, and where there is a concentration of state power, one would, on this account, expect a social movement to:

1   form around production processes;

2   increasingly address its demands to the state.

The ultimate aim of such movements, and also the reason for their eventual decline, is inclusion in central decision-making processes. Indeed, for Touraine this is what has happened to the workers' movement. As it has become politicized, and as its demands have increasingly been met by the state, it has become institutionalized within industrial society, and thus is no longer a social movement. In post-industrial society, conflict shifts from the workplace and from the political realm to civil society. Some of the imputed characteristics of movements of industrial and post-industrial society are set out in Table 3.3.

In Touraine's analysis, the characteristics of a post-industrial social movement represent something of an ideal against which actual movements can be judged; they represent the 'highest level of meaning' attainable. To reach this level of meaning a social movement must meet

Table 3.3   Industrial versus post-industrial social movements

	Industrial social movements	Post-industrial social movements
Focus of conflict	Workplace	Knowledge and technology
Social base	Economic class	Non-economic forms of identity
Location of movement	Increasingly absorbed into the state	Civil society
Aim	Integration	Defence of free public realm
Theme	Citizenship	Autonomy

a number of criteria: it must correctly identify its opponent (in a post-industrial society this opponent is not the owner of the means of production, but those who control knowledge, information, and technology); it must identify a social group in whose interest it acts (this is no longer an economic class, but citizens subject to technological control); finally, it must develop an alternative social model going beyond the single issue with which it was initially concerned. Post-industrial social movements are also said to be distinct in *form* as well as substance. In order to attain these goals they will develop alternative life-styles within civil society. Unlike the workers' movement, their aim is not the direct seizure of power, nor integration into processes of political decision-making, but the defence of culture and civil society against the technological state.

Ecological and anti-nuclear movements might be thought to conform to this model. Such an interpretation of the Green Movement would stress:

1 its self-identification in non-class terms (e.g. as 'citizens', 'the general public', 'consumers');

2 its identification of the forces to which it is opposed as technocratic production and the state;

3 that the social-base of the movement cannot be reduced to economic class;

4 that its aim is primarily couched in terms of limiting the power of technology and the state, and not in terms of integration or power.

Thus, Touraine argues that 'The anti-nuclear movement cannot be reduced to a political action. It is a voluntary action, and above all a different way of living, acting and thinking' (1983, p.178). One difficulty of such an interpretation is that it treats alternative strategies (e.g. formation of pressure groups, political parties, etc.) as deviant. For example, the ecology movement has developed in a variety of ways, including the formation of political parties which have drawn ecological issues into mainstream political debate. Whether such a development is to be viewed as 'success' or 'failure' for the movement depends on whether one accepts Touraine's claim that there is one and only one (potential) movement for each class in each society. The more integrationist social action theories which we shall examine in Section 5 would not accept that the survival of the movement is the primary or sole point of a social movement.

The assumption that there is some qualitative difference between old and new social movements is common within structuralist accounts. Dieter Rucht (1990), for example, distinguishes between instrumental/power-oriented and expressive/identity-oriented movements. Like Touraine, he views the former as primarily political, and the latter as primarily cultural.

ACTIVITY 3 You should now read **Reading C, 'The strategies and action repertoires of new movements'**, by Dieter Rucht. In this reading, Rucht examines new, more expressive and identity-oriented movements. He argues that these new movements display a wider range of activities and styles, or what Charles Tilly has called 'action repertoires'. Is Rucht right to argue that new movements have wider 'action repertoires' than older movements, such as the workers' movement?

Although Rucht also notes that 'power-oriented groups and movements need to maintain their collective identity by adopting cultural symbols' (1990, p.162), and although he recognizes the possibility of mixed orientations, he proposes this distinction between instrumental and identity-oriented movements in part as a means of periodizing social movements into old and new. New movements, he also argues, have a wider repertoire covering both instrumental and expressive activity. By 'instrumental' he means activity aimed at achieving specific ends; while 'expressive' action is that which demonstrates anger, discontent, disappointment, etc. Older movements have tended to be more narrowly instrumental and power-oriented. There is, however, an alternative interpretation. What the more structuralist writers take to be

Protest against the stationing of cruise missiles at Greenham Common illustrates the overlap between recent social movements, in this case feminism and the peace movement. The human chain was a common form of protest in the 1980s, particularly within the peace and ecology movements. Like the paintings on pages 134–5, it is an expression of solidarity and resistance, but with quite different connotations. Such actions reflect themes of non-violence and civil disobedience within those movements which may in turn have taken their cue from older pacifist arguments.

a qualitative difference in the action of social movements can be viewed as a cyclical effect — for example, 'expressive' action may be appropriate at an early stage of a movement's development when it is important to motivate people by engaging their feelings, while 'instrumental' action may come to dominate later as a movement engages other actors and institutions in order to place demands. Furthermore, political and cultural activity may constitute alternative 'action repertoires' (Tilly, 1984) open to *any* social movement. These differences of interpretation will be developed further in Sections 5 and in the Conclusion.

A vivid analysis of what Rucht has in mind can be found in Rowbotham's account of feminism (1989). Using examples such as the disruption of Miss World competitions in the 1960s, Rowbotham describes both the innovative nature of the types of mobilization used by feminists (which were themselves built on the 'action repertoires' developed within the black civil rights movement) and how many of these practices had both expressive and instrumental aspects:

> The passionate desire for union among women was a necessary first step towards the fused identity of a new social movement. The symbolic disruption of a spectacle with ordered divisive conceptions of our female identity was part of a wider challenge to the power of men to define and judge how we were to be valued. (Rowbotham, 1989, p.248)

But does any of this allow us to speak of a *qualitative* difference between 'old' and 'new' movements? One way of criticizing the post-industrial explanation of social movements is to radicalize its claims. If in contemporary society social conflict has become defused to the point where it has no single focus, then it must also be unrealistic to expect the appearance of a single, coherent social movement. This is Melucci's position: 'Touraine's idea of *the* central movement still clings to the assumption that movements are a *personage* — unified actors playing out the role on the stage of history. This idea simply doesn't correspond to present-day conditions in complex societies' (Melucci, 1989, p.202).

In Melucci's view, social movements in modern, post-industrial societies are too heterogeneous in their aims and modes of activity to play the role of substitute for the workers' movement. They have no meaning over and above what they do. Borrowing a famous phrase from Marshall McLuhan, Melucci argues that in contemporary movements 'the meaning is the message'. Their activities are as much symbolic as purposeful, and more cultural than political: 'The organizational forms of movements are not just "instrumental" for their goals, they are a goal in themselves. Since collective action is focussed on cultural codes, the *form* of the movement is itself a message, a symbolic challenge to the dominant codes' (ibid., p.60).

This radicalized form of the post-industrial interpretation raises an interesting question: namely, have the aims of social movements moved so far away from those of the workers' movement that it is no longer useful to talk of politics in traditional left–right terms?

Both theoretical and empirical support has been offered for such a proposition. So-called 'post-Marxist' commentators such as Laclau and Mouffe (1985) and Keane (1988) have argued that traditional socialist aims have been replaced by more nebulous demands for freedom, democracy, autonomy, etc. Laclau and Mouffe speak of 'radicalized democracy' rather than equality, and argue that modern movements (feminist, peace, anti-nuclear, etc.) are autonomous and incapable of any final 'synthesis'. This 'relativism' is as far from the orthodox Marxist interpretation as it is possible to get:

> To defend relativism requires a social and political stance which is thoroughly modern. It implies the need for establishing or strengthening a democratic state and a civil society consisting of a plurality of public spheres, within which individuals and groups can openly express their solidarity with (or opposition to) others' ideas.
>
> (Keane, 1988, p.238)

Aspects of such an analysis receive some support from the events in Eastern Europe, particularly the case of New Forum in the former GDR. New Forum's stated aims were to free society from the constraints of the Honecker regime. Its activities were focused on issues such as freedom of travel, public access to the information held by the *Stasi* (State Security Service), etc. They refused either to develop an ideological or utopian alternative to 'actually existing socialism', or to attempt to take political control as the regime collapsed. Attempts at pursuing a 'third way' between communism and capitalism lost out after New Forum's immediate demands — the opening of the border to the West and the calling of free elections — had been achieved. After this point, New Forum was unable to counter the influence of the West German economy and political parties and was forced to watch as other political forces, particularly the centre-right 'Alliance for Germany', took the political initiative.

The argument that there has been a qualitative shift in the nature of politics to the extent where left–right distinctions are largely redundant, or at least have been overlaid by other divisions, has received empirical support in the work of Ronald Inglehart. Inglehart argues that there has been a shift away from 'material' to 'postmaterial' values within those western societies in which basic material needs have been met. He identifies a generational effect here: since we receive our political socialization in our late teens, the conditions prevailing during that period will mould our values for life. Value changes will therefore be 'glacial'. For Inglehart, new social movements are a *reflection* of these deep value shifts within western publics:

> Postmaterialists emphasise fundamentally different value priorities
> from those that have dominated industrial society for many
> decades ... [They] place less emphasis on economic growth and
> more emphasis upon non-economic quality of life. Their support
> for environmentalism reflects this concern.
> (Inglehart, 1990, p.45)

Inglehart's arguments provide a link with the second major approach to
social movements, where they have been influential.

5   SOCIAL ACTION PERSPECTIVES: THE CAUSES AND COURSE OF SOCIAL MOVEMENTS

The approaches I have gathered under the title 'social action' reverse
the direction of explanation in the positions discussed above: rather
than view social movements as a *reflection* of social relations, collective
action and its institutional context are seen as interacting factors in both
bringing social movements about and influencing the course of their
development. From the action perspective, we need not look for a single
central agent or focus of conflict, as social relations are themselves
complex and multidimensional.

The difference is illustrated above all in the treatment of class.
According to the structural approach, despite the differences between
the industrial and post-industrial approaches, class is taken to be an
objective social location, and it is upon the basis of this location and the
interests which correspond to it that collective action is then built. As
we have seen, within this approach there can be disagreements as to
whether these classes are 'economic' classes in the classical Marxist
sense, or other types of social groupings around ethnicity, gender,
consumption, etc.

Action theories break from this paradigm. There are no objective
classes, merely *individuals* sharing similar life-chances, etc. 'Class',
according to the action approach, is purely a social actor. A class exists
only in so far as these individuals through collective action *constitute
themselves as a class*; that is, develop a sense of common (class)
identity and interests, and a sense of solidarity:

> Classes are not a datum prior to the history of concrete struggles.
> Social reality is not given directly through our senses ... What
> people come to believe and what they happen to do is an effect of
> a long-term process of persuasion and organization by political and
> ideological forces engaged in numerous struggles for the realization
> of their goals ... Social differences acquire the status of cleavages
> as an outcome of ideological and political struggles ...

It is not the proletariat that is being formed into a class: it is a
variety of persons some of whom are separated from the system of
production.
(Przeworski, 1985, pp.69 and 90)

On the basis of this shift of perspective, a quite distinct set of issues and
questions arises for research into social movements. How do social
movements mobilize their, mainly human, resources?. What factors
shape the course and outcome of a social movement's activities? What
counts as a 'successful' social movement? Section 5.1 will examine
some of these points.

5.1   SOCIAL MOVEMENTS AS ORGANIZATIONS: QUESTIONS OF RESOURCE MOBILIZATION

Questions about the workings of social movements as organizations are
addressed in so-called 'resource mobilization theory' (RMT). RMT treats
a social movement like any other organization. Like other organizations,
social movements have to secure resources in order to function. They
are distinct in having social mobilization as their central resource. So
the specific organizational dilemma they face is how to secure that
mobilization. Addressing, or failing to address, this question plays a
major role in determining the effectiveness and survival of social
movements. RMT theorists are, like Olson (see Section 2), exercised by
problems such as free-riding. In this sense RMT theories are variations
of 'economic decision-making' (or 'rational choice') models. They are
distinct from rational choice theory in allowing a variety of motivations
beyond that of the rational calculation of self-interest. They do however
stress individual calculation of risk versus reward as a key factor which
any social movement must take into account. J.C. Jenkins has
characterized RMT as follows:

> (a) movement actions are rational, adaptive responses to the costs
> and rewards of different lines of action; (b) the basic goals of
> movements are defined by conflicts of interest built into
> institutionalized power relations; (c) the grievances generated by
> such conflicts are sufficiently ubiquitous that the formation and
> mobilization of movements depend on changes in resources, group
> organization, and opportunities for collective action; (d)
> centralized, formally structured movements organizations are more
> typical of modern social movements and more effective at
> mobilizing resources and mounting sustained challenges than
> decentralized, informal movements structures; and (e) the success
> of movements is largely determined by strategic factors and the
> political process in which they become enmeshed.
> (Jenkins, 1983, p.528)

ACTIVITY 4   Read the account of the principle features of RMT in **Reading D, 'Social movements in an organized society'**, by J.D. McCarthy and M.N. Zald, two of its chief proponents. Note the application of terms from economics to social movements.

A number of differences in interpretation between the structural approach considered in Section 4 and resource mobilization approaches are evident in the extract from McCarthy and Zald. Rather than focusing on ideology and stakes, RMT is more concerned with a movement's organization and interaction with its institutional and political environment. Particular movements are thus not viewed as 'reflections' of underlying social change, and there is little interest in identifying *the* social movement, or in arguing that 'new' social movements are so qualitatively different from 'old' movements that they require some separate interpretative framework. All movements are viewed as organizations with the particular characteristic that they rely on mobilization as a central organizational resource. Success or failure of movements is explained in terms of what they do, their organizational characteristics, and their interaction with other organizations (e.g. the state, political parties, etc.). Likewise, social movements are placed in a continuum with other organizational forms (interest groups, parties, etc.), and the relationship between these organizational forms are regarded as fluid and changing. Thus, the social movement is not an

New Year's Eve celebrations at the Brandenburg Gate, Berlin, 31 December, 1989. Mass mobilization on a grand scale characterized the 'velvet revolutions' in the GDR and Czechoslovakia. Estimated crowd sizes included 300,000 (Leipzig, 23 and 30 October, 1989), 100,000 (Dresden, 25 October), over 500,000 (East Berlin, 4 November), and 200,000 (Wenceslas Square, Prague, 20 November).

end in itself. Actors tend in this account to be viewed as rational in the sense that they have clear instrumental grounds for participating in collective action.

5.2   THE COURSE AND EFFECTS OF A SOCIAL MOVEMENT

Action approaches tend to account for the course (and success or failure) of social movements not by referring to structure or ideology, but in terms of the interaction between other social groupings and institutions and social movement activity. This defines the second area of research within the social action paradigm: how do existing social arrangements affect the course and outcome of social movement action, and what effects do social movements in turn have on those arrangements? Implied in these questions is the view that the form and outcome of social movement activity is shaped by the dominant political arrangements in the society. Within this approach, the primary focus has been on the role of political institutions and arrangements. Action approaches also stress that the course and outcome of a social movement is decisively influenced by the *unintended and unforeseen consequences* of actions. Even in failing to achieve its aims, a social movement can have a powerful influence on decision-making processes and on the relationship between state and civil society.

One approach has been to ascribe to the 'political opportunity structure' a key role in shaping social movements in different national contexts. From a comparative perspective, Kitschelt (1986) argues that differences between national political arrangements present social movements with distinct 'political opportunity structures', and thus shape the course of their development. The lobby system in the US, for example, will tend to encourage movements to develop into interest groups, while an environment conducive to the development of new political parties (such as West Germany) will encourage movements to develop in this direction. We can see here the difference between this form of interpretation and that considered in Section 4. Whereas more structural theories ascribe the course of movement development to a mixture of structural and ideological factors, action approaches focus on the interaction between social movements and their institutional environment.

ACTIVITY 5   You should now read **Reading E, 'Political opportunity structures and political protest'**, by Herbert Kitschelt. How adequately does the concept of 'political opportunity structures' account for national differences in the form and development of social movements?

We can see this type of approach developed in more detail by examining an influential interpretation of the course of development of the workers' movement. The American 'analytical Marxist' Adam Przeworski (1985) is concerned to explain the course of the workers' movement within industrial capitalist societies through addressing the following question: 'Why have workers' parties which set out with revolutionary aims invariably transformed themselves into revisionist parties?' He answers this question with reference to:

1   the interests of the worker who is a rational individual calculating risks and rewards (cf. Olson in Section 2.2);

2   the nature of the political process (and particularly voting) in majoritarian democracies;

3   the unintended and unforeseen consequences of workers' collective action.

His analysis provides one of the most systematic and best supported examples of an interpretation of a social movement which links its fate to the political and institutional arrangements of capitalist democracies.

Przeworski does not wish to explain the shift to reformism in terms of a sell-out of the working class by its leaders, etc. Rather he approaches the issue historically and sociologically. Historically he traces the intellectual development of revisionist Marxism and the development of communist parties into social democratic parties in the modern sense. Sociologically, he tries to identify the forces which channel working-class politics in this direction. The historical and sociological aspects of the argument are closely intertwined.

Crucial to both the historical and sociological argument is the presence of democratic institutions already existing within capitalist society. Because democracy was already present at the inception of the socialist movement, that movement was faced with the tactical option of employing already existing democratic institutions to further working-class interests, and in the process extending and strengthening 'bourgeois democracy' — for example, universal male suffrage. Przeworski suggests that the workers' movement had little option but to adopt these means: 'as long as democratic competition offers to various groups an opportunity to advance some of their interests in the short run, any political party that seeks to mobilize workers must avail itself of this opportunity' (1985, pp.10–11).

Why is this so? Here Przeworski's argument is similar to that of Claus Offe and Helmut Wiesenthal in an important article 'Two logics of collective action' (in Offe, 1985). Przeworksi and Offe and Wiesenthal argue that workers and capitalists find themselves in a different strategic situation with respect to the best means they can employ to pursue their interests within capitalist society. Capitalists can act individually in the pursuit of their interests — for example, by making individual decisions about investment. Workers, on the other hand, can only pursue their interests as workers if they act collectively. One explanation for this is that individual workers are in competition with one another, or different groups of workers are in competition (e.g. poorer sections of the white working class are in competition with immigrant workers). It is only in acting collectively that common interests can be constructed for the working class as a whole *vis-à-vis* employers.

Przeworski identifies three stages through which the workers' movement has passed on the road to reformism:

Stage one

The crucial connecting element in Przeworski's argument here concerns workers' claims over the product of their labour. Przeworski agrees with Marx that a unique feature of capitalism is that workers have no rights over the products of their labour whatsoever. But, and this is the point, the existence of democratic institutions means that workers can claim some rights over the products of their labour or over the profits it produces *as citizens* (cf. Korpi, 1983). By shifting class conflicts to the political sphere, workers can hope to gain for their class concessions which at the individual plant or industry level they are unable to attain. Foremost among these gains are the institutions of the welfare state. In achieving this the socialist movement was propelled towards parliamentary forms of activity.

Stage two

Przeworski is chiefly interested in what happens once the step towards parliamentary forms of action is taken. His argument here is complex, and I can only outline its basic features. Przeworski's argument is essentially that once socialist parties adopt parliamentary democracy the shift from revolutionary to reformist politics has in effect already been made (even if this implication is not yet fully realized and their stated intentions are wholly tactical).

There are a number of points here. First, socialists never resolved the problem of how to socialize the means of production through parliamentary means. The question was never answered as to whether capitalists would accept the legal appropriation of their property, or whether they would destroy the democratic institutions upon which the socialist movement was now dependent in the attempt to defend their property rights. The fear that the attempt to socialize the means of production through legal means would remove the very conditions under which it was theoretically possible to do this (that is, liberal democracy) gradually led socialist parties to drop their plans to radically socialize the means of production. They were thus drawn into a situation in which they attempted to balance their furthering of workers' interests with the management of capitalist economies:

> Once this programme was suspended ... no socialist economic policy was left. Socialists behave like all other parties: with some distributional bias towards their constituency but full of respect for the golden principles of the balanced budget, deflationary anti-crisis policies, gold standard, and so on.
> (Przeworski, 1985, p.35)

Przeworski's second, and more central argument, concerns the nature of voting. The central principle of representative democracy is majoritarian: the party with the most votes rules. The majoritarian character of representative democracy provides the crucial push in the direction of reform politics. Initially, socialist parties believed that they would come to power on the back of the working class as it grew to become numerically the largest class in capitalist societies. But the simple polarization theories upon which this assumption was based were mistaken.

In the face of a shrinking working class, social democratic parties, if they were to retain hope of gaining power, were forced into a historic decision: the decision to become *mass* parties rather than *class* parties. To form governments they had to appeal to voters not as class members but as citizens, or the people, etc. Thus 'stage one' draws social democratic parties into parliamentary politics (though at this stage they think the choice is tactical). 'Stage two' locks them into parliamentary practices through the logic of the voting and the limits of the political road to the abolition of private property. Finally, in 'stage three', Przeworski identifies the feedback mechanisms which reinforce the hold of parliamentary methods on social democratic parties and further inhibit the development of radical policies.

Stage three

The process described above has one obvious and one less obvious consequence, to which Przeworski ascribes great significance. The obvious consequence is the necessity of diluting socialist politics to appeal to groups other than the working class. This becomes more and more significant as the size of the working class (i.e. manufacturing workers) shrinks with industrialization — thus widening and weakening the programme.

The less obvious consequence is that this move to mass parties undermines the significance of class as a ground for voting and political identity. At the beginning of Section 5, I mentioned that for Przeworksi and other social action theorists classes were constructed within collective action, within political discourse. Here this methodological principle becomes important in the substantive argument:

> Class shapes political behaviour of individuals only as long as people who are workers are organized politically as workers. If political parties do not mobilize people *qua* workers but as the 'masses', 'the people', 'consumers', 'taxpayers', or simply as 'citizens', then workers are less likely to identify themselves as class members and, eventually, less likely to vote as workers. (Przeworski, 1985, p.27)

What Przeworski has done here is to identify the internal contradiction of social democratic politics. The socialist movement actively creates a working class, and in the process of pursuing the interests of that class it undermines the existence of its creation, and of its own power base.

The process of consolidation of workers as a class is followed by its partial dissolution.

I have discussed Przeworski's arguments in some detail because they are challenging and they illustrate the possible effects of political institutions on the course of a social movement. But his stage model suggests a further hypothesis which has also become a contention of social action approaches — namely, that social movements have a life-cycle or career; a beginning, middle and end.

This view has been developed by Sidney Tarrow, notably in *Democracy and Disorder* (1989), where he examines in detail 'contentious collective action' in Italy during the 1960s and 1970s. In his analysis, Tarrow attempts to identify a wider cyclical pattern in incidents of contentious collective action. He does so by comparing them to business cycles: 'The dynamics of a protest cycle can be seen in a similar way to that of a business cycle, except that what carries a protest cycle forward are people's decisions to take disruptive collective action against elites, other groups or authorities' (Tarrow, 1989, p.26).

The cyclical view of social movements implicit in Przeworski and made explicit by Tarrow clearly marks another break with the structuralist approaches discussed in Section 4. The cyclical appearance and disappearance of social movements does not diminish their broader significance, but does suggest that the appearance of a single, all-encompassing movement is unlikely.

A contemporary example of social movement activity may serve to illustrate more concretely some of the implications of a social action interpretation, and also bring out the differences between structural and social action explanations.

ACTIVITY 6   Read Máté Szabó's account of the 'Danube Circle' in **Reading F, 'Social movements, mobilization and democratization in Hungary'**. What are the major similarities and differences between this ecology movement and those in Western Europe.

The account is interesting for a number of reasons, and throws light on the previous discussion. On some general points of interpretation, structural and social action approaches would probably agree. For example, it is striking that despite the institutional differences between Eastern and Western Europe there is a remarkable similarity between the developments Szabó describes and those in the social movement sector in the West. As in the Hungarian case, Western European ecology movements developed out of specific protests by local 'citizens' initiatives' (a term first applied in West Germany).

Nevertheless, these similarities pose theoretical and interpretative problems for both the structural and the more institutional, social action approaches we have been discussing. The case at first appears to lend support to Touraine's view that a single system-transforming movement can develop within contemporary society, and that such a movement can widen into a generalized opposition to the technocratic state. But there are a number of reasons why we must be cautious about drawing such a conclusion. While East European ecology movements like that described by Szabó do have the characteristics ascribed to post-industrial movements, they developed in a social context (state socialism) which can itself hardly be said to be 'post-industrial'. Furthermore, as Szabó points out, it was not the initial intention of ecologists (in contrast to dissidents) to oppose 'the system'. In common with other social movements which emerged in Eastern Europe in the 1980s, such as Civic Forum in the GDR, the ecological movement did not advocate a single alternative utopia to replace state socialism.

An alternative interpretation would be to view Eastern European social movements, as some commentators have viewed western movements, as responses to the failure of institutions of 'interest intermediation' such as political parties (see Offe, 1987; Nedelmann, 1987; and Scott, 1990). In other words, it was the specific failure of the Hungarian state to respond to ecological issues and to incorporate the groups who represented those interests which created the conditions for the emergence of an ecology movement. On such a view, the aim of these movements is to be included in the polity. Thus, Sidney Tarrow, quoting Charles Tilly, characterizes the aims of social movements at the most general level as follows: ' "All challengers seek, among other things, to enter the polity. All members seek, among other things, to remain in the polity", Tilly writes. Contentious collective actions is what challengers do to get into the polity and what members do to avoid losing their place' (Tarrow, 1989, p.123).

Although this argument was developed in the context of western social movements, it can be said to fit the Hungarian case. In terms of policy, social actors, and ideology, the modernization process (of which the barrage-project was part) excluded ecological issues and many groups within civil society from the polity. The institutional mechanisms and degree of exclusion, not the fact of it, is what distinguishes the Hungarian from Western European cases. Although sociologically the difference may be said to be qualitative rather than quantitative, this has a significant implication in terms of outcome. Neither the appearance of a coherent oppositional force nor the collapse of a social order in the face of social movement opposition is inevitable. A regime's reaction can be a decisive factor in determining the course of a social movement as well as its own fate. Thus, for example, as Albert Hirschman (1982) has argued, inflexible regimes are likely in the long-run to encourage the development of strong oppositional forces precisely because they are less able to incorporate new demands and social groups without endangering their stability.

The Hungarian example provides a kind of intermediate example between, on the one hand, some West European representative democracies (e.g. Sweden), which have quite successfully absorbed new political issues and the groups which bore them into political decision-making processes, and, on the other hand, cases such as the GDR where the failure to do this contributed to the de-legitimization and ultimate collapse of the regime. Thus, a more institutionally-minded sociological interpretation would explain the generalization of ecological and similar movements in state socialist societies in terms of the institutional structure and mode of social control exercised in those societies, and not in terms of some inevitable unravelling of a predetermined social process.

Szabó's account also illustrates the usefulness of Charles Tilly's notion of 'action repertoires'. We can illustrate this point by comparing the Danube Circle with an earlier but similar protest in Austria. The Austrian Government under Chancellor Sinowatz planned a barrage and power station on the Danube east of Vienna at Hainburg in 1984. The parallels with the Hungarian case are striking. First, the arguments of both the supporters and opposers of the project were later echoed in Hungary. The Government claimed that the project was not only vital for the Austrian energy supply, but also that it had desirable economic side-effects; for example, it would maintain economic growth and full employment at a time of international economic contraction. Ecologists disputed the validity of these claims both on technical and political grounds, but — as in the Hungarian case — the prime concerns were environmental: Hainburg was an important riverside forest (an *Au* or *Auenwald*) with a unique flora and fauna. Secondly, there are strategic similarities. Austrian Greens, as well as occupying the *Au* during Christmas 1984 as clearance was about to begin, demanded and — again like the Hungarians — started to collect signatures for a plebiscite. The time-lag and similarities between the two cases support an argument of Tilly that movements innovate forms of action (and, one might add, arguments) which are then taken up and adapted by later movements. Finally, as in the Hungarian case, support for the building project came to be viewed as a dividing line between the political old-guard and more 'modern' forces within the Austrian Socialist Party. The difference between the two cases lies in the fact that the Austrian Government acted with a degree of flexibility by giving in at an early stage to the ecologists' demands.

It will be interesting to see whether the contentious ecological issues around which the Danube Circle mobilized are further integrated into Hungarian politics, and politics in Eastern Europe generally. In so far as they are, from a more institutional social action perspective, one would expect similar developments to those in several West European societies where ecological movements have changed, in part at least, their character; either developing into pressure group-type organizations or political parties. If integration into the polity is the general aim of a social movement and of its social base, this would be a sign of its success rather than its failure. Since neither all social groups, nor all issues, are ever fully incorporated, the end of one round of movement activity is the precondition for the next.

Demonstration against a proposed toxic waste incinerator in Northern Ireland. *Greenpeace* adopts a flexible approach, moving back and forth between local and national/international issues, and between social movement and pressure-group tactics. It mobilizes support like a social movement, while at the same time lobbying governments, offering expert knowledge, etc. in the manner of a professional pressure group. This illustrates the permeability of the boundaries between social movements and related phenomena.

6 CONCLUSION

We have noted that the activities of social movements have been explained in terms of competing perspectives within social science. Despite this, a picture of the nature and significance of social movements is emerging within sociology and political science. By way of summary I shall review the main points:

1 Social movements achieve their effects in a number of ways. First, as Melucci emphasizes, they are a source of cultural and value innovation. Here their effects are wide-reaching: from dress style, through linguistic innovation, to their impact on gender relations, social movements have provided a central generator of new values and life-styles. This has an indirect effect on political institutions such as parties because it changes the cultural environment in which they operate. In other words, it changes political culture. Secondly, social movements have a more direct impact upon politics and other decision-making institutions through the absorption of their demands. One prime effect of social movements here is to challenge and move the boundary between state and civil society. As Rowbotham notes in the case of feminism, definitions of what constitutes a political issue can be altered: 'The

contested borders between public and private, evident in the changes in everyday life at home and at work, were beginning to find a political language in the late 1960s' (1989, p.247). If social movements have these indirect and direct effects it suggests that they work both within civil society *and* interact with the state.

2   The course and outcome of social movements is determined not exclusively by their ideological content, but also by their organizational features, the resources which they come to command, and the institutional context in which they operate (e.g. the political opportunity structures). Arguments to support this have been developed within theories of resource mobilization.

3   Social movement analysts influenced by theories of resource mobilization have also come to argue that social movements have a definite career or life-cycle. Tentative stage models have been suggested (Offe, 1990) in which the career of a social movement is said to run a course through a series of stages starting with high levels of mobilization around specific issues and ending, potentially at least, with the incorporation of the movement and those issues into mainstream decision-making institutions (particularly those of the state).

4   It would be consistent with such an interpretation to argue, as Tarrow does, that there are cycles of social movement activity as well as cyclical processes within a single movement.

5   If such stage and cyclical models are correct, it would mean that there are grounds for accepting the argument found in the work of quite diverse commentators, such as Tilly, Tarrow, and Offe, that social movements present the state, political parties and other social institutions with an opportunity to change or 'modernize'. For example, they may alter their policy base and thereby broaden their appeal in order to widen their electoral constituency. The incorporation of 'green issues' into the programmes of social democratic parties in Europe demonstrates both of these aspects: it can be viewed as an attempt to move away from a labourist policy base *and* thereby appeal to potential supporters within the 'new middle class'. Przeworski has provided us with a plausible explanation as to why modern representative democracies impose upon parties the need for this periodic revision and constant widening of their support base.

Over the next few years I would expect research into social movements to focus increasingly on the interaction between social movements and the political and institutional environment: not merely to show how the one shapes the other (as Kitschelt has done), but to identify the complex interactions and feedback mechanisms through which social movements are partly shaped by and partly shape their environment, and through which the impact they have in turn moulds the form of the next cycle of movement activity. Then we may even start to develop the means to talk about 'structural' and 'action' aspects of social life in a common language.

REFERENCES

Anderson, B. (1983) *Imagined Communities,* London, Verso.

Dalton, R.J. and Kuechler, M. (eds) (1990) *Challenging the Political Order,* Cambridge, Polity Press.

Esping-Andersen, G. (1990) *The Three Worlds of Welfare Capitalism*, Cambridge, Polity Press.

Gramsci, A. (1971) *The Prison Notebooks*, London, Lawrence and Wishart.

Guttsman, W.L. (1990) *Workers' Culture in Weimar Germany*, Oxford, Berg.

Hall, S. and Gieben, B. (eds) (1992) *Formations of Modernity*, Cambridge, Polity Press.

Hall, S., Held, D. and McGrew, A. (eds) (1992) *Modernity and its Futures*, Cambridge, Polity Press.

Hirschman, A. (1982) *Shifting Involvements*, Oxford, Basil Blackwell.

Hobsbawm, E. (1983) 'Mass-producing traditions: Europe, 1870–1914', in Hobsbawm, E. and Ranger, T. (eds) *The Invention of Tradition*, Cambridge, Cambridge University Press.

Inglehart, R. (1990) 'Values, ideology, and cognitive mobilization in new social movements', in Dalton, R.J. and Kuechler, M. (eds) (1990).

Jenkins, J.C. (1983) 'Resource mobilization theory and the study of social movements', *Annual Review of Sociology*, vol.9, pp.27–53.

Keane, J. (1988) *Democracy and Civil Society,* London, Verso.

Kitschelt, H. (1986) 'Political opportunity structures and political protest: anti-nuclear movements in four democracies', *British Journal of Political Science*, vol.16, pp. 58–95.

Korpi, W. (1983) *The Democratic Class Struggle,* London, Routledge and Kegan Paul.

Laclau, E. and Mouffe, C. (1985) *Hegemony and Socialist Strategy*, London, Verso.

Le Bon, G. (1947) *The Crowd*, New York, Macmillan (first published 1895).

McCarthy, J.D. and Zald, M.N. (1987) 'Resource mobilization and social movements' in Zald, M.N. and McCarthy, J.D. (eds) (1987).

Melucci, A. (1989) *Nomads of the Present,* London, Hutchinson Radius.

Müller-Rommel, R. (1990) 'New political movements and "new politics" parties in Western Europe', in Dalton, R.J. and Keuchler, M. (eds) (1990).

Nedelmann, B. (1987) 'Individuals and parties: changes in processes of political mobilization', *European Sociological Review*, vol.3, no.3, pp.181–202.

Offe, C. (1985) *Disorganized Capitalism,* Cambridge, Polity Press.

Offe, C. (1987) 'Changing the boundaries of institutional politics: social movements since the 1960s', in Maier, C.S. (ed.) *Changing the Boundaries of the Political*, Cambridge, Cambridge University Press.

Offe, C. (1990) 'Reflections on the institutional self-transformation of movement politics', in Dalton, R.J. and Keuchler, M. (eds) (1990).

Olson, M. (1965) *The Logic of Collective Action*, Harvard, Harvard University Press.

Przeworski, A. (1985) *Capitalism and Social Democracy*, Cambridge, Cambridge University Press.

Raschke, J. (1987) 'Zum Begriff der sozialen Bewegung', in Roth, R. and Rucht, D. (eds) *Neue soziale Bewegungen in der Bundesrepublik Deutschland*, Bonn, Bundeszentrale für politische Bildung.

Rowbotham, S. (1989) *The Past Is Before Us: Feminism in Action Since the 1960s*, London, Pandora Press.

Rucht, D. (1990) 'The strategies and action repertoires of new movements', in Dalton, R.J. and Keuchler, M. (eds) (1990).

Scott, A. (1990) *Ideology and the New Social Movements*, London, Unwin Hyman.

Smelser, N. (1962) *Theory of Collective Behaviour*, London, Routledge and Kegan Paul.

Szabó, M. (1991) 'Sozale Bewegungen, Mobilisierung und Demokratisierung in Ungarn', in Deppe, R., Dubiel, H. and Rödel, U. (eds) *Demokratischer Umbruch in Osteuropa*, Frankfurt am Main, Suhrkamp Verlag.

Tarrow, S. (1989) *Democracy and Disorder: Protest and Politics in Italy 1965–1975*, Oxford, Clarendon Press.

Tilly, C. (1984) 'Social movements and national politics', in Wright, C. and Harding, S. (eds) *Statemaking and Social Movements*, Ann Arbor, University of Michigan Press.

Touraine, A. (1982) *The Voice and the Eye*, Cambridge, Cambridge University Press.

Touraine, A. (1983) *Anti-nuclear Protest: The Opposition to Nuclear Energy in France*, Cambridge, Cambridge University Press.

Weber, M. (1930) *The Protestant Ethic and the Spirit of Capitalism*, London, Unwin.

Zald, M.N. and McCarthy, J.D. (eds) (1987) *Social Movements in an Organizational Society*, New Brunswick, NJ, Transaction Books.

READING A ON THE CONCEPT 'SOCIAL MOVEMENT'

Joachim Raschke

The first approximation of a definition might run: *a social movement is a collective actor/agent which intervenes in the process of social change.* This contains the first clues:

- *Collective actor:* movements provide a context for action which binds individuals together. They are not merely the 'medium' of social change, nor passive expressions of social trends; but they are agents who actively intervene in the course of events with the aim of influencing them. The agent is not to be characterized with reference to a specific form of organization. The concept 'agent' should not introduce homogeneity, rather we should expect by-and-large a multiplicity of tendencies, organizations, and forms of intervention within a social movement. More importantly, the organization does not define the movements, rather the social movement is always greater that the organization which it encloses.

- *Far-reaching aims*: these aims need not in any way be 'revolutionary' in the sense of a complete overthrow of the social system. Action is however aimed at changing more or less relevant social structures, or, in the case of a counter-movement, to prevent such change.

The definition of social movements must therefore contain pronouncements on at least two aspects:

(a) The particular structure of the group which forms the movements.

(b) The goals which the group sets itself.

Proposed definitions can be sorted by the ways in which they characterize these basic elements: the bearer-group and the goal ...

The definitional suggestion offered here runs: *a social movement is a mobilizing collective actor which pursues with a certain degree of continuity its aim of bringing about, preventing, or reversing a more fundamental social change, on the basis of high symbolic integration and little specification of role, and by means of variable levels of organization and forms of action.*

Some clarification of this definition:

- *Mobilization*: the power base of every social movement is precarious; it is not institutionally assured. Therefore, mobilizing support is, more than in other forms of intermediation, a condition of its existence. The active, permanent search for support — remaining in motion — is therefore a feature of a social movement.

- *A degree of continuity*: a certain level of continuity (say over several years) seems sensible in order to distinguish social movements from

Source: Raschke, J. (1987) 'Zum Begriff der sozialen Bewegung', in Roth, R. and Rucht, D. (eds) *Neue soziale Bewegungen in der Bundesrepublik Deutschland*, Bonn, Bundeszentrale für politische Bildung, pp.20–22 (translated by Alan Scott).

episodes of collective action. (In passing, the range of the goals is correlated with the durability of the movements.) On the other hand, continuity of activity shows that the movement is still a movement.

- *High symbolic integration*: the group which constitutes itself as a movement is characterized by a pronounced sense of common identity [*Wir-Gefühl*]. This consciousness of belonging together develops on the basis of a distinction between those who are 'for' and those who are 'against'. It manifests itself in, among other things, fashion (from sansculotte to jeans), manners, speech, habitus [disposition], and political symbols.

- *Low role specification/differentiation*: when compared to formal organizations, the social movement as a whole, which is always more than the organizations which form part of it, displays a low differentiation between the establishment of roles. Without or outside formal membership, varied and changing forms of participation are possible. The role specification grows with the degree of movement organization (it is therefore for example lower within new social movements than it was in the workers' movement). The undoubtedly present role differentiation (e.g. élites, activists, sympathizers) is less stable and binding than in formal organizations because of the superimposition of formal and informal elements. Role differentiation is, however, a clear expression of the division of labour and of power relations which are at work even within movements.

- *Goals*: the delimitation of aims to more fundamental social change (which is of course in need of further interpretation) stresses the aspect that structural transformation of the state and/or society is characteristic of social movements. It is not necessary to aim at transformation of the whole system, but to aim for change in at least some major specific parts of it. The greater range leads in the course of time to a systematization of the aims and to a, however rudimentary, ideology. An unfinished and searching nature is characteristic of most movements.

READING B   NOMADS OF THE PRESENT

Alberto Melucci

Visibility and latency

In complex societies social movements develop only in limited areas and for limited periods of time. When movements mobilize they reveal the other, complementary face of the submerged networks. The hidden networks become visible whenever collective actors confront or come into conflict with a public policy. Thus, for example, it is difficult to under-

Source: Melucci, A. (1989) *Nomads of the Present,* London, Hutchinson Radius, pp.70–3.

stand the massive peace mobilizations of recent years unless the vitality of the submerged networks of women, young people, ecologists and alternative cultures is taken into account. These networks make possible such mobilizations and from time to time render them *visible.*

Latency and visibility are the two interrelated poles of collective action. Those who view collective action from a professional–political standpoint usually confine their observations to the visible face of mobilization. This view overlooks the fact that collective action is nourished by the daily production of alternative frameworks of meaning, on which the networks themselves are founded and live from day to day. Consequently, there exists a physiological link between the visibility and latency of movements. The actors become visible only where a field of public conflict arises; otherwise they remain in a state of latency. Latency does not mean inactivity. Rather, the potential for resistance or opposition is sewn into the very fabric of daily life. It is located in the molecular experience of the individuals or groups who practice the alternative meanings of everyday life. Within this context, resistance is not expressed in collective forms of conflictual mobilizations. Specific circumstances are necessary for opposition and therefore of mobilizing and making visible this latent potential.

It follows that there is a major difference between mobilization and a movement. In most discussions, references to the movements' political effects and organizational tactics are commonly mistaken for the collective forms of mobilization which develop around specific issues. But movements live in another dimension: in the everyday network of social relations, in the capacity and will to reappropriate space and time, and in the attempt to practice alternative life-styles. This dimension is not marginal or residual. Rather, it is the appropriate response to new forms of control that no longer correspond solely to state action. Resistance and conflict also operate in this molecular dimension as well as bring about important changes. Paradoxically, the latency of a movement is its effective strength.

The latency and visibility of social movements points to the existence of two other paradoxes. First, collective conflicts are increasingly personal and revolve around the capacity of individuals to initiate action and to control the space, time and interpersonal relations that define their social existence. This paradox is already apparent. During the past decade collective action has displayed a tension between the need to publicly declare objectives and the need to practice directly and personally the innovations in daily life. This tension has produced some dramatic splits within the groups.

There is a second paradox: if the basis of contemporary conflicts has shifted towards the production of meaning, then they seemingly have little to do with politics. Instead collective action concerns everyday life, personal relationships, and new conceptions of space and time. Thus collective actors are prone to disperse, fragmented and atomized, into networks which quickly disappear into sects, emotional support circles or therapy groups. While collective action continually faces disintegration, it also poses questions about the production of symbols which transcend politics. As such, collective action can never be wholly represented by political mediation, in decisions (or 'policies') which translate collective efforts into institutional changes. The forms of action I am referring to are at one and the same time prior to and beyond politics: they are *pre-political* because they are rooted in everyday life experiences; and *meta-political* because political forces can never represent them completely. Paradoxically, unless collective action is represented it becomes fragmented and dispersed; at the same time, because it is never fully capable of representation it reappears later on new ground, with changed objectives and altered strategies.

There are numerous examples of this process. The anti-nuclear struggle, for instance, has been a strong mobilizing force in many countries. Initially, its actions addressed the problem of nuclear power stations, but later it raised more general questions, including the power to make decisions about the equilibrium of the eco-system. No governmental nuclear policy could ever fully incorporate these demands, and this is why particular mobilizations — concerning alternative sources of energy and the risks associated with nuclear power — tend to push conflicts on to different ecological fronts. ...

READING C   THE STRATEGIES AND ACTION REPERTOIRES OF NEW MOVEMENTS

Dieter Rucht

The political action of new movements: an historical perspective

In the European context, 'new social movements' (NSMs) has enjoyed increasingly widespread usage. In contrast, American scholars and movement activists are much less familiar with this concept, or are even baffled when confronted with it. In the United States, both the absence of a powerful and well-organized labor movement and the existence of radical liberal traditions — from the eighteenth-century revolution to left-wing populism, civil rights movements, New Left and student movements, and finally to various contemporary movements such as the women's, ecology, and nuclear freeze movements — make it relatively difficult to contrast the latter movements with the former. While in Europe the concept of NSMs usually refers to a distinct, although broad, political and ideological spectrum, 'new' movements in the United States tend to be associated simply with 'contemporary' movements, including salient countermovements such as those of the New Right. ...

Source: Rucht, D. (1990) 'The strategies and action repertoires of new movements', in Dalton, R.J. and Kuechler, M. (eds) *Challenging the Political Order*, Cambridge, Polity Press, pp.157–61.

In comparing the actions of social movements in the first half of the century to the actions of NSMs, I would like to point out some differences that deserve explanation. In contrast to the 'old' movements and in particular to the labor movement or the fascist movements in Europe, groups and organizations within the NSMs seem to act more independently from each other. They reject any hegemonic position or concept, in particular the Leninist model of the 'avantgarde.' Even protest parties claiming to represent movement issues in the field of national parliamentary politics and with a strong emphasis on locally based activities are met with strong reservations by significant parts of the NSMs. As a result of this quest for autonomy ... contemporary movements' activities do not necessarily focus on the national level. They emphasize the role of independent and small groups and the importance of local activities, and they promote grassroots politics ... . Of course, these tendencies can also be found in 'old' movements, particularly in their early stages of formation. Today, however, the NSMs seem to choose the form of loosely coupled networks deliberately, and not necessarily because of a lack of resources and organizational skills.

With respect to conventional participation, the significance of parliamentary representation (and thus the meaning of elections as well) seems to have decreased, whereas other conventional forms of participation, including court action, have apparently become increasingly relevant.

Some historical movements, such as the 'old' women's movement or the 'reformist' labor movement in the twentieth century, expected to achieve societal change via parliamentary majority. The role of the legislative was largely overestimated not only by these movements, but also by the wider public. Today a more realistic perception seems to prevail. Contemporary movements are less confident of achieving social change not only by revolution, but also by legislation. Moreover, voting for a party or a political leader today depends much more on situational considerations ('issue-voting') than on an overall world-view. People may vote for a party at the same time that they publicly oppose some of its particular policies. This would have been very difficult for a working-class voter at the turn of the century.

Litigation by social movements has also increased because possibilities to intervene in specific policies by using administrative and constitutional courts previously did not exist at all, or only to a very limited degree. This is also true for procedures such as public hearings and inquiries. Moreover, in many Western democracies the judicial system presently has a more independent position in relation to the holders of political and administrative power than it did in the nineteenth and early twentieth centuries. In addition, courts are more sensitive to certain issues and claims not propagated by strong interest groups. Finally, just as respect for authority seems to be lower than in earlier decades, the willingness to challenge legal decisions has grown. This is also due to the political schisms within societal elites on most issues raised by NSMs, be it abortion, biotechnology, nuclear power, or military defense.

With respect to unconventional behavior, acts of violence, and particularly the use of arms, have generally diminished in importance over the last few centuries, whereas acts of civil disobedience are becoming more and more relevant. The relative infrequence of armed violence is mainly the result of the institutionalization and extension of formal procedures for the expression of social and political discontent. Moreover, minority rights seem to be respected both socially and juridically to a greater extent than in earlier periods. Finally, the power of the modern state is so great as to discourage the use of violence by social movements, at least when conflicts are carried out in the public domain and do not escalate to the dimension of a civil war.

Still, all the institutionalized means of articulating interests and expressing discontent are powerless to prevent the relative deprivation of certain population groups and social strata, the deterioration of public goods such as the quality of water and air, or even the possible extermination of humankind. Consequently, there are still reasons to protest, and new ones are likely to emerge. In general, the concerns of social movements in the last century, even if these movements started as single-issue movements, tended to be embedded into broad and sharply contrasting ideological world-views. By contrast, the concerns of the NSMs are conceived much more as single issues, not to be solved by a redistribution of the means of production and wealth within a wholly new political system. This trend is a major reason why there is no longer *one* salient movement representing *the* subjected class, but a plurality of coexisting and cooperating movements whose significance can hardly be described in terms of class antagonisms.

In so far as institutionalized channels for expressing discontent are blocked (for example, by a broad coalition of the established parties, by a neocorporatist cartel of elites, or by high procedural thresholds) or are unsuited to the nature of the problems (for example, sexist role behavior), and in so far as a policy or social behavior as a whole cannot be changed via other means, acts of civil disobedience may be an adequate answer for protest groups. These acts allow the venting of specific and intense criticism without necessarily aiming at a general transformation of society.

Moreover, civil disobedience as an act with a highly symbolic and expressive component requires an audience to whom the actor can appeal. Unlike revolutionary or terrorist acts, which are directed specifically at the enemy and which do not necessarily involve or require the support of third parties, civil disobedience must take account of public opinion — and the dependence of power-holders on that opinion — as a crucial variable for its failure or success. Civil disobedience can only flourish when there is a large public which is not *a priori* partisan to the conflict and whose opinions cannot be directly controlled or easily manipulated by power-holders. Obviously, the presence of modern mass media enhances the efficacy of civil disobedience. The disobedient act can become audible and visible to millions of people; further, to a much greater degree than before, such acts are transferred immediately to the large public, without passing a long chain of transfer stations. Even if news is necessarily interpreted and filtered by journalists, competition between news outlets, professionals standards, and the ideological heterogeneity of the press combine to make it difficult for the media to ignore protest or to deny movement representatives a hearing.

A final difference between old and new movements is that at least particular parts of the former tended to rely on a narrow action repertoire, and they rarely shifted quickly from one kind of action to another. Today, cooperation and alliances between groups using different forms of action seem to be more common. Also the parallel use of different forms of action by the same group, or the shift from one form to another, seems more likely than in older movements. In consequence, a broad variety of forms of action, extending from moderate expressions of discontent to overt violence, is likely to be practiced at the same time and within a single movement. This observation is strongly supported by various case studies. Moreover, surveys of contemporary forms of political participation show that people tend to use both conventional and unconventional forms of action ...

These features may also be partially explained by a kind of reasoning which is determined less by general ideologies than by situational cost-benefit assessments. A still more relevant argument to account for the variety and flexibility of new movements' actions is the autonomous status of groups and organizations within these movements. For instance, in contrast to the German labor movement, there are no hegemonic organizations and elites that have enough authority to tell the rank and file what should be done, whether it is allowed to protest, or whether the time is ripe for radical action. In addition, the loose networks of many groups and activists as well as their overlapping issues and positions within the NSMs allow for a broad dissemination of ideas, experiences, and action forms. There is room for the parallel use of different forms of action by different groups in the same conflict, without forcing each group to legitimize every form of action that is used. Finally, one should take into account factors such as the enormous spatial mobility of people in modern societies, the involvement of many professionals in the NSMs, and the ensuing broad spectrum of knowledge, techniques, and other resources available to contemporary movements. Strikingly, even conservative groups such as those of the New Right tend to use a range of actions (including disruptive tactics) similar to that of their opposite numbers on the Left.

READING D   SOCIAL MOVEMENTS IN AN ORGANIZED SOCIETY

J.D. McCarthy and M.N. Zald

A *social movement* is a set of opinions and beliefs in a population representing preferences for changing some elements of the social structure or reward distribution, or both, of a society. A *countermovement* is a set of opinions and beliefs in a population opposed to a social movement. As is clear, we view social movements as nothing more than preference structures directed toward social change, very similar to what political sociologists would term *issue cleavages*. (Indeed, the process we are exploring resembles what political scientists term *interest aggregation*, except that we are concerned with the margins of the political system rather than with existing party structures.)

The distribution of preference structures can be approached in several ways. Who holds the beliefs? How intensely are they held? In order to predict the likelihood of preferences being translated into collective action, the mobilization perspective focuses upon the pre-existing organization and integration of those segments of a population that share preferences. Oberschall ... has presented an important synthesis of past work on the pre-existing organization of preference structures, emphasizing the opportunities and costs for expression of preferences for movement leaders and followers. Social movements whose related populations are highly organized internally (either communally or associationally) are more likely than are others to spawn organized forms.

A *social movement organization* (SMO) is a complex, or formal, organization that identifies its goals with the preferences of a social movement or a countermovement and attempts to implement those goals. ...

All SMOs that have as their goal the attainment of the broadest preferences of a social movement constitute a *social movement industry* (SMI) — the organizational analogue of a social movement. A conception paralleling that of SMI, used by Von Eschen, Kirk and Pinard ... the 'organizational substructure of disorderly politics,' has aided them in analyzing the civil rights movement in Baltimore. They demonstrate that many of the participants in a 1961 demonstration sponsored by the local chapter of CORE [the Congress of Racial Equality] were also involved in the NAACP [National Association for the Advancement of Coloured People], the SCLC [Southern Christian Leadership Conference], Americans for Democratic Action (ADA), or the Young People's Socialist Alliance (YPSA). These organizations either were primarily concerned with goals similar to those of CORE or included such goals as subsets of broader ranges of social change goals. ...

Definitions of the central term, *social movement* (SM), typically have included both elements of preference and organized action for change.

Source: McCarthy, J.D. and Zald, M.N. (1987) 'Resource mobilization and social movements', in Zald, M.N. and McCarthy, J.D. (eds) *Social Movements in an Organizational Society*, New Brunswick, NJ, Transaction Books, pp.20–5.

Analytically separating these components by distinguishing between an SM and an SMI has several advantages. First, it emphasizes that SMs are never fully mobilized. Second, it focuses explicitly upon the organizational component of activity. Third, it recognizes explicitly that SMs are typically represented by more than one SMO. Finally, the distinction allows the possibility of an account of the rise and fall of SMIs that is not fully dependent upon the size of an SM or the intensity of the preferences within it. ...

The definition of SMI parallels the concept of industry in economics. Note that economists, too, are confronted with the difficulty of selecting broader or narrower criteria for including firms (SMOs) within an industry (SMI). For example, one may define a furniture industry, a sitting-furniture industry, or a chair industry. Close substitutability of product usage and, therefore, demand interdependence is the theoretical basis for defining industry boundaries. ...

Given our task, the question becomes how to group SMOs into SMIs. This is a difficult problem because particular SMOs may be broad or narrow in stated target goals. In any set of empirical circumstances the analyst must decide how narrowly to define industry boundaries. For instance, one may speak of the SMI that aims at liberalized alterations in laws, practices, and public opinion concerning abortion. This SMI would include a number of SMOs. But these SMOs may also be considered part of the broader SMI commonly referred to as the 'women's liberation movement,' or they could be part of the 'population control movement.' In the same way, the pre-1965 civil rights movement could be considered part of the broader civil liberties movement. ...

Let us now turn to the resource mobilization task of an SMO. Each SMO has a set of *target goals*, a set of preferred changes toward which it claims to be working. Such goals may be broad or narrow, and they are the characteristics of SMOs that link them conceptually with particular SMs and SMIs. The SMOs must possess resources, however few and of whatever type, in order to work toward goal achievement. Individuals and other organizations control resources, which can include legitimacy, money, facilities, and labor.

Although similar organizations vary tremendously in the efficiency with which they translate resources into action ... the amount of activity directed toward goal accomplishment is crudely a function of the resources controlled by an organization. Some organizations may depend heavily upon volunteer labor, while others may depend upon purchased labor. In any case, resources must be controlled or mobilized before action is possible.

From the point of view of an SMO the individuals and organizations that exist in a society may be categorized along a number of dimensions. For the appropriate SM there are adherents and nonadherents. *Adherents* are those individuals and organizations that believe in the goals of the movement. The *constituents* of an SMO are those providing resources for it.

At one level the resource mobilization task is primarily that of converting adherents into constituents and maintaining constituent involvement.

However, at another level the task may be seen as turning nonadherents into adherents. Ralph Turner ... uses the term *bystander public* to denote those nonadherents who are not opponents of the SM and its SMOs but who merely witness social movement activity. It is useful to distinguish constituents, adherents, bystander publics, and opponents along several other dimensions. One refers to the size of the resource pool controlled, and we shall use the terms *mass* and *elite* to describe crudely this dimension. Mass constituents, adherents, bystander publics, and opponents are those individuals and groups controlling very limited resource pools. The most limited resource pool individuals can control is their own time and labor. Elites are those who control larger resource pools.

Each of these groups may also be distinguished by whether it will benefit directly from the accomplishment of SMO goals. Some bystander publics, for instance, may benefit directly from the accomplishment of organizational goals, even though they are not adherents of the appropriate SM. To mention a specific example, women who oppose the preferences of the women's liberation movement or have no relevant preferences might benefit from expanded job opportunities for women pursued by women's groups. Those who would benefit directly from SMO goal accomplishment we shall call *potential beneficiaries.*

In approaching the task of mobilizing resources an SMO may focus its attention upon adherents who are potential beneficiaries and/or attempt to convert bystander publics who are potential beneficiaries into adherents. It may also expand its target goals in order to enlarge its potential beneficiary group. Many SMOs attempt to present their goal accomplishments in terms of broader potential benefits for ever-wider groupings of citizens through notions of a better society, and so on (secondary benefits). Finally, an SMO may attempt to mobilize as adherents those who are not potential beneficiaries. *Conscience adherents* are individuals and groups who are part of the appropriate SM but do not stand to benefit directly from SMO goal accomplishment. *Conscience constituents* are direct supporters of an SMO who do not stand to benefit directly from its success in goal accomplishment. ...

An SMO's potential for resource mobilization is also affected by authorities and the delegated agents of social control (e.g., the police). While authorities and agents of control groups do not typically become constituents of SMOs, their ability to frustrate (normally termed *social control*) or to enable resource mobilization are of crucial importance. Their action affects the readiness of bystanders, adherents, and constituents to alter their own status and commitment. And they themselves may become adherents and constituents. Because they do not always act in concert, ... a strong case [can be made] that authorities and delegated agents of control need to be analyzed separately.

The partitioning of groups into mass or elite and conscience or beneficiary bystander publics, adherents, constituents, and opponents allows us to describe more systematically the resource mobilization styles and dilemmas of specific SMOs. It may be, of course, to the advantage of an

SMO to turn bystander publics into adherents. But since SMO resources are normally quite limited, decisions must be made concerning the allocation of these resources, and converting bystander publics may not aid in the development of additional resources. Such choices have implications for the internal organization of an SMO and the potential size of the resource pool that can ultimately be mobilized. For instance, an SMO that has a mass beneficiary base and concentrates its resource mobilization efforts toward mass beneficiary adherents is likely to restrict severely the amount of resources it can raise. Elsewhere ... we have termed an SMO focusing upon beneficiary adherents for resources a *classical SMO*. Organizations that direct resource appeals primarily toward conscience adherents tend to utilize few constituents for organizational labor and we have termed such organizations *professional SMOs*.

Another pattern of resource mobilization and goal accomplishment can be identified ... . It depends upon the interactions among beneficiary constituency, conscience adherents, and authorities. Typical of this pattern is an SMO with a mass beneficiary constituency that would profit from goal accomplishment (for instance, the Massachusetts Welfare Rights Organization) but that has few resources. Protest strategies draw attention and resources from conscience adherents to the SMO fighting on behalf of such mass groups and may also lead conscience elites to legitimate the SMO to authorities. As a result of a similar pattern, migrant farmworkers benefited from the transformation of authorities into adherents ...

But an SMO does not have complete freedom of choice in making the sorts of decisions to which we have alluded. Such choices are constrained by a number of factors, including the pre-existing organization of various segments of the SM, [and] the size and diversity of the SMI of which it is a part ... . Also, of course, the ability of any SMO to garner resources is shaped by important events such as war, broad economic trends, and natural disasters.

READING E   POLITICAL OPPORTUNITY STRUCTURES AND POLITICAL PROTEST

Herbert Kitschelt

Explaining strategies and impacts of social movements

Political opportunity structures can further or restrain the capacity of social movements to engage in protest activity in at least three different ways. Firstly, mobilization depends upon the coercive, normative, remunerative and informational resources that an incipient movement can extract from its setting and can employ in its protest. In Western

Source: Kitschelt, H. (1986) 'Political opportunity structures and political protest: anti-nuclear movements in four democracies', *British Journal of Political Science*, vol.16, pp.60–4; 66–7.

democracies, non-violent resources are crucial for the emergence of pro-test. Thus, if movements can appeal to widely shared norms, collect adequate information about the nature of the grievance against which they protest and raise the money to disseminate their ideas and information, the chances of a broad mobilization increase. Secondly, the access of social movements to the public sphere and political decision-making is also governed by institutional rules, such as those reinforcing patterns of interaction between government and interest groups, and electoral laws. These rules allow for, register, respond to and even shape the demands of social movements that are not (yet) accepted political actors. They also facilitate or impede the institutionalization of new groups and claims. Thirdly, a social movement faces opportunities to mobilize protest that change over time with the appearance and disappearance of other social movements. The mobilization of one movement, for example, may have a 'demonstration effect' on other incipient movements, encouraging them to follow suit. And the simultaneous appearance of several movements con-testing the institutions of social control often presents the best oppor-tunity to maintain movement momentum and to change established policies.

[A comparison of anti-nuclear protest movements in France, Sweden, the United States and West Germany is well-suited to discovering the effects of institutional constraints on social movement mobilization.] In the four countries compared here, the temporal opportunity structures encoun-tered by the anti-nuclear movements were quite similar; the protests reached a peak in the second half of the 1970s and they grew out of the broader environmental movement. Crucial differences, however, charac-terize the resource and institutional opportunity structures they faced. These configurations, which are relatively inert over time, may also be labelled as the 'political regimes' prevailing in each country. While they are not immutable, they respond only slowly to new policy demands. And inasmuch as they pattern policy demands and options independently of the preferences of shifting coalitions of interested political actors and social forces, they inject a decidedly non-pluralistic element into the pol-icy formation process.

Students of social movements at times distinguish relatively 'open' politi-cal opportunity structures from relatively 'closed' ones and note that the dominance of one type or the other sets limits to the responsiveness that movements can expect. A particularly useful outgrowth of this research is the identification of a curvilinear relationship between openness and movement mobilization, which shows that very closed regimes repress social movements, that very open and responsive ones assimilate them, and that moderately repressive ones allow for their broad articulation but do not accede readily to their demands.

This conceptualization of opportunity structures is useful but somewhat one-sided, for it considers only the input processes of political decision cycles. The other side of the coin is that the capacity of political systems to convert demands into public policy also affects social movement mobili-zation and impact: the output phase of the policy cycle also shapes social movements and offers them points of access and inclusion in policy-making. Indeed, this conclusion is supported by the many case studies which show that policies are often entirely renegotiated as they are implemented. Thus, the capacity of political opportunity structures to implement policies — as well as their openness to societal demands — ought to be seen to determine the overall responsiveness of politics to social movements.

While it is certainly the case that political opportunity structures vary among policy arenas within the same political regime, system-wide political properties and national 'policy styles' also play key roles in determining the dynamics of social movements. The nature of these properties and styles are of crucial importance because representatives of entirely new demands often cannot participate effectively in highly differentiated policy arenas and instead must appeal to actors and institutions in politics, such as parties, parliaments and courts, whose authority and decision procedures at least partially transcend those of particular policy arenas.

In this respect, at least four factors determine the openness of political regimes to new demands on the input side. (1) The number of political parties, factions, and groups that effectively articulate different demands in electoral politics influences openness. The larger this number, the more 'centrifugal' a political system tends to be and the more difficult it is to confine electoral interest articulation to the 'cartel' of entrenched interests that is represented by the established, bureaucratized parties. (2) Openness increases with the capacity of legislatures to develop and control policies independently of the executive. This is the case because a legislature is by definition an electorally accountable agent and is therefore much more sensitive to public demands, whereas only the uppermost positions in the executive are subject to such direct public pressure. (3) Patterns of intermediation between interest groups and the executive branch are another element shaping political openness. Where 'pluralist' and fluid links are dominant, access for new interests to the centres of political decision-making is facilitated. (4) Finally, political openness not only requires opportunities for the articulation of new demands, but new demands must actually find their way into the processes of forming policy compromises and consensus. For this to occur, there must be mechanisms that aggregate demands. Openness is constrained when there are no viable procedures to build effective policy coalitions.

In a similar vein, three operational dimensions characterize the capacity of political systems to implement policies. (1) National policies are implemented more effectively when the state apparatus is centralized. A complicated division of jurisdiction between a multitude of semi-independent government agencies and a federal stratification of state authority tends to make policy implementation more cumbersome. (2) Simultaneously, government control over market participants is a key variable for government effectiveness in many policy areas. The degree of state control over the finance sector, the relative size of the public sector's share of GNP and its share of total employment, and the state's co-ordination, control or exclusion of economic interest groups in policy-making, are some of the factors that influence policy effectiveness. The greater is the control of economic resources and decision centres through political insti-tutions, the more limited are the resources available with which to chal-lenge policies. (3) Policy effectiveness is also determined by the relative independence and authority the judiciary enjoys in the resolution of pol-itical conflict. Policy implementation becomes more hazardous and cum-bersome if courts are forums of political arbitration removed from execu-tive branch control. ...

How do these different national political opportunity structures affect the strategies and impacts of social movements? Two major hypotheses guide the present comparison of anti-nuclear movements. Firstly, with respect to strategies, political opportunity structures set the range of likely protest activities. For instance, when political systems are open and weak, they invite *assimilative* strategies; movements attempt to work through estab-lished institutions because political opportunity structures offer multiple points of access. In contrast, when political systems are closed and have considerable capacities to ward off threats to the implementation of pol-icies, movements are likely to adopt *confrontational,* disruptive strategies orchestrated outside established policy channels.

Secondly, political opportunity structures facilitate or impede movement impacts, among which we may distinguish three types: procedural, sub-stantive and structural. Procedural impacts or gains open new channels of participation to protest actors and involve their recognition as legitimate representatives of demands. Substantive gains are changes of policy in response to protest. And structural impacts indicate a transformation of the political opportunity structures themselves as a consequence of social movement activity.

To elaborate further, the second hypothesis leads us to expect procedural gains to covary with the openness of political systems. Thus, open regimes should be more willing to accept new groups, as it is likely that at least some established political actors wili seek to strengthen their own pos-itions by allying themselves with the newcomers. This incentive is miss-ing in closed systems, where policy-making is the prerogative of a circumscribed cartel of political actors. For substantive gains to be made, a polity must have not only relatively open institutions and policy-making procedures but a high capacity to implement policies. The more openness and capacity converge, the greater the likelihood of policy innovation. A variation should occur when a regime is closed and strong. In this instance, movement activities may prompt a limited range of elite-initiated reforms. Substantive gains are least likely to be found in weak regimes, be they open or closed. Here the likely outcome of protest activity is political stalemate, a situation in which neither old nor new policies can be implemented successfully. Finally, structural impacts will figure when a political system cannot bring about either procedural or substantive reforms. In this instance, a social movement will try to broaden its demands to include those for altering the existing political system funda-mentally.

READING F SOCIAL MOVEMENTS, MOBILIZATION AND DEMOCRATIZATION IN HUNGARY

Máté Szabó

The intensification of the economic, political and social crisis led in Hungary, as in other Eastern European socialist countries, to the expansion and organization of social protest. At the beginning of the 1980s a whole range of new types of social self-organization emerged, from the peace to ecology movements, acting alongside the 'traditional' intellectual opposition and partly widening its base ...

The clear lines of confrontation between state and society which were dominant during the Kádár period weakened: the legal recognition of conscientious objection to military service, the cessation of building on the Danube Dam, and the restructuring of the university curriculum were political concessions towards social movements' demands made before the first free elections. The possibilities for action were widened through the legalization of freedom of assembly and association, and by the introduction of press freedom. In contrast to other socialist countries, in Hungary there was no period of direct mobilization leading to the collapse of the old regime. One can speak rather of an amalgam of protest and concessions which transformed the structural framework through institutional innovation. The social movements, in contrast to the dissident movement, did not have as a purpose the transformation of 'the system'. Nevertheless they contributed to that process indirectly by acting as crises signal and potential for democratization. In Hungary the old system grew into a new one. Instead of mass demonstrations and mass protest, structural imperatives and a readiness to compromise were in the foreground and this is still the case. This dynamic was evident in the development of all movements.

Structure and dynamic of the development

With respect to the ecological movement, one marked difference from Western industrialized states is that in Hungary there is no conflict around atomic power. This, together with the regime's massive institutional barriers, resulted in the lack of strategic coordination of themes or actions at national level between the various initiatives of the ecological movement. However, there was a whole series of local conflicts around feared or already existing environmental damage which, however, remained limited to the locality and to particular protest aims. Examples here include the conflict over the atomic waste dump at Ófalu, a small southern hamlet; the resistance of the village of Zsámbék against a planned dump for dangerous waste, and the dispute over a refuse incinerator in the northern Hungarian industrial town of Dorog. The diverse conflict variations

Source: Szabó, M. (1991) 'Sozale Bewegungen, Mobilisierung und Demokratisierung in Ungarn', in Deppe, R., Dubiel, H. and Rödel, U. (eds) *Demokratischer Umbruch in Osteuropa*, Frankfurt am Main, Suhrkamp Verlag, pp.206–20 (translated and abridged by Alan Scott).

demonstrated that under Kádárism local worthies had a better chance of achieving something by using special routes and special pleadings than was possible within the framework of politically motivated protest movements.

The 'Danube Circle' became the largest and internationally the best known citizens' initiative. Under a variety of names ('The Blues', 'Friends of the Danube', 'Alliance for the Danube') and, at various times, in several groupings, the Danube Circle has fought since 1984 against the building of the Danube power station Bös-Nagymaros; that is to say against the Hungarian part of a joint barrage-project with Czechoslovakia which was financed with credit from the Austrian Government and built by Austrian firms. Against the state's assertion that the power station was indispensable for Hungary's energy supply and offered additional economic advantages because it made the Danube [at this point] navigable, the Danube Circle disputed the economic viability of the project and criticized the immense squandering of energy within the Hungarian economy. The barrage system was, however, opposed above all for its feared catastrophic ecological consequences. Unique flora and fauna as well as the supply of drinking water were endangered.

The opposition to the Danube power station originated with specialists who turned to the public after they had criticized the project to no avail within the scientific community. In 1984 a 'Committee for the Danube' collected 10,000 signatures to a protest letter to the Communist Party-dominated Parliament and Government. Government officials reacted with an array of repressive measures ranging from hindering the collection of signatures and forbidding demonstration and publications, to debarments from employment [Berufsverbote] for individual activities within the anti-power station movement. Every attempt by civilian environmentalists to found a legal and permanent organization was stopped. The official press was at best allowed to touch on the power station problem only through indirect allusion. As a result, the Danube Circle was forced to bring out its own unauthorized magazine, and otherwise had to rely on reports in the underground press of the democratic opposition from which it sought to clearly distinguish itself politically. In 1985 the dispute reached its then high point in the period leading up to the parliamentary elections when the power station project was criticized in many election meetings in which, under difficult and manipulated conditions, several independent candidates emerged for the first time. Among these were protest movement activists as well as dissidents. A conspiratorial group by the name of 'The Blues' distributed some 10,000 leaflets against the project, and 3,000 signatories demanded a plebiscite. For some time after this the protest movement was weakened to the point of marginalization by a mixture of internal repression and resignation brought about by external developments (the Hungarian Government received massive financial assistance from Austria).

In the course of 1988 under changed political conditions a quite new dynamic developed which affected the forms of protest, the number of participants, and, not least, the aims. Protest became in fact and in the self-understanding of its protagonists a part of a democratic movement. This development was assisted after Kádár's fall by the more liberal stance of the renewed political leadership, and by the differences between conservative and reform-forces at the top of the State Party. Support for or rejection of the barrage-project became one of the dividing lines between both groups, and was largely congruent with the division between those who blocked and those who supported the process of democratization.

In May 1988, 5,000 people demonstrated in front of the Austrian Embassy in Budapest against Austrian participation in the building of the Danube power station. For the first time a mass demonstration was tolerated, and fully and critically reported on Hungarian television. After this, parts of the official press began to report the barrage-project in a similar fashion. In June, in a parliamentary initiative of an independent MP, twenty-three MPs voted for a cessation of building on the Danube. In September 35,000 people demonstrated in Budapest. The immediate occasion for the demonstration was the speeding up of work by Austrian building firms. Beyond this the demonstrations marked a decisive political turning point in that the protest movement against the Danube power station became a rallying point for democratization. The thematically specific protest of the citizens' initiatives which had lasted over years and the general rejection of the system by the democratic opposition merged into a common show of strength which reinforced self-confidence even in the absence of immediate concrete success. One month later Parliament once more backed continuation of the barrage-project. However, it never came to the plebiscite demanded by the protest movement. In spring 1989 the Németh Government declared a stop to building. With this decision Party reformers wished to distance themselves visibly from the conservative forces around the Party Secretary Grosz. This was not least because they found themselves confronted with a rapidly growing opposition organized into parties which was about to push through democratization at Round Table negotiations.

The ecological movement itself, which up to this point had largely organized itself in associations, did not at first find a strong political form of integration. A Green Party has been formed in which one-time Danube activists participate, but this is hardly *the* representative of the ecological movement and gained no parliamentary seats in the first free elections. Today there is a wide range of ecological movements which form a spectrum from loose local amalgams and forms of protest to organized, institutionalized and stable forms.

CHAPTER 4 CITIZENSHIP AND THE WELFARE STATE

Denise Riley

CONTENTS

1   INTRODUCTION

It is impossible to conceptualize the liberal-democratic state in its modern form, which we have been examining in earlier chapters in this book, without the complementary notion of 'citizenship'. What does the term 'citizenship' mean? In what kinds of political language has it been embedded, and what meaning does it have now? It is a peculiar and a slippery concept with a long history. It is common to different political rhetorical forms, and the politics which have made use of it have varied enormously in character: conservative, social-democratic and revolutionary. Because the deployments of 'citizenship' have been and continue to be so wide and so dissimilar, it is hard to define, yet also hard to replace. 'Citizenship', and 'citizen', operate, in effect, as what the philosopher Wittgenstein called 'cluster concepts': that is to say, they have no immutable central core, but are more like a meeting-ground for several notions. In any particular instance it is, therefore, necessary to specify how the terms are being used: they need to be supplemented by some further fixing of the kind of political understandings which determine how the words operate and what they mean in practice.

In this chapter, we will examine how 'citizenship' and 'citizen' have been used, and look at the historical development of different sorts of citizenship. Notions of 'citizenship' have had an important role in the development of modern (western) societies and we will assess this by focusing on the ways in which an ideal of citizenship was invoked in the founding of the welfare state in Britain. From this analysis, a number of problematic issues associated with definitions of citizenship emerge. In particular, there is the issue of inclusion/exclusion: who are 'citizens' and who are excluded from the rights of citizenship? And, underlying this issue, there are further questions about the relationship between the private and public domains (and how these are defined), and about the active or passive nature of citizenship. Does citizenship depend exclusively on the state (public) and how do its rights and responsibilities relate to an individual's status within the family (private)? Must the citizen actively participate in political life? As you will see, these issues have been present, both in theory and in practice, throughout the history of the institution of citizenship. But they remain centrally important today with the ideal of equality firmly embedded in the notion of citizenship, but imperfectly attained in practice. So we will end this chapter by considering current debates about the limitations of citizenship in the context of the modern welfare state.

2   FORMATIONS OF CITIZENSHIP

The notion of 'citizenship' suggests some persuasively powerful, though loosely defined, claims about the standing of a person as a member of a society or a nation. It could even be extended to membership of the universe, as in the environmentalist ideal of a 'global citizenship' in which each would owe allegiance, not within national boundaries, but by virtue of possessing human status alone. Yet claims to citizenship are not, usually, interchangeable with general claims about human rights or duties: they point towards a more locally-defined ground, connected to that of nationality. To be a 'British citizen' is to enjoy the rights and privileges which flow from full membership of the United Kingdom as a nation-state.

The word 'citizen' derives from the Latin *civitas*, (meaning 'citizenship', 'body of citizens' and, more rarely, 'city'). In its classical origins, the notion of citizenship was intimately connected with membership of a city. Roman citizens enjoyed certain rights (e.g. voting in assemblies) and acquired certain responsibilities (e.g. military service) as a consequence of belonging to Rome. Initially limited to those belonging to the city of Rome, the rights of citizenship were later extended throughout the Roman Empire. Citizenship was thus associated from an early stage with membership of a state and the word has retained this sense in modern times, so that current usage is synonymous with membership of a nation-state, with being an enfranchised inhabitant of a country. As David Held has commented, the nation-state is 'the entity to which the language of citizenship refers, and within which the claims of citizenship, community and participation are made' (1991, p.24).

This modern use of the word 'citizen' as a rough equivalent of 'national' (i.e. belonging to a particular nation with settled and stable boundaries) has a predominantly western origin. In 1917 Max Weber suggested some reasons for this. He identified the difficulties experienced by some non-western societies in becoming 'nations' and located these difficulties in the different modes of development of religious cultures and forms of authority:

> The peculiar character of the Asian intellectual strata essentially prevents the emergence of 'national' political formations, even of the kind which have developed in the West from the later Middle Ages onwards — although even in our case, the full conception of the idea of the nation was first elaborated by the modern western intellectual strata. The Asian cultural regions lacked, and fundamentally so, any community of language. The language of culture was a religious language or the language of literati; Sanskrit among aristocratic Indians, the Mandarin dialect of Chinese in China, Korea and Japan.
> (Weber, 1978, p.205)

All these languages functioned in a similar manner to Latin in the middle ages in the West. This theological or highly aestheticized nature of the world's 'high' languages meant, as with Buddhism in Burma, or Confucianism in China, that only those who possessed access to such a language could have 'consciousness of common identity'; and such a consciousness was primarily of a religious, not a political or social kind.

'For the plebians', Weber held, 'there appeared no prophets with an ethical mission which might have imposed a national form on their everyday lives' (ibid.).

Weber also examined the bases of national identity in the context of the West in notes he made on the subject between 1910 and 1914. However, as Reading A demonstrates, the defining features of nationhood are not easy to pin down.

ACTIVITY 1   You should now read **Reading A, 'What is a nation?'**, by Max Weber, which you will find at the end of this chapter.

1   Note down those factors which Weber listed as important for national identity.

2   What are his qualifications and reservations about the idea of national solidarity?

Weber's examples reflect the pre-First World War state structure; his comments about Austria, for example, refer to the Austro-Hungarian Empire which both included different language groups and a German-speaking Austrian core. But some cases he cites (e.g. the Serbs and Croats who speak very closely related languages but adhere to distinctive Orthodox and Catholic versions of Christianity respectively) remain pertinent examples of conflicting national identities.

Essentially Weber argues that you cannot define a 'nation' in terms of the common shared characteristics of its members, since its citizens may not, in fact, belong to the same ethnic group, speak the same language or share the same religious or cultural values. It will be useful to bear Weber's reservations in mind when thinking about citizenship and the state, and the kind of conditions under which people may come to feel themselves a part of a whole — or may wish to break away from what they feel to be an imposed whole. The break-up of the USSR and Yugoslavia, in the early 1990s, dramatically demonstrated Weber's argument.

As his examples indicate, nations can coalesce around very different factors. Such varying political formations have given rise to quite different versions of citizenship, and it is not easy to generalize about how particular nationhoods were established, and what the attendant meanings of their citizenship were. As Bryan Turner has noted:

> [a] general theory of citizenship, as the crucial feature of modern political life, has to take a comparative and historical perspective on the question of citizenship rights, because the character of citizenship varies systematically between different societies. (Turner, 1990, p.195)

As we will see in Reading B, Turner's analysis provides illuminating examples of different citizenship formations in different societies. The comparative and historical approach he takes points to important underlying issues which have informed the development of citizenship rights in modern nation-states.

Turner, like Weber, is attentive to the broad impact of religious influences on how all states have constituted themselves, especially in helping to frame a distinction between the public and private spheres:

> ... both Christianity and Islam contributed to the development of citizenship by providing a universalistic discourse of political space (the City of God and the Household of Islam) which challenged ethnicity and kinship as the primordial ties of the societal community (Parsons, 1971). However, Christianity also produced an important limitation on the emergence of an active view of the citizen as a carrier of rights. ... The effect of Protestant doctrine was to create a private sphere (of devotional religious practice, the subjectivity of the individual conscience, the privatised confessional and familial practices) in which the moral education of the individual was to be achieved, and a public world of the state and the market place, which was the realm of necessity. ... This division did not provide an environment which was congenial to the full development of the citizen as an active and responsible member of the public arena.
> (ibid., pp.197–8)

Turner sees the roots of this public/private division as lying in the problems of late Roman antiquity, as classical philosophies attempted to adapt earlier notions of citizenship (which were closely tied to the polity of the city-state) to the changed political reality of the large, bureaucratic and absolutist Roman Empire (ibid, pp.201–3). But while tensions between public and private spheres passed from antiquity into the Christian legacy, the original ideal of the city-state citizen also had an important impact on the formation of citizenship in the West.

ACTIVITY 2   You should now read **Reading B, 'Comparative formations of citizenship'**, by Bryan Turner. It examines further the comparative origins of citizenship in different states.

1   What are the two key dimensions which Turner suggests should be the basis of any model of citizenship?

2   Establish clearly in your mind the distinctions Turner makes between French, German, English and American conceptions of citizenship, using the two dimensions in his model.

Turner's analysis shows how the ground upon which citizenship stands is historically changeable, fought over, and enormously politically variable. If, for example, we were to say that 'the citizen' is simply a member of civil society — the terrain which lies between the private sphere and the formal organizations of the state — then at once there arise complications of how this 'middle ground' has been established historically and politically, which particular concepts of 'public' and 'private' underpin it, and what hidden assumptions about the status of the family underlie it.

The ideal of German citizenship, for example, was embroiled in a vision of a developing realm of civil society in which it was necessary for a man to leave the sphere of the family to reach that of the properly public and thus to become a burgher, a privileged and cultured town-dweller. Hegel, the German philosopher, positioned civil society between the state and the family; in his schema the state alone had the capacity for the type of 'universality' required to constitute citizenship. His *Phenomenology of the Spirit* (1807) posited a link between the private emotional sphere of the family and its public, ethical incarnation as part of the community. The private and the public worlds were thus clearly distinguished through gender. The father moved in the outer world; the virtuous wife inhabited the domestic, natural, personal world of the family. Both universes were necessary, but only the citizen who was able to move in the communal world beyond the home could be endowed with a 'universally' ethical status, and this citizen was by definition masculine. In this model of citizenship, Bryan Turner argues, the stress fell at either end of two points: the family as the supposedly private realm, and the state as the main legitimate source of public authority (Turner, 1990, p.204). Civil society, poised between the two, with its elected assemblies, was consequently less prominent. By contrast, the English common-law tradition, grounded in the public rights of private citizens, placed considerable emphasis precisely in this 'middle ground' and its civil rights, and this was reinforced by the seventeenth-century revolution, the Civil War and the execution of King Charles I, and the subsequent strength of Parliament's authority and scope. The persistence of inequality in property ownership in England, however, and the continuing severe restrictions to the franchise, based on such ownership, set their own different but equally exacting limits to the democratic potential of these changes.

Contested property rights were also important in the French Revolution of 1789–1792. Its concepts of citizenship issued in part from a revulsion against a court-ruled society, tightly classified into estates. Here a

A debate in the French Assembly, 1799

conception of citizenship, which incorporated a standard of common worth, was used to attack the absolute rule of the sovereign. The philosopher Jean-Jacques Rousseau's dream, in his *Du Contrat Social* of 1762, was thus of citizenship as the logical antithesis of monarchy: direct participation by each and every (male) citizen, so that the state would embody the general (male) will. Political space was thus expanded, in his vision, into what has been described as a 'totalitarian democracy'. In this, there would be a tacit undertaking 'that whoever refuses to obey the general will shall be compelled to do so by the whole body. This means nothing less than that he shall be forced to be free; for this is the condition which, by giving each citizen to his country, secures him against all personal dependence' (Rousseau, 1913). Rousseau's forcible democracy was his answer to the problem of how to ensure active citizen participation, but apart from its practical implausibility it too enshrined exclusions.

2.1   THE PROMISE OF UNIVERSALITY AND THE PERSISTENCE OF EXCLUSION

Despite the capacity of the term 'citizenship' to be stretched over different historical and political structures, it is arguable that its definitions have never been wide enough. 'Citizenship' represents an ideal of inclusion, of some standard of entitlement for everybody. Yet its history demonstrates a series of battles against exclusion on the part of those denied full or effective membership of the society it promised. While the suffrage alone does not necessarily guarantee adequate citizenship, it is a precondition, so unpropertied men, and all women, had to fight for the vote as the initial entry into any hope of democracy. The Parisian feminist, Olympe de Gouges, appealed in vain in her 1791 *Declaration of the Rights of Woman* for the incorporation of women as citizens in the new French Republic, on the grounds that they possessed equal virtue to men; but other Republican women, who had argued instead for the 'special' capacities of their sex as a passport to incorporation, were also defeated. The influence of the writings of Rousseau (among others) upon the ideas of the Revolution suggested that there could be no other outcome.

For Rousseau, qualification for citizenship was to be based on the criterion of 'independence', so neither women nor the poor could qualify. While the theoretical claim of his social contract implied the full integration of political with social existence (so that citizens would hold political authority themselves rather than assigning it to others), Rousseau believed profoundly in the distinctiveness of the family as part of the order of nature, as well as of the order of civil society. Women, as guardians of the family, mediated between nature and society since they participated in both. Anchored in a natural world, they could not, by definition, become truly independent and thus achieve full citizenship, essential though they were as go-betweens.

The persistence of exclusion: *Homeless and poor*, a sketch by John Gilbert (*c.* 1890)

French, German and British theories of political participation were all coloured differently with a range of exclusions of the unpropertied and/or the differently-sexed. For example, in the English political philosopher John Locke's work, the 'natural right to liberty' was implicated with the ownership of property: women, not usually possessing property in their own right, and embedded in the 'private' realm of the family, were not considered adequate contenders for political subjecthood.

Locke's account of political representation, embodying these
assumptions, entailed a liberal-democratic 'fiction of citizenship', as
Carole Pateman has argued (1989, p.103). In this, the tacit exclusions
from citizenship of those without property are further complicated by
the nature of the political participation which is actually on offer. The
fiction is that citizens are supposed to be embodied by their
representatives, who make decisions on their behalf. Private individuals
are not bound together in any way, and while their interests are
supposed to be delegated to representatives in what becomes the
political sphere, those who are represented can only contemplate this
resulting 'thing' — 'the state'. Although citizens can exercise their right
to vote, they nevertheless remain 'private' citizens because they vote for
their own interests, as they see them. The political sphere is in effect
sublimated into a cloudy elevation, out of real reach of its citizens. The
vote effectively serves as a mechanism for the alienation of people's
participation, despite its theoretical aim to incorporate their wishes.

This is a pessimistic account of the reality of democratic participation.
Other writers have noted the problems of a system of delegation to
representatives, but have concentrated on the advantages of the ideal.
The American sociologist Talcott Parsons, for instance, described
modern citizenship as an idea which could only emerge when it became
possible to conceive of an abstract political being, irrespective of that
being's social rank, gender, or ethnic membership; the political status of
citizenship was therefore detached from the social status of the
individual and made 'universal' (Parsons, 1966). This ideal of
citizenship as a universality which rises above the accidents of personal
circumstances is vulnerable to the charge that it masks real differences.
Yet, importantly, it also possesses the strength of its own idealism.
Because of its claim to universality, such an ideal can form the basis for
arguments for participation by everyone, as well as for entitlements and
responsibilities for all, and it is close to broad arguments about human
rights. Citizenship as a theory sets out a claim and an egalitarian
promise, about real democratic participation; it envisages participation
as a *potential*. But how can the formal equalities conferred on citizens
by law be transformed into a practical equality, and how in particular
can a free market economy encompass this hope? One of the main
arenas in which the tensions between formal and substantive equality
and between the egalitarian promise of citizenship and the inequalities
of the market economy have surfaced and been negotiated is that of the
welfare state.

2.2 CHANGING CONCEPTIONS OF WELFARE AND THE 'MODEL' CITIZEN

Marx's writings from the 1840s onwards highlight the tension between
the promise of equality, given at least formally by modern democracies,
and the obstinate fact of the wide discrepancies of ownership and
wealth and power in free market economies. The issue is: Is the ideal of

OVERDOING IT.

"WHAT? GOING ALREADY? AND IN MACKINTOSHES! SURELY YOU ARE NOT GOING TO WALK!"
"OH, DEAR NO! LORD ARCHIBALD IS GOING TO TAKE US TO A DEAR LITTLE SLUM HE'S FOUND OUT NEAR THE MINORIES—SUCH A FEARFUL PLACE! FOURTEEN POOR THINGS SLEEPING IN ONE BED, AND NO WINDOW!—AND THE MACKINTOSHES ARE TO KEEP OUT INFECTION, YOU KNOW, AND HIDE ONE'S DIAMONDS, AND ALL THAT!"

citizenship in an unequal society only a smoke-screen to hide real differences of opportunity? Or, is the egalitarian promise inherent in citizenship valuable in itself?

The battles for an enlarged suffrage for men and for women's suffrage concentrated on widening access to the formal equality conferred by the franchise. It would be wrong to characterize the possession of the vote as a merely 'passive' form of citizenship, for this would be to overlook the vehemence and length of this struggle which dominated late nineteenth- and early twentieth-century European history. However, in the course of this struggle, Liberal and emergent Labour social policies (concerned to address substantive questions of equality) also gradually took their shape. The development of a welfare state was thus an attempt to realize the promise of citizenship entitlements conferred by the technical political equality entailed in universal suffrage.

The establishment of anything approaching a welfare state is dependent on what the shape of the public sphere is held to be, what degree of responsibility for meeting the common good the state is believed to bear and what it is prepared to organize its economy to support. Any public welfare network will only flourish or survive when a government assents to this conception; the very different political and administrative history of the United States of America, for example, has entailed only a minimal subscription to public welfare as an ideal. Nor, of course, do governments which support social provisions necessarily do so out of humanitarian motives unalloyed by other calculations: the generous family allowances and crèche provisions in France can be traced to turn of the century fears about the falling birthrate, resulting in pronatalist policies (those designed to encourage a higher birthrate). And, in times of war, state help to families has been provided principally in order to release women's labour — a phenomenon evident in wartime Europe on all political sides. Another instance of social provision, stemming from governmental calculations about a possible labour shortage, is visible in the early 1990s' anxieties about a threatened shortage of women workers. This produced some hesitant governmental debate about practical measures to help, although this was hampered by ideological uncertainties since it seemed to contradict the philosophy of self-help conservatism; it was in any event subsequently offset by the prospect of increasing unemployment.

The sociologist T.H. Marshall has spoken of a 'war' between capitalism and citizenship (we will turn to his arguments in more detail later). This can be traced in continuing policy skirmishes across a whole period over the proper scope of the state. The 1980s' Conservative philosophy developed in Britain under the Thatcher government promoted self-reliance, independence, enterprise and efficiency — the virtues of individual self-help — and was suspicious of any emphasis on entitlements to benefit conferred on people as part of their social rights as citizens. Rather, this particular Conservative philosophy saw the theories of citizenship entitlements as an aspect of 'the nanny state' fostering dependence via costly bureaucratization, leading to an apathetic clientele of claimants. Such an apprehension of state provision as axiomatically reflecting an overbearing, invasive and wasteful socialism echoed earlier themes in this debate and included both political and economic anxieties.

It is true that the vocabulary of 'rights' and 'entitlements' must face the limits of constraints on resources if it is to avoid mere wish-fulfilment; but to acknowledge that there must be constraints does not answer the question of *how* welfare is to be allocated, which is a political question. The popularity of the National Health Service persists despite its visible strains, and this is often ascribed to the power of the democratic ideal that it embodies — the fair and equal access of the vulnerable to treatment. Yet recent changes in accounting and budgeting procedures in the NHS are making visible the extent to which this ideal is not met in practice: drugs are rationed where their costs are high, and covert criteria (of social usefulness) have long been applied in decisions as to which renal patients, for instance, shall be permitted access to dialysis to save their lives.

Nevertheless, as Raymond Plant has pointed out, it is not only the social rights of citizenship that place a strain on public expenditure in the shape of welfare benefits. Civil and political rights also have their cost; the police, courts, and prisons are hardly self-financing. And if the solution of 'workfare' (a 'market welfare' system in which all recipients of welfare must work to receive it) is espoused in Britain, following the

American model, then such 'earned' benefits would also entail an extra cost on public expenditure since it would commit the government, as the employer of last resort, to manufacturing jobs, which would be an expensive business in itself (let alone, one could add, the cost of ancillary provisions like crèche facilities for single parents) (Plant, 1991, p.56).

The American model of 'weak' national welfare rights reflects the distinctive political history of America as an assemblage of local states, whereas the British welfare state from the Second World War onwards constituted a national arena for the better distribution of social rights, and designedly so. No British political party wishes to concede the discourse of social concern to its opposition, and the Conservative Party's interest in establishing the model of an 'active citizen' who pursues neighbourhood and neighbourly helpfulness and personal philanthropy is a tribute to the persistence of citizenship as an ideal with some life in it, despite the anti-statist rhetoric of the Thatcher years.

How could a more 'active' idea of citizenship be developed, in which the gender-differentiated separation of realms (public/private) and the distancing of the political sphere from the citizen might be lessened? The problem is that of replacing a passive 'citizenship from above', which is bestowed, with little real content, by the state, with a 'citizenship from below', perhaps using local participatory or voluntary channels. This conception of an 'active citizenship' has been proposed by both social-democratic and conservative opinion, the former in the 1940s and the latter in the 1980s. Others have argued that this vocabulary of 'active citizenship' does not really illuminate the problem of how to achieve democratic participation, and may even be counter-productive if it implies a trade-off between obligations and rights, furthering a two-tier citizenry in which those who are able to participate most should receive greater rewards (Dahrendorf, 1990).

One familiar (and recurring) argument against the welfare state is that it enables a passive survival, if at minimal standards of living; that it takes away the 'economic incentive' to self-advancement; and that it may offer a 'perverse incentive', an inducement to remain on benefit so as to gain further advantage (as with young women who *supposedly* become pregnant to gain council housing). These arguments are not new. The tightened-up proscriptions of the revised Poor Law at the end of the nineteenth century, and the tenets of the Charity Organization Society (established in 1869) both incorporated versions of this conviction that people had to be stung by need into the vigorous pursuit of their own and their dependants' well-being. Or, to express it more benevolently, that the giving of 'doles', or charity inspired by an unsystematic philanthropy, sapped the morale of those who most needed to learn to manage their lives more effectively. Whatever the poor's initial disadvantages might be, these were held to be the result of individual propensities rather than socio-economic factors. So charity, if it were

West and East: a party of slummers: charity visitors in the 1880s

not to be positively disempowering, was to be used judiciously, and the Society's 'visitors' (caseworkers) relied on exhortation to improvement as well as aid (which might well not include giving money), according to the 'visitor's' assessments of what would be effective. The Society established a school of social work training in London in 1873 embodying this philosophy. By 1903 it had become a School of Sociology, offering a practical and theoretical course.

The revised Poor Law of 1834 had been designed to make certain that nobody in receipt of relief was at any possible advantage over those who were in some kind of work. The 'indoor relief' of the Workhouse was accompanied by loss of citizenship rights, including the separation of family members. When a fundamental reworking of the Poor Law was being considered, by means of a Royal Commission set up in 1905, discussions still centred on arguments about the limits of philanthropy and the scope of state intervention, the nature of charity, and the most efficient way of relieving or preventing poverty in the first place. These broad arguments endured until the outbreak of the First World War. By then, however, many social and political movements had taken on some commitment to the idea of collectivism (sometimes called socialism). Collectivism was set against individualism, but there was every shade of intermediate alliance or overlap between the two philosophies. Collectivist conviction — which was a broad doctrine of social (i.e. collective) responsibility towards the amelioration of society's problems — looked to state or local authority provision and intervention on matters of health and housing, education and training, employment and culture. Individualism — far more indeterminate and less systematized — emphasized a more conventional liberal philosophy of self-help and the market economy; but this vague philosophy did not fit easily with the increasingly radical preoccupations of the Liberal Party itself (Freeden, 1986).

Social welfare philosophy, the then-developing formal study of sociology, and political and social theories were all immersed in this collectivist versus individualist debate. The New Liberal political philosophers, of whom the most prominent had strong sociological interests (such as L.T. Hobhouse who became a professional sociologist), were far from espousing the 'classical' liberalism which emphasized the protection of individual rights in the context of the market. Rather, they presented a philosophy which kept the liberal virtues of respect for the individual citizen and the importance of character and self-development, but also emphasized the need for social reform to make these virtues more democratically approachable (Collini, 1979).

Although New Liberalism as a distinctive voice fell into decline during the First World War, it left strong traces of its original concerns in subsequent beliefs about social provision, even though their ancestry has been largely forgotten. The citizenship ideal of these collectivist-inclined Liberals (as well as the Fabians to whom they were close) of the 1890s and 1900s included a strong element of local government provision for schools, housing, libraries, museums, as well as what was satirically referred to as 'gas and water socialism', the provision of certain essential services by local authorities. The Fabian Society leaders, committed to establishing a framework for national reforms in part through advancing a comprehensive 'municipal socialism', were much given to analysing the respective rights and duties of citizens and the democratic state. Their version of an 'active citizenship' emphasized the responsibilities of those who would benefit from Fabian plans for a comprehensive welfare service to replace the Poor Law, and the installation of minimum wages. They also advocated 'the endowment of motherhood', a nationally-based system of payments to cover some of the costs of children (a scheme which, after the long campaign conducted by Eleanor Rathbone and others, finally resulted in the payment of family allowances — now called child benefit — after the Second World War).

All these initiatives to attack poverty, put forward under the banner of 'citizenship', demanded a reciprocal set of duties from those who would benefit. This insistence on mutuality went along with a suspicion of the individualism inherent in some of the new social movements which preceded the First World War. Beatrice Webb, for example, was concerned that aspects of what she saw as a feminism of self-fulfilment or personal liberation were antithetical to the interests of 'the community' (Webb, 1914). Mabel Atkinson of the Fabian Women's Group was also exercised by the reciprocal nature of the duties of the woman citizen. These, she held, included avoiding a middle-class 'parasitism' by both pursuing work and raising families in response to

Beatrice and Sidney Webb

contemporary theories of eugenics (eugenics is the study of means to breed an 'improved' population): 'Women, too, must be citizens and fully conscious of the privileges and duties of their citizenship if socialism is to be attained. Not least among the duties of that citizenship should be what Plato long ago demanded of his women guardians: that they should bear children for the service of the State' (Atkinson, 1914, p.199). So the collectivist ideal was highly susceptible to becoming entangled with pronatalism, and both were portrayed as an essential part of civic dutifulness, whether advocated from Right or Left.

The development of sociology as a separate field of study in Britain had proceeded in tandem with the political interest in establishing a clear foundation for 'citizenship'. After the First World War, some sociologists pursued a widely-voiced concern with the apparent 'failure of citizenship'. Trying to ascertain the empirical basis for this anxiety, they tracked down evidence of electoral and social 'apathy' across the newly-developing municipal housing estates, such as those the London County Council were building. This 'apathy' was seen as a refusal by the working classes to contribute as citizens with much conviction. However, by the 1940s, this notion of 'apathy' had narrowed to mean the supposed 'defeatism' of the working-class couple who lacked eagerness to have what was assumed by inter-war demographers to be a socially-responsible number of children (four per family was the suggested ideal).

3   THE POST-WAR WELFARE STATE: HOPES, PLANS AND CRITICISM

The eugenic and demographic anxieties which rose and subsided in successive waves during the nineteenth and early twentieth centuries thus effected an intimacy of association between family responsibilities and citizenship responsibilities . The conviction about the mutuality of obligations, the active duty of citizen to state, ran through the whole contributory philosophy of the plans for the new post-war welfare state when it finally emerged. Benefits were to be paid, 'up to subsistence level, as of right and without means test' as William Beveridge, the architect of post-war welfare, wrote (1942, p.7). These were firmly based on the principle that they were a return for what had been paid in, either directly via stamped insurance cards or indirectly via taxation.

What Beveridge did was to enlarge upon and to systematize an already existing but poor and piecemeal range of benefits and allowances. Although his Plan was greeted as new, it is arguable that a great deal of its thinking, including its aspirations for democratic citizenship rights, were in a line of descent from Liberal thinking of the 1890s, including collectivist ambitions for governmental control and comprehensive delivery of services. Victorian distinctions between the deserving and undeserving poor and the older individual casework and self-help philosophy of the Charity Organization Society did not reappear; clear entitlement was aimed at, together with a comprehensive meeting of needs 'from the cradle to the grave', akin to the early socialists' hopes for a machinery which would attend to the needs of all family members for housing, health, and education (as, for example, in the work of Sidney and Beatrice Webb).

Through this political history, the association of the concepts of 'citizenship' and 'the welfare state' was cemented. War may bring to light national social weaknesses and highlight neglected aspects of society, such as the degree of malnutrition revealed by the extent of unfitness for military service, or of poverty discovered in evacuated families. Nevertheless, the Second World War did not in and of itself generate the immense speculative interest in the social fabric, of which Beveridge's plan for welfare was a formalization. What it did was rather to provide the grounds for the reorganization and redescription of already established concerns and political philosophies. The post-Second World War intensification of interest in 'citizenship' mingled nationalistic with social ambitions, and was part of a broad social-democratic structure of feeling, diffused across the boundaries of the main political parties and other smaller progressive groups, tendencies and religious persuasions in the aftermath of the war. All of this was in part the fruition of inter-war agitation about economic depression and unemployment, about the evidence of children's undernourishment and constant family poverty, and the inadequacy of new house-building programmes to deal with existing needs.

William Beveridge

There was a huge literature during the Second World War which argued for nurseries, play-centres, family tickets on trains, after-school play facilities, holidays as part of social services for poorer families, more communal restaurants and municipal laundries — all in the name of 'citizenship'. Those worried about the apparent decline in family size wanted marriage-guidance clinics, child management courses, and training in 'civic values' both in adult education classes and in schools. The Fabian evidence to the 1945 Royal Commission on Population proposed, again under the rubric of 'citizenship', nursery schools and aids to parents, including a marriage bonus in the shape of entitlement to utility furniture and household goods, or prams for new mothers. Beveridge himself recommended council-sponsored holidays for exhausted housewives. This mesh of domestic innovations and pronatalist hopes (all aimed ostensibly at 'the family' but in practice at the mother) was threaded through by the language of 'social citizenship' as the apposite voice of the new post-war national democracy.

This long-established background accounts for the enthusiastic reception of the 'Beveridge Report', *Social Insurance and Allied Services*, published in 1942 and the founding text for the post-1945 welfare state. Its author was insistent, however, that a system of truly national insurance to provide a safety-net for all was merely one step towards the alleviation of poverty and other social ills. Health, education, and cultural provision were imperative too, as was the reorganization of labour policies so as to provide full employment. Beveridge's proposals for the latter were set out in 1944 in *Full Employment in a Free Society,* effectively the second part of his national plan for citizenship rights and entitlements. As he had expressed it in his Report of 1942:

> Now, when the war is abolishing landmarks of every kind, is the opportunity for using experience in a clear field. A revolutionary moment in the world's history is a time for revolutions, not for patching ... Social insurance fully developed may provide income security: it is an attack upon Want. But Want is one only of five giants on the road of reconstruction and in some ways the easiest to attack. The others are Disease, Ignorance, Squalor, and Idleness. ... The State should offer security for service and contribution. The State in organising security should not stifle incentive, opportunity, responsibility: in establishing a national minimum, it should leave room and encouragement for voluntary action by each individual to provide more than that minimum for himself and his family. (Beveridge, 1942, p.6)

So Beveridge believed that his Plan would offer at least a floor of subsistence for everybody, and one which could be achieved under the post-war capitalist economy. He was, though, agnostic as to whether a capitalist or a fully socialist economy would best provide for social needs in the future, and he took a cheerfully pragmatic view on this question in *Full Employment in a Free Society.* In a discussion of 'the State and the Citizen' he claimed:

> Full employment cannot be won and held without a great extension of the responsibilities and powers of the State exercised through organs of the central Government. No power less than that of the State can ensure adequate total outlay at all times, or can control, in the general interest, the location of industry and the use of land. (Beveridge, 1944, p.36)

But while such control was necessary, it could not be an all-encompassing source of social maintenance: 'all the essential liberties of local government for health, housing and education must be preserved'. The need for public ownership of industry via full nationalization had not, he believed, 'yet been demonstrated': 'This implies no judgment on the general issue between socialism and capitalism, which remains for debate on other grounds' (ibid.).

To the criticism that his policies for organizing the labour market would subordinate the individual to the state, Beveridge retorted that the truth was the opposite. A state which regarded its responsibilities as unimportant would be content to sacrifice individuals to mass unemployment, in the name of the prosperity of the better-off, whereas if:

the state is regarded as existing for the individual, a state which
fails, in respect of many millions of individuals, to ensure them
any opportunity of service and earning according to their powers
or the possibility of a life free from the indignities and inquisitions
of relief, is a state which has failed in a primary duty. Acceptance
by the state of responsibility for full employment is the final
necessary demonstration that the state exists for the citizens — for
all the citizens — and not for itself or for a privileged class.
(Beveridge, 1944, p.252)

Beveridge's conception of the welfare state was essentially that of a
social service, secured through insurance; it was an enabling device,
and the question of 'active' or 'passive' citizenship was not pertinent
within that framework. His conception, though, of the responsibilities of
government was wide and it was not restricted to the narrowly
economic:

> Learning should not end with school. Learning and life must be
> kept together throughout life: democracies will not be well
> governed till that is done. Later study should be open to all, and
> money, teaching and opportunities must be found for that as well.
> In the development of education this is the most important, if not
> the most urgent, of all the tasks of reconstruction. The needs of
> civilized men are illimitable, because they include the wise, happy
> enjoyment of leisure.
> (Beveridge, 1944, p.256)

This broad conception is in a direct line of descent from the hopes of
the 1890s' Liberal reformers.

ACTIVITY 3   Now read **Reading C, 'The five giant social evils'**, from the 1942
Beveridge Report. When you have finished, ask yourself:

1   Do Beveridge's plans and hopes strike you as optimistic, or as
realistic, or both?

2   If you do perceive a lack of realism in the Report, to what extent is
your reaction due to the hindsight of recent history? How much is it
a result of changes in our political language?

In recent years, with the critique of the welfare state by the New Right
and the disillusionment with socialist ideals, it is plain that the
optimistic assumptions which underpinned the Beveridge Report have
been under siege. In fact, some of Beveridge's critics were critical of
claims made for the Report from its inception. It was argued at the time
that its breadth was more apparent than real, and that the phrase 'the
needs of civilized men', democratic though it was intended to be,
indicated serious deficiencies. Who was this citizen for whom
Beveridge was constructing his welfare state? Was the concept as truly

inclusive as it sounded? There was nothing novel about the separate demarcation of the 'woman citizen', and the Fabian Women's group in particular had concentrated on discussing this character, her needs and her contributions. But this was an awkward and ambiguous figure. It implied the existence of a tacitly male, if supposedly, universal, citizen, to whom the woman citizen was a supplement, with special capacities or deficiencies.

The inter-war years witnessed several attempts by feminists to break open the existing rhetoric of citizenship, principally by the tactic of emphasizing the particular needs (which were dictated by existing social arrangements) of women — largely, as mothers. However, the vestiges of some of the former suffrage organizations joined other women's organizations under the umbrella of the National Union of Societies for Equal Citizenship, and they followed the tactic of pressing for equality on all fronts, rather than that of emphasizing difference.

Did the citizenship inherent in post-war planning, then, fail to embody true universality, whatever the progressive aims of reconstruction? Some critics of Beveridge argued just that. The proposals of the Report, they said, while in many ways genuinely progressive for women, nevertheless fell short of the universality they were supposed to have. On the one hand, 'housewives' (married women who did not go out to work) were not treated by the Report as persons in their own right, and as separately insurable; whereas, on the other hand, married women who also were waged workers would receive lower benefits, or if they elected to exempt themselves from contributing, would receive none at all. (This option to opt out was withdrawn in 1975.) The feminist writers and equalitarian campaigners, Elizabeth Abbott and Katherine Bompas, felt that an inducement to 'social irresponsibility' was being waved in front of married women workers — the invitation not to contribute — while housewives, the majority of married women not busy with 'gainful employment', were being made into a vast class of non-persons. They produced a pamphlet in 1943 which detailed how the sexually democratic intentions of the Beveridge Plan were not actually realized within its own provisions. Many of the improvements to it which they suggested have never been incorporated in the welfare provision system.

ACTIVITY 4   Now read **Reading D, 'Does the Beveridge Plan meet the needs of women?'**, which is taken from *The Woman Citizen and Social Security* by Elizabeth Abbot and Katherine Bompas.

1   How did Abbot and Bompas analyse the ways in which the Beveridge Report drew a distinction between:

(a)   unmarried women,

(b)   married women who were wage-earners, and

(c)   married women who only worked in the home?

2   What conclusions do the authors draw?

Beveridge had argued, against the inclinations of his own advisers, that housewives did need to be insured, but that, given the 'social facts' of the dependence of the great majority of married women on their husbands' wages, it was unrealistic to place them on the same level of benefit as unmarried men. But if marriage and housekeeping and child-bearing did constitute an 'occupation' for the bulk of women citizens, did it not follow that loss of this occupation should become an insurance risk? Beveridge did consider including some insurance against marriage breakdown; the prospects for deserted wives worried him particularly. But in the end, fears of 'complications' caused such plans to be dropped: collusion between husband and wife to obtain benefit was a spectre, as were 'guilty' wives who might divorce a husband in order to benefit. These would need casework enquiries to check their entitlement, and Beveridge wanted a universal benefit, free from scrutinies of people's personal circumstances.

However, by the time of the publication of the 1953 edition of his Report, Beveridge's hopes had already foundered. Full employment had indeed been secured, but as an effect of the Cold War and not of a principled social policy. National Insurance benefits had already become rather inadequate, and increasingly they were being means-tested, rather than being given as of right. Within a very few years of the generally warm reception of the Beveridge Report, it was widely observed that the welfare state had huge shortcomings. The question was whether these were the effects of the practical exclusions which had been written into the Plan. Or whether its limitations were an inevitable result of its existence within a market economy? Welfare provisions were less generous than had been originally hoped and the Plan's aspirations to fair treatment for all citizens had not, in practice, met the needs of women citizens.

3.1   WELFARE AND THE LIMITS OF EQUALITY

The sociologist T.H. Marshall developed an interest in the concept of citizenship in the late 1940s. He worked at a time when the separation between academic sociology and social policy was less marked than it is now. We need to think of his work in the context of the powerful Second World War and post-war fascination with the hopes of a reconstructed society, in which a decent standard of living, housing, education and culture would be democratically available to everyone — to all citizens irrespective of where they stood in the labour market. What Marshall did was to take the set of general concerns about social renewal — which were most famously crystallized in the Beveridge Report and the discussions which surrounded it — and to argue them through in the more specialized language of post-war sociology, which was then working out its own vocabulary. Marshall's hopes and ambitions for citizenship were very much of their period. But the anxiety he felt about the concept was: How did it fit with the rapid growth of a post-war capitalist society, some of whose tenets about

T.H. Marshall

profitability would be at odds with it? How far could citizen rights reinstate some of the theoretical equalities which were at risk in the open market?

At the end of the 1940s, Marshall was optimistic about these issues: 'Apparent inconsistencies are in fact a source of stability, achieved through a compromise which is not dictated by logic', although he saw that the balance would be fragile: 'It may be that some of the conflicts within our social system are becoming too sharp for the compromise to achieve its purpose much longer' (Marshall, 1950, p.84). At the same time, he tried to systematize and clarify the meaning of citizenship by dividing it into the civil, the political, and the social, and these three divisions he mapped (perhaps too tidily) on to three centuries. The eighteenth century, he suggested, saw the flowering of civil rights — access to the law, and rights before it. The nineteenth century saw the development of political rights — the growth of new parties, and of rights to parliamentary representation (the Chartist-led struggle for the working man's suffrage, for example). The twentieth century he described as the period of social rights — of the formulation of claims for social protection against destitution, for instance. The law, Parliament and the welfare state were the three main institutions corresponding to his tripartite chronology of citizenship. However,

Marshall saw the smoothness of this sequence as being interrupted by the capitalist context in which 'citizenship' was embedded — the need to make a profit and to raise taxes.

From his post-war vantage-point, Marshall (like many other liberal, social-democratic and socialist observers at the time) hoped that the state (a Labour government was in power between 1945 and 1951) would be the arena in which citizenship claims would be contested and supported. This supposition, it must be emphasized, is only intelligible in its context; it is a product of those local social democratic aspirations, and not a deduction which Marshall would have drawn had he examined the long international history of battles for enfranchisement. The linked concepts of 'citizenship and the welfare state' which Marshall entertained were indeed largely evolutionary, and restricted in Marshall's analysis to one country, Britain (although in the same period Sweden and Norway used similar concepts). As such they were characteristic of the post-war social democracy which sustained them, if only briefly.

ACTIVITY 5   Now read **Reading E, 'Citizenship and social inequalities'**, by T.H. Marshall. As you read, look for answers to the following questions:

1   What are Marshall's three components of citizenship?

2   What factors does he claim led to the blurring of class distinctions after the nineteenth century?

3   How does Marshall's tone compare with Beveridge's? Is he optimistic or sceptical?

Marshall argues that people's continuing economic inequality would be significantly offset by their enjoyment of their new citizenship entitlements, while the market would continue to generate enough wealth to sustain these benefits. Poverty was not to be tolerated; yet some degree of inequality — an inevitable concession to the capitalist market, but certainly to be distinguished from poverty — was a necessary motor for generating economic growth. So a mixed economy, with all its paradoxes, was still, he held, the best guarantor of a welfare system which would underpin citizenship rights. But Marshall's analysis embodied serious doubts about whether citizenship rights within the welfare state would further social equality:

> Is it still true that basic equality, when enriched in substance and embodied in the formal rights of citizenship, is consistent with the inequalities of social class? I shall suggest that our society today assumes that the two are still compatible, so much so that citizenship has itself become, in certain respects, the architect of legitimate social inequality.
> (Marshall, 1950, p.9)

How could this sharp reversal of the expectations of the Beveridge Plan have come about? Marshall believed that the growth of 'citizenship' should bring about a more comprehensive equality, but he observed that the continuities of social class maintained systematic inequalities. 'How is it that these two opposing principles could grow and flourish side by side in the same soil? ... The question is a pertinent one, for it is clear that, in the twentieth century, citizenship and the capitalist class system have been at war' (Marshall, 1950, p.29).

He answered it by pointing to a historical congruence between the growth of civil rights and the rise of both the market economy and modern democracy: the eighteenth century, he argued, 'saw the birth, not only of modern civil rights, but also of modern national consciousness'. Nineteenth-century political rights confirmed this setting up of the potential for citizenship to flourish. Then 'social rights', Marshall claimed, enabled a radical 'class-abatement' (by this phrase he implied the gradual erosion of class privileges) which was inherent in the notion of citizenship:

> Class-abatement is still the aim of social rights, but it has acquired a new meaning. It is no longer merely an attempt to abate the obvious nuisance of destitution in the lowest ranks of society. It has assumed the guise of action modifying the whole pattern of social inequality. It is no longer content to raise the floor-level in the basement of the social edifice, leaving the superstructure as it was. It has begun to remodel the whole building, and it might even end by converting a skyscraper into a bungalow.
> (Marshall, 1950, p.47)

This flattening out of the stratifications of the class system would come about, Marshall thought, because while income differentials remained, what he saw as a more significant 'equality of status' would be ensured through insurance and welfare benefits, a new National Health Service and reforms of education. The differences in what people earned would be compensated for through such social provisions. However, the success of individual expectations within this newly democratized framework would be subject to what the national economy could manage. Here the individual and the collective rights of citizenship would come into conflict, for national planning would concentrate not on individual needs, but on stratifying and sorting and classifying groups of people — as in the case of cohorts of children being put through education.

> In the end the jumble of mixed seed originally put into the machine emerges in neatly labelled packets ready to be sown in the appropriate gardens. I have deliberately couched this description in the language of cynicism in order to bring out the point that, however genuine may be the desire of the educational authorities to offer enough variety to satisfy all individual needs,

they must, in a mass service of this kind, proceed by repeated classification into groups, and this is followed at each stage by assimilation within each group and differentiation between groups. (Marshall, 1950, p.66)

So, despite the egalitarian aims of public education, a sort of inegalitarian undertow would accompany the actual process. The ideal of citizenship would result in an actual operation of 'social stratification'. This, however, did not undo Marshall's conviction that such a flawed welfare democracy was better as a context extending citizenship than the old structures of privilege. The new balance of power, he felt, was more benign: the broad tendency still remained egalitarian, directed towards flattening the skyscraper.

ACTIVITY 6   Look again through Reading E. Does the case of education, for example, justify his mix of optimism plus a tolerance for some lack of equality? Is such a tolerance a serious drawback to his own theory of improving citizenship rights?

Historical, political, and economic changes have scarcely borne out Marshall's post-war hopefulness. In the late 1950s, the sociologist Richard Titmuss was arguing against the belief that 'Britain is approaching the end of the road of social reform; the road down which Eleanor Rathbone and other reformers and rebels laboured with vision and effect' (Titmuss, 1958, p.34). The welfare state could not be seen as a piece of engineering whose construction had successfully finished in 1948. Pointing to contemporary feelings of resentment, he commented on 'a stereotype or image of an all-pervasive Welfare State for the Working Classes. Such is the tyranny of stereotypes today that this idea of a welfare society, born as a reaction against the social discrimination of the poor law may, paradoxically, widen rather than narrow class relationships'. For, he concluded (arriving at a position comparable to that of Marshall), the stereotyping assumptions of the critics of the welfare state blurred and distorted the truth. They narrowed down the multiplicity of those social services such as occupational benefits and allowances for taxpayers which helped the better-off, to the one demeaning conception of a social service — the welfare state for the working classes. The search for equity between taxpayers took precedence over the need for equity between citizens, Titmuss claimed:

The lack of any precise thinking about what is and what is not a 'social service' confuses and constrains the social conscience, and allows the development of distinctive social policies based on different principles for arbitrarily differentiated groups in the population.
(Titmuss, 1958, p.54)

Titmuss gave examples of these enormous 'confusions' about what was and wasn't a social service. Pointing to the benefits enjoyed by 'professionals', he wrote: 'The training of doctors is a social service. Marriage guidance services are not'. And: 'Technological training and further education is a social service. Subsidised housing for miners is not'. So the equation of 'social' services with one narrow conception of a 'welfare state' for the use of the working class alone was a form of bias, and this inaccurate perception, Titmuss argued, only served to enlarge and to consolidate social inequalities. In this he agreed with Marshall's earlier thoughts about the new inequalities which were paradoxically being thrown up by post-war welfare, but he did not share Marshall's hopes for any prospect of 'class-abatement'. By the end of his career, Marshall himself was concentrating on the persistent tensions between human needs, what a welfare state could achieve by way of meeting them, and the dictates of a market economy (Marshall, 1981).

4   CONTINUING PROBLEMS FOR CITIZENSHIP AND THE WELFARE STATE

It is widely believed now that the welfare state has failed to act as an adequate safety-net, let alone as a guarantor of more elaborate rights, and that it is unable to respond adequately to the demands placed upon it. Different political interpretations are advanced to account for its decline or to proffer remedial means, but the decline of the national economy had not been anticipated. Bryan Turner has written:

> Marshall's nationally-based analysis is no longer relevant to a period of disorganized capitalism. The British state, in fact, has very little scope for manoeuvre: while capital operates on a global scale, labour tends to operate within a local national market, articulating its interests in terms of a national interest group. (Turner, 1990, p.195)

Given this internationalization of capital and an apparent global recession in the early 1990s, can a market economy *sustain* both its own growth and an adequate welfare state? To what extent is this a question of economics and to what extent one of politics? These are questions which assail us if we try to make use of Marshall's framework now and its supposition that, although tensions might characterize the relations between state and welfare and citizenship, these were, on balance, creative tensions.

There has been some recent interest, among political philosophers, in reanimating the concept of citizenship. Much of this has developed from an interest in using the term to argue for civil or 'human' rights, fuelled by the spread of capitalization and democratization in Eastern

Europe. Nevertheless, the political and economic upheavals in these countries and the profound social alterations accompanying their democratization have had ambiguous interim results for the practical implementation of social citizenship. As a state-supported network of welfare provision and housing subsidies falls into decline, and in East Germany, for instance, nursery places for the children of working parents diminish while unemployment multiplies, so a gap appears anew between the theoretical and civil realization of citizenship and its daily possibilities.

The anticipation of a common European market in 1992 has brought the prospect of greater parity between Western European countries in respect of their labour laws and entitlements — as specified in the Social Charter, which sets out directives for the European Community (some of which the British government, at the time of writing, dissents from). Claims for a revived standard of citizenship may be invoked here. Those who, in Britain, have advocated a written constitution or a Bill of Rights (including the supporters of 'Charter 88') have used the idea of a common standard of safeguards to liberty as a defence against perceived erosions to civil liberties during the 1980s. Most of these recent rehabilitations of the language of citizenship have not been directly concerned with claims to a minimum standard of living. Ruth Lister, however, has argued for the reassociation of citizenship with entitlement to an adequate minimal support and proper access for all to educational and cultural provision (Lister, 1990).

Others claim that this idea of a reinvigorated citizenship would require a great deal of overhauling of the concept to be successful. The late nineteenth- and early twentieth-century arguments that 'women citizens' possessed, by virtue of their sex, special capacities for 'humanizing' citizenship, and the inter-war and wartime egalitarian feminist claims, have left a residue of unresolved problems. The political philosopher Carole Pateman has recently returned to these, to show that they are products of an underlying structural shortcoming in the concept of 'citizenship': its very construction, she argues, is flawed.

Taking up Marshall's architectural metaphor of the remodelling of the social edifice from the skyscraper of privilege to the bungalow of equality, Carole Pateman asks: 'are women in the building or in a separate annexe?' (1989, p.185). For Marshall's confidence that citizenship is a status accorded to those who are full members of a community overlooks the fact that, 'as shown graphically and brutally by the history of blacks in the United States', the formal status of being a citizen can be held by categories of people who, though they possess the right to vote, do not thereby possess full and effective social membership. Although women are theoretically equal as citizens, the continuing sexual division of labour, the 'feminization of poverty' and the far greater involvement of women with the unpaid care of children and the elderly, contradict this formal parity. Carole Pateman's argument is that in addition to the fact that benefits, allowances, support systems and pension entitlements may well be neither adequate nor properly distributed to claimants in general, the broad architecture of the welfare state repeats a 'patriarchal' division, in which full citizenship is associated with waged work (done full-time outside the home), and its benefit structure is predicated on the superiority of this mode. The dilemma for women can then be solved neither by an ideal of a strictly 'gender-neutral' welfare, which would ignore the facts of gendered social arrangements as they are, nor yet by a recognition of a separate 'women's citizenship', which would only tend to perpetuate its secondary nature, given the existing framework. She argues that, while women, who constitute the vast majority of single parents, do draw heavily on the state, on the other hand the strain on the state to produce public care provision would be infinitely greater if women did not work at home, often as unacknowledged carers. This caring constitutes unwaged welfare work, which, since it is 'private', is not recognized as a significant contribution to the public good.

Only a radical re-evaluation of the associations between being a citizen, possessing human worth, and being a wage-earner, she suggests, could truly incorporate women's citizenship. As 'the social basis for the ideal of full (male) employment is crumbling', so there is a chance 'to move from the welfare state to a welfare society without involuntary social exiles, in which women as well as men enjoy full social membership. Whether the opportunity can be realized is not easy to tell now that the warfare state is overshadowing the welfare state' (Pateman, 1989, p.204).

ACTIVITY 7   Now read **Reading F, 'Are women full citizens of the welfare state?'**, by Carole Pateman. Pateman makes a radical claim for the 'hidden' contribution of women to the welfare state.

1   Does Pateman's argument require a rethinking of the usual distinctions between the private and the public spheres?

2   How do Pateman's criticisms compare with those made by Elizabeth Abbott and Katherine Bompas in Reading D?

Carole Pateman's analysis indicates the omissions inherent in Marshall's perspective. From a rather different standpoint, the political theorist Ralf Dahrendorf is also worried by exclusions from the ideal of 'citizenship'; these are not, for him, so much flaws in the construction and history of the concept itself, but rather the products of a worsening social decline (Dahrendorf, 1990). He stresses (against the drift of current American and British conservative emphases on 'obligations') the 'unambiguous' nature of citizenship social rights: most importantly, the guaranteed right 'not to fall below a certain level of income and the right to an education' — ideas which today sound radical, yet would have been part of the Fabian and social-democratic stock-in-trade in the debates concerning citizenship between the 1890s and 1940s. The contemporary growth of a 'new minority' at the bottom of the social ladder which has no voice or representation is, he holds, a serious

undermining of the universality implied in 'citizenship': a (low) basic
income, guaranteed by right, would be essential to reintegrate people
presently consigned to the new 'underclass':

> I do not expect the basic income to be a minimum wage. To me the
> most important point about the unconditional quality of a basic
> income is that it would institutionalize an element of people's
> income for which they do not have to fill out forms, queue in
> offices, or divulge their innumerate debts to a bureaucrat.
> (Dahrendorf, 1990)

Reminiscent of Beveridge's 1940s ambitions for an entitlement as 'of
right', Dahrendorf's hopes for a new 'decade of citizenship rights'
include arguments drawn from recent historical developments. If these
rights are anchored in a purely national framework, they become
illogical, he argues. The rights of people of multinational parentage, of
refugees, of immigrants within a nation-state are pushing at the
boundaries of that rough identification of 'citizen' with 'national':
'Citizenship implies pluralism. It requires exercising the right to be
different'. The new enemy for citizenship is a mixed brand of political,
cultural and religious fundamentalism, with the emphasis on the
homogeneity of the group. Such fundamentalism runs the risk of the
associated possibilities of intensified racism and xenophobia.
Dahrendorf's speculations underline the main problem for any
contemporary theories of social need now: how differences, of whatever
order — cultural, sexual, national — are to be understood and reflected
within the framework of social citizenship.

Many enfranchised inhabitants of a country cannot be fitted neatly into
the model which assumes a common and democratically accessible
civic and cultural status. In different ways, ethnicity, gender, sexual
orientation and habits of living, chosen or imposed, may all make this
general universalistic model inapplicable or unreachable. The very
distinct cases, for example, of travellers or 'gypsies', or those caught up
in immigration procedures, all offer enormously different examples of
the way in which a standard social citizenship may prove hard to meet,
or be hedged about with daunting bureaucracy (as with the
requirements of the Immigration and Nationality Department for proof
of the 'genuine' nature of arranged or other marriages contracted
abroad). The egalitarian ideal of citizenship suffers under the realities of
diffused racism and other xenophobic hostilities; prospects of an anti-
semitic revival, for instance, hardly accord with the dream of a tolerant
civic life. A poverty of public resources, too, erodes this vision. A
formally equal access to the law is dependent on the health of the
system of Legal Aid. A culturally-alive citizenship assumes some
foundation in a nationally sound and effective system of education;
whereas, for instance, in the late 1980s it was reported that the nominal
right to education for a child was worthless in London boroughs such as
Tower Hamlets which, partly owing to the continuing shortage of
teachers, were failing to be able to supply places within schools for

some of the children requiring them. An effective welfare citizenship presumes an economy designed to supply certain standards and availability of housing. All these examples could be multiplied. They imply questions about how the availability of resources interacts with social policies which determine how social needs are to be assessed and considered.

4.1 CONCLUSION: CAN A TRANSCENDENT IDEAL OF EQUALITY ACCOMMODATE DIFFERENCES?

The common cultural standard embodied in the ideal of citizenship is tested again and again by the realities of a pluralist society in which cultural differences abound. Some legal concessions are discreetly made to such differences, while in other cases they are not. Polygamy and female circumcision are not tolerated by law and the appeal in Britain (following the *Satanic Verses* furore) from some factions within the Muslim community to extend the scope of the blasphemy laws has not succeeded. The rights of religious minorities to local-authority funded schooling in their faith for their children is not currently extended beyond the Jewish and Christian 'mainstream'. Where religious conviction clashes with civic belief about proper conduct, the secular claim to reason will often override the appeal to faith; but in America the invoking of 'freedom of religion' clauses in the constitution has ensured a fuller public debate on such issues as the 'right' of parents who are convinced Jehovah's Witnesses to refuse life-saving blood transfusions to their children. These clashes between general codes of conduct and particular feelings, religious or otherwise, concerning entitlements to exemplary rights are not, in theory, central to citizenship debates. Yet they are more powerful than being mere indicators of the boundaries of such debates. We are familiar with demands from those who have been historically excluded from being citizens to be allowed in, but the set of problems posed by the special pleas for tolerance of religious and cultural differences also have profound implications for citizenship. If it is understood to embody what we might all have or aspire to have in common, then, inherent in that wish for the highest common factor, is an ideal of transcendence. As Anne Phillips says, citizenship

> implies a contrast with all the more differentiated descriptions of capitalist and worker, male and female, black and white, for it accentuates the rights and responsibilities we share. It is a concept that deliberately abstracts from those things that are particular and specific, and seems to lift us onto a higher terrain. ... When we are called upon to act *as citizens* we are by implication not acting simply as women or men, black or white, manual worker or professional, homeowner or council tenant, however powerful these affiliations are that bind us to a particular social definition or location.
> (Phillips, 1991, pp.80–1)

Yet working against this transcendence is the wish for a proper
recognition of the different needs and perspectives of different groups.
How are these ideals to be harmoniously implemented? Given that the
social world is itself so fragmented, is it not inevitable that any realistic
conception of citizenship must be internally divided too, or else if it
implicitly imposes a homogeneity which obscures real differences, be at
risk of reproducing the features of domination in a society upon which
it hopes to improve? But would a citizenship of groups or of 'special
needs' be plausible? Would it not undermine the claim to universal
entitlements upon which citizenship campaigns have based themselves
in the past? Historically, citizenship has aimed to distribute rights to
individuals on the basis, supposedly, of their personhood, but
effectively, as is frequently argued, on the basis of their power.

Citizenship, especially when invoked in the same breath as the welfare
state, embodies a purposeful dream which has never been fully realized.
The question is how far this egalitarian drive within citizenship remains
convincing as an aspiration, given the proliferation of claims for the
recognition of differences. Yet this strong ideal within citizenship is
unlikely to fall into neglect because it insists on some standard of rights
which inhere in each person, simply by virtue of that person's being in
society.

REFERENCES

Abbott, E. and Bompas, K. (1943) *The Woman Citizen and Social Security: a criticism of the proposals made in the Beveridge Report as they affect women*, London, Bompas.

Andrews, G. (ed.) (1991) *Citizenship*, London, Lawrence and Wishart.

Atkinson, M. (1914) *The Economic Foundations of the Women's Movement*, London, Fabian Tract No. 175.

Beveridge, W. (1942) *Social Insurance and Allied Services,* London, HMSO, CMD 6404.

Beveridge, W. (1944) *Full Employment in a Free Society,* London, George Allen & Unwin.

Collini, S. (1979) *Liberalism and Sociology*, Cambridge, Cambridge University Press.

Dahrendorf, R. (1990) 'Decade of the citizen', interview with John Keane, *Guardian*, 1 August.

Freeden, M. (1986) *Liberalism Divided*, Milton Keynes, Open University Press.

Held, D. (1991) 'Between state and civil society' in Andrews, G. (ed.) (1991).

Lister, R. (1990) *The Exclusive Society: Citizenship and the Poor*, London, CPAG Ltd.

Marshall, T.H. (1950) 'Citizen and social class', in *Citizenship and Social Class and other Essays*, Cambridge, Cambridge University Press.

Marshall, T.H. (1981) *The Right to Welfare and other Essays*, London, Heinemann.

Parsons, T. (1966) *Societies, Evolutionary and Comparative Perspectives*, Englewood Cliffs, Prentice Hall.

Parsons, T. (1971) *The System of Modern Societies*, Englewood Cliffs, Prentice Hall.

Pateman, C. (1989) *The Disorder of Women: Democracy, Feminism and Political Theory,* Cambridge, Polity Press.

Phillips, A. (1991) 'Citizenship and feminist theory' in Andrews, G. (ed.) (1991).

Plant, R. (1991) 'Social rights and the reconstruction of welfare' in Andrews, G (ed.) (1991).

Rousseau, J.-J. (1913) *The Social Contract and Discourses*, New York, E.P. Dutton.

Titmuss, R. (1958) 'The social division of welfare' in *Essays on 'The Welfare State',* London, George Allen and Unwin.

Turner, B. (1990) 'Outline of a theory of citizenship', *Sociology*, vol.24, no.2, pp.189-217.

Webb, B. (1914) *The New Statesman*.

Weber, M. (1979) *Economy and Society*, vol. 2, Roth, G. and Wittich, C. (eds), University of California Press.

READING A   WHAT IS A NATION?

Max Weber

If the concept of 'nation' can in any way be defined unambiguously, it certainly cannot be stated in terms of empirical qualities common to those who count as members of the nation. In the sense of those using the term at a given time, the concept undoubtedly means, above all, that *it is proper* to expect from certain groups a specific sentiment of solidarity in the face of other groups. Thus the concept belongs in the sphere of values. Yet, there is no agreement on how these groups should be delimited or about what concerted action should result from such solidarity.

In ordinary language 'nation' is, first of all, not identical with the 'people of a state', that is, with the membership of a given polity. Numerous polities comprise groups who emphatically assert the independence of their 'nation' in the face of other groups; or they comprise merely *parts* of a group whose members declare themselves to be one homogenous 'nation' (Austria is an example for both). Furthermore, a 'nation' is not identical with a community speaking the same language; that this by no means always suffices is indicated by the Serbs and Croats, the North Americans, the Irish, and the English. On the contrary, a common language does not seem to be absolutely necessary to a 'nation'. In official documents, besides 'Swiss People' one also finds the phrase 'Swiss Nation'. And some language groups do not think of themselves as a separate 'nation', for example, at least until recently, the White Russians. As a rule, however, the pretension to be considered a special 'nation' is associated with a common language as a culture value of the masses; this is predominately the case in the classic country of language conflicts, Austria, and equally so in Russia and in eastern Prussia. But this linkage of the common language and 'nation' is of varying intensity; for instance, it is very low in the United States as well as in Canada.

'National' solidarity among men speaking the same language may be just as well rejected as accepted. Solidarity, instead, may be linked with differences in the other great culture value of the masses, namely, a religious creed, as is the case with the Serbs and Croats. National solidarity may be connected with differing social structure and mores and hence with 'ethnic' elements, as is the case with the German Swiss and the Alsatians in the face of the Germans of the Reich, or with the Irish facing the British. Yet above all, national solidarity may be linked to memories of a common political destiny with other nations. ...

It goes without saying that 'national' affiliation need not be based upon common blood. Indeed, especially radical 'nationalists' are often of foreign descent. Furthermore, although a specific common anthropological type is not irrelevant to nationality, it is neither sufficient nor prerequisite to nation founding. Nevertheless, the idea of the 'nation' is apt to include the notions of common descent and of an essential, though frequently

Source: Weber, M. (1979) 'The nation', in *Economy and Society*, vol.2, Roth, G. and Wittich, C. (eds), University of California Press.

indefinite, homogeneity. The 'nation' has these notions in common with the sentiment of solidarity of ethnic communities, which is also nourished from various sources, as we have seen before. But the sentiment of ethnic solidarity does not by itself make a 'nation'. ...

READING B   COMPARATIVE FORMATIONS OF CITIZENSHIP

Bryan S. Turner

The notion of the city and the historical evolution of autonomous cities played a critical role in the development of philosophical thought about freedom, individuality and civility. Weber thought this constellation was unique to the West:

> only in the Occident is found the concept of citizen (*civis Romanus, citoyen, bourgeois*) because only in the Occident again are there cities in the specific sense.
> (Weber, 1966, p.233)

The issue of citizenship was consequently an important issue in his view of the unique character of Western rationalism. These terms were also closely related to ideas about civility and civilization. To leave the countryside in order to enter the city was typically connected with the process of civilization; to become urban was to 'citizenise' the person. The city emerged as a topic in social philosophy with very contradictory meanings. Whereas Voltaire thought that the city was the core of individual freedoms which challenged the false hierarchies of traditional rural society, by the beginning of the nineteenth century the city came to be more frequently seen as the great centre of social corruption and moral decadence. ... In Germany the radical humanists generated an ideal vision of the Greek city-state as a major alternative to the urban society which was developing alongside capitalism. Thus Schiller, Fichte and Hölderlin merged the features of the Greek polis with those of the medieval town to create an image of burgher culture as an alternative to the emerging industrial cities of Germany (Barasch, 1968). We can therefore identify a rather significant distinction between the emerging concept of citizenship in Germany and the more revolutionary idea of citizenship which had developed in France out of the French Revolution. ...

These comparisons between different histories of citizenship in Europe suggest a model of citizenship development in terms of two dimensions. The first dimension is the passive-active contrast depending on whether citizenship grew from above or below. In the German tradition, citizenship stands in a passive relationship to the state because it is primarily an effect of state action. It is important to note that this distinction is in fact fundamental to the western tradition and can be located in medieval political philosophy, where there were two opposed views of citizenship. In the

Source: Turner, B. (1990) 'Outline of a theory of citizenship', *Sociology*, vol.24, no.2, pp.189–217.

descending view, the king is all powerful and the subject is the recipient of privileges. In the ascending view, a free man was a citizen, an active bearer of rights. ... The second dimension is the tension between a private realm of the individual and the family in relationship to the public arena of political action. In the German case, an emphasis on the private (the family, religion, and individual ethical development) was combined with a view of the state as the only source of public authority. This typology allows us to contrast Germany with other historical trajectories. ...

By contrast with both the English and German cases, the French conception of citizenship was the consequence of a long historical struggle to break the legal and political monopoly of a court society within a social system which was rigidly divided in terms of estates. The very violence of this social transformation resulted in a highly articulate conception of active citizenship in the revolutionary struggles of the eighteenth century. The old myth that the king represented, combined and integrated the multiplicity of orders, groups and estates had become transparent during the political conflicts of the eighteenth century. Revolutionary political theories, acting against the absolutist conception of sovereignty, followed Rousseau in conceptualising society as a collection of individuals whose existence would be represented through the general will in popular parliamentary institutions. What bound Frenchmen together into a common nation was again the concept of citizenship (Baker, 1987). Frenchmen had ceased to be merely subjects of the sovereign and had become instead common citizens of a national entity. ...

Finally, the American case represents another variation on the history of western citizenship. The American example shared with the French a strong rejection of centralised power, adopting also the discourse of the rights of man and privileges of independent citizens. The Boston Tea Party was a symbolically significant expression of the idea 'no taxation without representation'. The radical nature of the 'democratic revolution' in America struck observers like Alexis de Tocqueville with great force; he came to regard America as the first macro-experiment in democracy in modern history. For de Tocqueville, the democratic foundation of the nation was explained by the absence of aristocracy, the frontier, and the exclusion of an established church. Although there was a radical tradition of citizenship expressed in the idea of an independent militia, American democracy nevertheless continued to exist alongside a divisive racist and exploitative South. In addition America's welfare state was late to develop and provided very inadequate forms of social citizenship and participation for the majority of the population. This weak tradition of citizenship in welfare terms has been explained by the very strength of American individualism, and by the checks and balances of the federal system; American citizenship was expressed in terms of localism versus centralism, thereby limiting the development of a genuinely national programme of welfare rights. To some extent the dominance of individualism and the value of personal success have meant that the 'public arena' is typically understood in terms of individual involvement in local voluntary associations. ...

The point of this historical sketch has been partly to provide a critique of [a] monolithic and unified conception of citizenship ... and partly to offer a sociological model of citizenship along two axes, namely public and private definitions of moral activity in terms of the creation of a public space of political activity, and active and passive forms of citizenship in terms of whether the citizen is conceptualised as merely a subject of an absolute authority or as an active political agent. ...

The analysis of citizenship has in recent years become a pressing theoretical issue, given the problems which face the welfare state in a period of economic recession. However, the problem of citizenship is in fact not confined merely to a question of the normative basis of welfare provision; its province is global. It includes, on the one hand, the international consequences of perestroika and glasnost in the Soviet Union, and, on the other, the implications of medical technology for the definition of what will count as a human subject/citizen. ...

[A]ny further development of the theory of citizenship will have to deal more fundamentally with societies in which the struggle over citizenship necessarily involves problems of national identity and state formation in a context of multiculturalism and ethnic pluralism. ... We may in conclusion indicate two possible lines of theoretical development of the (western) notion of citizenship. The first would be the conditions under which citizenship can be formed in societies which are, as it were, constituted by the problems of ethnic complexity (such as Brazil), and the second would be an analysis of the problems which face the development of global citizenship as the political counter-part of the world economy.

References

Baker, K.M. (1987) 'Representation' in Baker, K.M. (ed.) *The French Revolution and the Creation of the Political Culture of the Old Regime*, Oxford, Pergamon Press.

Barasch, M. (1968) 'The city' in Weiner, P.P. (ed.) *Dictionary of the History of Ideas*, vol.1, pp.427-34, New York, Charles Scribner's Sons.

Weber, M. (1966) *The City*, Glencoe, Ill., Free Press.

READING C   THE FIVE GIANT SOCIAL EVILS

William Beveridge

Twice in this century the onset of cyclical depression has been arrested by the outbreak of war, just after the culmination of an upward movement of the trade cycle. After the boom of 1913 employment had already begun to fall in 1914. After the half-hearted boom of 1937 employment fell in 1938. In each case an incipient depression was stopped or reversed, but it needed a war to bring this about. The test of statesmanship in the near future lies in finding a way to avoid depressions without plunging into war.

Source: Beveridge, W. (1953) *Full Employment in a Free Society*, originally published in 1944, London, George Allen & Unwin, paras 377–9 and 382–3.

That is the aim and hope of this Report. We cure unemployment for the sake of waging war. We ought to decide to cure unemployment without war. We cure unemployment in war, because war gives us a common objective that is recognized by all, an objective so vital that it must be attained without regard to cost, in life, leisure, privileges or material resources. The cure of unemployment in peace depends on finding a common objective for peace that will be equally compelling on our efforts. The suggestion of this Report is that we should find that common objective in determination to make a Britain free of the giant evils of Want, Disease, Ignorance and Squalor. We cure unemployment through hate of Hitler; we ought to cure it through hate of these giant evils. We should make these in peace our common enemy, changing the direction and the speed rather than the concentration and strength of our effort. Whether we can do this, depends upon the degree to which social conscience becomes the driving force in our national life. We should regard Want, Disease, Ignorance and Squalor as common enemies of all of us, not as enemies with whom each individual may seek a separate peace, escaping himself to personal prosperity while leaving his fellows in their clutches. That is the meaning of social conscience; that one should refuse to make a separate peace with social evil. Social conscience, when the barbarous tyranny abroad has ended, should drive us to take up different arms in a new war against Want, Disease, Ignorance and Squalor at home.

Want, arising mainly through unemployment and other interruptions of earnings, to a less extent through large families, is the subject of my earlier Report on Social Insurance. It could, without question, be abolished by the whole-hearted acceptance of the main principles of that Report. The worst feature of Want in Britain shortly before this war was its concentration upon children. Wages were not and probably could not be adjusted in any way to family responsibilities; the various social insurance schemes for providing income when wages failed either ignored family responsibilities entirely — as in health insurance or workmen's compensation — or made inadequate provision for them — as in unemployment insurance. By consequence there followed a sinister concentration of Want on those who would suffer from it most helplessly and most harmfully. Nearly half of all the persons discovered in Want by the social surveys of British cities between the wars were children under fifteen. Nearly half of all the working-class children in the country were born into Want. It is certain on general principles and can be shown by experiment that the bodies and minds of children respond directly and automatically to a better environment, that the citizens of the future will grow up taller, stronger, abler, if in childhood all of them have had good feeding, clothing, housing and physical training. Want and its concentration on children between the wars represented a destruction of human capital none the less real because it did not enter into any economic calculus. The decision to destroy Want should be taken at once, for its own sake, to free Britain from a needless scandal and a wasting sore. That decision would deliver at the same time the first blow in the war against Idleness. The redistribution of income that is involved in abolishing Want by Social Insurance and children's allowances will of itself be a potent force in helping to maintain demand for the products of industry, and so in preventing unemployment. ...

Squalor means the bad conditions of life for a large part of our people which have followed through the unplanned disorderly growth of cities, through our spoiling more and more country by building towns without building good towns, through our continuing to build inadequate, ill-equipped homes that multiply needlessly the housewife's toil. The greatest opportunity open in this country for raising the general standard of living lies in better housing, for it is in their homes and in the surroundings of their homes that the greatest disparities between different sections of the community persist today. Better housing means not merely better houses but houses in the right environment, in the right relation to places of work and recreation and communal activity. Town and country planning must come before housing, and such planning, as one enquiry after another has shown, is impossible, until we resolve justly but firmly the problem of land values. Here is the greatest urgency of all. The attack on Squalor cannot wait, but it must be a planned attack. The war will leave a yawning gap, which must be filled without delay by building more homes. We must have housing at once but we must have town and country planning before housing.

The policy for Full Employment outlined in this Report is a policy of spending and doing. It is a policy of common action. If we attack with determination, unity and clear aim the four giant evils of Want, Disease, Ignorance and Squalor, we shall destroy in the process their confederate — the fifth giant of Idleness enforced by mass unemployment. The carrying out of the policy depends on the positive acceptance of a new responsibility by the State, that of ensuring adequate demand for the products of industry, however industry itself may be organized. The policy preserves all the essential British liberties; it uses Britain's political advantages to carry through a task which can be carried through only by the power of the State. These political advantages are great and should be used. The constitution of Britain concentrates in the Government of the day the great power without which the problems of a great society cannot be solved. It makes the use of that power subject to continual scrutiny by the citizens and their representatives, and the power itself subject to recall; the essence of democracy is effective means of changing the Government without shooting.

READING D DOES THE BEVERIDGE PLAN MEET THE NEEDS OF WOMEN?

Elizabeth Abbott and Katherine Bompas

It must be emphasised, then, that it is not upon the denial of equal economic status to women that the Plan comes to grief. Indeed the unmarried woman worker has equal economic status but is divorced from equal

Source: Abbott, E. and Bompas, K. (1943) *The Woman Citizen and Social Security: a criticism of the proposals made in the Beveridge Report as they affect women.*

responsibility. It is with the denial of any personal status to a woman because she is married, the denial of her independent personality within marriage, that everything goes wrong and becomes unjust and ungenerous, sometimes comic, always unrealistic and inevitably antagonistic to the best interests of marriage and social life. In place of the famous phrase of Blackstone: 'I and my wife are one, and I am he.' the author of the Report has substituted his special version: 'Every woman on marriage becomes a new person.' Nearly two hundred years may lie between the two phrases. The thought behind them is the same: that a married woman is not a person at all. Today, as so many years ago, injustice and complication are the inevitable result. That this may be quite other than the aim of the Plan is apparent, since its author refers to the married woman as 'an equal partner', as 'occupied on work which is vital' etc. etc. The tribute of the word is a sad commonplace to women. What is here of concern is not what the Report may say in praise of women, but what it proposes shall be done and the social tendencies which will be thereby encouraged. Far from putting a premium on marriage, as it purports to do, the Plan penalises both the married woman and marriage itself.

Nevertheless it would be unjust and ungenerous not to recognise that some new features and improvements, both evolutionary and revolutionary, will benefit women as well as men. The pity is that a Plan which went so far did not go further and in a better direction where women are concerned. ...

Reference has already been made to the good and progressive features of the Report as a whole, and the fact that many women will be helped in various ways, some directly, as by the equal benefits for single women; others indirectly by the extension of the health service to the woman in the home; others by the realistic and just reform of widowhood aid, and the plan for bringing younger widows back into employment.

Nevertheless, the scheme as a whole is marred by the general plan for insuring women, particularly the married woman.

The critic is too often denounced for not being creative, and there is a tendency to ignore the fact that demolitions and constructions are rarely carried out by the same hands. This memorandum has dealt with what is considered to be a basic failure in the Plan; the failure to treat women as full and independent fellow citizens with men. It offers only general recommendations which are set forth below. ...

Recommendations.

1 An equal retirement age.
2 Safeguarding of pension and other rights of unpaid domestic workers by compulsory insurance on their behalf.
3 Direct insurance of the married woman — the housewife — with benefits adjusted to her needs, including cash benefit when she is disabled by sickness or accident and retirement pension in her own right.

4   Maintenance of insurance rights upon marriage, subject to general tests of genuine desire for and availability for work.

5   No exemption from insurance of the married woman worker save the general exemption for any person who earns less than £75 a year.

6   Full normal benefit for the married woman worker when unemployed or disabled.

7   Full pension in her own right for the insured married woman.

8   Payment by single women of an equal contribution for an equal benefit.

9   Removal from the Plan of all moral tests.

10   Widowhood benefit should be recognised as and called Temporary Loss of Livelihood Benefit.

11   Maternity Grant and Benefit and Guardian Benefit should be acknowledged for what they are: not individual benefits, but Family Benefits, designed to safeguard the bearing, rearing, sustenance, health, home life and general well-being of children.

Practically all the disabilities and anomalies criticised could have been obviated had there been a different approach to the whole subject. At present the Plan is mainly a man's plan for man: it remains selective instead of being truly national. A great part of what is offered to women is in the spirit of that mistaken benevolence from which perhaps more than anything else women need to be emancipated before they can take their place as partners in marriage and in work.

READING E   CITIZENSHIP AND SOCIAL INEQUALITIES

T.H. Marshall

I shall be running true to type as a sociologist if I begin by saying that I propose to divide citizenship into three parts. But the analysis is, in this case, dictated by history even more clearly than by logic. I shall call these three parts, or elements, civil, political and social. The civil element is composed of the rights necessary for individual freedom — liberty of the person, freedom of speech, thought and faith, the right to own property and to conclude valid contracts, and the right to justice. The last is of a different order from the others, because it is the right to defend and assert all one's rights on terms of equality with others and by due process of law. This shows us that the institutions most directly associated with civil rights are the courts of justice. By the political element I mean the right to participate in the exercise of political power, as a member of a body invested with political authority or as an elector of the members of such a body. The corresponding institutions are parliament and councils of local government. By the social element I mean the whole range from the right to a modicum of economic welfare and security to the right to share to the full in the social heritage and to live the life of a civilised

Source: Marshall, T.H. (1950) 'Citizen and social class', in *Citizenship and Social Class and other Essays*, Cambridge, Cambridge University Press.

being according to the standards prevailing in the society. The institutions most closely connected with it are the educational system and the social services. ...

The Poor Law treated the claims of the poor, not as an integral part of the rights of the citizen, but as an alternative to them — as claims which could be met only if the claimants ceased to be citizens in any true sense of the word. For paupers forfeited in practice the civil right of personal liberty, by internment in the workhouse, and they forfeited by law any political rights they might possess. This disability of disenfranchisement remained in being until 1918, and the significance of its final removal has, perhaps, not been fully appreciated. The stigma which clung to poor relief expressed the deep feelings of a people who understood that those who accepted relief must cross the road that separated the community of citizens from the outcast company of the destitute.

The Poor Law is not an isolated example of this divorce of social rights from the status of citizenship. The early Factory Acts show the same tendency. Although in fact they led to an improvement of working conditions and a reduction of working hours to the benefit of all employed in the industries to which they applied, they meticulously refrained from giving this protection directly to the adult male — the citizen *par excellence*. And they did so out of respect for his status as a citizen, on the grounds that enforced protective measures curtailed the civil right to conclude a free contract of employment. Protection was confined to women and children, and champions of women's rights were quick to detect the implied insult. Women were protected because they were not citizens. If they wished to enjoy full and responsible citizenship, they must forgo protection. By the end of the nineteenth century such arguments had become obsolete, and the factory code had become one of the pillars in the edifice of social rights. ...

A new period opened at the end of the nineteenth century, conveniently marked by Booth's Survey of Life and Labour of the People in London and the Royal Commission on the Aged Poor. It saw the first big advance in social rights, and this involved significant changes in the egalitarian principle as expressed in citizenship. But there were other forces at work as well. A rise of money incomes unevenly distributed over the social classes altered the economic distance which separated these classes from one another, diminishing the gap between skilled and unskilled labour and between skilled labour and non-manual workers, while the steady increase in small savings blurred the class distinction between the capitalist and the propertyless proletarian. Secondly, a system of direct taxation, ever more steeply graduated, compressed the whole scale of disposable incomes. Thirdly, mass production for the home market and a growing interest on the part of industry in the needs and tastes of the common people enabled the less well-to-do to enjoy a material civilisation which differed less markedly in equality from that of the rich than it had ever done before. All this profoundly altered the setting in which the progress of citizenship took place. Social integration spread from the sphere of sentiment and patriotism into that of material enjoyment. The components of a civilised and cultured life, formerly the monopoly of the few, were brought progressively within reach of the many, who were encouraged thereby to stretch out their hands towards those that still eluded their grasp. The diminution of inequality strengthened the demand for its abolition, at least with regard to the essentials of social welfare.

These aspirations have in part been met by incorporating social rights in the status of citizenship and thus creating a universal right to real income which is not proportionate to the market value of the claimant. ...

The extension of the social services is not primarily a means of equalising incomes. In some cases it may, in others it may not. The question is relatively unimportant; it belongs to a different department of social policy. What matters is that there is a general enrichment of the concrete substance of civilised life, a general reduction of risk and insecurity, an equalisation between the more and the less fortunate at all levels — between the healthy and the sick, the employed and the unemployed, the old and the active, the bachelor and the father of a large family. Equalisation is not so much between classes as between individuals within a population which is now treated for this purpose as though it were one class. Equality of status is more important than equality of income.

Even when benefits are paid in cash, this class fusion is outwardly expressed in the form of a new common experience. All learn what it means to have an insurance card that must be regularly stamped (by somebody), or to collect children's allowances or pensions from the post office. ...

In the second phase of our educational history, which began in 1902, the educational ladder was officially accepted as an important, though still small, part of the system. But the balance between collective and individual rights remained much the same. The State decided what it could afford to spend on free secondary and higher education, and the children competed for the limited number of places provided. There was no pretence that all who could benefit from more advanced education would get it, and there was no recognition of any absolute natural right to be educated according to one's capacities. But in the third phase, which started in 1944, individual rights have ostensibly been given priority. Competition for scarce places is to be replaced by selection and distribution into appropriate places, sufficient in number to accommodate all, at least at the secondary school level. In the Act of 1944 there is a passage which says that the supply of secondary schools will not be considered adequate unless they 'afford for all pupils opportunities for education offering such variety of instruction and training as may be desirable in view of their different ages, abilities and aptitudes.' Respect for individual rights could hardly be more strongly expressed. Yet I wonder whether it will work out like that in practice. ...

I have tried to show how citizenship, and other forces outside it, have been altering the pattern of social inequality. To complete the picture I ought now to survey the results as a whole on the structure of social class. They have undoubtedly been profound, and it may be that the inequalities permitted, and even moulded, by citizenship do not any longer constitute class distinctions in the sense in which that term is used of past societies. ...

We have to look for the combined effects of three factors. First, the compression, at both ends, of the scale of income distribution. Second, the great extension of the area of common culture and common experience. And third, the enrichment of the universal status of citizenship, combined with the recognition and stabilisation of certain status differences chiefly through the linked systems of education and occupation. The first two have made the third possible. Status differences can receive the stamp of legitimacy in terms of democratic citizenship provided they do not cut too deep, but occur within a population united in a single civilisation; and provided they are not an expression of hereditary privilege. This means that inequalities can be tolerated within a fundamentally egalitarian society provided they are not dynamic, that is to say that they do not create incentives which spring from dissatisfaction and the feeling that 'this kind of life is not good enough for me', or 'I am determined that my son shall be spared what I had to put up with.' ...

We are not aiming at absolute equality. There are limits inherent in the egalitarian movement. But the movement is a double one. It operates partly through citizenship and partly through the economic system. In both cases the aim is to remove inequalities which cannot be regarded as legitimate, but the standard of legitimacy is different. In the former it is the standard of social justice, in the latter it is social justice combined with economic necessity. It is possible, therefore, that the inequalities permitted by the two halves of the movement will not coincide. Class distinctions may survive which have no appropriate economic function, and economic differences which do not correspond with accepted class distinctions. ...

The unified civilisation which makes social inequalities acceptable, and threatens to make them economically functionless, is achieved by a progressive divorce between real and money incomes. This is, of course, explicit in the major social services, such as health and education, which give benefits in kind without any *ad hoc* payment. In scholarships and legal aid, prices scaled to money incomes keep real income relatively constant, in so far as it is affected by these particular needs. Rent restriction, combined with security of tenure, achieves a similar result by different means. So, in varying degrees, do rationing, food subsidies, utility goods and price controls. The advantages obtained by having a larger money income do not disappear, but they are confined to a limited area of consumption. ...

ARE WOMEN FULL CITIZENS OF THE WELFARE STATE?

Carole Pateman

In the story of the creation of civil society through an original agreement, women are brought into the new social order as inhabitants of a private sphere that is part of civil society and yet is separated from the public world of freedom and equality, rights, contract, interests and citizenship. Women, that is to say, are incorporated into the civil order differently from men. But women's inclusion within the private sphere is not the whole story. Women have never been completely excluded from participation in the institutions of the public world — but women have been incorporated into public life in a different manner from men. Women's bodies symbolize everything opposed to political order, and yet the long and often bitterly contested process through which women have been included as citizens has been structured around women's bodily (sexual) differences from men. Women have been included as 'women'; that is, as beings whose sexual embodiment prevents them enjoying the same political standing as men. Women's political position, before and since we have won citizenship, is full of paradoxes, contradictions and ironies, but both women's exclusion from the public world and the manner of our inclusion have escaped the notice of political theorists. ...

Democratic theorists have concentrated on the link between men's participation in the workplace and their wider political participation. They have had nothing to say about men's position as husbands or breadwinners and how that is connected to their citizenship — or to women's citizenship. The terms of the fraternal pact and the patriarchal criteria for participation in the public world have been embodied in the structure of the workplace and in the structure of the state. Women are now citizens, but the continuing uncertainties and paradoxes of our citizenship have been illustrated in the large body of empirical and theoretical research by feminist scholars into the welfare state. Political theorists still manage to write on the 'normative justification' of democratic citizenship in the welfare state without taking any account of women, the 'feminization of poverty' or feminist arguments. They are still silent about women's indirect constitution as citizens of the welfare state as men's (workers') dependents, and about the fact that women have not been called upon to make the same 'contribution' to the welfare state as men.

Men's 'contribution' derives from their construction as free and equal 'individuals'. As 'individuals' all men are owners, in that they all own the property in their persons and capacities over which they alone have right of jurisdiction; they are self-governing. Work and citizenship come together around the criterion of ownership. A 'worker' is a man who contracts out a specific piece of the property in his person, namely his labour power, and, as owners, all men are able to be incorporated on the same

Source: Pateman, C. (1989) *The Disorder of Women: Democracy, Feminism and Political Theory*, Cambridge, Polity Press, pp.5, 9-10, 183-97.

footing as citizens of the welfare state. One of the main arguments advanced by democratic theorists in defence of the welfare state is that all 'individuals' (workers) make a 'contribution' that allows them to be 'insured' against times when they are unable to participate in the labour market. Thus the welfare state provides the resources that (in principle) enable all men to enjoy their citizenship, even if their material circumstances are impoverished through, say, unemployment. All men are thus entitled by right of citizenship to the resources that enable the equal worth or equal enjoyment of their citizenship to be maintained.

The attack from the right on public provision of resources over the past decade has brought renewed interest in political theory in arguments justifying citizenship in the welfare state. But neither these discussions nor radical democratic theory pays attention to the question of women and self-ownership or to women's 'contribution' to the welfare state. The 'contribution' exacted from women by the state has reflected the political significance given to sexual difference. In the case of the welfare state, as I argue in 'The Patriarchal Welfare State', the irony is that women have been required to contribute welfare. The welfare in question is the private, unpaid 'welfare' provided by women in their homes for the young, the aged, the sick and infirm, and for their husbands. More generally, the demands made upon women by the state have always taken a form suited to those held to have their own private tasks and whose status as citizens is thus ambiguous and contradictory. Women's 'contribution' is not seen as part of, or as relevant to, their citizenship, but as a necessary part of the private tasks proper to their sex. Political theorists have not pondered about this state of affairs, even though the complex question of the demands placed upon women and the paradoxes surrounding their public standing is of considerable importance for a problem central to political theory: the issue of what, if any, political obligation is owed to the state by citizens. ...

Women have now won the formal status of citizens, and their contemporary social position may seem a long way removed from that prescribed by Hegel. But Hegel's theory is still very relevant to the problem of patriarchy and the welfare state, although most contemporary political theorists usually look only at the relation between civil society and the state, or the intervention that the public power (state) may make in the private sphere (economy or class system). This view of 'public' and 'private' assumes that two of Hegel's categories (civil society and state) can be understood in the absence of the third (family). Yet Hegel's theory presupposes that family/civil society/state are comprehensible only in *relation* to each other — and then civil society and the state become 'public' in contrast to the 'private' family.

Hegel's social order contains a double separation of the private and public: the *class* division between civil society and the state (between economic man and citizen, between private enterprise and the public power); and the *patriarchal* separation between the private family and the public world of civil society/state. Moreover, the public character of the sphere of civil society/state is constructed and gains its meaning through what it excludes — the private association of the family. The patriarchal division between public and private *is also a sexual division.* Women, naturally lacking the capacities for public participation, remain within an association constituted by love, ties of blood, natural subjection and particularity, and in which they are governed by men. The public world of universal citizenship is an association of free and equal individuals, a sphere of property, rights and contract — and of men, who interact as formally equal citizens. ...

The exiles from society who need the welfare state to give moral worth to their citizenship are male workers. Hegel showed deep insight here. Paid employment has become the key to citizenship, and the recognition of an individual as a citizen of equal worth to other citizens is lacking when a worker is unemployed. The history of the welfare state and citizenship (and the manner in which they have been theorized) is bound up with the history of the development of 'employment societies'. In the early part of the nineteenth century, most workers were still not fully incorporated into the labour market; they typically worked at a variety of occupations, worked on a seasonal basis, gained part of their subsistence outside the capitalist market and enjoyed 'Saint Monday'. By the 1880s full employment had become an ideal, unemployment a major social issue, and loud demands were heard for state-supported social reform (and arguments were made against state action to promote welfare). But who was included under the banner of 'full employment'? What was the status of those 'natural' social exiles seen as properly having no part in the employment society? Despite many changes in the social standing of women, we are not so far as we might like to think from Hegel's statement that the husband, as head, 'has the prerogative to go out and work for [the family's] living, to attend to its needs, and to control and administer its capital.'

The political significance of the sexual division of labour is ignored by most democratic theorists. They treat the public world of paid employment and citizenship as if it can be divorced from its connection with the private sphere, and so the masculine character of the public sphere has been repressed. For example, T.H. Marshall first presented his influential account of citizenship in 1949, at the height of the optimism in Britain about the contribution of the new welfare state policies to social change — but also at the time (as I shall show) when women were being confirmed as lesser citizens in the welfare state. ...

As the governor of a family, a man is also a 'breadwinner'. He has the capacity to sell his labour-power as a worker, or to buy labour-power with his capital, and provide for his wife and family. His wife is thus 'protected'. The category of 'breadwinner' presupposes that wives are constituted as economic dependents or 'housewives', which places them in a subordinate position. The dichotomy breadwinner/housewife, and the masculine meaning of independence were established in Britain by the middle of the last century; in the early period of capitalist development, women (and children) were wage-labourers. A 'worker' became a man who has an economically dependent wife to take care of his daily needs and look after his home and children. Moreover, 'class', too, is constructed as a patriarchal category. 'The working class' is the class of working *men*, who are also full citizens in the welfare state.

This observation brings me back to Marshall's statement about the universal, civil right to 'work', that is, to paid employment. The democratic implications of the right to work cannot be understood without attention to the connections between the public world of 'work' and citizenship and the private world of conjugal relations. What it means to be a 'worker' depends in part on men's status and power as husbands, and on their standing as citizens in the welfare state. The construction of the male worker as 'breadwinner' and his wife as his 'dependent' was expressed officially in the Census classifications in Britain and Australia. In the British Census of 1851, women engaged in unpaid domestic work were 'placed ... in one of the productive classes along with paid work of a similar kind.' This classification changed after 1871, and by 1911 unpaid housewives had been completely removed from the economically active population. In Australia an initial conflict over the categories of classification was resolved in 1890 when the scheme devised in New South Wales was adopted. The Australians divided up the population more decisively than the British, and the 1891 Census was based on the two categories of 'breadwinner' and 'dependent'. Unless explicitly stated otherwise, women's occupation was classified as domestic, and domestic workers are put in the dependent category.

The position of men as breadwinner-workers has been built into the welfare state. The sexual divisions in the welfare state have received much less attention than the persistence of the old dichotomy between the deserving and undeserving poor, which predates the welfare state. This is particularly clear in the United States, where a sharp separation is maintained between 'social security', or welfare-state policies directed at 'deserving workers who have paid for them through 'contributions' over their working lifetimes', and 'welfare' — seen as public 'handouts' to 'barely deserving poor people'. Although 'welfare' does not have this stark meaning in Britain or Australia, where the welfare state encompasses much more than most Americans seem able to envisage, the old distinction between the deserving and undeserving poor is still alive and kicking, illustrated by the popular bogey-figures of the 'scrounger' (Britain) and the 'dole-bludger' (Australia). However, although the dichotomy of deserving/undeserving poor overlaps with the divisions between husband/wife and worker/housewife to some extent, it also obscures the patriarchal structure of the welfare state. ...

Although so many women, including married women, are now in paid employment, women's standing as 'workers' is still of precarious legitimacy. So, therefore, is their standing as democratic citizens. If an individual can gain recognition from other citizens as an equally worthy citizen only through participation in the capitalist market, if self-respect and respect as a citizen are 'achieved' in the public world of the employment society, then women still lack the means to be recognized as worthy citizens. Nor have the policies of the welfare state provided women with many of the resources to gain respect as citizens. Marshall's social rights of citizenship in the welfare state could be extended to men without difficulty. As participants in the market, men could be seen as making a public contribution, and were in a position to be levied by the state to make a contribution more directly, that *entitled* them to the benefits of the welfare state. But how could women, dependents of men, whose legitimate 'work' is held to be located in the private sphere, be citizens of the welfare state? What could, or did, women contribute? The paradoxical answer is that women contributed — welfare.

The development of the welfare state has presupposed that certain aspects of welfare could and should continue to be provided by women (wives) in the home, and not primarily through public provision. The 'work' of a housewife can include the care of an invalid husband and elderly, perhaps infirm, relatives. ...

In the 1980s the large changes in women's social position, technological and structural transformations within capitalism, and mass unemployment mean that much of the basis for the breadwinner/dependent dichotomy and for the employment society itself is being eroded (although both are still widely seen as social ideals). The social context of Hegel's two dilemmas is disappearing. As the current concern about the 'feminization of poverty' reveals, there is now a very visible underclass of women who are directly connected to the state as claimants, rather than indirectly as men's dependents. Their social exile is as apparent as that of poor male workers was to Hegel. Social change has now made it much harder to gloss over the paradoxes and contradictions of women's status as citizens.

However, the question of how women might become full citizens of a democratic welfare state is more complex than may appear at first sight, because it is only in the current wave of the organized feminist movement that the division between the private and public spheres of social life has become seen as a major *political* problem. From the 1860s to the 1960s women were active in the public sphere: women fought, not only for welfare measures and for measures to secure the private and public safety of women and girls, but for the vote and civil equality; middle-class women fought for entry into higher education, and the professions and women trade unionists fought for decent working conditions and wages and maternity leave. But the contemporary liberal-feminist view, particularly prominent in the United States, that what is required above all is 'gender-neutral' laws and policies, was not widely shared. In general, until the 1960s the focus of attention in the welfare state was on measures to ensure that women had proper social support, and hence proper social respect, in carrying out their responsibilities in the private sphere. The problem is whether and how such measures could assist women in their fight for full citizenship. In 1942 in Britain, for example, many women welcomed the passage in the Beveridge Report that I have cited because, it was argued, it gave official recognition to the value of women's unpaid work. However, an official nod of recognition to women's work as 'vital' to 'the nation' is easily given; *in practice,* the value of the work in bringing women into full membership in the welfare state was negligible. The equal worth of citizenship and the respect of fellow citizens still depended on participation as paid employees. 'Citizenship' and 'work' stood then and still stand opposed to 'women'.

The extremely difficult problem faced by women in their attempt to win full citizenship I shall call 'Wollstonecraft's dilemma'. The dilemma is that the two routes toward citizenship that women have pursued are mutually incompatible within the confines of the patriarchal welfare state, and, within that context, they are impossible to achieve. For three centuries, since universal citizenship first appeared as a political ideal, women have continued to challenge their alleged natural subordination within private life. From at least the 1790s they have also struggled with the task of trying to become citizens within an ideal and practice that have gained universal meaning through their exclusion. Women's response has been complex. On the one hand, they have demanded that the ideal of citizenship be extended to them, and the liberal-feminist agenda for a 'gender-neutral' social world is the logical conclusion of one form of this demand. On the other hand, women have also insisted, often simultaneously, as did Mary Wollstonecraft, that *as women* they have specific capacities, talents, needs and concerns, so that the expression of their citizenship will be differentiated from that of men. Their unpaid work providing welfare could be seen, as Wollstonecraft saw women's tasks as mothers, as women's work *as citizens,* just as their husbands' paid work is central to men's citizenship.

CHAPTER 5 FORDISM AND MODERN INDUSTRY

John Allen

CONTENTS

1   INTRODUCTION

If the emergence of a modern industrial economy can be epitomized by the rise of factory production and a factory workforce, its characteristic image must surely be that of the giant industrial workplace in which car after car, or other consumer durable, is turned out on a seemingly endless assembly production line. A sea of men in blue overalls pouring through factory gates at the sound of a hooter that marks the end of the working day, or mass, open-air union meetings attended by men with raised hands are all part of this dominant imagery. The period in question is post-1945 rather than the nineteenth century, and the typical form of industry can be summed up under the heading of *large-scale, mass production.*

As a process, mass production can be traced back to the volume production of goods such as (Singer) sewing machines and bicycles at the end of the nineteenth century, but the real development of mass production began with the combination of moving assembly lines, specialized machinery, high wages, and low cost products at the Ford Motor Company between 1913 and 1914. Henry Ford's heyday was the 'Model T' era in which car production at the Ford Motor plant soared from three hundred thousand in 1914 to more than two million in 1923, but the industrial era which he initiated and which subsequently became known as 'Fordism' is best described as a post-war affair. If large-scale, mass production is one specific form of modern industry, its zenith was reached after the Second World War across a range of industrial economies. After a brief look at Henry Ford's development of mass production methods, the rest of the chapter takes this post-war moment of 'Fordism' as its central focus.

As you work your way through this chapter, you should bear in mind that the use of the term 'Fordism' to depict an industrial era is a highly contentious issue. The very idea that the term 'Fordism' helps us to understand the dynamics of the long post-war boom is deeply contested. For some, the concept of 'Fordism' captures all things modern about an economy: it is associated with scale, progress, science, control, technology, rationality, including the sea of disciplined workers that poured through the factory gates each working day. More than this, the concept of Fordism has been held up as a symbol of a new kind of society, indeed as a modernizing discourse: one that involves a new type of worker, a different kind of life-style, and a specific form of state and civil society.

For others, it is precisely the sweeping nature of such claims that irritates. The use of the term 'Fordism' to make sense of the rather complex set of events and circumstances that lie behind the long post-war economic boom is regarded as at best misleading, at worst a gross caricature. Mass production has performed an important role in post-war economic history, but the conceptual leap from mass production to 'Fordism', taking in mass consumption and the mass worker along the way, is said to offer a reductive image. It obscures more than it reveals. It obscures the varied organization of manufacture across different modern economies, the diversity of markets, the different types of labour and work, as well as simplifying post-war political developments in the advanced economies. In short, Fordism is rhetoric: it is part of a discourse of industry that sets out a powerful but misleading image of what a modern economy looks like in the second half of the twentieth century.

In this chapter, we are going to explore these claims, and in particular some of the *economic* implications that are entailed by the concept of Fordism. One of the initial aims of the chapter is to spell out what it is about Ford and Fordism that has generated such disagreement and caught the imagination of many. Section 2 looks at this issue and explores the relative importance of the mass production industries in the post-war period. A major concern of this section is to examine the claim that Fordist industries performed some kind of 'lead' role or established an economic 'dominance' in the post-war industrial economies. What does it mean to say that an economy is Fordist? Is there some kind of checklist of features involved which, if present, add up to an economy organized along Fordist lines? Or does the concept of Fordism draw its explanatory power from its ability to highlight the structural connections that shape an economy?

Section 3 extends this assessment of Fordism by widening the topic of enquiry to include an evaluation of the role of services in a modern economy. Fordism as usually understood is taken to represent a modern *manufacturing* economy. Growth and modern industry are invariably taken to be synonymous with a thriving manufacturing sector. What interests us in Section 3 is why a modern economy should be regarded as manufacturing based. What kind of economic discourse is in play which suggests that only certain kinds of economic activity generate growth and represent real wealth? Why are services usually represented in modern economies as unproductive or frequently seen as a poor form of economic progress?

Finally, in Section 4, the chapter concludes with a summary of the arguments explored and also a brief consideration of the implications that an era of increased global interdependence may have for the pattern of growth in modern, national economies. But first let's consider Henry's part in all this.

2 FORD, FORDISM AND MODERN INDUSTRY

The name of Henry Ford is synonymous with the advent of the moving assembly line and mass production. The name conveys a sense of technological progress as well as a model of how manufacturing production is or should be organized. In contrast with the early stages of industrialization, Ford*ism* is conceived as an era of mass, standardized goods produced for mass markets, created by an interventionist state which gave people the spending power to make mass consumption possible. The two, however, are linked by a particular history.

2.1 FORD AND MASS PRODUCTION

In the Introduction, it was noted in passing that mass production began with the combination of:

1   moving assembly lines;
2   specialized machinery;
3   high wages; and
4   low-cost products.

The stress here should be placed upon the term *combination*, for it was the manner in which these elements were brought together at Ford's Highland Park factory in Detroit between 1913 and 1914 which gave rise to the *system of mass production*. It was this combination of elements that lay behind the shift from craft to mass production. We shall take a closer look at these elements before considering the system as a whole.

First, let's consider the development of the moving assembly line and specialized machinery. Before the opening of the Highland Park factory in 1910, Henry Ford had already put into place one of the keystones of assembly-line production at the company's Piquette and Bellevue plants: the interchangeability of parts. Although much of the production at Ford's early plants was craft-based, Ford and a handful of skilled mechanics had already designed and developed fixtures, jigs and gauges with which unskilled workers could turn out uniform parts. Special- or single-purpose machine tools followed, as did the practice of arranging the flow of materials to follow the sequence of operations. Hounshell (1984) has shown how these innovations drew upon and extended earlier attempts to attain a high volume of production of interchangeable parts, first in the American firearms industry and then in the manufacture of sewing machines, agricultural machinery and bicycles. By 1913, Ford's refinements to the American process of repetition manufacture had laid the foundation upon which the technique of continuous-flow or assembly-line production rests: the standardization and simplification of the product, the use of special-purpose equipment together with the interchangeability of parts, and the reduction of skilled labour. All that remained was to connect these elements together through the introduction of the moving assembly line.

ACTIVITY 1   Now turn to **Reading A, 'Ford and mass production'**, by David Hounshell, which you will find at the end of this chapter. This extract provides an insight into the development of the first moving assembly lines at Ford's Highland Park plant.

One of the most interesting aspects is the way in which the development of the moving assembly line took an incremental and experimental form. Refinement and adjustment, attention to detail, flexibility, were all part of the innovative process. Also of interest are the differences that Hounshell highlights between the approaches of Frederick W. Taylor and Henry Ford to the *relationship* between labour and machinery. The ideas of Taylor will be considered in greater detail in Chapter 7, but for the moment I would like you to pull out the main differences in their approach to that relationship.

One of the clearest differences that I noted between the approaches of Taylor and Ford was that whereas Taylor sought to organize labour around machinery, Ford sought to eliminate labour by machinery. Where Taylor took for granted the existing level of technology and sought greater efficiency from workers through the reorganization of work, Ford and his mechanics used technology to mechanize the work process. A second difference concerns the pace of work, which, for Taylor, was set by the workers themselves or the supervisors, whereas for Ford it was set by the machinery, the speed of the assembly line. Despite these radical differences, however, this new technology led to similar consequences for the modern workforce: fragmentation of tasks and a more detailed division of labour. With the introduction of fixed-speed, moving assembly lines, tasks were broken down and simplified

The first moving assembly line at Ford's Highland Park Factory, 1913

further, removing previous skill requirements for the job. Such benefits achieved by the company from gaining greater control over the production process were not without their disbenefits however. The most serious, as Hounshell points out, was the rapid increase in the turnover rate of labour, growing absenteeism and broad dissatisfaction with work at the Ford plant. Yet, paradoxically, it was the growth in labour unrest on the shop floor that led to the introduction of the third element which was to give rise to the system of mass production, namely the payment of high wages or the 'Five-Dollar Day' policy.

The high wage system which became known as the 'Five-Dollar Day' effectively doubled the earnings of Ford workers (or rather those workers who qualified for the profit-sharing scheme if their private lives met the standards laid down by Ford's new Sociological Department). The impact on absenteeism, labour turnover and labour productivity was dramatic: profits soared as absenteeism and turnover stabilized and productivity leapt. Ford's Five-Dollar Day had in effect laid the basis for a new contractual system whereby workers stayed 'on the line' in return for high wages paid for by the dramatic increases in labour productivity. A new 'mass worker' had been created — highly paid and unskilled — to accompany the introduction of the new mass technology.

The fourth and final element in the system of mass production, a low-price strategy, is perhaps the most understated feature of Ford's system of manufacture. Unlike most of his contemporaries, Ford recognized that there was an enormous demand in the US at that time for cheap, basic, reliable cars. Where companies like Singer had dominated the US sewing-machine market in the 1870s and 1880s by producing quality products at a high price, Ford sought to manufacture *low*-priced cars and to use a strategy of successive price reductions to boost demand further. Ford's Model T, a robust car, easy to repair and available in 'any colour as long as it was black', sold in unprecedented numbers at a price well below that of its industrial competitors. Thus, alongside mass technology and the mass worker, the growth of mass markets represented the sum of Ford's *system* of mass production or modern manufacture.

Prior to Ford's technical innovations, the factory system of manufacture was based largely upon the division of the production process into a number of tasks which varied in terms of the degree of skill required. Thus, each worker would perform a specialized task within the factory, drawing upon their own craft skills to manufacture the required part of the overall product. (See Book 1 (Hall and Gieben, 1992), Chapter 4, for discussion of this type of low-technology production.) What broadly distinguished modern manufacture from the factory system was primarily those aspects of Ford's approach to manufacture that were identified in the discussion of Reading A, namely:

- the introduction of machinery to eliminate labour and skills;
- the introduction of machinery to wrest control from labour over the nature and pace of work.

Ford's giant River Rouge plant

In many ways it is the moving assembly line, accompanied by a high degree of specialization among workers and standardization of products, that symbolizes this shift to modern industry. But modern industry is not only characterized by technical innovations; the social innovations introduced by Ford — the high pay, the enforced labour discipline, and the attempt to cater for a mass market by continually dropping prices — are all part of what we take to be the fabric of modern industry.

By the early 1920s, the Model T had captured 55 per cent of the US car market, brought about in part by the economies of scale reaped through large-scale mass production at Ford's new River Rouge plant. A massive complex with its own deep water port and railway, the plant was designed as a fully integrated manufacturing operation from steelmaking through to final assembly, employing tens of thousands of workers. With high fixed costs in plant and machinery, Ford's efficiency was achieved by high volume production which reduced the cost per car as output rose. As a giant industrial workplace it looked capable of satisfying the demands of an expanding mass market and, in terms of economic efficiency, it had all the hallmarks of competitive advantage. The operation was widely admired and the diffusion of Fordism as an industrial model looked set to occur.

2.2 FORDISM AS AN INDUSTRIAL ERA

In the years that followed Ford's successful market performance in the 1920s, the methods of mass production were borrowed liberally by US firms in housing, furniture and other consumer goods industries. As Hounshell points out, Ford was neither slow nor reticent to bring his economic innovations to the attention of US manufacturing industry. In particular, the mass production technology was quickly seized upon as a recipe for economic growth. However, the economic Depression of the 1930s across the industrial economies was soon to remove the gloss from Ford's ideas and methods. Alongside mass production, a different kind of mass phenomenon was about to arise: mass unemployment. Cyclical crises and recurrent disruptions in economic production as a result of the time-lags between effective demand and productive investment were a known feature of industrial economies. But the coupling of mass production and mass unemployment was a new experience — especially for those workers laid off by Ford and other car manufacturers in the Detroit area. The limited consumption levels of the mass of the population on the one hand and the sharp increase in the productivity growth of industry on the other had brought about what many considered to be a crisis in the very functioning of capitalism itself. President Roosevelt's New Deal staved off the US crisis, but it was not until after the Second World War that this mismatch between the amount of goods produced and the effective ability of the population to consume them was to be resolved in any general way. What became known as a crisis of 'underconsumption' was about to give way to what others have termed 'Fordist' growth.

Fordist growth — that is, a mode of economic growth based upon a system of mass production and sustained by mass markets — is widely regarded as a feature of the US, UK and other European economies in the 1950s and 1960s. Such growth, it is argued, was fostered by what Chapter 2 referred to as 'managed capitalism', an institutional arrangement which owed much to the experience of state wartime mobilization and large-scale planning. It was this experience which enabled governments confidently to take an ever-increasing role in the regulation and direction of their national economies. In the UK, for example, Keynesian demand management policies (over levels of taxation, interest rates, and public expenditure) and the introduction of welfare payment systems helped to raise the spending power of the mass of the population to within a level capable of sustaining mass markets. In other modern industrial economies, the actual political forms of intervention by national governments in the regulation of their economies varied widely, although the outcome — in terms of the promotion of mass markets — is said to have varied less. The *bulk* of the additional spending power however was considered to be a direct result of real wages rising at an unprecedented rate in the industrial economies, broadly in line with the sustained growth in productivity. With the formation of mass markets across much of the industrialized world, a stable link between mass consumption and mass production was considered to be firmly in place. And it was this connection, this match between mass production and mass consumption, that was taken to be one of the hallmarks of the modern industrial era. However, of equal importance was the Depression of the inter-war period and the severe onslaught by employers and governments on labour movements in the late 1940s which, many now argue, cleared the way for the introduction of the new type of work discipline and economic trade-offs between high wages and high productivity that an economy organized along Fordist lines entailed.

We shall examine some of the general features of this Fordist era, especially the notion of a Fordist mode of growth. Before we do so, however, it is worth spelling out precisely what those general features are, primarily to avoid any potential misunderstandings over the sense in which I intend to use the term 'Fordism'.

Sayer (1989) has helpfully provided four different meanings attached to the term.

1   Fordism as a *labour process* involving moving assembly line mass production.

This refers to the tasks and technologies that should be familiar to you from the above account of the labour process developed by Ford at the Highland Park plant. A Fordist labour process involves the use of semi-skilled labour performing few tasks at a pace determined by 'the line'. Control over all aspects of production is exercised by management through a hierarchical chain of authority. This aspect of Fordism is explored in greater detail in Chapter 7.

2   Fordist sectors as the *lead growth sectors* capable of transmitting growth to other sectors of an economy.

This refers to the *dominant* role performed by the mass production industries in the post-war period. Such industries, it is argued, take a lead role in an economy because of their ability to *generate* growth. Thus, the car industry may literally be seen as the 'motor' of an economy, setting both the pace and the direction of growth through rising productivity and ascending output levels (achieved through economies of scale). The lead sectors may also *transmit* growth to other sectors through their network of supply relationships. Taking the example of the car industry again, a range of industries from steel, rubber, and glass through to upholstery and electronics, as well as a host of services, are seen to depend upon it, wholly or in part, for their own growth.

The sum total of this growth may be referred to as 'Fordist' growth.

3   Fordist organization as *hegemonic*.

The term 'hegemonic' refers to the pervasive influence of Fordist ways of organizing production, work, and labour. It can be considered as another aspect of a sector's *dominance*, although in this instance the criterion by which the influence of the mass production sector is measured concerns the *extent* of that influence. If, for example, a range of industries outside of the mass production sector are seen to adopt, say, collective bargaining procedures, contracts on a rate-for-the-job basis, management hierarchies which leave little discretion to the workforce, or the technical innovations of mass production, then the Fordist influence may be regarded as widespread throughout the economy.

4   Fordism as a *mode of regulation.*

In this sense of Fordism, the term 'regulation' refers to more than the labour process or the lead sectors of growth in an economy, and moves beyond the strictly economic to include both political and cultural considerations. We have already noted some of the more central political considerations, in particular the kind of policy interventions made by national governments in their attempts to balance mass production and mass consumption, and thus underpin long-term growth. Indeed, it could be said that *all* modes of regulation, of which there are a considerable variety, are geared towards the regulation of a particular pattern of growth, in this case Fordist growth. Thus, the continuation of Fordism as a pattern of growth can be considered to be as dependent upon self-regulation by organized labour and leading industrial enterprises as it is dependent upon the state to secure a balance between profit and wage levels so that mass purchasing power is maintained.

Our concerns in the rest of Section 2 are more narrowly economic, and will address in particular the meanings of Fordism outlined in (2) and (3) above, through an assessment of the relative importance of the mass production industries in modern industrial economies. The coverage will none the less include a consideration of Fordist forms of regulation, as these are regarded as indispensable to an understanding of the character of economic growth in the long post-war boom.

Thus far, we have loosely referred to a Fordist mode of growth as a feature of the advanced industrial economies in the 1950s and 1960s. However, in terms of actual growth rates, a more precise periodization is usually given, starting in the early 1950s, and tailing off in the early 1970s around the time of the 'oil crisis' of 1973 and the economic downturn of 1974. If we look back at that period, it is difficult not to be impressed by the sheer scale and pace of growth across the economies of Europe and the US, as well as that of Japan. Industrial output across the advanced economies virtually trebled between 1950 and 1973, with more produced in this period than in the whole of the previous seventy-five years — itself a period of not inconsiderable growth, especially in the late nineteenth century (Armstrong *et al.,* 1991, p.117). Also, in terms of the quality of life, the development and availability of a whole string of consumer goods — from washing machines, vacuum cleaners, fridges, cars, to colour TVs — represented a real leap in living standards for a large part of the working population. Judged in either quantitative or qualitative terms, the pattern of post-war growth in the 1950s and 1960s can only be described as phenomenal. While it would be wrong to suggest that everybody in the industrial nations benefited from this development or indeed benefited equally, or to suggest that everyone was content with the direction of change towards standardized, mass consumer durables, none the less in aggregate output terms this pattern

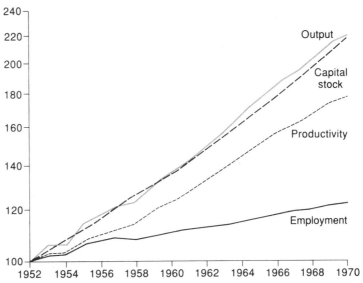

Figure 5.1   Output, capital stock, productivity, and employment in
the advanced industrial economies, 1952–70 (index numbers,
1952=100, log scale)

Source: Armstrong *et al.*, 1991, p.118

of growth was taken to be a clear sign of modernist progress. The
question we need to ask now is, what makes this pattern of growth
distinctively Fordist?

Armstrong *et al.* (1991) provide a framework within which we can
pursue this question. Figure 5.1. lays out the context.

A wealth of information is presented in Figure 5.1, but the main point of
interest to note is the contrast between output growth and employment
growth over the period. As you can see, the increase in output is far
higher than the growth in employment, which suggests that output per
person, the productivity rate within industry, grew rapidly in the 1950s
and 1960s (as Figure 5.1 also indicates). This growth in productivity
could conceivably have stemmed from people working longer hours, but
as the length of the 'normal' working week declined during this period,
the most likely factor behind the shift in productivity was the sharp rise
in the amount of machinery and plant (as measured by capital stock) at
the workplace. If you look again at Figure 5.1, you will note that the
amount of capital stock at the workplace more than doubled in the
1950s and 1960s, giving the impression that 'each worker was
confronted by two machines where one had stood before' (Armstrong *et
al.*, 1991, p.119). However, the change in the *type* of machinery that
confronted workers was just as important as (or even more important
than) the multiplication of machinery. Increased mechanization of
industrial production, in particular the forced pace of production, is
singled out by Armstrong and his co-authors as one of the main causes
of the rapid growth in productivity, along with changes in both work
practices and the design of jobs. So, in both quantitative and qualitative

terms, the new production technologies and their embodiment in new machinery lay behind the post-war boom in production. But, to restate the main question, how far was this pattern of rapid growth actually tied to Fordist production?

Certainly the car industry, that icon of Fordist production, was at the hub of post-war growth. Motor vehicle production rose dramatically in the 1950s across all the advanced industrial economies. In the UK, France and Germany, annual average production went way above the million mark for the first time, while in the US it topped seven million. By the second half of the 1960s, annual average car production in Japan had risen to above four million from a low base in the 1950s; vehicle output in France, Germany and Italy had more than doubled; and in the UK car industry production reached its highest post-war figure of just over two million per year (Lee, 1986). Other industries geared directly to consumer durables, especially those concerned with the mass production of electrical goods, were at the forefront of post-war growth trends. Indeed, those industries involved in the production of complex standardized goods excelled as a result of the introduction of mass production techniques. But they were not alone.

Clearly those industries geared to the mass consumption of consumer durables were among the high growth sectors in the post-war period, but the performance of other industries — notably those in the capital and intermediate goods sector which supply and feed into the manufacture of washing machines, cookers, cars and the like, or those, such as chemicals, which do not — also exhibited strong growth rates. Technological advances and the introduction of new machinery were not restricted to the assembly of complex consumer goods, and nor was the pattern of post-war growth simply the result of a boom in consumer durables. None the less — and this is an important observation — technological innovation and economic growth were unduly concentrated upon the manufacture and consumption of such consumer durables. And those who place Fordist production at the heart of the post-war boom would see much of the rest of the economy as *dependent* upon the growth of mass produced consumer goods.

The car industry is also seen to hold a central position in the creation of mass markets and mass production. If real wages had not risen broadly in line with the rate of productivity growth in the 1950s, then (apart from a greater share of profits accruing to industry) production would have outstripped consumption and the industrial economies would have faced another 'underconsumption' crisis similar to that of the 1930s. If we follow Murray (1989), the development of a national system of collective wage bargaining which effectively tied wage rises to rising productivity levels throughout industry in the 1950s and 1960s owed much to the *dominant* role of the car industry within the US and the UK. Although conditions varied between the two countries, the annual pay settlement negotiated by the mass unions within the vehicle industry, the 'going rate' for the year as it were, was regarded as a kind of benchmark for wage settlements in the rest of the economy. As a 'lead' industry, in this case one which had substantial connections with a range of other industries and their workforces through its supplier network, it was in a position to influence the wage pattern for much of the rest of the economy, especially in manufacturing. In wage negotiations with their own managerial bureaucracies, the unionized workers in dependent and other sectors would be guided by the pay settlement agreed in the vehicles sector. And so, it is argued, a predictable pattern of wage increases and a stable pattern of differentials between sectors occurred which, when linked to rising productivity, created the initial conditions for consumer spending to rise in line with increased goods production.

To this we can add a further condition which was also a characteristic of the post-war car industry as well as many other consumer durable industries, namely the domination of national markets by a few large firms. The significance of large firms in this period, apart from their ability to enjoy economies of scale, is usually taken to be their power to regulate the price of their products in domestic markets. The ability to operate oligopolistic markets — that is, markets which are run by a few large-scale enterprises who tend to use marketing ploys such as easy credit facilities or minor design changes (remember the chromework, 'tail-fins', and 'portholes' on the larger American cars in the 1950s?) to distinguish and sell their product rather than compete directly on price terms — can create long periods of price stability. Thus, the regulation of national markets by a few large firms can and arguably did provide another part of the post-war economic framework which enabled prices,

Design detail on a post-war Ford

wages, productivity and investment to sustain one another. Under these conditions Fordist growth would certainly predominate.

We have covered a lot of ground in this sketch, perhaps more economic than historical, in order to bring the conditions that gave rise to Fordism as an industrial era to the fore. As with any historical generalization, we have sacrificed some of the rich detail that brings a period to life and we have been selective in our focus, concentrating on Fordist growth within national economies at the expense of the global economic and political regulatory structures that also enabled Fordist growth to continue. Chapter 2 touched upon some of the structures that lay behind the rapid growth in international trade in the early post-war period, such as the dominance of the US in the field of international finance and the range of institutions and networks that made up the Bretton Woods system, namely the International Monetary Fund, The World Bank and The General Agreement on Tariffs and Trade (GATT). On a broad scale, these arrangements were responsible for the long periods of stability in world trade and investment in the 1950s and 1960s and thus mirrored the stable pattern of growth within national domestic markets.

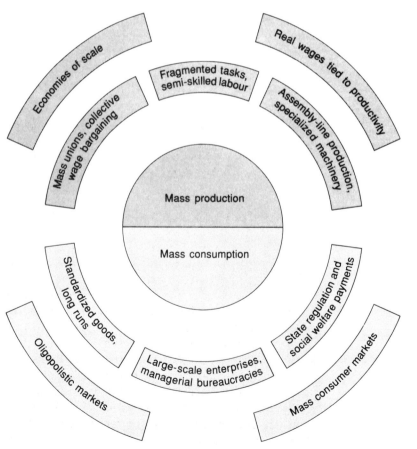

Figure 5.2   Fordism as an industrial era

We shall return to the international dimension in Section 4, but for now it is worth standing back to take stock of the general features of Fordist growth that we have highlighted. Figure 5.2 provides a diagrammatic representation of Fordism as an industrial era.

One of the things that always strikes me about this kind of general representation and, in this case, quite forcibly, is the number of different processes — economic, political, and cultural — that overlap and interact over a relatively short period to give rise to something that we now call Fordism. We have moved a fair way beyond the four elements in Henry Ford's system of mass production — moving assembly lines, specialized machinery, high wages, and low prices. And yet those four elements are clearly part of the preconditions for the emergence of Fordism as an industrial era. Whether or not Fordism as the contingent outcome of many elements and processes was ever as developed or as dominant a post-war model as many now take it to be remains, however, an open question.

2.3 WAS FORDISM EVER DOMINANT?

It is possible to approach this question by considering 'Fordism' as a mode of growth (in Sayer's second and third meanings of the term, outlined in Section 2.2), or, in a broader way, through a consideration of Fordism as a mode of national regulation. In practice, it is not particularly easy to separate the two senses. Having said that, the intention here is initially to separate the two senses of Fordism for analytical purposes and then to bring them together through the work of Jessop (1989).

The first thing that we need to do is to clear some ground. Earlier it was noted that the dominance of Fordist industries could be gauged by their ability to generate and transmit growth in the national economy, as well as influence ways of organizing work and labour. Let us take the issue of growth generation and transmission first.

A judgment that Fordist industries are dominant in an economy does not entail the simple view that mass production has spread throughout industry, or that assembly line production and dedicated machinery are now typical of factory work. On the contrary, mass production industries may represent a small part of the manufacturing sector, in both output and employment terms, yet remain dominant in terms of their ability to stimulate growth in small and medium batch production, especially in those industries that supply inputs to the mass production sector. In this case, 'dominance' is a question of the structural *reach* of large-scale, mass industry; that is, how far it can transmit growth as a *propulsive industry*. Much depends upon the extent to which the mass production sector is integrated with other sectors of an economy. If it is well integrated, other firms — whatever their size — may prosper as suppliers of component parts or raw materials. If the ties are loose then, at the level of the national economy, imports will be sucked in to meet the needs of the Fordist industries and little growth transmission will take place. Indeed, it may be the case that batch production in the capital goods sector (for example, in the mechanical engineering industry) retains a critical national importance and assembly industries remain just that, plants which assemble complex products.

Turning to the second aspect of an industry's dominance, its ability to influence ways of organizing work or labour in its own and other sectors, then the issue *is* one of how widespread those changes are. For example, Tolliday (1986) has drawn attention to the fact that, among British car manufacturers in the inter-war period and beyond, there was extensive adaptation, rather than imitation, of Ford's production methods and labour strategies. Both Austin and Morris combined various aspects of Ford's moving assembly line production with a continued use of labour-intensive methods, and operated piece-work incentive systems rather than a payment system based upon fixed daily rates. More generally, within Europe, even after 1945, few of the major car manufacturers ran plants which closely resembled the highly integrated River Rouge model. Most in fact relied upon operations outside of their plants to sustain their internal production processes (Williams *et al.*, 1987). Indeed, it was the Ford Motor Company itself, through its multinational transplants (at Dagenham and Cologne), which brought about the direct diffusion of Fordist ways of organizing production.

At this *fine* level of detail it is of course possible to show that no other firm or industry provides a perfect imitation of the Fordist model (other than Ford's own multinational transplants). But this type of exercise tends to underestimate just how far Fordist ways of doing things, rather

Fast food as a standardized product

than the whole package, influenced the modern car industry and spread across other industries, such as electrical engineering. And although it is accurate to point out that mass production techniques are best suited to a narrow range of industries concerned with the manufacture of *complex* consumer durables, such as cars and electrical goods (Williams *et al.*, 1987), this observation does not negate the pervasive influence or appeal of the *idea* of large-scale, mass produced, standardized products throughout the post-war period, in areas as diverse as clothing, construction, furniture, food processing, and, in some countries, schools and hospitals (Murray, 1989 and 1991).

You should bear in mind these two aspects of an industry's dominance as we consider the development of Fordism in its broadest sense in two European economies during the post-war period.

ACTIVITY 2   Now turn to **Reading B, 'Fordism in Britain and Germany'**, by Bob Jessop, which looks at the different forms assumed by Fordism in Britain and (West) Germany.

A number of definitional terms are introduced in this extract, but their exact meaning need not concern us here. Rather you should concentrate upon the significant differences that Jessop points to in the development of Fordism in the two economies. In particular, he stresses their distinctive modes of growth and traces the differences to their particular industrial profiles and relationship to the global economy. I would like you to reflect upon the distinct character of each economy for a moment and then to consider the degree to which Fordist industries in either economy could have been characterized as dominant. Jessop's concluding remarks offer a useful starting point. Remember that we are only looking for some general indicators, not a comprehensive assessment.

Clearly Jessop is sympathetic to the heuristic value of the term Fordism as a way of describing the post-war industrial era in Britain and (West) Germany, but what is of particular interest is his willingness to accept considerable national variation in how that Fordist era held together. Take, for example, the issue of mass production.

So far we have referred to the mass production sector primarily in terms of 'lead' consumer industries, high productivity growth, domestic markets, and semi-skilled workers. In the UK, there is some degree of 'fit' between this characterization and the profile of manufacturing industry in the 1950s and 1960s. The consumer goods industries were among the lead growth sectors and the mass worker did indeed have a presence at the workplace. Yet, if we follow Jessop's account, it is apparent that a thorough-going Fordist transformation of industry did not occur in Britain. Industry failed to obtain the productivity levels from mass production techniques that had been secured elsewhere (recall the above reference to British car manufacturers *adapting* rather than imitating Ford's innovations), and one of the consequences of this failure was an increase in the level of imports of mass consumer durables. Thus, in terms of growth generation and indeed growth transmission through linkages to other parts of the economy, it is debatable how far the mass production sector in Britain occupied a dominant role.

In (West) Germany the situation appears to be more clear-cut. The post-war growth of the German economy owed as much if not more to the export-orientated capital goods sector than to the consumer goods sector. Moreover, the dynamism and growth of the capital goods sector was largely attributable to the technologies employed and the use of highly skilled labour rather than to the operation of economies of scale in large firms and the use of a semi-skilled workforce. While it is important not to slip into the simple error of equating all mass production with the manufacture of consumer durables (think for example of the mass production of standard chips in the electronics industry), it is none the less unusual to talk about an export-orientated economy (like the German one), based upon the lead role of the capital goods sector, in strictly Fordist terms. Industries such as iron and steel or mechanical engineering may well perform a propulsive role in an economy, but they are more likely to be characterized by small and medium batch production than by mass production.

If we turn our attention from the issue of growth generation and transmission towards the question of economic influence, then it is possible to see Fordist industries as in some measure hegemonic. In both Britain and (West) Germany, Jessop notes the practice of oligopolistic pricing by large firms (described in Section 2.2), and he points to the formation of institutionalized collective bargaining arrangements which more or less tied real wages to rising productivity levels. What is more, he is prepared to argue that a Fordist wage relation was evident in the UK, despite the relative absence of mass industrial trade unions. Indeed, this is part of Jessop's portrayal of the British post-war economy as one of 'flawed' Fordism.

So perhaps the broadest indication that we have from Jessop of the Fordist character of post-war Britain and Germany has less to do with the nature of modern industry and more to do with the manner in which it is regulated. This focus is certainly consistent with Jessop's concern to show how institutions such as the state attempted to secure and maintain the conditions for stable, Fordist patterns of growth. Although he is very careful to show the varied ways in which the two national governments actually intervened to engineer and sustain rising living standards and a growth profile, it is evident that the common threads of economic management represent a Fordist form of regulation for Jessop. Indeed, other commentators equally sympathetic to the characterization of post-war growth in industrial economies as Fordist go to considerable lengths to show how the forms of state regulation were nationally specific. For example, post-war France is usually characterized as a strong interventionist state concerned with the

regulation of wages and prices; Italy is generally regarded as a state
which was rather late in adopting a strategy of direct intervention;
Germany, as we have seen, is said to have operated a decentralized,
federal system which made it difficult to pursue a strategy of demand
management; the Japanese state is depicted as one which coupled a high
level of public investment in industrial infrastructure with a low level
of social welfare provision, and so on.

If we place this political diversity alongside the industrial diversity that
we have just witnessed in the cases of Britain and (West) Germany, and
consider too Jessop's point about the different ways in which those two
countries are inserted into the global economic order, then we are faced
with a considerable *plurality* of Fordist economies. If the forms assumed
by Fordism across a range of industrial economies in the post-war
period are indeed the contingent outcome of many elements and
processes which come together in specific ways in different countries,
can we legitimately talk about Fordism as an industrial era or refer to
Fordist industries as in any way dominant? Is the general notion of
Fordism too broad, too encompassing, to convey such diversity?

We can start to answer this question by considering what strengths and
weaknesses are attached to Fordism as a broad historical abstraction. On
the plus side, it does point to a remarkable string of general
characteristics that, in different forms, were part and parcel of the long
post-war boom across the industrial economies. Those general
characteristics were set out in Figure 5.2 and indeed act as a *vision* of a
particular industrial era. The articulation of those features through the
concept of Fordism provides a fixed image of an industrial landscape —
with its large manufacturing plants and big industrial cities — which
despite its reductiveness clearly strikes a chord with many. But perhaps
a more important strength of the concept of Fordism, in economic terms
at least, is that it represents *more* than a simple checklist of features on
which to tick-off the extent of Fordist-type development. Implicit within
the concept of Fordism is an evident prioritization of features, with, for
example, collective wage bargaining, oligopolistic markets, economies
of scale, and mass standardized consumer durables each receiving a
high weighting. If few of these features were widespread in a national
economy, then it is unlikely that we would refer to it or describe it as
Fordist. The point however is not simply that a range of prioritized
features should appear for the first time in one place; rather, it concerns
the presence of *actual* connections between these features. For without
such interconnections the concept of Fordism is sapped of its
explanatory power. This takes us closer to the critical question of
whether Fordist industries have performed a *dominant* role in post-war
national economies. As we have seen, this can only be judged in terms
of the extent of their integration or interconnectedness in a national
economy or their degree of influence over issues of work and labour
organization — issues which, it has to be said, can only be settled by
empirical evidence on a country by country basis.

On the debit side, a central weakness of the concept of Fordism is not so much its inability to adequately convey a pattern of national diversity as its failure to see beyond large-scale mass production. There is a tendency in the Fordist literature to overstate the key importance of the mass production industries within an economy at the expense of other kinds of manufacturing production. Equally, there is a tendency to foreshorten the history of mass production by dating its demise across the industrial economies from the early 1970s. As Sayer (1989) has pointed out, 'western Fordist' mass production may have its problems today, but no such problems are apparent in South-East Asian mass production. We thus need to be alert to the twin dangers of overstating the significance of mass production in a national economy and mass production in the West. (In one sense this is just another example of how the discourse of 'the West and the Rest' is played out; see Book 1 (Hall and Gieben, 1992), Chapter 6.)

A further major weakness of the concept of Fordism is that its reference does not include some of the most important developments in the post-war economies. When we fix the reference of a concept, we offer a description of its general features, as in Figure 5.2. However, this industrial vision leaves out two prominent characteristics of the 1950s and 1960s: the activities of multinational firms and their impact on national economies, and the role of the service industries. In the US economy for example, at the height of the long post-war boom, multinationals were increasingly locating plants offshore, in Europe and other parts of the globe. The relative neglect of this phenomenon in Fordist accounts can, in part, be traced to the emphasis they place upon the regulation of *national* economies. As for the limited attention paid to the service industries within the Fordist literature, this may be traced directly to the broad assumption that it is *manufacturing* which acts as the 'engine' of growth within an economy. Service industries, for example those concerned with finance and commerce, are regarded as dependent upon the Fordist manufacturing sectors for their economic well-being. In the next section, we explore this representation of services further, and examine the kind of 'history' that tells us that modern manufacture equals progress. In the final section, the position of multinational and transnational firms within a system of national markets is briefly considered.

3   PROGRESS AND MODERN INDUSTRY

In discussing Ford's economic innovations and the relative importance of Fordist industries in the post-war period we have generally taken it for granted that the kind of modern economy which we have before us is a modern *manufacturing* economy. In fact, it is quite difficult to think otherwise. Modern progress is after all associated with the making of things, not in a craft sense, but rather, as noted in the Introduction, with

Charlie Chaplin in *Modern Times*

the mass manufacture of objects: the ability to act on raw materials and to transform them into tangible goods in unprecedented quantity and volume. As the twentieth century progressed, the rise of assembly line manufacture represented for many the very apex of modern industrialism. In one sense it can be regarded as the culmination of a long line of economic development that reaches back to the rise of industry in the eighteenth century (see Book 1 (Hall and Gieben, 1992), Chapter 3). What interests us here is why the modern economy should be seen in this particular way. Why, for instance, is our image of industrialism linked so closely with that of heavy machinery, large workforces, physical outputs, and the overall process of manufacture? Why is manufacturing regarded as so important to a modern economy?

3.1 MANUFACTURING GROWTH?

At one level the answer to the above question may appear quite straightforward: yes, industrialism and the process of manufacture are closely linked because the latter is the most dynamic, productive sector of an economy. Other sectors such as services are less able to generate high productivity gains, and act as adjuncts to the manufacturing process, keeping the factory going and ensuring that the goods reach the marketplace. So the line of argument that was used to justify the lead role of Fordist mass production industries earlier can also be extended to the *whole* of the manufacturing sector. Manufacturing represents the engine of growth within an economy in so far as it is capable of achieving increasing returns to scale. Put simply, this means that if the scale of production were to double in size, the increase in output would more than double. Unlike services, so the argument runs, the manufacturing industries can achieve successive productivity gains through the introduction of new machinery and the operation of larger plants. In the UK in the 1960s and 1970s this argument had strong political support (principally through the ideas of Nicholas Kaldor, an advisor to the Labour Government in the second half of the 1960s) and quickly became a version of economic common sense.

Certainly there is strong empirical support for this line of argument in the post-war period. Across the advanced industrial economies there was a significant association between manufacturing growth and overall growth rates. And in the UK, Lee (1986) has shown how much of the growth in Gross Domestic Product was attributable to a strong manufacturing performance. Lee's work on the UK economy is however interesting for a number of other reasons.

Even though manufacturing exhibited a certain dynamism throughout the 1950s and 1960s in the UK, the service sector was not far behind in its overall contribution to growth. While the service sector may not have experienced the increasing returns to scale that manufacturing clearly did in this period, it did contribute just under half the rate of national growth. Indeed, Lee's study of growth rates in the UK economy over the past century and a quarter showed that the service sector consistently generated around half of GDP growth, with finance and commerce among the main contributors. Table 5.1 provides a breakdown of output growth rates in two selected periods, 1856–1913 and 1951–73.

Table 5.1   Weighted sectoral output rates (per cent per annum), United Kingdom

	1856–73	1873–1913	1951–64	1964–73
Agriculture, forestry, fishing	0.03	-0.01	0.12	0.11
Mining, quarrying	0.19	0.12	-0.02	-0.07
Manufacturing	0.61	0.51	1.14	1.11
Construction	0.11	0.04	0.23	0.11
Gas, water, electricity	0.02	0.06	0.13	0.15
Transport, communications	0.21	0.24	0.18	0.28
Commerce	0.59	0.52	0.74	0.75
Public and professional services	0.12	0.22	0.21	0.27
Ownership of dwellings	0.12	0.10	0.07	0.09
GDP	2.00	1.80	2.80	2.80

Note: The growth rate of each sector is weighted by its share in GDP.
Source : Lee, 1986

ACTIVITY 3   The two main periods shown in Table 5.1 were chosen because they represent moments of strong growth in the UK economy. The latter period, as you know, covers the long post-war boom and the former period includes a time when Britain was regarded by many as the 'workshop of the world'.

The bottom row of figures in the table represents the growth rate of the national economy in each selected period, and the contribution of each sector towards Gross Domestic Product is listed in the columns above. Bearing in mind that we are looking at two periods which arguably have shaped our understanding of industrialism, I would like you to do the following:

1   Cast your eye down the first column, 1856–73, and compare the rate of manufacturing growth with that of services (transport and communication, commerce, and public and professional services). Remember that this was a period in which Britain was seen to be something of a manufacturing powerhouse.

2   Now read across the columns and compare the profile of industry in the periods 1856–1913 and 1951–73. Which sectors have grown and which have declined? In the inter-war period, especially in the decade after the First World War, virtually all sectors declined, but it is the comparison of the two strong growth periods that we are after.

In response to (1) above, I noted that, overall, service growth exceeded that of manufacturing in this period, as indeed it did up to 1914. In particular, there was a close similarity in the rates of growth for commerce and manufacturing: 0.59 and 0.61 per cent respectively. However, what is perhaps surprising about the half century up to 1914 is the prominence of services in what is taken to be an era of manufacturing, an industrial age.

In response to (2), I picked out a couple of features. Most sectors experienced higher growth rates in the post-war boom, in particular manufacturing, although services were not far behind. Mining had declined and agricultural output (which is not exactly known for its Fordist character) had grown at a rapid pace.

Taking the two periods together, however, it is the contribution of the service sector to GDP, especially commerce, that catches Lee's attention and leads him to ask why so little attention has been paid to services in accounts of the development of UK industry. Or, to put it another way, why is so much attention paid to manufacturing in accounts of the rise of modern industry?

The answer that he offers is reminiscent of the 'increasing returns to scale' argument, in so far as he notes the pervasive assumption that services are dependent upon the dynamism of industry. The close interconnection of services and manufacturing in an industrial economy is regarded as a one-way relationship, with services growing, as we have seen, in response to manufacturing growth. Thus, the relative size of the service sector in output terms is *not* an issue in this context; it could exceed the contribution of manufacture (as it often did in the UK and other industrial economies) yet still remain firmly dependent upon manufacturing as the 'engine' of growth to drive the national economy. In some cases, this line of thought has been extended to refer to manufacturing as the part of an economy which produces wealth, and services as the part which is paid for and sustained by that wealth. The

Lloyd's of London
New Building

Finance as an 'engine of growth'? The Lloyds of London Building

crucial issue for Lee, however, is not the productive capacity of services, but whether or not services only generate growth *through* manufacturing. His findings for the British economy are especially interesting.

Throughout much of the nineteenth century he found little evidence to show that services had grown in response to demands from manufacturing industry. On the contrary, he found strong links between services but few between manufacturing industries and services. Among banking, insurance, commerce, and several other sectors he found little dependence on manufacturing, and he argued that many such services may have actually paved the way for industrial development in the UK. A similar stress upon the diversity of sources which gave rise to service sector growth is also evident throughout the twentieth century, although perhaps less marked. Manufacturing was certainly an important stimulus for service sector growth in this period, but again no strong pattern of dependence was evident across the UK economy.

It is important to recognize that Lee is not suggesting here that there was a virtual absence of links between the manufacturing and service sectors in a modern economy such as the UK. Clearly most manufacturers require the services of banks, insurers, communication and transport firms as well as retail distribution networks. His point is that such relationships are not simply one-way or dependent relationships. Banks and commercial practices require a variety of manufacturers too, as well as a range of services. In modern economies, services generate growth for one another, and those such as finance and banking may look beyond the national boundaries for global business — including that of international service firms. Of course the pattern and form of such relationships varies from economy to economy, although few if any follow the example of the UK where the City and financial services have acted as a source of wealth creation independently from the rest of the national economy.

Having outlined Lee's concerns, we can now draw together the threads of the argument in this subsection. The significance of services may well have been underestimated in our understanding of what it is that holds together and drives a modern economy. The exclusive focus upon manufacturing as a dynamic sector has perhaps presupposed more than we had been aware of; in particular, it tends to regard as irrelevant the volume of output generated by services. No one however is suggesting that services and not manufacturing have held central ground throughout the industrial age; only that services have lost out to manufacturing as the dominant discourse of industry and industrialism.

3.2 INDUSTRY AND THE REST

So far, the discussion of the relationship between manufacturing and services has centred on growth statistics and growth dynamics. In this section, I want to alter that focus slightly by looking at how the relationship between manufacturing and services has been *represented* in the discourses about the modern economy. A *discourse* provides a language for talking about a topic which makes it difficult to think about that topic in any other way. *Representations* are part of a process of binding and work as a system; that is, they generate meaning as a cluster or set of images and ideas rather than standing alone. (For a discussion of the concept of 'discourse', see Book 1 (Hall and Gieben, 1992), Chapter 6.)

ACTIVITY 4 Bearing that in mind, what do the following terms represent to you? Jot down your first thoughts on each one in turn before you read on.

- industry
- production
- service industry
- service production.

If your first thoughts were anything like my second thoughts, there should be a few knots to untangle. When we talk about *industry,* many of the things that we have discussed in this chapter naturally come to mind: manufacturing, tools, machines, skilled labour, unions, factories, set perhaps against an urban backdrop. To this picture we can add one thing that we have yet to talk about: men, invariably in full time work. When we talk about the *service industries* however, a somewhat different picture tends to emerge. It is not quite the mirror image, but it is centred on the office or the shop and involves people, often women, working with people and information rather than with machines or tools. Both accounts are exaggerations, one-sided in their coverage, but that is of less importance here. What interests me is that when we refer, quite legitimately, to services *as* industries we obtain one view of work and production, yet when we refer to industry on its own we obtain quite another view. Once the term 'services' is disconnected from the term 'industry', the latter seems to refer exclusively to manufacturing. One part of industry — manufacturing — has been substituted for the whole.

The meanings we attach to *production* appear to bind us to manufacturing in much the same way. Production is about making things; it calls up images associated with power sources, raw materials, physical labour, technology, and a productivity rate that can be measured down to the last nut and bolt. Yet when we connect services to production, a different, rather blurred image is evoked. There is a product, but it is more difficult to pin down exactly what it is, how it is produced, and what measure of productivity and output is best. In some cases, for example in health care, education, entertainment, and a range of personal services, the output is essentially intangible, produced at the same time as it is consumed, and judged by a measure of quality rather than quantity. But not all services fit this snug picture and many in fact possess characteristics which are not that dissimilar to the industries which make things. The production of audits, consultancy reports, legal briefs, insurance policies, advertisments, transport systems, communication systems, restaurant meals, and even haircuts all take tangible forms. Electricity is just as much a power source as coal or steam in modern production; technologies have been a feature of much service production long before computers arrived; and although one needs to be cautious about interpreting productivity and output statistics in the service industries a range of quantitative measures operate across the sector.

In lots of ways, therefore, the distinction between making things and providing services is a *constructed* distinction. This is not to deny that there are differences between manufacturing and service production; rather it points to the fact that the differences between the two are less than are commonly thought. Yet the moment that we return to talking about production in a general way, the opposition between manufacturing and services reasserts itself and production connects with making things. Once again, we find ourselves back in the language of manufacturing. If you can touch it, it can only be something that has been manufactured, or so it would seem.

That some things are tactile, suggestive of touch, and other things are not is of especial interest here. Some things are easily grasped in our minds as tangible, whereas others, such as a haircut or a legal service, *seem* intangible. Arguably this is because the notion that services may actually be produced or the idea that services may possess a 'hard' form lack legitimacy. Such views contradict the language of industry and manufacturing. The image of services as industrial production remains unconvincing primarily because we appear to know what services are *not*. After all, services are not industry; it would seem that they are not machine-based, skill-based, exportable or measurable, and above all they do not make things. Accordingly, they are not manufacturing. And it is this representation of services in terms of their *difference* from manufacturing which gives it its strength. It fixes the image, even though only certain services fall in the frame (for example, telecommunications and computing services fall outside), and thus limits the number of ways in which we can talk about services.

It is important to be aware that we are not only talking about a stereotype of services here. We have also seen how the *relationship* between manufacturing and services is represented through the language of industry. That language is not of recent origin and nor is it a seamless web of meaning which has remained intact since the Industrial Revolution. As a *discourse* of industry it contains statements that differ in form, statements that on occasions appear to contradict one another, and conceptions of economic life that do not sit easily alongside one another. Yet within this pattern of dispersion it may be possible to discern a certain regularity in the relation between statements which provides a constant way of talking about such differences. This unity of a discourse was described by Foucault (1972) as a 'system of dispersion' (see Book 1 (Hall and Gieben, 1992), Chapter 6). We can think of this as a group of statements which systematically govern the different ways in which it is possible to talk about a particular topic. It is as if there are certain ground rules which allow us to make all sorts of comments and observations about the nature of industry, manufacturing, services, and yet the very same rules restrict the number of things that it is possible to say about these aspects of an economy.

Let me spell this out further.

3.3   A DISCOURSE OF INDUSTRY

What makes it possible to talk about a discourse of industry is the system according to which the different sectors of the economy can be specified and related. In talking about services, it is difficult to think of their role outside of their relation to manufacturing, the form of the connection, and the direction in which it flows. The discourse of industry thus only makes sense from this position and it is from this position that the sectors can be specified in terms of their contribution to society's wealth. Or rather a nation's wealth, because the discourse itself makes its appearance first within a system of national economies: 'engines of growth', 'motors of the economy' refer to *national* modes of growth. In this way, a national economy can be systematically split into two: the productive, wealth-creating part and the other part — seen either as supportive of growth at the core, an obstacle to growth at the core, or a drain upon wealth created at the core.

In consequence, there are theoretical choices to be made within this discourse. As we have stressed, not all the statements within a discourse point to the same set of conclusions or co-exist without contradiction. In the first place, given that the rules of industrial discourse presuppose that there is a productive core within a national economy, there are choices to be made over where that core is located — in which sector, or in what part of a sector, or in what combination of sectors.

For example, both the physiocrats, a group of eighteenth-century French economists, and Adam Smith specified economic sectors according to their capacity to generate wealth, yet each chose to locate that productive core in different parts of the economy (see Book 1 (Hall and Gieben, 1992), Chapter 3). The physiocrats held that agriculture was the only source of wealth, whereas Smith ranked agriculture, manufacturing, and commerce in descending order. In both cases, their choices were linked not simply to the development of 'industry' at that time but also to wider views of how an economy works and how it *should* work (for Smith, questions of the economy were linked with questions of morality, government, law, and jurisprudence). Since the eighteenth century, the productive core of an economy has been located in various positions, sometimes quite narrowly, as with its identification with the mass production industries of the post-war period, or, more recently, with the high technology industries of advanced economies, and sometimes quite broadly to include the whole of manufacturing. The choices, however, are guided by questions of what is considered a *valid* form of wealth and how this is best understood through an analysis of the relationships that hold within and between sectors of the economy.

Thus, there are also choices to be made about how the sectors connect and relate. At various times in the past, the relationship between sectors, especially manufacturing and services, has been regarded as mutually beneficial at one extreme or mutually antagonistic at the other, with services representing a 'drain' on the 'surplus' created in the rest of the economy. It is of less importance here to spell out the various gradations in between the two extremes and of greater interest to note how statements about the sectors (even the concept of 'sector' itself) presuppose a national economy as a complete interdependent system with interlocking parts. So the very act of formulating a theoretical opinion about how services relate to manufacturing requires a regular practice of seeing an economy as first, *national*, and second, as a *system of internally related sectors — with links out to the wider international economy*. It is only within such a conception of the economy that statements about 'engines of growth', 'motors of the economy', 'lead sectors', and 'productive cores' are possible. In choosing to locate these phenomena, we find ourselves speaking from *within* this economic discourse.

And when we speak the discourse of industry today, we locate that core in a sector called manufacturing. However, such a location is neither innocent nor without its consequences. We can note two in passing.

One consequence of the discourse of industry is that the qualities of manufacturing and service jobs tend to be regarded as quite different. Where manufacturing jobs tend to be associated with full-time employment and a full range of work skills, many service sector jobs are often seen as part-time and low-skilled. Where jobs in engineering and the car industry are accepted without thought as 'real jobs', jobs in for example catering and cleaning have to battle for the accreditation. The origins of these ideas are to be found in nineteenth-century notions of which jobs are the most suitable for men and women (see Book 1 (Hall and Gieben, 1992), Chapter 4). In the following chapter, the discussion of modern divisions of labour will show how such notions remain linked to conceptions of technology which, in turn, are related to the 'worth' of a job. If services are not regarded as a valid source of wealth, especially labour-intensive services, then this estimation is likely to be reflected in the payment of low wages for such work.

Another consequence of the discourse of industry is that it differentiates between a positive and negative direction of economic change. In its weakest version, we are told that an economy (for which read 'national economy') cannot survive on services, by 'taking in laundry' or 'selling its heritage'. This is probably true, although 'niche economies' can specialize in tourism, off-shore data processing, specific financial practices, and the like. In its stronger and more plausible version, the importance of industry (for which read 'manufacturing') is that it generates more exports (for the national economy). Invisibles (an interesting representation) — services such as banking, insurance, shipping, travel, and other activities that earn income abroad — account for a relatively small proportion of international trade. It is hard to see, therefore, how any (national) economy can rely upon services to maintain a broad balance between imports and exports. This is particularly so in an open economy such as the UK, which has a high propensity to import goods in comparison with other less open economies. Hence the importance accorded to mass production export industries in the post-war modern economies.

The logic is fine, but it is perhaps too much of an industrial logic. Visible trade is about the export of things that are made; goods produced in one country and then sold in another. But what does it mean to export a service? As the dominant representation of services is one of intangibility (which has helped to strengthen the view of service exports as 'invisible'), statements about the measurement of service trade consistently refer to those aspects of the trade which are tangible — that is, which approximate to trade in goods. This 'hard' service trade element is however increasingly difficult to isolate in a modern global economy, characterized by large international flows of money in the financial sector and an increased transnationalization of services ranging from cleaning and security through to property and advertising (UNCTC, 1988).

4   CONCLUSION: GLOBALIZATION AND INDUSTRY

Much of the previous section illustrated the importance of the national economy as the discursive framework within which discussions of the role and significance of modern industry have taken place. A modern economy is conceived as an 'economy-in-one-country', which has a 'core' or an 'engine of growth' and it is this part of the economy which is assumed to shape the pattern and trajectory of a national mode of growth. The state's management of the national economy, which took on such importance in the post-war period across the advanced industrial economies, sustained this view of an economy as a system of interdependent sectors — mining and agriculture, manufacturing, and services — whose borders coincided with those of the nation-state.

The concept of Fordism fitted neatly within this discursive framework. The explanatory power of the term 'Fordism' could be demonstrated by tracing the connection between industries and sectors within a national economy. The dominance of Fordist industries could be assessed by the extent of their integration within a national economy. This led us to note the relative neglect of the activities of multinational and transnational firms within Fordist discourse, especially in terms of their impact upon the regulation of national economies. We now need to consider briefly the relationship between national economies and the processes of internationalization that move across them. For if the modern economy takes its shape from a national mould, does that imply that the globalizing of modernity will break that mould?

The intention here is merely to clear some ground for the examination of this question and to raise some of the issues that flow from the topics discussed in this chapter (the question is dealt with in greater depth in Book 4 (Hall *et al.*, 1992)). The first point to bear in mind is that internationalization is not a recent phenomenon. There have been international trade flows of some significance for much of the past two centuries, as well as considerable flows of portfolio (financial) investment between countries, and in both cases, in the early period, the UK economy was at the hub of these flows. Direct foreign investment, the establishment of production facilities in different countries, is a different form of internationalization and is connected with the rise of multinational firms. Multinationals are simply large firms which have spread their operations beyond their country of origin, and they are an important feature of the post-war period.

Given this history, it is quite possible therefore that none of these international movements, of trade, of finance, of production, will lead to the fragmentation of the modern national economy. On the contrary, it often argued that multinational (manufacturing) industry is usually headquartered in one country and operates between countries. Similarly, the flows of finance, money and jobs which take place occur between national economies. The stress here then is upon relations *between* national economies of the kind that we have been concerned with in this chapter (i.e. the fully interlocking economy). There is, however, an alternative interpretation of global relations. With the contemporary growth in the volume of financial transactions across the globe, more specifically between a relatively small number of 'world cities', and the expansion of *trans*national service firms alongside the many multinational concerns, it could be argued that national economies are increasingly becoming 'sites' *across* which international forces flow. Note here that the emphasis has switched from processes which operate *between* countries to processes which operate *across* national economies.

The significance of this change in emphasis is profound as the latter approach points to the formation of dislocated 'national' economies; economies that are characterized by co-existing modes of growth rather than one model of growth. On this interpretation, as the global processes themselves take an uneven pathway across countries, taking in some regions while passing around others, the 'national' economy will exhibit lines of dislocation. In the UK, for example, it could be argued that the contemporary role of the City of London in the global financial system has shaped much of the southern economy while leaving the north relatively untouched. The notion of a 'national' economy as a system of interdependent sectors thus falls away somewhat. Similarly, in the US, the rising industrial energies of the South West and California, resting on a high technology base, are very loosely connected to the decline of the mass production industries in the Midwest, around Chicago and Henry Ford's Detroit. Are we therefore witnessing the break up of modern industrial economies in an era of greater global economic interdependence? If so, then this also calls into question the validity of the national growth models based upon 'lead' sectors that we have considered in this chapter. As noted at the end of Section 2.3, if mass production was the high point of modern industry, it is not so much disappearing as moving across the globe. The next chapter explores this issue further in the context of recent shifts in the international division of labour.

The full picture, however, will only become clear when we pick up the implictions of globalization in Book 4 (Hall *et al.*, 1992). We shall also explore the nature of a modern economy *after* Fordism — or rather, *possibly* after Fordism, since the concept of 'post-Fordism', signifying the end of the industrial era, is just as contested within the social sciences as we have discovered Fordism to be in this chapter.

REFERENCES

Armstrong, P., Glyn, A., and Harrison, J. (1991) *Capitalism Since 1945*, Oxford, Basil Blackwell.

Foucault, M. (1972) *The Archeology of Knowledge*, London, Tavistock Publications.

Hall, S. and Gieben, B. (eds) (1992) *Formations of Modernity*, Cambridge, Polity Press.

Hall, S., Held, D. and McGrew, A. (eds) (1992) *Modernity and its Futures*, Cambridge, Polity Press.

Hounshell, A. (1984) *From the American System to Mass Production 1800–1932*, Baltimore, Johns Hopkins.

Jessop, B. (1989) 'Conservative regimes and the transition to post-Fordism: the cases of Great Britain and West Germany', in Gottdiener, M. and Komninos, N. (eds) *Capitalist Development and Crisis Theory: Accumulation, Regulation and Spatial Restructuring*, London and Basingstoke, Macmillan.

Lee, C.H. (1986) *The British Economy Since 1700: A Macroeconomic Perspective*, Cambridge, Cambridge University Press.

Murray, R. (1989) 'Fordism and post-Fordism', in Hall, S. and Jacques, M. (eds) *New Times*, London, Lawrence and Wishart.

Murray, R. (1991) 'The State after Henry', *Marxism Today*, May.

Sayer, A. (1989) 'Post-Fordism in question', *The International Journal of Urban and Regional Research*, vol.13, no.4, pp.666–95.

Tolliday, S. (1986) 'Management and labour in Britain 1896–1939', in Tolliday, S. and Zeitlin, J. (eds) *The Automobile Industry and its Workers: Between Fordism and Flexibility*, Oxford, Polity Press.

United Nations Centre on Transnational Corporations (1988) *Transnational Corporations in World Development: Trends and Prospects*, New York, United Nations.

Williams, K., Cutler, T., Williams, J. and Haslam, C. (1987) 'The end of mass production?' (review of Piore, M.J. and Sabel, C.F. *The Second Industrial Divide: Possibilities for Prosperity*, New York, Basic Books, 1984), *Economy and Society*, vol.16, no.3, pp.405–38.

READING A   FORD AND MASS PRODUCTION

David Hounshell

On April 1, 1913, workers in the Ford flywheel magneto assembling department stood for the first time beside a long, waist-high row of fly-wheels that rested on smooth, sliding surfaces on a pipe frame. No longer did the men stand at individual workbenches, each putting together an entire flywheel magneto assembly from the many parts (including sixteen permanent magnets, their supports and clamps, sixteen bolts, and other miscellaneous parts). This was no April Fool's joke. The workers had been instructed by the foreman to place one particular part in the assembly or perhaps start a few nuts or even just tighten them and then push the fly-wheel down the row to the next worker. Having pushed it down eighteen or perhaps thirty-six inches, the workers repeated the same process, over and over, nine hours, over and over. Martin, Sorensen, Emde, and others had designed what may have been the first automobile assembly line, which somehow seemed another step in the years of development at Ford yet somehow suddenly dropped out of the sky. Even before the end of that day, some of the engineers sensed that they had made a fundamental breakthrough. Others remained sceptical. Twenty-nine workers who had each assembled 35 or 40 magnetos per day at the benches (or about one every twenty minutes) put together 1,188 of them on the line (or roughly one every thirteen minutes and ten seconds per person). There were prob-lems, to be sure. The workers complained about aching backs because of stooping over the line; raising the work level six or eight inches would solve that problem. Some workers seemed to drag their heels while others appeared to work too fast. Although a piece rate system would probably eliminate the slow ones, the engineers knew that Henry Ford would never tolerate such a system. Soon they found that by moving magnetos at a set rate with a chain, they could set the pace of the workers: speed up the slow ones, restrain the quick. Within the next year, by raising the height of the line, moving the flywheels with a continuous chain, and lowering the number of workers to fourteen, the engineers achieved an output of 1,335 flywheel magnetos in an eight-hour day — five man-minutes compared to the original twenty.

One can only imagine how excited the Ford production engineers were about the problems and possibilities of the assembly line. It became an object of study not only by Martin, Sorensen, and Emde but also by the heads of other assembling departments. Almost immediately after seeing the flywheel magneto assembly line, William Klann, head of the engine assembly, received permission to build an engine assembly line. The rush to implement such a line — beginning with putting the crankshaft in the engine block — led to an accident on the second day of operation which injured a workman seriously enough to bring James Couzens into the fac-tory to inspect this 'Goldberg job.' Couzens wanted to call a halt to Klann's

Source: Hounshell, D.A. (1984) *From The American System to Mass Production 1800–1932: The Development of Manufacturing Technology in the United States*, Baltimore, Johns Hopkins, pp.247-61.

experiments. But when Klann assured Martin and Sorensen that the line 'could be made foolproof,' he received their permission to continue. Klann recalled that he started the line again the next day after adding certain safety devices to keep the engines from falling off the conveyors. 'In a few weeks we had the job licked,' Klann boasted. Arnold wrote that new attempts were not made until November 1913. In any case, productivity gains were enormous. Klann and the Ford production engineers also turned to transmission assembly.

The Model T's transmission consisted of three distinct subassemblies: the transmission mechanism, the flywheel magneto assembly, and the transmission cover. Assembly of the transmission mechanism onto the back side of the flywheel was put on the line soon after the line had been built for the permanent magnets onto the front side of the flywheel. (Or, if one believes Klann, this was done first.) Beginning with the flywheel, workers added the triple gears, the driven gear, three drums, and the numerous parts of the clutch to form a complete subassembly. This line was developed so that when the transmission mechanism was completed, the flywheel was simply flipped over, ready for the magnets to be installed further down the line.

In June 1913, Klann changed transmission cover assembly into a line operation. On this subassembly, the production engineer had to resort to flat-top metal tables instead of rail slides because the shape of the cover did not lend itself to rails. Line operation immediately brought cover assembly time down from eighteen man-minutes to nine minutes and twelve seconds. As Klann pointed out about the adoption of line assembly techniques, 'There wasn't any discussion on whether this would work. You couldn't go wrong because the first one worked all right.'

By November 1913, Klann, Emde, and others put the entire engine assembly — made up of several subassemblies — on an integrated assembly line. This was not one long line but two lines at right angles with several machine tools, babbitting ovens, and other miscellaneous machinery interspersed. Engine line assembly proved to be a matter of constant experiment and refinement. As Klann remarked, 'We monkeyed with that thing all kinds of ways before we got it to work on a moving line.' By the time Klann and his colleagues had gotten 'all of the kinks' worked out, lowering engine assembly from 594 man-minutes to 226 man-minutes, Charles Sorensen and his assistant Clarence W. Avery had tried moving line assembly principles on the chassis. This operation became, in the public's mind, 'the' assembly line.

Horace Arnold described the Ford chassis assembly line as 'a highly impressive spectacle to beholders of every class, technical or non-technical.' Charles Sorensen called it 'the most spectacular one.' Sorensen may have imagined such a spectacle in 1908 and may have even tried to realize it. But in August 1913 the apparent success of the flywheel magneto line and the unqualified productivity gains of the engine and transmission assembly lines led Sorensen and others to begin experimentation with chassis assembly. Sorensen was not to be denied this time. Appointed

directly by Henry Ford, Sorensen's assistant Clarence Avery (who had
been Edsel Ford's manual training teacher in high school) proved to be a
decisive factor in the success of the assembly line at Ford. As Avery said in
1929, 'It was my good fortune to have [been assigned] the problem of
developing the first continuous automobile assembly line.' Avery was a
bright, well-educated young man who had wanted to get out of teaching
into the 'real world' of manufacturing. When assigned to him by Ford,
Sorensen had instructed Avery to master conceptually every manufacturing operation at Highland Park. After eight months of study, Avery was
ready to help Sorensen. As Fred Colvin had pointed out in the *American
Machinist,* stationary chassis assembly at Ford was not a matter of guess-
work. With several assembly gangs moving up and down the rows of chassis and with delivery of parts at each station demanding correct
scheduling, the orchestration of the assembly process had required
motion and time studies (albeit perhaps elementary ones) to avoid chaos.
It was from these studies or from this knowledge about how long certain
operations took that Sorensen and Avery laid out the basic plans of the
first chassis assembly lines.

The use of time and motion studies for the layout of the final or chassis
assembly line at Ford raises an important question: To what extent did
Taylorism or scientific management or any other contemporary form of
systematic management shape or influence the developments at Ford's
Highland Park factory? The Ford Motor Company, after all, arose in the era
when Taylorism was approaching the height of its influence. The widely
publicized *Eastern Rate* case (1910) and the publication of Frederick W.
Taylor's *Principles of Scientific Management* (1911) occurred just before
the innovations at Highland Park, and it is natural to assume that there
was a connection. Whether that was in fact the case, however, is by no
means certain, because the contemporary sources are not adequate to
assure a definitive answer. In addressing this issue, the initial problem is
arriving at a reasonable definition of Taylorism or systematic management.

If by Taylorism we mean rationalization through the analysis of work
(time and motion studies to eliminate wasteful motions) and the 'scientific' selection of workmen for prescribed tasks, then we can agree with the
recent judgement of Stephen Meyer III that Ford engineers 'Taylorized' the
Highland Park factory. Indeed, this was the conclusion of Allan Nevins in
his standard work on Henry Ford and the Ford Motor Company. Ford's
engineers, Nevins suggested, 'had doubtlessly caught some of his
[Frederick W. Taylor's] ideas.' Moreover, Nevins wrote that Clarence
Avery, who was clearly critical in the development of the moving chassis
assembly line, had 'kept in touch with the ideas of men like Frederick W.
Taylor.' Meyer generalized by arguing that 'Ford managers and engineers
may not have followed a specific programme [of systematic or scientific
management], but they surely followed general principles.'

Unquestionably, Ford engineers standardized work routines at Highland
Park after they analyzed jobs and work flow patterns. With the widespread
use of special-purpose machine tools at Ford, the engineers hired semi-

skilled and unskilled workers to operate these machines (scientific selection of workmen, as Taylor called it). As early as 1912 or 1913, the Ford factory had a time study department, although some Ford employees later recalled that it was first known as the work standards department. The very idea of establishing work standards — how much output a manufacturer could expect from a certain machine tool, a work process, or a series of processes if labor did a fair day's work — is the very heart of Taylorism in particular and systematic management in general. Moreover, in the Ford factory, there was a clear division of labour between management and workers along the lines advocated by Taylor in his *Principles of Scientific Management* (for example, machine tenders did not perform any maintenance on their machines but left this to specialists).

Despite these facts, there is much reason to doubt that Taylorism contributed significantly to the new assembly system at Highland Park. Henry Ford himself claimed that the Ford Motor Company had not relied on Taylorism or any other system of management. As Horace Arnold noted in 1914, 'In reply to a direct question he [Henry Ford] disclaimed any systematic theory of organization or administration, or any dependence upon scientific management.'

Four months before he died, Frederick W. Taylor spoke in Detroit to some six hundred superintendents and foremen of 'leading' manufacturers of the city. In reflecting upon his experience in Detroit, Taylor proudly declared that the manufacturers there 'were endeavouring to introduce the principles of scientific management into their business and that they were meeting with large success.' This especially interested Taylor because it was 'almost the first instance, in which a group of manufacturers had undertaken to install the principles of scientific management without the aid of experts.' According to Allan Nevins, however, many of those who heard Taylor saw the matter differently. They argued that 'several Detroit manufacturers had anticipated his ideas.' The Ford Motor Company could have been 'Taylorized' without Taylor.

By focusing on those elements of the Highland Park factory that were Taylorized, one runs the danger of misjudging the fundamental differences between the Ford philosophy (Fordism) and that of Taylor (Taylorism). It was Henry Ford himself, or, more accurately his ghostwriter, who pointed up these differences. To explain his system, Taylor often resorted to his tale about Schmidt, the scientifically selected worker who was told how to load pig iron scientifically (that is, after time and motion studies had been carried out) and was placed on an incentive wage system. Previously, Schmidt had hand carried each day twelve and a half tons of pig iron up a ramp and dumped it into a railroad car. But after he underwent the magic of scientific management, Schmidt was able to hand carry forty-seven and a half tons of the ninety-two-pound pigs each day. The Taylor approach was to assume that the job of loading pig iron was a given; the task of scientific management was to improve the efficiency of the pig iron carrier. Ford's production experts saw the problem differently. Why, they asked, should pig iron be hand loaded? Could this not be done by some mechanical means? (Ford engineers would later ask why one had to bother with pig iron at all. Why not pour castings directly out of the blast furnace and dispense entirely with handling and reheating pigs?)

The Ford approach was to eliminate labour by machinery, not, as the Taylorites customarily did, to take a given production process and improve the efficiency of the workers through time and motion study and a differential piecerate system of payment (or some such work incentive). Taylor took production hardware as a given and sought revisions in labour processes and the organization of work; Ford engineers mechanized work processes and found workers to feed and tend their machines. Though time and motion studies may have been employed in the setup of the machine or machine process, the machine ultimately set the pace of work at Ford, not a piecerate or an established standard for a 'fair day's work.' This was the essence of the assembly line and all the machinery that fed it. While depending upon certain elements of Taylorism in its fundamentals, the Ford assembly line departed radically from the ideas of Taylor and his followers.

The first attempt at line assembly in August 1913 was crude but phenomenally successful in increasing productivity. At one end of a long open space in the Highland Park factory, the Ford engineers put a windlass and stretched out a rope 250 feet down the open space. Based on their knowledge about optimal installation times for various chassis components, the engineers placed these components at different intervals along the path. Whereas the man-hour figure had been slightly under twelve and a half with static assembly, the first assembly line attempt (in which six assemblers followed the slowly moving chassis as it made its way past the various components) reduced the figure to five and five-sixths man-hours.

Experiments continued. On October 7, 140 assemblers had been placed along a 150-foot line. Man-hour figures dropped to slightly less than three hours per chassis. By December, Avery and those working with him had extended the line to 300 feet and had increased the assembly force to 177 men. Time: two hours, thirty-eight minutes. After Christmas, 191 men worked along the 300-foot line but pushed the assembly along by hand. Man-hour time increased rather than dropped. Sixteen days later, the engineers had installed a line on which the car was carried along by an endless chain. In the next four months, lines were raised, lowered, speeded up, slowed down. Men were added and taken off. As Charles Sorensen wrote, all of 'this called for patient timing and rearrangement until the flow of parts and the speed and intervals along the assembly line meshed into a perfectly synchronized operation.' By the end of April 1914, three lines were fully in operation, and the workmen along them put together 1,212 chassis assemblies in eight hours, which worked out to ninety-three man-minutes. Assembly figures became consistently predictable. Horace Arnold noted the effects of these developments: 'Very naturally this unbelievable reduction in chassis-assembling labor costs gave pause to the Ford engineering staff, and led to serious search for other labor-reduction opportunities in the Ford shops, regardless of precedents and traditions of the trade at large.'

Experiment and refinement continued on the existing subassembly lines. These adjustments provided productivity gains comparable to those achieved with chassis assembly and led the company to adopt entirely new lines. On June 1, 1914, chain-driven assembly lines began to roll out front axle assemblies. These reduced assembly time from 150 minutes (a January 1, 1913, figure) to $26\frac{1}{2}$ minutes (July 13, 1914). Other subassemblies followed. All of the assembly stands over which Fred Colvin had marveled only months before and which were characteristically Yankee had been taken to the scrap pile.

The Ford engineers next designed and installed conveyor systems to feed these hungry lines. As Arnold wrote in July 1914, 'Besides these almost unbelievable reductions in assembling time [wrought by assembly line], the Ford shops are now making equally surprising gains by the installation of component-carrying slides, or ways, on which components in process of finishing slide by gravity from the hand of one operation-performing workman to the hand of the next operator.' Reductions in labour costs were thus achieved by assembly lines, conveyor systems, gravity slides, and the like along with the Ford system of machining, which had removed virtually all skill requirements for operation and whose fixtures and gauges allowed foremen to demand speed. But these great achievements had wrought serious labour problems at the Ford factory. Henry Ford's five-dollar day was an attempt to eliminate these problems.

Although the motives behind the five-dollar day are rooted in a sort of industrial beneficence on Henry Ford's part and a consciousness on James Couzen's part that such a wage and profit-sharing system would pay for itself in free advertising, the five-dollar day must be seen as the last step or link in the development of mass production. During 1913 the labor turnover rate at the Ford factory had soared to a phenomenal figure. Keith Sward points out that turnover in 1913 reached 380 per cent: 'So great was labor's distaste for the new machine system that toward the close of 1913 every time the company wanted to add 100 men to its factory personnel, it was necessary to hire 963.' Not only did this burden the administrative machinery at Highland Park, but it also affected the operations within the factory. High turnover was also accompanied by growing signs of unionization at the Ford factory. Other Detroit automakers had already experienced strikes. The Ford management sought to relieve these pressures by carrying out labour reforms in 1913. Jobs were re-evaluated and brought into parity with each other. The company gave special raises to efficient employees. And finally, an across-the-board pay increase, averaging 13 per cent, was announced on October 1, 1913. The company set $2.34 as the minimum daily wage for every employee.

These reforms, however, did not stem the rising tide of labour problems. The growth in output of the factory, the installation and rigorous improvement in the efficiency of assembly lines in three different departments, and the promise of one being installed in every department added additional force, swelling the tide of labour turnover and dissatisfaction higher and higher in the final months of 1913. Attempting to reward workers who had stayed with the company for three years or more, the Ford directors gave a 10 per cent bonus on December 31, 1913. Out of some 15,000 employees only 640 qualified for the bonus, a figure that indicates the extent of worker turnover. The following day, or perhaps a few days later, Henry Ford, James Couzens, P. E. Martin, Charles Sorensen, Harold Wills, John R. Lee (the personnel department head), and Norvel Hawkins (the sales manager) met, discussed the labour problems, and considered increasing daily earnings (wages and 'shared' profits) to $3.00, $3.50, $4.00, $4.00, $4.50, $4.75, or $5.00. Ford had clearly become concerned about the inequity between the salaries and profits of directors (as well as the salaries and bonuses paid to the production experts) and the wages earned by the majority of workers in the factory. The turnover rate, the signs of unionization, and the manifest inequity of income combined in Ford's mind (and Couzen's) to produce a quick solution to all three. Ford, Couzens, and Horace Rackham (a director of the company) met on January 5, 1914, and adopted the five-dollar day. Since Ford owned controlling stock, the meeting was pro forma. Couzens had been convinced of the desirability of the plan — perhaps he had engineered it — so he and Ford encouraged Rackham to make the vote unanimous. Couzens got his free advertising, Ford his hero-worship, 'acceptable' workers extraordinarily high earnings. The basic psychology of the plan, however, and its basic effect were that now the company could ask its workers to become for eight hours a day a part of the production machine that the Ford engineers had designed and refined during the past four years.

The five-dollar day assured the company that the essential human appendages to this machine would always be present. This 'bonding' effect of extremely high earnings was evident within a month after Ford announced it. As an anonymous housewife of a Ford assembly line worker wrote to Henry Ford on January 23, 1914, 'The chain system you have is a *slave driver! My God!*, Mr. Ford. My husband has come home & thrown himself down & won't eat his supper — so done out! Can't it be remedied? ... That $5 a day is a blessing — a bigger one than you know but *oh* they earn it.' As part of the five-dollar day scheme, Henry Ford also scaled up the paternalistic operations of the Ford sociological department, which determined if workers qualified for profit-sharing by investigating their private lives — an extra burden on top of those already imposed by Ford production technology.

The story of mass production at the Ford Motor Company was not something that only historians of a later generation would delve into and try to understand. Henry Ford's contemporaries, many of whom were competitors, closely watched the doings at Highland Park, attempting to understand and emulate the revolutionary developments. Henry Ford encouraged their interest. Unlike the Singer Manufacturing Company, the Ford company was completely open about its organizational structure, its sales, and its production methods — at least after Henry Ford was satisfied that his company was on the road to mass production. As Horace Arnold wrote in 1914, 'The Ford company is willing to have any part of its commercial, managerial or mechanical practice given full and unrestricted publicity in print.' Ford engineers had no skeleton closets in their factory.

Proud of their work, they were anxious to have technical journalists tour the shops and write extensive articles about Ford methods. When Horace Arnold was writing the series of articles for *Engineering Magazine* Henry Ford himself devoted attention to the author. Fay Faurote experienced the same cooperation and developed a friendship with Ford over the next fifteen years.

As a consequence of Ford's openness, Ford production technology diffused rapidly throughout American manufacturing. The *American Machinist* series of 1913, *Engineering Magazine*'s series of 1914 and 1915 (which resulted in Arnold's and Faurote's *Ford Methods and the Ford Shops*), a series in *Iron Age* in 1912–13, and occasional but incisive articles in *Machinery* were the primary agents of this diffusion. One can thumb through the pages of these and other technical and trade periodicals in the days after the assembly line appeared in print and find automobile companies that were trying moving line assembly techniques even though they made only one or two thousand cars. Manufacturers of other products also tried the assembly line. Within a decade, many household appliances such as vacuum sweepers and even radios were assembled on a conveyor system. The Ford Motor Company educated the American technical community in the ways of mass production.

READING B FORDISM IN BRITAIN AND GERMANY

Bob Jessop

Fordism in Britain and Germany

[G]eneral models of Fordism and post-Fordism have obvious limitations in comparing different social formations. For each national mode of growth has its own specific features deriving from its own mix for Fordist and non-Fordist elements and its particular industrial and political profiles. ... Each national economy also has its own specific mode of insertion into the international economic system and the forms of crisis and this is reflected in its tendency to ascend or fall in the hierarchy of nations (Mistral 1986). Britain and West Germany clearly differ in both respects. The nature of Fordism in each society is different and so are their insertions into the international economy. This has affected the forms of crisis and the forms of transition to post-Fordism.

Flawed Fordism in Britain

Fordism first struck firm roots in Britain in the 1930s. But the economic expansion and prosperity which this brought to *some* regions only became general in the years of the post-war boom. The extension of the Fordist wage relation was not so much rooted in the expansion of [a] ... mass production system as in two other factors: the post-war settlement (1942–

Source: Jessop, B. (1989) 'Conservative regimes and the transition to post-Fordism: the cases of Great Britain and West Germany', in Gottdiener, M. and Komninos, N. (eds) *Capitalist Development and Crisis Theory: Accumulation, Regulation and Spatial Restructuring*, London and Basingstoke, Macmillan, pp. 266–72; 288–9.

48) with its precocious commitment to full employment and a universal welfare system and the favourable economic conditions created by an advantageous shift in the terms of trade with less developed economies and the sellers' market created by economic growth in the other advanced economies. The Keynesian welfare state (hereafter 'KWS') system provided the political shell and the organising myth in and through which a Fordist regime of sorts extended its hold over most parts of British society.

The extension of Fordism in Britain was flawed at all three nodal points in the virtuous circle of mass production–high wages–mass consumption. Productivity did not increase to the same extent as in other countries; the Fordist wage relation was defective; and mass consumption was financed through demand management and the social wage as well as productivity increases.

The relative retardation of Fordist mass production was reflected not only in lower levels of productive investment but also in two other aspects of investment. It was more often 'add-on' in nature, that is, concerned to compensate for deficiencies in existing techniques and processes of production rather than to introduce entirely new processes and products. And British firms failed to reach the same levels of *productivity* from similar production processes, machinery and so on, which were obtained in other advanced capitalist economies. This failure becomes even clearer if one discounts the impact of the higher levels of productivity and investment which were obtained by incoming *foreign* concerns and/or from British firms setting up on *greenfield* sites. Its long-term impact was evident in recurrent balance of payments problems tied to poor productivity, inflation and progressive de-industrialisation.

The voluntaristic collective bargaining system also contributed to the problems of Fordism in Britain. Trade unions were organised on overlapping craft, industrial and general lines and this resulted at plant level in multi-unionism; employers' associations at branch or industry level were weak, peak organisations lacked power and there is still no peak organisation for business as a whole. In the private sector bargaining was decentralised, fragmented, informal, *ad hoc* and disorderly; its scope and outcome depended far more on the prevailing balance of forces between 'the two sides of industry' than on any institutionalised procedures and rules of engagement. There was only a long-term and imperfect link between productivity increases and real wages; and labour market conditions had little impact on collective bargaining. In the short term, stagflationary tendencies [inflation at a time of static or declining output] became more marked. This was not reversed by increasing state intervention through wages policies (as often concerned to support the exchange rate as to further industrial policy) nor growing centralisation in the 1960s. Instead the combination of relative decline and global crisis provoked greater conflict among all three social partners from 1969 onwards and this led to repeated attempts to reform industrial relations.

Thirdly, despite the failure to consolidate mass production, the British state was committed, through the post-war settlement and the continuing bipartisan consensus about jobs for all, to validating full employment levels of demand. Industry's failure to complete a thorough-going Fordist transformation in relevant sectors was therefore reflected in a structural propensity to compensate for deficiencies in domestic production through the import of mass consumer durables. This was not compensated by the export of capital goods — indeed increasing import penetration and export failure were also evident here. An expanding welfare state further aggravated these problems through an increase in public sector employment and the growth of the social wage — both of which served to generalise Fordist mass consumption norms. Overall the economy was affected by rising unit wage costs, rising imports of mass consumer goods, expanding social expenditure, and an emergent fiscal crisis.

This flawed Fordism was reinforced by the manner in which Britain was inserted into the international economy. British firms tended to look towards imperial markets in Africa and Asia and/or to the more slowly developing and fragmented markets overseas (Latin America) at a time when fast growth and integrated mass markets were found in North America, Japan and Western Europe. This reinforced the traditional industrial profile of British firms and did little to encourage modernisation. These problems were aggravated by the dominance of financial capital within the market hierarchy in Britain and by government's concern to maintain the reserve and transaction roles of sterling even when this meant deflation. Modernisation and growth policies were blocked by this external dependence. Conversely the weakness of Fordism led to payments problems which affected the City's role and at one time seemed destined to restrict it to the overseas sterling area. The result was a gradual descent down the international hierarchy.

The crises which have unfolded over the last twenty years in the British political economy involve more than the economic and political forms of the Keynesian welfare state. They are rooted in the failure even to complete the transition to Fordism in key respects and the emerging crisis of Fordism on a world scale. In particular this flawed Fordism has had significant effects both during the post-war boom and during its collapse.

Firstly, because the boom years were mistakenly identified with the Keynesian welfare state system, efforts were made to shore this 'KWS' system up through corporatist bargaining over prices, incomes, and productivity and through eleventh hour, state-sponsored Fordist modernisation aimed at securing economies of scale through mergers, more stable growth through indicative planning and re-industrialisation through investment subsidies. But the corporatist strategies lacked a continuous tradition of social partnership instituted before the economic crisis, a corporatist social base in well-organised industrial unions and strong business associations and corporatist structural supports. Likewise state intervention was attempted without first constructing an interventionist state with the strategic capacities to define, co-ordinate and implement a coherent industrial policy (Jessop 1980). Industrial policy for the purposes of Fordist modernisation was too often confused with job preservation and/or regional policy and too often subordinated to exchange rate, fiscal and electoral priorities.

And secondly, the flawed character of British Fordism aggravated the impact of the second oil shock and the deflationary policies pursued by the Thatcher government, leading to a rapid process of de-industrialisation. ...

Export-oriented Fordism in Germany

Fordism in West Germany has also assumed a specific form. This can only be understood by considering how its economic, social and political systems were reconstructed after 1945 and how it was inserted into the international economy during the 1950s. Whereas Britain survived the war undefeated and its organisational and institutional structures remained much the same, the occupying powers led by the US presided over the reconstruction of West Germany's systems of industrial relations, unions, parties, governance and education. In addition the heavy industrial base which the future Federal Republic inherited after the division of Germany could only operate at full capacity if it found markets abroad.

Thus the German post-war settlement was quite different from that in Britain and it was considered somewhat later (1949–52). The labour movement secured co-determination and worker participation but was also obliged to work within the limits of a strong market rationality embodied in the social market economy (*soziale Marktwirtschaft*). This involved the dominance of private sector capital, a key co-ordinating role for banking capital, only limited direct and open state intervention and a welfare state organised along corporatist rather than liberal lines. The distribution of powers between federal and regional (*Land*) government and the legally entrenched autonomy of the central bank (*Bundesbank*) made it difficult for the federal state to engage in *dirigisme* [strategies of economic control] and/or demand management; but high levels of nominal taxation and access to Marshall Aid (together with counterpart funds) did enable the federal state to discriminate among different economic activities through selective tax concessions and subsidies. The Erhard government encouraged investment, exports and capital formation in specific industries and, despite rhetoric to the contrary, penalised consumption and imports (Abelshauser 1982, pp.49–51; Markovits and Allen 1984, pp.91–102; Deubner 1984, pp.519–23). This pattern of massive tax concessions and subsidies has continued to the present (Webber 1986, pp.25–8).

The German post-war settlement also gave a central role to the unions and employers' organisations in managing the wage relation. The industrial relations system was marked by a strong juridification — or the penetration of law into industrial relations, well-organised social partners (with a system of unitary industrial unions and highly organised employers' bodies at both regional and national level), and commitment to wage bargaining. Protected from state interference through the legal principle of *Tarifautonomie,* unions and employers met each other on two levels. Whereas unions bargained over wages and hours at industry and regional levels, works councils (*Betriebsraete*) negotiated over conditions at plant level. In bargaining the social partners take account of conjunctural factors (especially export markets) as well as past productivity gains (Hager 1980, p.6; Markovits 1986, pp.416–17; Streeck 1985, p.16).

The post-war expansion of German industry was marked less by mass production of consumer durables than by an export-oriented capital goods sector. The expansion and productivity of this key sector depended less on Fordist economies of scale and the semi-skilled labour of the Fordist 'mass worker' than on technological rents and the highly skilled labour of *Facharbeiter*. Mass consumer durables (for example cars) penetrated West Germany more slowly than in other big West European countries and were important only from the mid-1960s onwards (Deubner 1984, p.510). Likewise the consumer goods sector has lost out from internationalisation of the West German economy and has suffered from rapid import penetration (Deubner 1984, p.512).

Initially sustained by the clear undervaluation of the DM, this export orientation has since become structurally necessary. For West Germany's industrial profile and production are oriented towards foreign markets, and conversion to serve the home market would be difficult — especially as the capital goods sector is so dominant (Deubner 1984, p.506). This sector lies at the centre of a relatively coherent industrial core.

The development of this core is co-ordinated and, where necessary 'crisis-managed', in at least three inter-related ways: through the system of universal banks, which control four-fifths of shares; through formal cartels, cross-investment, interlocking directorates, and subcontracting ties; and, especially from 1966–67, through regional and federal government (Dyson 1986; Esser 1986; Webber 1986). The state system has been active in promoting modernisation since the 1960s in order to maintain West Germany's position at the top of the international hierarchy in civilian capital goods: it has invested in nuclear energy, infrastructure, production technologies, industrial research and development, education and so forth (Hager 1980, p.5). From 1966 there has also been a shift towards state sectoral intervention and Keynesianism. More recently *Ostpolitik* has had important commercial as well as political implications. Finally, although they play no significant co-ordinating role (except in structural crisis cartels), the trade unions recognise West Germany's export dependence and generally support the modernisation strategies necessary to maintain a high wage export oriented economy (compare Deubner 1979).

The dominance of the capital goods sector (and export-oriented industries more generally) has underpinned a virtuous circle in wage relations. Exports long maintained full employment, monopolistic pricing at home maintained profits, real wages tracked productivity, and the social partners took account of the export market in collective bargaining (Henkel 1980, p.29; Boyer 1986; Markovits 1986).

The crisis in the West German mode of growth took, as might be expected, a form different from that in Britain. The crisis is one of a mature, export-oriented mode of growth rather than a flawed, uncompetitive Fordism. The first export-led slump came in 1975 but the problems were already apparent earlier in slackening productivity and declining profits. They provoked the social-liberal coalition to develop the *Modell Deutschland* solution in the early 1970s. On the macro-level this sought to secure the international competitiveness of German capital through corporatist arrangements aimed at modernisation and austerity. It also sought to block the movement from economic to political crisis by integrating the unions into the crisis-management process (Huebner 1986, p.375). The continuing problem has been to maintain export-driven growth despite high wages and a slackening in productivity increases in Fordist sectors (such as cars).

A crucial role in this adaptation process has been played by the state at regional and federal level: it has provided finance to modernise old branches and to develop high value-added products for export, promoted international co-operation to stabilise existing export markets and create new ones; financed retraining of the labour force; underwritten the social costs of change; and mobilised union support at plant, branch, regional and national levels in an effort to minimise the political costs of modernisation (Esser 1986). ...

Concluding Remarks

... Neither Britain nor Germany reveal a clear-cut case of Fordism if this is defined simply in terms of mass production and mass consumption. Britain failed to secure the productivity growth which Fordist methods could have brought to mass production and was hard-hit by de-industrialisation as a result. West German growth owes as much to the capital goods sector as to mass production of consumer goods and has also relied as much on its highly qualified *Facharbeiter* as on semi-skilled, Fordist mass workers. In its minimal sense, therefore, 'Fordism' serves mainly as an 'ideal type' against which to assess the specificity of the British and German regimes of accumulation. The broader concept of Fordism is, however, both directly relevant and powerful. For the Fordist wage relation based on institutionalised collective bargaining around a wage tied to rising productivity and inflation characterised both Britain and West Germany. Likewise private credit and monopolistic competition played key roles in capital accumulation; and state credit and tax expenditures were central elements in economic management. If we adopt the broader concept of Fordism as a regime of accumulation, therefore, we can treat both Britain and West Germany as having Fordist regimes.

The related concepts of 'mode of regulation' and 'mode of growth' have proved even more relevant for our analysis. They are clearly more concrete concepts and can generate significant insights into the differential dynamic of the British and West German regimes. The institutions of collective bargaining, the relations between banks and industry, and the state play key roles in a mode of regulation; and their contrasting natures in the two cases investigated emerges very clearly. Likewise the modes of growth in Britain and Germany are also significantly different — reflecting their different industrial profiles and modes of insertion into the international economy. By examining the contrasting modes of regulation and growth in these two economies we can better grasp the specificity of their post-war development and of the forms assumed by the crisis of Fordism.

References

Abelshauser, W. (1982) 'West German economic recovery, 1945–1951: a reassessment', *Three Banks Review*, vol.135, pp.34–53.

Boyer, R. (1986) *La Théorie de la Régulation: Une Analysis Critique*, Paris, La Découverte.

Deubner, C. (1979) 'Internationalisierung als Problem alternativer Wirtschaftspolitik', *Leviathan*, vol.7, no.1, pp.97–116.

Deubner, C. (1984) 'Change and internationalisation in industry: towards a sectoral interpretation of West German politics', *International Organisation*, vol.38, no.3, pp.501–34.

Dyson, K. (1986) 'The State, banks and industry: the West German case', in Cox, A, (ed.) *The State, Finance and Industry*, Brighton, Wheatsheaf.

Esser, J. (1986) 'State, business and trade unions in West Germany after the "political wende" ', *West European Politics*, April.

Hager, W. (1980) 'Germany as an extraordinary trader', in Kohl, W.L. and Baseri, G. *West Germany: A European and Global Power*, London, Gower.

Henkel, W. (1980) 'Germany: economic nationalism in the international economy', in Kohl, W.L. and Baseri, G. *West Germany: A European and Global Power*, London, Gower.

Huebner, K. (1986) ' "Modell Deutschland": Karriere einer "oekonomischen Kampfformation" ', in Thien, H.G. and Wienold, H. (eds) *Herrschaft, Krise, Ueberleben*, Muenster, Westaelisches Dampfboot.

Jessop, B. (1980) 'The transformation of the state in post-war Britain', in Scase, R. (ed.) *The State in Western Europe*, London, Croom Helm.

Markovits, A. (1986) *The Politics of the West German Trade Unions*, Cambridge, Cambridge University Press.

Markovits, A. and Allen, C. (1984) 'Trade unions and the economic crisis: the West German case', in Gourevitch, P. *et al., Unions and Economic Crisis*, London, Allen & Unwin.

Mistral, J. (1986) 'Regime internationale et trajectoire nationale', in Boyer, R. (ed.) *Capitalismes: Fin de Siècle*, Paris, PUF.

Streeck, W. (1985) 'Industrial relations in West Germany 1974–1985: an overview', *Discussion Paper IIM/LMP 85–19*, Wissenschaftszentrum, Berlin.

Webber, D. (1986) 'The framework of government–industry relations and industrial policy making in the Federal Republic of Germany', University of Sussex, Working Paper Series on Government–Industrial Relations, no.1.

CHAPTER 6 THE DIVISIONS OF LABOUR AND OCCUPATIONAL CHANGE

Peter Braham

CONTENTS

1   INTRODUCTION

This chapter will examine issues surrounding the division of labour and sectoral changes in the labour market. This will be done not only in relation to the UK but, where appropriate, in a way that is both international and comparative, and that reflects the growing globalization of the economic system. (In the context of the series *Understanding Modern Societies*, this chapter extends the discussion of the emergence of the economy (see Book 1 (Hall and Gieben, 1992), Chapter 3), though in a more sociological direction, and it serves as a stepping-stone to the chapter on post-industrialism and post-Fordism (see Book 4 (Hall *et al.*, 1992), Chapter 4).)

The notion of a modern economy takes certain things for granted. Prominent among these is a specialized and educated workforce organized to produce a highly differentiated range of goods for a worldwide market. However, the extent to which an economy has become modernized is also assessed according to the relative importance of different sectors in terms of output and employment. Conventionally a modern economy is seen as one where manufacturing industry is much more important than agriculture, but the history of the twentieth century has demonstrated that this sectoral composition is neither final nor predetermined. Perhaps the most obvious development in most industrially advanced countries (IACs) has been the decline of the manufacturing sector and the rise of the service sector.

The term 'division of labour' originally referred to these sectoral divisions, as well as to occupational structures and to the organization of tasks. More recently, the term has been applied to the gender and racial divisions of labour, and to the spatial division of production and the movement of some elements outside the factory (Cohen, 1987, p.228). For example, the boundaries between male and female labour have altered markedly; and the location of production may change too: a typical case may involve a multinational corporation withdrawing from the established industrial areas of the UK to set up factories in low-wage, newly industrialized countries (NICs), while its headquarters are relocated to the South East of England.

The most obvious labour market developments in all western IACs since the Second World War concern the decline of manual and industrial occupations and the rise of white-collar and service occupations. Once-familiar jobs have disappeared and new jobs have appeared — often involving new skills or demanding new categories of worker. These developments — together with the erosion of the norm of full employment — have raised a number of important questions. For example, can 'work' still be seen as a full-time, regular, job-for-life performed by men, while women merely 'housekeep'? Or is full-time employment now too limited an area for study, and does part-time employment — and the role of women within it — demand our attention?

The difference between part-time and full-time employment provides a good starting point for introducing the contrast between 'core' and 'periphery' in the labour market, which provides the underlying connecting theme of this chapter.

The Penguin Dictionary of Sociology offers a definition of CENTRE/ PERIPHERY the second part of which focuses on the loci of economic power and relates quite closely to the so-called new international division of labour (NIDL). And in Book 3 (Bocock and Thompson, 1992), Chapter 1, Harriet Bradley cites Wallerstein's view that colonialism produced an integrated world economy in which western 'core' societies exploited 'peripheral' Third World societies. My own use of the terms 'core' and 'periphery' is, however, both wider and less specific than these usages. I shall treat the contrast between 'core' and 'periphery' as providing valuable insights into the labour market position of women and of migrant workers, as well as helping our exploration of labour market segmentation, the new international division of labour, and the concept of flexible specialization, each of which will be explored in a separate section of this chapter.

Thus, a woman or a migrant worker is more likely to be directed to 'peripheral' employment, while a man or an indigenous worker is more likely to be found in 'core' employment. This process reflects long-standing beliefs about what *type* of work is appropriate for particular *types* of worker. And, by extension, if a worker can be adversely or positively categorized in more than one way — say as a female migrant — then the disadvantage or advantage is likely to be commensurately greater. We can use the terms 'core' and 'periphery' not only to refer to workers and to jobs, but also to refer to contrasts between industries in a society and to refer to contrasts between developed and less developed societies. Through the use of these twin concepts then, we can bring out connections between ostensibly disparate groups of workers in different locations.

Before proceeding it is worth saying that to use the terms 'periphery' or 'peripheral' is not to suggest that the entity or group so described is not of central importance to economic life or to production. Thus, if we categorize part-time workers — most of whom are women — as 'peripheral', this is not intended to diminish the importance of female waged labour. Nevertheless, it does reflect the fact that part-time workers *are* seen by many employers and trade unionists as *marginal*, whether their work is of marginal or central importance to the production process. As Hakim points out, this prevailing view of part-timers has had substantive consequences for jobs which are low-graded, low-paid, lacking in promotion, and denied the range of benefits generally given to full-time employees (Hakim, 1990, p.163).

2   FROM A MANUFACTURING TO A SERVICE ECONOMY?

Perhaps the most conventional way to describe the industrial structure of a country like the UK is to divide it into three sectors namely:

1   the primary sector (extractive industries and agriculture);
2   the manufacturing sector (the production of commodities);
3   the service sector (where commodities are circulated or a service is provided).

The changing balance between these sectors may then be evaluated in accordance with, for example, the proportion of GDP accounted for by each sector or, as in Figure 6.1, the proportion of workers employed in each sector at various times.

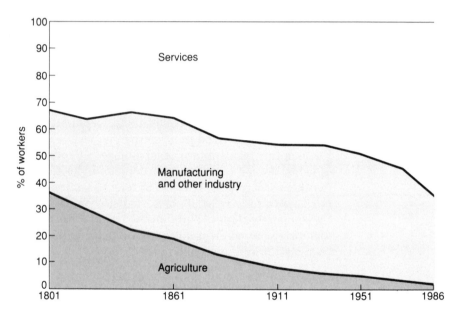

Figure 6.1   Approximate proportions of workers in different economic sectors, 1801–1986
Source: based on Abercrombie, Warde *et al.*, 1988, p.84

In the UK over the last two centuries there has been a significant change in the percentage of people employed in each of these three sectors, as shown in Figure 6.1. As the proportion of workers entering the primary sector fell steadily, so more people entered manufacturing. It also shows that the growth in the proportion of the workforce entering the service sector is of long-standing and that by the 1980s about two-thirds of all workers were in service industries.

The decline in employment in manufacturing in the UK has been very swift: for instance, between 1966 and 1985 it fell from 8.6 million to 5.4 million workers (Abercrombie *et al.*, 1988, p.82). But the decline of manufacturing and the rise of services is a feature of all the IACs and is taken as signifying a new type of economy, a *post-industrial* economy (see Book 4 (Hall *et al.*, 1992)). This is not simply a statistical extraction of the sort that can be derived from Figure 6.1 (for instance, far fewer people now work in textile manufacture, shipbuilding or car production, whereas many more people work in shops, hotels, the provision of financial services and in health care and education). It also involves a view of historical change whereby the most developed service-based economies are held to chart the course that other aspiring economies will eventually replicate (see Chapter 5 of this volume for discussion of this point).

The current emphasis on manufacturing decline may cause us to neglect the point that, as a source of employment, manufacturing in Britain has contracted quite consistently since the mid-1950s, and that at no time since the Second World War has manufacturing employed as many people as services. A number of reasons may be suggested for this decline, prominent among which are factors such as the loss of employment that often accompanies mechanization and automation, and the declining competitiveness of British manufacturing in the face of competition not only from low-wage, Third World countries but also from other IACs with higher rates of capital investment. It is not suggested that this decline is universal, but viewed solely in terms of aggregate employment even the expansion of the so-called 'sunrise' industries, such as electronics, is more than matched by the contraction and/or demise of the so-called 'sunset' industries, such as steel and shipbuilding.

But the UK economy can be described as a service economy not only because the majority of *employment* is service employment and has been so since the Second World War but also because the majority of *output* is service output and has been so since the 1960s. It would be a mistake to consider the employment implications of 'de-industrialization' and the emergence of a service economy as if they are quite separate and as if what 'services' are is self-evident. As Gershuny and Miles (1983) point out, services comprise:

1   industries where the final output is non-productive — thus, 'services' encompasses both manual and non-manual occupations;

2   occupations, whether in agriculture, manufacturing or services, where there is no *direct* involvement in the production of material products;

3   service products, such as maintenance contracts, which may be delivered by manufacturing firms as well as by service enterprises; and

4   service functions — a more specialized usage, which reminds us that all products, whether material or otherwise, incorporate a service function.

What is important to note here is that services such as marketing, technical expertise and finance are often integral components of modern manufacturing activities. Gershuny and Miles also argue that service jobs have grown in number in response to an increased demand for manufactured goods which is, in reality, a consequence of what they describe as a 'self-service' economy. They therefore emphasize not the separateness of manufacturing and services, but the links between them. The view that there is, indeed, a linkage between the service and the manufacturing sector is also central to Porter's analysis of national competitive advantage (1990, pp.252–3). In Porter's view, this link has become an important part of the argument that a nation cannot afford to neglect its international competitive position in manufacturing, assuming that services will fill the gap. This is not only because many service industries have been created through the de-integration of service activities by manufacturing concerns, but also because services are often tied to the sale of manufactured goods *and* manufactured goods are often tied to the sale of services.

The emergence of a post-industrial society, as evidenced by the decline of manufacturing and the rise of services, should not be seen only in domestic terms, and our attention should not be confined solely to sectoral movement within the IACs. In addition to taking into account the nature of the linkage between services and manufacturing, we should also emphasize the importance of the effect of the global relocation of manufacturing industry to NICs on the balance between services and manufacturing in the IACs.

3   LABOUR MARKET SEGMENTATION

The scale of the long-term changes in the proportion of the population employed in each of the sectors and the degree of occupational change discussed in the previous section might almost convey a picture of free and unhindered movement, such that the labour market seems to be undifferentiated and unitary. However, this is not the case: the labour market is not a single entity, but a whole series of labour markets marked by divisions not only between industries, but also between employing organizations, skills, hierarchies of authority, geographical locations, and so on. For example, geographical divisions are apparent in Harris's summary of developments in the UK economy of the 1930s and 1940s, in which he refers to the decline of large-scale industries located mainly in Scotland and North-East England and to the rise of new industries in the Midlands and South-East England (Harris, 1988, p.12). Similarly, the 'sunset' and 'sunrise' industries of the 1970s and 1980s display a very unequal geography. And more generally there is a clear *inverse* relationship between de-industrialization and the rise of services: those regions that have experienced the largest falls in manufacturing employment have gained the least from the expansion of the private service sector; both trends have therefore dispersed inequalities between British regions (Massey, 1988, p.60). If we see the labour market in terms of these various divisions we can appreciate that movement within it is not free, but is constrained by one or more of a number of impediments, as well as by means of controls on entry operated by different 'gatekeepers'.

Yet there are a number of powerful concepts relating to the labour market which, though they acknowledge divisions — particularly divisions based on skill, qualifications and experience — seem to suggest that less relevant divisive factors (those unrelated to job performance) are of little or diminishing importance. For example, for the classical economists who examined the division of labour, relations of cooperation involving specialization of complementary tasks were of crucial importance. Their approach was set firmly within a framework of *laissez-faire* capitalism, where the relationship between worker and employer is treated purely in market terms: the worker selling labour and the employer hiring him or her. In this exchange it is irrelevant whether an individual worker is male or female, young or old, or white or black, provided the efficiency of production is maintained or enhanced. The status achieved by the worker is thus solely dependent on his or her individual efforts, skill, ability and so on (Worsley *et al.*, 1977, pp.279–81).

It requires no significant conceptual leap to relate this perspective to contemporary characterizations of *meritocracy* in Britain:

> ... more and more it becomes possible for talent and hard work to reap their reward through an upward progress in what is sometimes called a meritocracy — a new aristocracy based on individual ability and effort instead of on birth and social rank. (Fox, 1974, p.7)

A belief in an emerging meritocracy was particularly pronounced in the UK of the 1960s and was strengthened by a number of developments, prominent among which were educational reforms and changes in industrial structure. These in turn promised not only greater opportunities, but also more objective and achievement-related methods of selection and promotion.

Nowadays the word 'meritocracy' seems to have been supplanted by the idea of 'equal opportunity', which Seear defines as meaning 'that no one is denied training or a job for reasons that have nothing to do with their competence or capacity' (Seear, 1981, p.295). In one sense these concepts seem mutually beneficial to employee and employer: thus, if it is to the advantage of a suitably qualified job applicant to be chosen on merit, it is equally to the advantage of the employer to have the widest and best choice for selecting personnel. That this is so seems borne out by Offe's *achievement principle*, which suggests that there are qualitative differences between employees which can be objectively identified and rewarded by selection, promotion and so on (Offe, 1976). However, there are a number of problems in applying the 'achievement principle', particularly in respect of non-skilled jobs. The low skill

content of many jobs is indicated in Blackburn and Mann's survey of
manual jobs in Peterborough, carried out in the late 1970s. They found
that the *absolute* level of skill in all but the very highest jobs was
minimal: their research showed that 87 per cent of workers exercised
less skill at work than they would have done by driving to work
(Blackburn and Mann, 1979, p.280). In these circumstances it is
comparatively easy for employers to establish apparently objective entry
and promotion requirements which, though generally irrelevant to the
job in question, serve to exclude, deliberately or otherwise, certain
categories of worker. More widely, the definition of skill may turn out to
be somewhat elastic, as in the way in which it has been manipulated to
exclude or restrict the employment of women (Cockburn, 1983). Thus,
Offe prefers to see the 'achievement principle' not as a process of
objective evaluation, but as an ideology within the context of employer
authority and control which, because of its very imprecision, helps to
support *partiality* in deciding whom to select or promote. Functional or
relevant criteria are likely to be overlaid 'by a second level of ascriptive
qualifications ... [which] then become important as an additional
criterion for occupational status and mobility chances' (Offe, 1976,
p.90).

Yet it is sometimes argued that, with the steady upgrading of
employment as western IACs switch from having a preponderance of
manual and manufacturing occupations to being white-collar and
service based, so the functioning of labour markets becomes
increasingly homogenized. On this view, the labour market is conceived
as perfect in so far as it is atomistic: that is, irrelevant criteria do not
intrude in determining wages and conditions of employment, and the
existence of segmentation, whereby workers of equal efficiency are
differently rewarded, is regarded as of only marginal significance. Thus,
the elimination of undesirable, dirty and routine factory jobs and the
proliferation of what are assumed to be more desirable, cleaner and
varied jobs in the service sector seem to promise both more attractive
and less segmented employment.

But, as Wilkinson points out, there is absolutely no evidence that the
atomistic or non-segmented labour market has ever existed. On the
contrary, labour markets have always been, and continue to be,
structured such that the higher the skill and status of workers, the better
organized is their position, whereas where workers are continuously
obliged to compete with their fellows, pay and conditions are much
worse (Wilkinson, 1981, p.x). We can see this empirically too: many
jobs in services have never offered more attractive pay and conditions
than routine factory jobs, and many service occupations — notably
those in clerical work — are being deskilled and rationalized
(Abercrombie *et al.*, 1988, p.85).

The concept of the dual labour market (DLM) is perhaps the most
influential theoretical perspective to challenge the assumption that the
trend in IACs is towards economic homogeneity. It is premised on the
belief that social and economic difference in these labour markets

continues and may even become deeper. In essence the DLM hypothesis treats the labour market as separated into a primary sector, where jobs are categorized as skilled and where pay and conditions are good, and a secondary sector where jobs are categorized as unskilled and semi-skilled and where pay and conditions are markedly inferior (Roberts *et al.*, 1985, p.5, see also *Penguin Dictionary of Sociology*: DUAL LABOUR MARKETS, which gives a full summary and which relates the concept to 'core' and 'periphery').

The DLM thesis was developed in the 1960s to analyse labour market segmentation in the USA, but subsequently applied to the UK and to other western economies. Later variants of this thesis suggested that not only employers but also trade unions had an interest in maintaining these divisions. What was common to early and late versions alike, however, was the idea that firms had to devise a satisfactory means to adjust their labour force to fluctuations in demand, while contriving to retain more skilled workers in whom their investment was commensurably greater. What was expected of such 'core' workers might be seen in terms of *functional flexibility* whereby they might have to perform different tasks or utilize different skills as the demand for the firm's output varied in type and quantity. By contrast 'peripheral' workers — whether directly employed or employed by subcontractors — were required to provide necessary *numerical* flexibility: that is, they could more readily be hired and fired or move in and out of the labour market. This is a contrast to which we shall return in Section 7. Typically, primary sector or 'core' workers are to be found in large-scale enterprises whose strong market position permits them to offer reasonably good pay and conditions. By contrast, secondary workers are likely to be employed in smaller-scale enterprises whose market position is more precarious. In the secondary sector, the ease with which work tasks may be learnt by newly appointed employees, and the constant pressure to reduce labour costs, means that there is little incentive to retain staff by matching the pay and conditions on offer in the primary sector.

As Hakim points out, labour market segmentation theory in general (and the DLM thesis in particular) represents a substantial sociological contribution to a field which is otherwise the province of labour market economists (Hakim, 1990, pp.159–60). Its key elements are presented in Figure 6.2 (overleaf) which shows the fourfold classification developed by Loveridge.

This classification is derived by cross-cutting internal and external labour markets with primary and secondary sectors. Thus, most jobs in the primary internal sector are permanent and full-time and offer a high degree of discretion and reasonable earnings; the primary external sector includes professional or skilled craft work supplied on a self-employed or sub-contracted basis; the secondary internal sector refers most notably to part-time employment; and the secondary external sector involves, for example, seasonal, casual and homeworking and unskilled labour.

High span of discretion
and
long-term stable earnings

Primary
internal
market

Primary
external
market

Flexible but
specific skills

Specialized but
general skills

Secondary
internal
market

Secondary
external
market

Low span of discretion
and
unstable earnings

Figure 6.2   Organizational and firm-specific labour markets
Source: based on Loveridge, 1983, Figure 7.1, p.159

Though DLM theory has been criticized on a number of grounds (for example, for neglecting the influence of worker organization on labour market structure and on the protection of vulnerable groups in the labour market), the basic distinction that is made between full-time employees in regular, stable and permanent jobs and other forms of peripheral work remains a valuable one. Hakim prefers to use the term 'flexible', not only because for her it avoids the perjorative connotations of 'peripheral' and 'unstable', but also because it points to the advantages accruing to employees, as well as to employers, in the availability of flexible work (Hakim, 1987, p.550). The three most important groups within this flexible workforce are part-time workers, the self-employed, and those in temporary work. Although there is a considerable overlap between these categories, by far the largest element of the flexible workforce in the UK is part-time work, which accounts for half the total. In the UK, the growth in part-time employment has been dramatic: for example, in the 1970s alone, more than one million part-time jobs were created.

As Hakim points out, in the mid-1980s, the relative proportions of the 'traditional' and 'flexible' workforces in the EEC as a whole and in the USA were very similar to those in the UK: in each case roughly two-thirds worked in the 'core' workforce and one-third worked in the flexible workforce (Hakim, 1987, pp.553–4). However, the temptation to see the changing balance between traditional and flexible sectors of the UK workforce solely as a response to the recession of the early 1980s should be resisted. Though the total labour force has grown by more than 2 million since 1951, there has been a consistent and marked decline in the number of full-time jobs over the same period. Thus, in 1951 only 800,000 or 4 per cent out of a total workforce of 22 million worked part-time, whereas by 1987 part-time workers accounted for 5.6

million or 23 per cent of a total workforce of just over 24 million. Similar trends, amounting to a restructuring of the labour force, can be observed in other IACs (Hakim, 1987, pp.555–6).

Technological changes have helped to deskill and routinize many primary sector jobs, some of which have been relocated to low-wage labour countries. The advantages and bargaining power of primary sector workers have also been diminished by the tendency of many large-scale western enterprises to detach part of their production by means of subcontract to smaller concerns. This trend, while designed to protect large enterprises against fluctuations in demand and labour market rigidities, often results in the creation of peripheral jobs as the subcontractor tries to minimize costs. According to Goldthorpe, this practice is particularly pronounced in France and Italy (1985, p.142), but as Hudson reports it is also widely practiced in the UK by, for example, shipbuilding, coal, chemical and steel companies. He notes in particular that the common practice of subcontracting services once performed within these companies has led to increasing competition between subcontracting companies, with predictable adverse effects on the latter's wages and working conditions. Similarly, many previously 'core' workers have been re-hired by big companies on a casual or part-time basis to meet temporary surges in demand, and on terms which involve foregoing holiday entitlement, waiving redundancy rights, and agreeing to work any pattern of shifts or days that management might specify (Hudson, 1988, pp.154–6). In other words, not only may flexible or peripheral work grow in relation to or at the expense of primary work, but primary workers may become transformed into peripheral workers.

Though Goldthorpe sees this 'dualistic' strategy being based in no small measure on phenomena like subcontracting, he also places particular emphasis on the recruitment of exceptionally vulnerable migrant labour, which was of great value to employers in many western IACs, especially in terms of its elasticity of supply and its tractability (Goldthorpe, 1985, p.439). This type of dualism forms an important element of Phizacklea's analysis of the British garment industry and of the role of ethnic minority labour within it. She contrasts the development before the Second World War of factory-based production outside London with the traditional sweatshop — with its cluster of homeworkers — based in the inner cities. According to Phizacklea, the two sectors — one stable, employing capital-intensive techniques, the other precarious and undercapitalized — are sometime linked by a complex web of sub-contracting: the dualism in this relationship is reflected not only in technology and markets, but also in working conditions and in an ethnic division of labour (Phizacklea, 1990, pp.30 and 53).

In the next section the role of women in the labour force will be explored, while the general significance of a reliance on migrant labour will be discussed in Section 5. However, before we end our consideration of labour market segmentation, we should note the relationship between location in either the primary or secondary sectors on the one hand, and the risk of unemployment on the other. In IACs,

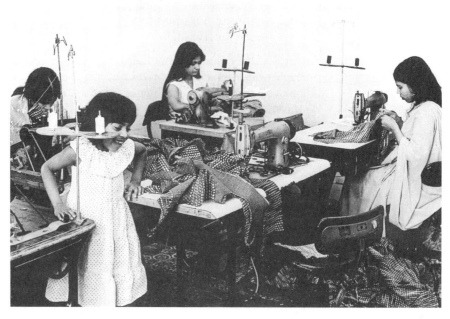

Parts of the UK garment industry have relied heavily on ethnic minority labour

the least likely to become unemployed are those who would normally fill the primary sector of the labour market: namely, men between the ages of 24 and 54. Conversely, those who normally fill the secondary labour market — the young and old, women and minorities — are more likely to be unemployed. The position in IACs in the early 1980s can thus be summarized as follows:

> ... ten persons out of 100 are unemployed. Of these ten persons, five are young and three of these are women. [A]mong the unemployed queuing up for unskilled jobs, the successful applicants will be the first adult males (between 24 and 54 years of age), then women of the same age, followed by young persons; the last will be minorities and older workers.
> (ILO, 1984, p.46)

4 GENDER AND LABOUR MARKET SEGMENTATION

In nineteenth-century Britain the majority of women did not enter regular waged employment — though many of them were engaged as homeworkers and domestic servants. Nevertheless, speaking of those who *were* in regular employment in the East End of London in 1988, Fishman says that 'the crime of being born female meant that women were at the bottom of the pecking order'. He cites a contemporaneous six-month research project carried out by Harkness, which revealed a picture of unmitigated exploitation: women were working in some 200 separate trades and, despite their low rates of pay and poor conditions of employment, Harkness found that 'many a family is at present kept by the labour of one or two such girls' (Fishman, 1988, pp.115–6).

Since 1945 the number of women in regular employment has grown sharply. For example, between 1951 and 1986 their number increased from almost 7.5 million to 9.4 million, at which point they accounted for more than 40 per cent of the economically active workforce; and of the nearly 3 million growth in the civilian labour force between 1971 and 1989, some 90 per cent has been among women. As for the future, of the projected increase between 1989 and 2001, again more than 90 per cent is expected to be among women (*Employment Gazette*, April 1990, pp.186 and 188).

This continuing 'feminization' of the UK labour force reflects not only the expansion of services but also the decline in the number of jobs for men in manufacturing. For example, while in 1986 female employment levels were slightly below their peak of 1979, male employment fell in the same period by 1.5 million to 11.5 million, a decline of 11 per cent (McDowell, 1988, p.165). Thus, the 1989 Labour Force Survey shows that 81 per cent of working women were employed in service industries as against just over 50 per cent of men. By contrast, manufacturing industries employed only 16 per cent of women as against 28 per cent of men. Moreover, there was an even greater concentration in the service industries of women who worked part-time (88 per cent) (*Employment Gazette*, December 1990, p.640). The expansion of part-time work and the dominant role of women within it is a continuing feature of the UK labour market and is a reflection of sectoral restructuring: while manufacturing and extractive industries employing full-time workers have declined as sources of employment, service industries have expanded. It is in these industries — often characterized by extended opening hours to meet consumer demand, as in the case of retailing — that part-time and women's employment is concentrated.

However, the concentration of women in the service sector of the economy, and in part-time work particularly, suggests that the idea of the 'feminization' of the labour force should be used with caution. It might be more accurate to describe certain activities within the service sector and certain occupations as having become 'feminized', rather than simply referring to the labour force as a whole having become so. Thus, as Werneke observes:

> Today, throughout the industrialized countries, one of the fundamental characteristics of the labour markets is the marked segregation by sex. Women are concentrated in a limited range of occupations and are most likely to be found working in relatively less skilled and lower paying jobs than their male counterparts. (Werneke, 1985, p.400)

In the labour market, two kinds of segregation by gender can be distinguished:

1   *Horizontal segregation,* which refers to the extent to which men and women are concentrated in different jobs. In the UK, for example, in 1986, half of all employed men worked in jobs where at least 90 per cent of the workforce was male and half of the women worked in jobs where at least 75 per cent of the workforce was female (McDowell, 1988, pp.167–8).

2   *Vertical segregation,* which refers to the differences within occupations in respect of pay, skill, status, promotion prospects, and the like. In broad terms we usually find women at the bottom of such hierarchies and men occupying more of the supervisory and managerial positions.

The degree to which women are concentrated in a narrow range of occupations, and are situated more often than not in the lower grades within occupational groups, owes much to the importance that part-time work has assumed for the growing number of women in employment. It was widely held in the period from the 1950s to the early 1970s that, against a background of shortages of labour, married women constituted the only major untapped source of labour. If this was so, then it seemed to follow that the most effective means to remedy the shortages was to expand part-time employment. Though very little part-time work was available in Britain prior to the Second World War, by the late 1980s this position had been transformed. In 1989, although over 76 per cent of employees and self-employed people were working full-time, this proportion was much higher among men (93 per cent) than among women (55 per cent) (*Employment Gazette,* April 1990, p.202). As Hakim explains, the enormous growth in part-time employment can be dated from the Second World War when the marriage bar for female workers was rescinded. It is worth quoting her comments in full:

> The marriage bar was the rule, jointly enforced by employers and trade unions, that women had to leave paid employment on marriage — effectively excluding married women from the labour market. The marriage bar became widespread in the second half of the nineteenth century, and was abolished from the 1940s onwards, after a long campaign by women's organizations against employers' organizations and trade unions. For example, the marriage bar was abolished in the Civil Service in 1946, but the Union of Post Office Workers ensured its operation until 1963. (Hakim, 1987, p.555)

The marriage bar clearly constituted a major obstacle to the employment of women. And its abolition therefore represented a fundamental change in their position and was a key factor in the subsequent growth of part-time work. Yet, as Hakim adds, it is rarely referred to by social historians, sociologists or economists (ibid.). However, the rise of part-time work represents both a breakthrough and a trap for women seeking employment. This is because part-time workers often work under much less favourable conditions than do full-time workers. For example, part-time workers who work only a few hours per week are not covered by many of the items of employment protection legislation introduced in the last decade.

Women in employment — despite the extent of their participation — tend to be regarded differently from men. At one level they are seen as a *labour reserve*; that is, as a body of workers who may be tempted to move into work when and where labour is in short supply, yet who equally ought to be prepared to move out of the workforce once more if unemployment levels rise significantly. This expectation was perhaps demonstrated most graphically when, in the period after the Second World War, talk of the vital contribution of women's work was replaced by an emphasis on the 'secondary' nature of women's earnings and on the virtues of domesticity. If women continue to be seen as a labour reserve or, equally, if they are regarded first and foremost as part-time workers, this gives credence to the idea that:

> ... paid work is held to be of central importance in men's lives, but not as important in women's lives. This reflects the widespread view in our society that women have a choice about employment, at least at certain stages of their lives, in a way that men do not as they will be primarily concerned with rearing children during their lives and so will either withdraw from the labour market or combine domestic responsibilities with part-time work.
> (Roberts, 1983, p.236)

The significance of such attitudes and their implications for the organization of work are indicated in Beechey and Perkins' investigation of part-time work in Coventry. They found, for instance, that it was invariably women's jobs that were arranged on a part-time basis; that part-time work was closely bound up with occupational segregation; and that employers and trade unionists alike made assumptions about the sort of work that was suitable for women and about why women did part-time work (Beechey and Perkins, 1985, p.261). The attitudes of employers and trade unionists which they report demonstrate that the consequences of the domestic division of labour strongly influence the circumstances under which women — and especially married women — present themselves to the labour market: women can be characterized as having limited availability and limited ambition. Equally, the demands of women workers for shorter working hours to match the school day, the provision of crèche facilities, or for paid leave in case of family illness and so on — whether or not seen as legitimate — can be said to reinforce the stereotype of women as primarily responsible for care in the family. Although one of the most important factors affecting women's participation in the labour market *is* the need to care for their children (economic activity rates for women range from as high as 91 per cent for those aged 25–39 without children to as low as 38 per cent for 16–24-year-olds with pre-school-aged children (*Employment Gazette*, December 1990, p.628)), we may nevertheless assume that *beliefs* about responsibilities for child-care are extended to justify the secondary status of women in the workforce more generally, even where their activity rates virtually match those of men.

How should we understand these different processes? At a general level, we can say that gender is central to the way work is organized. This is so not merely because of the implications that the domestic division of labour has for the employment of women, often in part-time jobs. The concentration of women in work that is labelled 'unskilled' or 'semi-skilled', and which is largely segregated from male employment, also reflects the way in which skill is attributed to a task (or to a number of tasks) depending on who is doing it. As Barker and Downing remark:

> ... conventional notions of skill and deskilling cannot be applied to a predominantly female labour process because the very fact of a job being labelled as 'women's work' brings in enormous ideological determinations which enable its skill content 'somehow' to be devalued.
> (quoted in Harvey, 1987, p.72)

We can apply the concept of the dual labour market to the employment profile of women by suggesting that, if it is in the interests of employers to maintain and expand the primary sector, it may be equally in their interests to maintain instability and low earnings in the predominantly female secondary sector. However, 'this strategy is necessarily related to the availability of a supply of workers willing to accept the poor pay, insecurity, low status and poor working conditions of secondary jobs' (Barron and Norris, 1976, p.52). This 'availability' is well illustrated in the UK clothing industry where, according to Phizacklea (1990), the workforce is 80 per cent female, but where women are concentrated in work which is gender-specific, low-paid, and which is ranked as low-skilled. In Phizacklea's view, this way of classifying women is not simply the product of the domestic division of labour: it is also the result of male workers succeeding in defining their own work in the industry as 'skilled' and persuading management to accept their demand, as breadwinners, for a 'family wage'. Thus, she quotes the following view of minority women clothing workers, expressed by an Asian entrepreneur:

> I see the majority of women working for me as benefiting from my job offer. They are illiterate and have no skills, hence no British factory will make use of them. Their £20 a week will help towards the family income, and we are like a big family here.
> (quoted in Phizacklea, 1990, pp.92–3)

5   MIGRANT WORKERS AND DIVISIONS OF LABOUR

At first sight, the differences between the position of women in the labour market and that of migrant workers exceed the similarities: for example, many women are part-time workers, but most migrants work full-time. Nevertheless, they are believed to share two important characteristics. First, their participation in the labour market is seen by employers and others to offer a (much-needed) degree of *numerical* flexibility. Secondly, both groups are seen as entering the labour market with lower expectations as to pay, conditions and prospects than do other workers.

The continuing shortages of labour that afflicted the British economy between 1945 and 1970 were also apparent in other IACs to a greater or lesser degree. One solution to these problems was to import foreign workers, though the extent to which these migrants satisfied the requirements to be available as demand for labour rose and to depart when demand for labour subsided varied from case to case. Their importance is to be understood not merely in terms of their overall numbers, but also in terms of their marginal contribution in particular sectors or in certain types of employment. For example, in the car industry, Cohen reports that 60 per cent of the workforce at Ford's largest British plant (Dagenham) was black; that the proportion of Turkish workers in Ford's plants in Germany was higher still; and that migrant labour-power predominated in car factories generally in France and Germany (Cohen, 1987, p.128).

Some observers believed that the importing of foreign workers had the effect of prolonging the life of relatively labour-intensive forms of production in the IACs, and thus, in the long-run, economic growth was constrained. Others (for example, Kindleberger, 1967) argue that migrant labour was integral to economic growth as well as to developments in the production process. In the case of West Germany, for instance, foreign workers provided much needed additional labour, particularly in growth industries such as engineering, chemicals and plastics, at times when the numbers of indigenous German workers were stagnant or in decline (Castles, 1984, p.127).

In general terms it can be argued that migrant workers in West Germany offered a number of advantages both to employers and to the receiving economy more widely: for example, they could be paid less than other workers; given their origins in less developed countries (LDCs), they had lower economic and social expectations than other workers; and they were easier to recruit *and* to dismiss. But possibly the greatest advantage that they offered lay in what it was that most obviously distinguished these migrants from their counterparts who left Europe to settle in North America in the nineteenth and early twentieth centuries. This concerns the range of *political* restrictions that post-1945 international migrants have faced and, in particular, their exclusion from, or their limited opportunities to obtain, full citizenship in receiving countries. They can thus be seen as belonging to the category *unfree labourers* which Cohen describes as being 'destined to be deployed either at the core or at the edge of the regional political economy' (Cohen, 1987, p.26).

In these circumstances, migrant workers offered the additional advantage that, if and when they were discarded by employers, it could be expected that they would return to their families who, because of restrictions at the point of entry, had remained in the country of origin. The receiving economy would then be responsible only for the wage at the point of production, and the 'social wage' (that is, the cost to society of providing for the worker's family and especially the costs associated with birth, education and health) would be eliminated or sharply reduced. As far as employers and governments alike in the labour-importing countries were concerned, there were good reasons for seeing migrant workers not only as a source of labour that would perform jobs others were unwilling to perform but also as a *flexible* source of labour. In part, this could be ascribed to migrants themselves who were believed to act as 'target' workers. What this meant was that workers arrived intending only to earn enough to improve their position in their country of origin. Once this was achieved, they would depart. In addition, there were strong grounds for preferring temporary labour migration to permanent settlement of immigrants together with their families. In the words of the Chairman of the Committee on Foreign Workers of the German Employers Association, 'the great value of the employment of foreigners lies in the fact that we have here at our disposal a *mobile labour potential*. It would be dangerous to limit this mobility through a large-scale assimilation policy' (quoted in Ward, 1975, p.24, emphasis added).

This 'mobile labour potential' was referred to by the West German government as the *Konjuncturpuffer* (meaning 'boom-buffer'): that is, the import of migrant labour during an economic boom serves to protect the indigenous labour force from some of the adverse consequences of labour shortages — such as lay-offs or short-time caused by production bottlenecks — and, equally, the export of migrant labour in time of economic recession cushions the indigenous labour force against unemployment. It was believed that such an objective would be obtained by having a partially rotating workforce: new migrants on short-term contracts would replace existing migrants whose contracts had ended; the number of migrants could then be adjusted by the government according to prevailing economic conditions, either by increasing recruitment or (aided by the migrants' normally high rate of return because they acted as 'target' workers) by restricting it or suspending it altogether.

But even in West Germany, where the system of controlling the inflow and outflow of foreign workers was particularly elaborate, only a proportion of the workforce remained 'flexible' in the manner just described. A larger element became an integral component of the labour

'Europe Patent': squeezing the best out of migrant workers

force, and as such were hardly more mobile than indigenous labour either individually or collectively. One persuasive explanation of this phenomenon is provided by Böhning's hypothesis (1981, pp.28–9) that, in what he termed a post-industrial society (which he defined as comprising a relatively small agricultural sector, a large semi-automated manufacturing sector which is in relative decline, and an equally large but expanding service sector), committed to high economic growth and to full employment:

1   because such a society is unable to change its traditional job structure, endemic labour shortages will arise in socially undesirable and low-wage jobs;

2   an attempt will be made to ameliorate these labour shortages by engaging foreign workers from LDCs; and consequently

3   the social-job structure will become rigidified, so forestalling an effective remedy to the initial problem of labour shortages and setting in motion a process of migration which, under current trends of technological developments is unending and self-feeding.

The transition from a 'mobile labour potential' to a 'self-feeding' process hints at the transformation of migrant workers into settled immigrant communities. Though it is true that migrants could be more easily hired and fired according to the dictates of the economy, it is also true that they were engaged as *replacement labour* to perform the dirty and socially undesirable jobs vacated by indigenous workers, who had taken advantage of expanding employment opportunities to secure more desirable jobs.

A recruitment centre for migrant workers in Istanbul

We can see this pattern clearly in the UK textile industry. In the post-war period, it faced severe labour shortages because indigenous workers had been generally unwilling to work in what was perceived as a declining industry in which pay and conditions were poor. The employers' response was to recruit large numbers of New Commonwealth immigrant workers, particularly for permanent night-shifts where the level of wages they judged to be low enough for them to remain competitive had failed to attract indigenous workers in any numbers. In performing this role, New Commonwealth immigrants followed in the footsteps of previous immigrants to Britain, for industries like textiles, iron foundries, clothing, and brickmaking have traditionally depended on immigrant labour.

The use of immigrant labour in the post-war period was not, however, simply the result of overall economic growth; it also reflected the form that this growth took — or, in the case of industries like textiles, the form of its retrenchment. The replacement of relatively labour-intensive methods of production by more capital-intensive methods involving the spread of automation and semi-automation did not eliminate poorly-paid, boring, or otherwise undesirable jobs. Indeed in some respects, as in the need to work some capital equipment on a continuous-shift basis in order to justify the cost of investment, it multiplied such jobs by necessitating the creation of permanent night-shifts. Much of the machinery that the expensive new capital equipment replaced had been worked by female labour. But there were both legal and social impediments to the employment of women on night-shifts. Given the reluctance of white males to accept the proffered rates of pay for this work, the introduction of the new machinery therefore resulted in black male immigrant labour being substituted for white female indigenous labour (Cohen and Jenner, 1981, pp.109 and 126). In some textile factories in Lancashire and Yorkshire which operated night-shifts, almost the entire shift would consist of Asian workers. More generally, a Political and Economic Planning Report found that 32 per cent of factories in which ethnic minorities formed the majority of the workforce had permanent night-shifts, compared with only 12 per cent of factories where only white workers were employed (Smith, 1974, p.41).

Though immigrant labour was an important element in the textile industry, its contribution to the continuing survival of the UK clothing industry throughout the 1980s may have been more vital still. While it is often assumed that garment workers in Britain will be undercut by low-paid counterparts in the Third World bent over sewing machines for twelve hours and more at a time, this is to neglect the extent to which certain types of clothing worker in *Britain* are paid very low wages for very long hours. For example, in 1989, according to Phizacklea, clothing homeworkers in the UK typically earned about 80 pence an hour with no provision for ill-health and no job security (Phizacklea, 1990, p.1). Whereas clothing manufacturers in West Germany offloaded less stable elements of their production by subcontracting to low-wage countries (as will be discussed in Section 6), in the UK such flexibility and competitive advantage tended to be gained by subcontracting to the plethora of small inner-city firms where ethnic entrepreneurs and labour were dominant. These firms could compete effectively with firms in low-wage countries only by intensifying the pace of work and casualizing its organization through the employment of homeworkers, who constitute an almost perfect solution to the need for a flexible workforce. These mainly ethnic enterprises also relied heavily on access to 'family' (i.e. female) labour, who had come to join the original male immigrants and who could be employed at low cost (Phizacklea, 1990, p.49).

An examination of the role of immigrant workers in both the textile and garment industries thus provides strong evidence that their employment was associated with unpleasant working conditions and intensification of work. They were obliged or willing to do such work where indigenous labour was not forthcoming because, as Cohen and Jenner concluded in their analysis of the UK textile industry:

> [Immigrant labour] is usually more willing to take this work than local labour for a variety of reasons. Firstly, the undoubted discrimination in employment against the immigrant restricts his choice of jobs severely. Secondly, his lack of suitable qualifications and language problems further restrict opportunities. Thirdly, one can hypothesize that the immigrant newly established in this

> country is much nearer the economist's ideal of economic man.
> The majority of immigrants are simply adult males less
> constrained than the English worker by non-economic factors such
> as socially awkward hours of work, and are willing to work as long
> hours as possible to earn as much as possible.
> (Cohen and Jenner, 1981, p.122)

In this process, immigrant labour became a permanent part of the
workforce, not only in the UK, but in France, West Germany and
Switzerland too (Castles and Kosack, 1973). Immigrant workers
performed jobs that indigenous workers were reluctant to undertake,
even in time of recession: 'Who else, after all, would shift the muck in
Munich or do the dirty work in Stuttgart or Frankfurt? Certainly not the
German unemployed' (*The Economist,* 25 January 1974). This is not to
say they were made welcome: the attitude of many employers in Britain
towards immigrant workers from the New Commonwealth is, perhaps,
encapsulated in the comment, 'We haven't got to the point where we
have to take them on. I suppose if things got bad enough we would'
(Daniel, 1968).

Nevertheless, and notwithstanding this replacement role of immigrant
labour, there is no doubt that the attraction of the 'migrant solution' as a
means of solving the sort of problems addressed in Böhning's self-
feeding hypothesis had virtually disappeared by the mid-1970s. To
some extent this was because the cost of maintaining what had
gradually evolved into immigrant communities (the social wage) had
become much higher than in the early stages of inward-migration. But
of equal, if not greater, importance was the realization by many
employers, for example in the garment and electrical industries, that
their labour requirements could be better met by relocating all or a part
of their production outside the national economy. A key question
became, is it not more rational to move the machines to the workers
than to bring the workers to the machines?

Though, of course, this 'reversal' could not be applied in certain
inherently immobile (immobile, that is, in international terms) spheres
such as public transport and the health service, the consequence of this
changing emphasis was that, in summary, 'an internal racial division of
labour could be replaced by an international division of labour, and the
sites of production could be switched to take account of market,
transportation and labour conditions' (Cohen, 1987, p.141). In broader
terms, however, this involves more than the internal racial division of
labour: it concerns the way employment opportunities in one part of the
world are related to those in another. Thus when, in pursuit of lower
labour costs, capital migrates in search of its own comparative
advantage, this relocation will come at the expense of both indigenous
and imported workers in the metropolis, where job prospects are
thereby reduced. It may be anticipated that this process will be
particularly marked in labour-intensive and easily-relocatable industries
such as textiles and clothing. Lipietz refers to this as a process whereby

not very well paid workers at the centre are replaced with women workers at the periphery who receive minimal wages: in his view this is a 'zero-sum game' involving no increase in world demand, in which it is employment at the centre which is the loser, thus explaining protectionist reactions aimed at curbing NIC exports (Lipietz, 1987, p.77).

Yet there is reason to suppose that in the face of this relocation it is the remaining immigrant workers who will experience higher levels of unemployment than will indigenous workers. This is not only because of discrimination and because it is less skilled workers who tend to lose their jobs first, but also because immigrant workers are disproportionately represented in declining and vulnerable industries such as textiles. In the UK, for example, in the middle and late 1980s, the unemployment rate for ethnic minority workers fluctuated at between two-thirds above that of the white population and twice their level (*Employment Gazette*, February 1991, p.65). But this differential rate of unemployment should not cause us to overlook an important change in labour market dynamics that Wilkinson (1981) notes with reference to West Germany. In the period from 1960 to the early 1970s, when labour shortages were at their most pronounced and West German employers relied heavily on immigrant workers to fill secondary occupations, it would hardly be an exaggeration to say, argues Wilkinson, that the West German labour force was segmented along international lines. However, the subsequent economic slowdown permitted a much more selective provision of primary employment conditions by employers: while unemployment was concentrated among workers with 'secondary characteristics', nevertheless 'the margin between the primary and secondary segments of the West German labour force has shifted from that country's border to include a significant proportion of the domestic labour force' (Wilkinson, 1981, p.ix).

6   A NEW INTERNATIONAL DIVISION OF LABOUR?

As a rule, the discussion of employment prospects for migrant labour in the metropolis has been conducted in domestic terms. Most attention has been paid to questions of racial discrimination on the one hand, and labour market segmentation on the other. Conversely, little attention has been devoted to the connections between international migration of labour and international movements of capital. Yet, as suggested in the previous section, changing attitudes towards the recruitment of foreign workers are strongly related to mobility of capital in general and to the operations of multinational corporations (MNCs) in particular.

As their name suggests, MNCs can operate 'geocentrically', planning the location of their production and the pattern of their investment according to the balance of advantage across the whole capitalist world economy. For example, in the short-term these geocentric MNCs have the ability to increase the level of production in one country at the expense of another and in the longer term they could even shift the entire balance of their production between countries. The importance of MNCs can be illustrated by the fact that something like two-fifths of international trade occurs *within* firms, a proportion that becomes even higher if we take into account the flows between companies and their partners in subcontracting agreements. This and other considerations causes some observers to visualize national economies as mere organic elements within an all-embracing world system (e.g. Fröbel *et al.*, 1980, p.8).

In this section our interest is not, however, in the pursuit of comparative advantage in general, but in the way in which production is located to take advantage of differential wage rates (and by implication of the social and economic conditions which influence these wage rates). We shall explore this further by examining the idea of a 'new international division of labour' (NIDL) developed by Fröbel *et al.* (1980). NIDL draws attention to the impact of MNCs, but its specific purpose is to point to the development of a world market in which manufacturing production (services are not addressed in their thesis) can be divided up into fragments and located in any industrialized or *less developed* part of the world, depending on where the most profitable combination of labour and capital can be obtained. Though this analysis is strong on contemporary empirical detail, it also presents a historical contrast between (i) a 'classical' international division of labour, in which a minority of industrialized countries produced manufactured goods and less developed countries were integrated into the world economy solely as producers of food and raw materials, and (ii) NIDL, in which the traditional 'bisection' of the world economy is undermined (Fröbel *et al.*, 1980, pp.44–5).

In brief, what NIDL entails is the shutting down of certain types of manufacturing operations in IACs, and the subsequent opening up of these same operations in the foreign subsidiaries of the same company. In Fröbel *et al.*'s view, the Federal German garment and textile industries represent one of the best examplars of this process (though these industries in other IACs too have, in most cases, drastically cut production at traditional sites of manufacture as output became less competitive in world markets), and an archetypal instance of it is that 'Trousers for the Federal German market are no longer produced for example in Mönchengladbach, but in the Tunisian subsidiary of the same Federal German company' (Fröbel *et al.*, 1980, p.9).

The extent to which for manufacturing the most profitable combination of labour and capital is no longer to be found in the IACs is frequently explained with reference to a supposed crisis of Fordist production at the 'centre' (see Chapter 5 of this volume). However, we should not underestimate the extent to which the optimum location for production shifts away from the centre in response to the erosion of the *initial* advantages derived by IACs from the employment of imported labour. Thus, as action by trade unions on behalf of immigrant workers, action by immigrant workers on their own behalf, or the beneficial effects of health and safety legislation combine to improve the pay and conditions of immigrant labour, so the advantages of decamping to areas of low-cost labour — particularly for firms in labour-intensive spheres — become ever more appealing. It is therefore not surprising to discover that the industries that once expanded by using immigrant workers, or those industries which forestalled decline by the same means, were in the forefront of the drive to relocate production, often to the same countries from which their imported workers originated.

ACTIVITY 1   You should now read **Reading A, 'The new international division of labour'**, by F. Fröbel *et al.*, which you will find at the end of this chapter.

In this extract Fröbel *et al.* refer to the creation of a virtually inexhaustible and easily exploitable supply of labour in developing countries, and elsewhere in their book they specify the characteristics of this labour force and the conditions under which these workers are employed. According to Lipietz, most of the jobs that are created in the developing countries involve 'Taylorism' rather than 'Fordism' — and 'primitive Taylorism' at that. (Taylorism and Fordism will be discussed in Section 7 of this chapter; for further discussion, see Chapters 5 and 7 of this book.) What he means by this is that the sort of jobs that are relocated — mostly in textiles and electronics — are not linked by any automatic machine system, yet they are fragmented and repetitive and thus labour-intensive in the strictest sense of the term (Lipietz, 1987, p.74).

It is no wonder then that the preferred labour force in this environment is invariably female: this is not simply because in developing countries, as in the IACs, the price of female labour-power is lower, and often very much lower, than that of male labour-power; it also reflects beliefs about the intensity with which women may work when sitting at a sewing machine in textile production or in an electronics factory. The ideological character of these beliefs can be gauged from a variety of sources. For example, an article in the *Far Eastern Economic Review* stated that:

> Most manufacturers prefer female workers because they have a longer attention span than males and can adjust more easily to long hours on the assembly line. In addition they are willing to accept lower pay and are said to have more agile hands, which is especially important in electronics.
>
> (2 July 1976; quoted in Fröbel *et al.*, 1980, p.348)

And in a feature on Mauritius in the *Financial Times* it was stated that:

> There has been some criticism of the fact that most zone
> industries, especially in the textile and electronic factories, employ
> mainly women. Some 85 per cent are women, and efforts are being
> made to switch the trend ... [It] is not necessarily due to the fact
> that women in Mauritius receive lower wages than men, but rather
> because industrialists have found that women are more adaptable
> than men to most of the skills required.
> (18 June 1976; quoted in Fröbel *et al.*, 1980, p.348)

The role of female labour in what Fröbel *et al.* call 'world market
factories', and in particular the way in which the domestic division of
labour is seen to prepare them for this role (women are referred to in
another Malaysian investment brochure as being qualified 'by both
nature and tradition' for work on the assembly line requiring great
manual dexterity) is further clarified by this impression gained on a
visit to a British-owed Malaysian factory which assembled integrated
circuit boards:

> ... well qualified young women who, whilst awaiting their parent-
> chosen bridegroom, work on flow lines doing minutely routinized
> assembly tasks under the supervision of generally less or equally
> qualified males. The latter have what they regard as a career in a
> 'high tech' industry: the former seem well aware of their
> subjugation to market, domestic and religiously sanctified
> hierarchy.
> (Loveridge, 1987, p.185)

Though Fröbel *et al.* emphasize the contrast between the old
international division of labour and the new, they see the latter as
deepening rather than reversing the historical underdevelopment of
LDCs: what applied to their agriculture and to mining is now replicated
in the industrial sector. In their view there is no discernible transfer of
technology. In part, this is because the technology being employed is
generally simple (and in any case is dependent on the expertise of
foreigners), but it is also because the skills acquired by the workforce in
world market factories are seen as minimal because training rarely lasts
for more than a few weeks. For these and other reasons, no significant
improvement is envisaged in either the material conditions of the
population or in its level of skill: only a fraction of the population is
employed — at very low wage levels — while the remainder forms a
permanent reserve army. In addition to this, Fröbel *et al.* see world
market factories remaining as industrial enclaves, unconnected to the
local economy except in so far as the latter provides new labour to be
freshly trained when the existing labour force is discarded (Fröbel *et al.*,
1980, p.6).

The great majority of workers in 'world market factories' are women

There are, nevertheless, a number of criticisms to be made of this general thesis. First, as we saw in the last section, Phizacklea contends that the German pattern of relocating the production of garments in the way described by Fröbel *et al.* was not replicated on the same scale in the UK: in Britain, similar ends were often achieved by subcontracting production to inner-city, secondary sector firms. However, though this strategy was indeed widely adopted in the UK, it should be noted that the structure of the UK garment industry is diverse: textile MNCs exist alongside inner-city sweatshops. And if we examine the conduct of British MNCs such as Coats Patons we see that, just like their German counterparts, their response to being undercut by imports from developing countries was to move much of their own production to such countries in order to take advantage of lower labour costs. (According to a report in the *Financial Times*, in 1981 comparative labour costs for Coats Patons were as low as 10 per cent of British levels in the Phillipines and 6 per cent in Indonesia (*Financial Times*, 29 June 1981).)

A second criticism is that NIDL theorists have exaggerated the scale of the relocation of production, for expressed as a proportion of world-wide industrial output, that of the Third World remains small. There is some truth in this, but what may be of more significance for NIDL theorists is that in the 1970s and 1980s the employment forces of MNCs in their home countries fell quite markedly as world-wide economic activity slackened, whereas their employment levels fell much less or even expanded in LDCs (Thrift, 1988, p.34).

Thirdly, some commentators (e.g. Jenkins, 1984, and Lipietz, 1987) have argued that where MNCs do relocate production they are as likely, if not more likely, to do so to establish a market position in the economy in question as to be in pursuit of cheap labour.

Though these are powerful criticisms, advocates of NIDL were generally well aware that the amount of direct foreign investment in LDCs was limited. What they sought to draw attention to was the likelihood that, given the three preconditions identified by Fröbel *et al.*, future flows of such investment would escalate, attracted in particular by the prospect of cheap labour. Thus, the path established by the relocation of garment and textile production would be followed by other industries, notably the car component industry. The logic of this argument is that MNCs have in their operations transcended national boundaries. But what this logic overlooks is that reducing direct labour costs — whether by relocation or otherwise — is only one route to competitive advantage, and perhaps one of diminishing importance. An alternative approach is to increase labour productivity by means of technical innovation. And in achieving this objective, as Porter argues, the role of the national environment is profoundly important: 'It shapes the way opportunities are perceived, how specialized skills and resources are developed, and the pressures on firms to mobilize resources in rapid and efficient ways … Globalization makes nations more, not less, important' (Porter, 1990 p.736). It is to aspects of this argument, and particularly to those which concern the concepts of 'core' and 'periphery' in the labour process, that we turn in the next section.

7 THE DIVISION OF LABOUR AND FLEXIBLE SPECIALIZATION

In drawing attention to the relocation of manufacturing consequent upon the division and subdivision of production processes into fragments, often requiring only minimal skill, Fröbel *et al.* also assert that this has overtaken the traditional means of rationalizing production in IACs. This rationalization is perceived quite differently by other commentators however. For example, according to Piore and Sabel (1984), contemporary capitalism is undergoing a period of restructuring which can be seen in terms of a divide between the eras of *mass production* and *flexible specialization*, the latter being linked to the new type of flexible electronics-based automation technologies.

In the era of mass production, particular models (whether cars or washing machines) were manufactured in large batches on assembly lines that required great investment in inflexible plant. In the era of flexible specialization, on the other hand, small batch production is possible. In this era, *flexibility* is at a premium not only in terms of the organization of production — one important aspect of flexible specialization is sometimes referred to as the system of just-in-time (or JIT) production, because one of its chief characteristics is its capacity to operate with minimal levels of inventory as components arrive on a just-in-time basis (Hoffman and Kaplinsky, 1988, p.51) — but also in terms of the *workforce*.

The transition to mass production associated with Taylorism and Fordism should be seen in terms of an evolving labour process which has both earlier and later manifestations (Kaplinsky, 1988, pp.453–4; Hoffman and Kaplinsky, 1988, p.330; see also the discussion in Chapters 5 and 7 of this volume). These developments have their roots in:

1   the division of labour discerned by Adam Smith, in which jobs are broken down into ever more specialized tasks, each of which can be done by a dedicated worker (however, it was the economies of scale associated with machine production of goods that vastly increased output, when complemented with the requisite pattern of work and production organization, rather than the division of labour in itself);

2   the so-called *Babbage principle*, which involved the identification and separation of unskilled tasks, thus simultaneously deskilling some work, permitting the employment of cheaper labour, and increasing managerial control by sacking recalcitrant workers (or threatening so to do);

3   the attempt to compensate for the unreliability of skilled labour by mechanizing hitherto skilled sub-processes;

4   the introduction of Taylorism in an effort to maintain control of workers in larger factories;

5   the incorporation of Taylorism into a mass production system of moving production lines and standardized products (Fordism) in which one of the key elements was the keeping of high levels of inventory as an insurance against interruptions in the system; and finally

6   as we saw in the previous section, the three preconditions mentioned by Fröbel *et al.* allow the process of task fragmentation, deskilling and large-scale production to be conducted on a worldwide basis in a 'new international division of labour'.

These developments need not and should not be seen as flowing inevitably from technological advances. Thus, the transition to mass production reflects *beliefs* about the gains to be derived from standardizing products, or about the economies of large-scale production. The choices between one form of technology and another are often shaped by a variety of non-technological, non-economic, and ideological considerations (Piore and Sable, 1984, p.57). We can see this type of influence, for example, in the success which Taylorism has had in establishing deskilling, task fragmentation and decreased worker discretion as key elements of managerial control, to the extent that they are widely taken-for-granted as the way to approach the organization of work. Yet as Rosenbrock observes, if the urge is to seek subsequently to automate 'unsatisfactory' (i.e. fragmented, deskilled) jobs out of existence, we must not overlook the extent to which, in order to apply the cure, to abolish the trivialized job, one first has to create the disease, the supply of trivialized jobs' (Rosenbrock, 1982, p.109). Nevertheless, it is precisely this creation of trivialized jobs that is presented by Braverman (1974) as the dominant and inevitable form of the way work is organized in capitalist industrial production. For Braverman, a continuous process of fragmentation and deskilling was visible in IACs from the 1890s onwards. Eventually, work for virtually the whole labour force would have become routine, fragmented and lacking in skill, and the distinctions between skilled and unskilled workers or between manual and non-manual workers would therefore be devalued. As Lane notes in Reading B, which you will be asked to read shortly, in Braverman's opinion Taylorism represented capitalism in its purest form, embodying the maximum division of labour and, in so far as labour is regarded as a factor disruptive of production, the minimal amount of worker discretion (Lane, 1988, p.141).

There are, however, a number of reasons for questioning the continued viability of Taylorism and Fordism at the centre over and above the competition emanating from peripheral NICs taking advantage of lower labour costs. For example, as Lane suggests, markets have become less stable and predictable, and the inflexibility of the established mass production model with its reliance on dedicated machinery operated by semi-skilled workers has therefore become more evident (1988, p.142). In addition, the diminishing returns associated with the Fordist labour process can be attributed to the denial of human creativity in the workplace: if worker discretion is minimized, it is unlikely that the enterprise will benefit from incremental improvements which workers may suggest on the basis of their detailed observations of production — improvements which in other, more enlightened, circumstances would be a vital element of technical innovation (Kaplinsky, 1988, p.455). It was in the light of these and other problems associated with Fordism that Piore and Sabel (1984) proposed a solution based on the concept of 'flexible specialization'.

Flexible specialization emphasizes flexibility in a number of areas: in terms of a response to the market, in terms of an ability to produce economically in small batches, and in terms of the flexibility demanded of the workforce. Piore and Sabel accept that the enhancement of workers' skills associated with more flexible forms of work organization may be balanced against, or even constrained by, the extension of management control which the introduction of new technology — particularly information technology — facilitates. Thus worker discretion may still be sharply circumscribed under flexible specialization. Nevertheless, they see the changes that flow from fragmented product markets as offering benefits to capital, labour and consumers alike: instead of workers with narrowly defined jobs using dedicated machines to produce a standard product, broadly skilled workers use capital equipment capable of making different models to produce specialized goods.

It is apparent that this represents a significant break with two of the key elements of Fordism: an increased division of labour and the deskilling of work. For example, whereas in Fordist car production the line is halted while specialist die-changers key in their work, in flexible specialization production workers are 'multi-tasked': not only are they responsible for changing the dies, but they have undergone training in routine maintenance and in a range of allied tasks. In addition to this, the new labour process is multi-skilling in so far as, in order to perform a range of tasks, workers must command a range of skills (Kaplinsky, 1988, pp.457–8; Hoffman and Kaplinsky, 1988, p.52).

What then is the evidence that a shift to flexible specialization has occurred or is occurring in IACs? In Meegan's opinion, in the UK the evidence is fragmentary and what evidence *is* discernible suggests caution in accepting what the advocates of flexible specialization claim. He concludes that although there are important changes going on of the type described by Piore and Sabel, they are happening more slowly and on a smaller scale than is sometimes claimed — claims that are often based on exaggerated accounts of the spread of flexible technologies like computer-integrated automation. In addition, Meegan argues that significant difficulties have been encountered in trying to automate 'flexibly' many of the assembly line operations that epitomize Fordism (Meegan, 1988, p.171).

ACTIVITY 2   You should now read **Reading B, 'The pursuit of flexible specialization in Britain and West Germany'**, by Christel Lane. As you read Lane's article, consider the following questions:

1   Why might it be argued that the established model of mass production in IACs has become less viable?

2   On the basis of Lane's article, what criticisms can be made of Braverman's central tenet concerning the labour process?

3   According to Lane, what evidence is there that 'flexible specialization' is a significant trend in West Germany?

4   What role should be assigned to skilled labour in achieving competitive advantage?

You will have seen in Reading B that, although she speaks of flexible specialization only as an emergent trend, Lane gives a rather different estimation of its development in Germany. She makes particular reference to the importance widely given there to organizational and technological innovation and to the links between them, which seem to signify 'an important change in capital's attitude to labour deployment which has more positive consequences for labour than the old Taylorist concept' (1988, p.159). At a general level, Lane discerns an important difference between employer strategies in Britain and those in Germany with regard to the workforce: drawing on Friedman's distinction between a labour process in which workers are given a measure of control over their working arrangements (*responsible autonomy*) and one where little or no discretion is granted *(direct control)* (Friedman, 1977), she explains the predisposition of German employers to adopt the former rather than the latter strategy both in terms of the availability of a large pool of skilled labour and in terms of how skill is produced. Lane describes how in Germany since 1945 there has been a predominance of skilled workers, possessing a high degree of qualifications. She calls such workers 'polyvalent'; that is, they have knowledge or capabilities in at least two areas gained in a systematic type of training.

On the basis of a review of several studies of industrial transformation in Germany in the 1970s and 1980s, Lane emphasizes the importance of developing forms of work organization which facilitate worker autonomy, job enrichment and upskilling. Though she is uncertain whether this denotes a new industrial strategy or merely indicates islands of change, Lane emphasizes that in Germany a successful competitive strategy is widely seen to depend on a range of factors: not *only* on the availability of worker skills, as Piore and Sabel suggest, but also on high levels of investment and managerial competence.

One of the main criticisms of Braverman's deskilling thesis is that it portrays a relationship between technology and the labour process which is ineluctable. It therefore ignores the extent to which the same sets of machinery located in similar modes of production can, nevertheless, be linked to quite different forms of workforce organization. These differences are evident, for example, in the 'extreme malleability of CNC [computer numerical control] technology' described by Hartman *et al.* They found that CNC could be operated either within a system where unskilled operators were neatly differentiated from skilled setters and technician planners, or near conventional machinery involving a skilled homogenous workforce (1985, p.359). More generally, it can be argued that, contrary to Braverman, it has *not* been equally true in all IACs that the labour process in the twentieth century has been one of deskilling. Thus, although the conditions described in *Working for Ford* (Beynon, 1973) seem to symbolize the deskilling thesis, according to which work is boring, repetitive and fragmented, other ways of manufacturing cars have been developed. For example, in the 1970s Volvo experimented with a system of flexible workgroups within which there was frequent rotation of a wide range of tasks.

The deskilling thesis seems also to neglect the extent to which new technology is conducive to the creation of new or extended skills, as well as to the disappearance of existing skills. In other words, management may pursue a variety of strategies, some of which may have a deskilling effect, others not. For example, we can see this in the way that management in the Japanese car industry seems to be able to give a substantial degree of control back to the workforce without having to worry that such control will be employed against company interests. Though some accounts of this phenomenon describe it as a matter of worker self-discipline rather than an indication that the workers control the production process, it seems more useful to see it in

A flexible workgroup at Volvo

terms of the distinction drawn by Hoffman and Kaplinsky between
'interior determination' and 'exterior control'. While the latter is a
product of Taylorism, the former entails providing the workforce not
just with quality circles, but also with the means to bring production to
a halt, something that cannot be easily envisaged under Taylorism
(Hoffman and Kaplinsky, 1988, p.338). The most arresting example of
this — and the word is used advisedly — is the installation of Andon
lights and switches by Toyota on many of their production lines. Not
only do these allow each line worker to bring the line to a standstill if a
fault is noted, but it is *expected* that this power will be exercised. (ibid.,
1988, p.337).

In contrast to the German approach to technological innovation, Lane
reports evidence of hesitancy (and worse) in the approach of British
firms. But even where British management pursues a 'new market
strategy' and makes extensive use of technical innovations, she argues
that labour force problems impede the realization of flexible
specialization. In particular, this is attributed to an insufficient supply
of skilled polyvalent labour. Similarly, Hartmann *et al.* conclude their
Anglo-German comparison by predicting that British companies will
train and utilize fewer skilled workers than their German counterparts,
which are able to draw on a greater supply of trained labour at all levels
(1985, pp.352–3).

We can visualize Anglo-German skill structures being different in at
least two important respects: first, there may be an absolute difference
in the level of skills (as in the decline of the apprenticeship system in

A Toyota production line on which the Andon system has been installed. Elevated cords run down both sides of the assembly line. When a segment of this cord is pulled by a worker, a corresponding light on the numbered overhead Andon board illuminates. The assembly line then halts automatically unless a supervisor overrides the stoppage.

Britain and the effect that this decline has had on the availability of skilled labour); and second, there may be a gulf in the differentiation between types and levels of skills (as in the extent to which 'demarcation' in Britain raises questions about the viability of utilizing multi-skill workgroups). At a more profound level it has been suggested that the UK may be caught in a 'low-skills equilibrium': manufacturing processes are based on low skill levels because the average skill level of the labour force is low, and this in turn dissuades management from investment in training because high skills are not deemed necessary for such processes (*Lloyds Bank Review*, February 1990).

As we have seen, central to the flexible specialization thesis is the view that changes in the markets for products have had or will have extensive implications for the sort of labour force that is needed to satisfy the market. Broadly speaking, one designated path for IACs can be summarized in terms of a reliance on the production of highly sophisticated goods and services for fast changing needs. This will require highly qualified workers capable of selecting data and handling strategic information. But if this is so, it may be asked whether the 'mixed strategy' that some commentators discern in the UK, which demands 'functional flexibility' from a core workforce and 'numerical flexibility' from a peripheral workforce (Hakim, 1990, p.164), or a 'polarized qualification pattern' (Hartmann *et al.*, 1985, p.358), is best suited to the posited product market.

We need to express some hesitation here, otherwise we may suggest, misleadingly, that a uniformly appropriate labour strategy is being pursued in one country whereas in another the strategy is wholly inappropriate to changes in the product market. In reality the difference is not so extreme. Thus, if we consider Kaplinsky's analysis of the reasons for the success of Japanese manufacturers in fostering the creation of a multi-skilled, multi-tasked workforce and entrusting this workforce with a measure of control over the production process, we note that the working conditions prevailing in Toyota stand in sharp contrast to those which exist in its subcontractors. In both the 200 highly specialized enterprises to which Toyota subcontracts directly and in the further 38,400 enterprises to which they, in turn, subcontract, wages are much lower than in Toyota, and there is no job security. In Kaplinsky's view, this constitutes a dual labour market so pronounced that it permits a structure of production costs that has traditionally been beyond the capacity of the older IACs to obtain (1988, p.466). Thus, in assessing trends towards 'enskilling', 'upskilling' and the like, which may be associated with 'interior determination' and the 'manufacture of consent', we should note that these concepts may apply only in certain parts of the production process and to certain types of worker. Those who work part-time or are employed by subcontractors may be excluded from these improvements; flexible specialization does not therefore entail the obsolence of the concepts of 'core' and 'peripheral' worker.

8   CONCLUSION

In this chapter I began my consideration of the division of labour in a conventional way by looking at sectoral divisions in the economy. But in emphasizing not only different aspects of the divisions of labour (in respect of gender, migrant workers, NIDL, and flexible specialization), but also the concepts of 'core' and 'periphery' as providing a theme which connects these disparate aspects, my approach has been somewhat less conventional.

Perhaps the key point, and one which can be applied to each of the groups and types of worker that I have dealt with, was set out in my reference in Section 3 to the idea of a 'dual labour market'. In the general context of a labour market being separated into *primary* and *secondary* sectors — or more accurately where workers can be categorized as being 'primary' or 'secondary' workers — reference was made to the need for employers to find a suitable means of adjusting their labour forces to fluctuations in demand. Broadly speaking, they will contrive to retain more skilled workers, in whom training and investment is relatively high, while shedding less skilled workers, in whom investment is relatively low and who are easy to replace. If this is so, we can go on to specify that the former group of workers are seen to be adaptable or 'functionally flexible', while the latter group need only be disposable or 'numerically flexible'. But we must not exaggerate the permanence of this posited boundary. It does not follow that 'once a primary worker, always a primary worker': for example, as we have seen, if large-scale enterprises detach part of their production to subcontractors, primary workers may be transformed into secondary workers.

Nor is it wise to exaggerate what different groups of workers share. For example, if we compare the situation of women workers and migrant workers, we see immediately that part-time work is considered appropriate for women because work is not regarded as centrally important to women's lives, whereas the term 'economic migrant' indicates that the desire to *work* is understood to explain the very act of migration itself. Nevertheless, women and migrants entering the labour market *do* have much in common. They are both perceived as being more easily disposable than are other groups of workers (though for different reasons): each is seen as providing a *labour reserve,* moving in and out of employment according to the demand for labour. And each is seen as suited to less-skilled work and to jobs with few prospects. The case of migrant workers in West Germany is particularly instructive. As was indicated in Section 5, although they were employed to provide a 'mobile labour potential', if anything, they turned out to be permanent, not temporary, replacements for indigenous labour. None the less, the differences between the high water mark of dependence on migrant labour and the subsequent recession, which also saw the growth of relocation of production to less developed countries described by Fröbel *et al.,* reveals a significant movement in the boundary between 'primary' and 'secondary' employment in West Germany. When migrant workers were at their most numerous, it was, according to Wilkinson, not much of a distortion to say that the German economy was segmented along international lines: that is, to be an indigenous worker was to be a primary worker. Thereafter, however, the boundary between primary and secondary employment shifted to include a significant percentage of indigenous workers amongst the secondary workforce. In essence this means that *who* was disposable changed: at one point the use of migrant workers guaranteed the employment of indigenous workers *and* protected them from unemployment; at the next point both the guarantee and the protection disappeared.

We saw the element of *disposability* most clearly, however, when we examined NIDL in Section 6. According to Fröbel and his colleagues, NIDL depends on a virtually inexhaustible and easily exploitable (thus disposable) supply of labour which, far from incidentally, is invariably female. Here there is no debate about work being of marginal importance to women's lives; instead, female workers are preferred because the price of their labour is lower, because of beliefs about the intensity with which they work (or can be made to work), and because of their perceived 'dexterity' (an attribute which diminishes by about the age of thirty, when they can be replaced by younger workers).

At first sight, the discussion of *flexible specialization* as an emergent trend seems to fit less easily into this framework of 'core' and 'periphery' — with its attendant emphasis on 'disposability'. However, a careful reading of Section 7 will show evidence to the contrary. We can see this most obviously in relation to the points about functional and numerical flexibility made at the beginning of this conclusion. As you will note, central to the flexible specialization thesis is the view that changes in the markets for products have far-reaching implications for the sort of workforce needed to satisfy those markets. These implications concern the degrees of skill that workers are required to possess and the degrees of control and autonomy that they are expected to exercise. However, you will also note that this emergent trend towards flexible specialization — if that is what we are witnessing — does not preclude a reliance on or a coexistence with forms of production where wages and conditions are much less attractive and where job security is much lower, and this often involves subcontracting relationships. In essence, therefore, a scenario in which workers are multi-skilled, relatively autonomous and, perhaps, indispensable, does not mean that other workers do not remain readily disposable.

REFERENCES

Abercombie, N., Hill, S. and Turner, B.S. (eds) (1988) *The Penguin Dictionary of Sociology*, 2nd edn, Harmondsworth, Penguin.

Abercrombie, N., Warde, A., Soothill, K., Urry, J. and Walby, S. (1988) *Contemporary British Society*, Cambridge, Polity Press.

Allen, J. and Massey, D. (eds) (1988) *The Economy in Question*, London, Sage Publications.

Barron, R. and Norris, E. (1976) 'Sexual divisions and the dual labour market', in Barker, D. and Allen, S. (eds) *Dependence and Exploitation in Work and Marriage*, London, Longman.

Beechey, V. and Perkins, T. (1985) 'Conceptualizing part-time work', in Roberts *et al.* (1985).

Beynon, H. (1973) *Working for Ford*, London, Allen Lane.

Blackburn, R. and Mann, N. (1979) *The Working Class and the Labour Market*, London, Macmillan.

Bocock, R. and Thompson, K. (eds) (1992) *Social and Cultural Forms of Modernity*, Cambridge, Polity Press.

Böhning, W. (1981) 'The self-feeding process of economic migration from low-wage to post-industrial countries with a liberal capitalist structure', in Braham *et al.* (eds) (1981).

Braham, P., Rhodes, E. and Pearn, M. (eds) (1981) *Discrimination and Disadvantage in Employment*, London, Harper and Row.

Braverman, H. (1974) *Labour and Monopoly Capital: the Degradation of Work in the Twentieth Century*, New York, Monthly Review Press.

Castles, S. (1984) *Here for Good: Western Europe's New Ethnic Minorities*, London, Pluto Press.

Castles, S. and Kosack, G. (1973) *Immigrant Workers and the Class Structure in Western Europe*, Oxford, Oxford University Press.

Cockburn, C. (1983) *Brothers: Male Dominance and Technical Change*, London, Pluto Press.

Cohen, R. (1987) *The New Helots: Migrants in the International Division of Labour*, Aldershot, Avebury.

Cohen, B. and Jenner, P. (1981) 'The employment of immigrants: a case study within the wool industry', in Braham, P. *et al.* (eds) (1981).

Daniel, W. (1968) *Racial discrimination in England*, Harmondsworth, Penguin.

Employment Gazette (monthly) London, Department of Employment.

Fishman, W. (1988) *East End 1888*, London, Duckworth.

Fox, A. (1974) *Man Mismanagement*, London, Hutchinson.

Friedman, A. (1977) *Industry and Labour: Class Struggle at Work and Monopoly Capitalism,* London, Macmillan.

Fröbel, F., Heinrichs, J. and Drey, O. (1980) *The New International Division of Labour*, New York, Cambridge University Press.

Gershuny, J. and Miles, I. (1983) *The New Service Economy: The Transformation of Employment in Industrial Societies*, London, Frances Pinter.

Goldthorpe, J. (1985) 'The end of convergence: corporalist and dualist tendencies in modern western societies', in Roberts, B. *et al.* (1985).

Hakim, C. (1987) 'Trends in the flexible workforce', *Employment Gazette*, November, pp.549–60.

Hakim, C. (1990) 'Core and periphery in employers' workforce strategies: evidence from the 1987 ELUS survey', *Work, Employment and Society*, vol.4, no.2, pp.157–88.

Hall, S. and Gieben, B. (eds) (1992) *Formations of Modernity*, Cambridge, Polity Press.

Hall, S., Held, D. and McGrew, A. (eds) (1992) *Modernity and its Futures,* Cambridge, Polity Press.

Harris, L. (1988) 'The UK economy at a cross-roads' in Allen, J. and Massey, D. (eds) *(*1988).

Hartmann, G., Nicholas, I., Sorge, A. and Warner, M. (1985) 'Computerised machine tools, manpower consequences and skill utilisation: a study of British and West German manufacturing firms', in Rhodes, E. and Wield, D. *Implementing New Technologies*, Oxford, Basil Blackwell.

Harvey, J. (1987) 'New technology and the gender divisions of labour', in Lee, G. and Loveridge, R. (eds) *The Manufacture of Disadvantage*, Milton Keynes, Open University Press.

Hoffman, K. and Kaplinsky, R. (1988) *Driving Force: The Global Restructuring of Technology, Labour and Investment in the Automobile and Components Industry*, San Francisco, Westview Press.

Hudson, R. (1988) 'Labour market changes and new forms of work in "old" industrial regions', in Massey, D. and Allen, J. (eds) (1988).

ILO (1984) *World Labour Report 1. Employment, Incomes, Social Protection, New Information Technology*, Geneva, International Labour Organization.

Jenkins, R. (1984) 'Divisions over the international division of labour', *Capital and Class*, no. 22, pp.28–57.

Kaplinsky, R. (1988) 'Restructuring the capitalist labour process: some lessons from the car industry', *Cambridge Journal of Economics*, vol.12, pp.451–70.

Kindleberger, C. (1967) *Europe's Post-war Growth: The Role of Labor Supply*, Cambridge, Mass., Harvard University Press.

Lane, C. (1988) 'Industrial change in Europe: the pursuit of flexible specialisation in Britain and West Germany', *Work, Employment and Society*, vol.2, no.2, pp.141–68.

Lipietz, A. (1987) *Mirages and Miracles: The Crisis of Global Capitalism*, London, Verso.

Loveridge, R. (1983) 'Labour market segmentation and the firm', in Edwards, J. *et al.* (eds) *Manpower Planning: Strategy and Techniques in an Organisational Context*, Chichester, John Wiley.

Loveridge, R. (1987) 'Social accommodations and technological transformations: the case of gender', in Lee, G. and Loveridge, R. (eds) *The Manufacture of Disadvantage*, Milton Keynes, Open University Press.

Massey, D. (1988) 'What's happening to UK manufacturing?', in Allen, J. and Massey, D. (eds) (1988).

Massey, D. and Allen, J. (eds) (1988) *Uneven Redevelopment*, London, Hodder and Stoughton.

McDowell, L. (1988) 'Gender divisions', in Hamnett, C. *et al.* (eds) *The Changing Social Structure,* London, Sage.

Meegan, R. (1988) 'A crisis of mass production?', in Allen, J. and Massey, D. (eds) (1988).

Offe, C. (1976) *Industry and Inequality*, London, Edward Arnold.

Penguin Dictionary of Sociology: see Abercrombie *et al.* (1988).

Phizacklea, A. (1990) *Unpacking the Fashion Industry: Gender, Racism and Class in Production*, London, Routledge.

Piore, M. and Sabel (1984) *The Second Industrial Divide*, New York, Basic Books.

Porter, M. (1990) *The Competitive Advantage of Nations*, London, Macmillan.

Roberts, C. (1983) 'Research on women in the labour market: the context and scope of the women and employment survey', in Roberts, B. *et al.* (1985).

Roberts, B. *et al.* (1985) *New Approaches to Economic Life: Economic Restructuring: Unemployment and the Social Division of Labour*, Manchester, Manchester University Press.

Rosenbrock, H. (1982) 'Can human skill survive microelectronics?', in Rhodes, E. and Wield, D. (eds) *Implementing New Technologies*, Oxford, Basil Blackwell.

Seear, N. (1981) 'The management of equal opportunity', in Braham *et al.* (eds) (1981).

Smith, D. (1974) *Racial Disadvantage in Employment*, London, PEP.

Thrift, N. (1988) 'The geography of international economic disorder', in Massey, D. and Allen, J. (eds) (1988).

Ward, A. (1975) 'European capitalism's reserve army', *Monthly Review Press*, vol.27, part 6.

Werneke, D. (1985) 'Women, the vulnerable group', in Forester, T. (ed.) *The Information Technology Revolution*, Oxford, Blackwell.

Wilkinson, F. (ed.) (1981) *The Dynamics of Labour Market Segmentation*, London, Academic Press.

Worsley, P. *et al.* (1977) *Introducing Sociology*, Harmondsworth, Penguin.

READING A   THE NEW INTERNATIONAL DIVISION OF LABOUR

F. Fröbel *et al.*

... [T]he old or 'classical' international division of labour is now open for replacement. The decisive evidence for this hypothesis is the fact that developing countries have increasingly become sites for manufacturing — producing manufactured goods which are competitive on the world market. ... [C]ase studies ... [will] provide extensive documentation of this world market oriented production of manufactures which is now being established and developed on new industrial sites, especially those in the developing countries.

This world market oriented industrialisation which is emerging today in many developing countries is not the result of positive decisions made by individual governments or companies. Industry only locates itself at those sites where production will yield a certain profit, sites which have been determined by five centuries of development of the world economy. In the 'classical' international division of labour which developed over this period, industrial sites for manufacturing basically only existed in Western Europe, and later in the USA and Japan. Since it is evident that the developing countries are now providing sites for the profitable manufacture of industrial products destined for the world market to an ever-increasing extent, we quickly come up against the question: What changes are responsible for this development?

Three preconditions taken together seem to be decisive for this new development.

Firstly, a practically inexhaustible reservoir of disposable labour has come into existence in the developing countries over the last few centuries. This labour-force is extremely cheap; it can be mobilised for production for practically the whole of the year, and all hours of the day, on shift work, night work and Sunday work; in many cases it can reach levels of labour productivity comparable with those of similar processes in the developed countries after a short period of training; companies can afford to exhaust the labour-force by overwork as it can easily be replaced, and they can also select their employees very specifically according to age, sex, skill, discipline and other relevant factors as there is an oversupply of people who are forced to take any job which is available.

Secondly, the division and subdivision of the production process is now so advanced that most of these fragmented operations can be carried out with minimal levels of skill easily learnt within a very short time.

Thirdly, the development of techniques of transport and communication has created the possibility, in many cases, of the complete or partial pro-

Source: Fröbel, F. *et al.* (1980) *The New International Division of Labour*, New York, Cambridge University Press, pp.12–15.

duction of goods at any site in the world — a possibility no longer ruled out by technical, organisational and cost factors.

The coincidence of these three preconditions (which are supplemented by other, less important ones) has brought into existence a world market for labour and a real world industrial reserve army of workers, together with a world market for production sites. Workers in the already industrialised countries are now placed on a world-wide labour market and forced to compete for their jobs with their fellow workers in the developing countries. Today, with the development of a world-wide market in production sites, the traditional industrialised and the developing countries have to compete against one another to attract industry to their sites.

In other words, for the first time in the history of the 500-year-old world economy, the profitable production of manufactures for the world market has finally become possible to a significant and increasing extent, not only in the industrialised countries, but also now in the developing countries. Furthermore, commodity production is being increasingly subdivided into fragments which can be assigned to whichever part of the world can provide the most profitable combination of capital and labour.

The term which we shall use to designate this qualitatively new development in the world economy is the *new international division of labour.*

Of those countries which were able to supply vast reserve armies of potential industrial workers and to offer these workers' labour-power at a low price, the first to attract the relocation of parts of the production process were countries with close geographical and commercial links to existing industrial centres. The first shifts of US industry were to Western Europe and to countries 'south of the border'; West European companies transferred production to other regions in Europe, such as Eire, Greece, Portugal and the south of Italy; Japanese industry moved into South Korea and Taiwan. At the same time, industrial firms recruited labour from countries with high rates of unemployment and drew it in to the traditional sites of industrial production. Hence the appearance of *Gastarbeiter* [guestworkers] in Western Europe, and Mexican and Puerto Rican immigrant workers in the USA.

Since then, sites for relocated manufacturing are not only being supplied in the border areas of Western Europe, Central America, North Africa, and South East Asia, but increasingly in Eastern Europe, South America, Central Africa and South Asia. The transfer of production to places with cheap labour not only affects the more or less labour-intensive production processes but also processes which are heavily dependent on raw materials and energy, and those which are a source of environmental pollution, given that the new sites can also offer favourable conditions as far as other factors of production are concerned. It has even affected capital-intensive production processes, contrary to the unsubstantiated prejudices of a number of international economists. Not only are investments, production capacities and output expanded and developed at these new sites, but existing facilities at the traditional sites which have become obsolete in terms of profitability are closed down.

This means that any company, almost irrespective of its size, which wishes to survive is now forced to initiate a transnational reorganisation of production to adapt to these qualitatively new conditions.

By far the most important means by which companies have secured their continued survival in the past has been through 'investment in rationalisation' — the installation of more efficient machinery and a reduction in the size and skills of the labour-force. This device alone (along with other 'classical' devices) is no longer adequate. The development of the world economy has increasingly created conditions (forcing the development of the new international division of labour) in which the survival of more and more companies can only be assured through the relocation of production to new industrial sites, where labour-power is cheap to buy, abundant and well-disciplined; in short, through the transnational reorganisation of production.

READING B   THE PURSUIT OF FLEXIBLE SPECIALIZATION IN BRITAIN AND WEST GERMANY

Christel Lane

Introduction

Braverman's (1974) work on the labour process introduced the claim that, in advanced capitalist society, the pressure for capital accumulation compels management to assume full control over the labour process in order to enhance economic exploitation. Tayloristic work organisation, entailing the maximum possible division of labour and the minimum possible worker discretion, is regarded as the tool ideally suited to the achievement of management goals. For Braverman, as Wood and Kelly (1982: 76) point out, management under capitalism has reached its purest expression in Taylorism. Braverman does not envisage the possibility that capitalist production organisation allows for the development of any alternative strategy of work organisation.

Subsequent critiques have challenged this claim and have shown that the goal of capital accumulation can be pursued by other means or that control over labour can be achieved by a variety of strategies. But most of these critiques still hold the Taylorist model to be the predominant one during the post-war period. The recent books by Sabel (1982) and Piore and Sabel (1984), in contrast, claim that the dominance of the Taylorist approach and of the whole model of industrial production in which it is embedded, is now being challenged and that an alternative manufacturing policy, referred to as 'flexible specialisation', has emerged. They envisage such fundamental industrial change to talk of the occurrence of a 'second industrial divide'. ...

Source: Lane C. (1988) 'Industrial change in Europe: the pursuit of flexible specialisation in Britain and West Germany', *Work, Employment and Society*, vol. 2, no.2, pp.141–8; 153–5; 157–65; 167.

The Piore and Sabel Thesis on 'Flexible Specialisation'

World-wide economic changes, particularly a shift in the international division of labour, have rendered problematic the old form of industrial development which has prevailed in advanced capitalist societies for most of this century. Greater competition in world markets from newer, low-wage industrial countries and a general decrease in market stability and predictability have rendered less viable the established model of mass production of standardised goods with the use of special-purpose machinery and of semi-skilled labour. A search for alternative markets and the emergence, at the same time, of a new and more flexible technology has caused industrial producers to reconsider their strategy of both capital and labour utilisation. The new market strategy aims to compete by offering product diversity and/or high quality, and the new technology facilitates the frequent adaptation to changing market demands as well as the attainment of higher quality standards and smaller batches, without increasing production costs. The advantages of the new technology for the pursuit of the new market strategy can be most fully exploited, Piore and Sabel argue, if it is allied to a new form of labour deployment. The Taylorist strategy of designing high specialisation/low discretion jobs needs to be replaced by one seeking a high degree of overlap between specialisms and flexibility of deployment, as well as the exercise of 'craft' judgement and skill. Lastly, these authors suggest, such a strategy of flexible specialisation is more likely to succeed in industrial communities with systems of industrial relations, based on co-operation, rather than on competition and conflict. ...

Managerial Practice in the Post-War Period

In the more recent past — from 1950 to the middle 1970s — German industry has stood out as being the least penetrated, though by no means unaffected, by Taylorist strategy, whereas British employers have been more receptive to Taylorist techniques. The following examination of the two national patterns of work organisation during this period will utilise Littler's (1982) comparative schema and analyse employer strategies in terms of three dimensions: division of labour/degree of discretion; structure of control; and employment relationship. This analysis, summarised in Table 1, makes it possible to characterise national patterns in ideal-typical form and place them on a continuum from the strategy of 'responsible autonomy' at one end of the pole to that of full Taylorism at the other. ...

In *Germany* the craft paradigm and the managerial strategy of 'responsible autonomy' remained central to the national economy. The first factor predisposing German management towards a strategy of 'responsible autonomy' in work organisation is the skill profile of the manual working class. All through the post-war period, there has been in German industry a predominance of skilled workers with high, formally labelled and certified qualifications. This proportion has stayed almost constant up to the late 1970s (Mooser 1984). Although there is not always a correlation between official skill labels and actual skill exercised, in Germany this correspondence is widely held to be close. The expansion of mass production industries has to a large extent drawn on un- and semi-skilled immigrant (*Gastarbeiter*) and female labour but also on skilled workers from economically declining industries and the artisan (*Handwerk*) sector. The nature of the skills imparted to skilled workers is best summed up by the concept of polyvalency, i.e. knowledge and capabilities in two or more areas, acquired through systematic rotation during training. Polyvalency of skill permits a broad and flexible utilization of labour across boundaries between production work, on the one side and technical and maintenance work, on the other. Polyvalency has not, as in the case of British craftsmen, been undermined by the erection of highly formalised boundaries between skills. Polyvalency of the German type also furthers co-operation within work groups across hierarchical divisions and thus provides a natural foundation for the institution of semi-autonomous work groups. German semi-skilled workers' training, although less broad and deep, is nevertheless also systematically oriented towards polyvalency.

This existence of a large pool of skilled, polyvalent workers has predisposed employers to implement the strategy of 'responsible autonomy'. (The concept used here is adapted from Friedman (1977).) It refers to a strategy which allows workers a reasonable scope in utilising their skills and trusting them to use them responsibly, i.e. in the interest of their employing organization. This form of work organization implies a structure of control which minimises task control and instead exerts ideological control. The control process utilises an ideology, inculcated during the training process. Contrary to Friedman, however, the inculcation of the tenets of this ideology does not require a complex ideological apparatus but occurs almost imperceptibly as a by-product of the technical training process. The ideology is based on the idea of a professional community in which superiors are respected as 'experts' rather than as punitive controllers, and a common task orientation dwells on unity of purpose and de-emphasises hierarchical divisions. Reduced task control in German industry is indicated by the facts that the authority over the organisation and monitoring of work in progress is vested in the chargehand and that the foreman is regarded more as a technical expert than as a punitive supervisor. This ideology is also expressed in, and reinforced by, the system of industrial relations which is characterised by a co-operative style. Lastly, the foregoing makes clear that, contrary to Friedman, the implementation of the strategy of responsible autonomy constitutes not merely a management reaction to worker unrest but has been a much more enduring feature of German management control, deeply embedded into the general institutional framework. ...

In *Britain* Taylorist employer strategies have become more widely established than in Germany during the post-war period, but they have been applied in a very half-hearted and inconsistent form. Inconsistency or ambiguity flows from two sources. The first, and by now less significant one, is the co-existence in British industry of a small 'craft' sector, in which work is still characterised by a relatively low division of labour and high level of discretion, with a large mass production sector, dominated by semi-skilled workers engaged in monotonous, deskilled detail work. (For examples of work in the craft sector, see accounts of work organisation in the engineering industry in Wood 1982). The second, and more formidable inconsistency lies in employer strategy. In the mass production industries, a high division of labour (including that between direct and indirect labour) and a fairly rigid separation of planning and implementation is accompanied by a structure of control which, while eschewing ideological control, is neither fully committed to task control nor to a strategy of 'responsible autonomy'. By international standards British workers have achieved a relatively high degree of control over the organisation of the labour process (e.g. joint regulation in the areas of job definition, task allocation, manning). But this control has not been granted as part of a strategy stressing worker 'responsible autonomy' which, indeed, is quite incompatible with deskilled detail work. This control orientation on the part of British management can be attributed to both the social origins and the relatively low level of technical training of managers which foster social distance and hinder the development of a task- and production-orientation among them. ...

Thus, to summarise, although Fordist employer practices have been widespread during the post-war period in both societies, their penetration has been more thoroughgoing in Britain than in Germany. The differences, it has been argued, are due not only to the differing numerical preponderance in the workforce of skilled workers but also to the differential processes by which skill is produced among all types of workers and the uses to which it has been put. This has, on the one side, led to differing worker identities, expectations and attachments to the employing organisation and, on the other, has channelled employer goals and practices in differing directions. These differences are summarized in schematic form in Table 1.

Table 1   Capitalist employer strategies on work organization up to the early 1980s

	Responsible autonomy	Taylorism
	Germany	*Britain*
Division of labour	Large proportion of high skilled	Deskilled (pockets of high skill in craft sector)
	Low formalisation of boundaries	High formalisation of boundaries
	High level of discretion	Low level of discretion
Structure of control	Predominantly ideological control	Weak task control
Employment relationship	High degree of employment security* for the core labour force	Complete substitutability of workers*
	Elements of paternalism	Minimum interaction

Adapted from Littler 1982: 193, Table 12.2

* In 1986, the unemployment rates in Germany and Britain were 7.8 and 12.02 respectively (*CEDEFOP News*, 2, 1986)

Flexible Specialisation in Germany

... The case for an emergent new industrial strategy in German manufacturing has been most cogently stated and most fully supported by empirical evidence in the work of Kern and Schumann (1984a and b). Their theoretical claims and empirical data are based on a follow-up study of several industries — the car, machine tool, chemical and, to a lesser extent, food-producing and shipbuilding industries — which they first investigated in the middle 1960s. ...

The evidence of industrial transformation in Germany during the late 1970s/early 1980s ... leaves no doubt that, at least in the core industries, changed market and technology strategies have led to the creation of more flexible production arrangements which have involved job enrichment, enlarged autonomy and upskilling for significant numbers of workers. It is more contentious, however, whether these developments amount to a new industrial strategy or new production concepts, to use Kern and Schumann's term (1984a and b). The latter make it clear that, at the present time, only a minority of production workers in the core industries are engaged in new forms of production work and that the full development of the new production concepts will not occur until the late 1980s/early 1990s. They also suggest that labour needs to exert more influence both on management to follow the new strategy more broadly and on the state to distribute the ensuing costs and benefits more widely.

The Implications

The question, therefore, remains whether the new forms of labour utilisation signal an emergent trend which will eventually become a fully-fledged industrial strategy or manufacturing policy, or whether, as some German commentators suggest (e.g. Düll 1985), they constitute merely island solutions which will remain confined to small sections of production and leave the overall Taylorist pattern intact. My own view is that in the German industrial context there exist a number of distinctive features which make the Kern and Schumann scenario at least very likely, if not inevitable. Some of these features which support a move towards a broader application of the policy of flexible specialisation and which were not recognised or under-emphasised by Piore and Sabel (1984) will be outlined in the following section.

Firstly, analysis of industrial change in the 1980s requires that a stronger emphasis be put on the key role the new technology plays in the process of change. Kern and Schumann (1984b) and Jürgens *et al.* (1986: 273) make it clear that the new technology is an indispensable factor in realising the new market concept and in facilitating and, sometimes, stimulating changes in work organisation. But this emphasis on new technology is not to be interpreted as the adoption of a stance of technological determinism. Kern and Schumann underline that the new technology can be exploited the more broadly the stronger the policy of labour utilisation has created the preconditions for such an exploitation. The computer-controlled technology has made the enterprise more transparent and hence more amenable to organizational integration. The new flexibility in worker deployment is mainly desired because the complexity and high degree of integration of technology makes machine down-time more disruptive and costly, and upskilling is practised because it is believed that the new technology can only be fully exploited with a skilled, autonomous workforce (*Industriemagazin,* April 1987). In each of the four industries where significant moves away from Taylorist work organisation had occurred, these had been preceded by the introduction of new technological processes. The most highly automated industry — the auto industry — has also been the most innovative one in terms of work organisation.

For German management maximum technical sophistication appears to be a central weapon in all the core industries surveyed. This technology-led competitive strategy presupposes the availability of both a high level of managerial technical competence and of investment resources. Thus, whereas Piore and Sabel (1984) stressed only the availability of worker skill as a precondition for achieving flexible specialisation, the German evidence also highlights the critical importance of managerial competence.

Secondly, German sources stress the situation on the labour market as an equally important intervening variable. The unemployment of even skilled workers guarantees an ample supply of skilled labour. This is further increased by the fact that, to alleviate youth unemployment, employers have yielded to union pressure and have trained apprentices in excess of their own immediate needs. This makes non-Taylorist work organisation a feasible goal and renders the conversion process suggested by the new strategy relatively painless. ...

... German sources see flexible deployment of labour only in functional terms. The pursuit of numerical flexibility, i.e. the adjustment of labour inputs to meet fluctuation in output, receives no mention. ... The lack of attention to numerical flexibility is probably due to the fact that external numerical flexibility was not very prominent in German industry during the early 1980s. Generally speaking, German employment legislation has made it difficult for employers to solve the problem of fluctuating demand by casualisation of the labour force. The high degree of *de facto* employment security and the strong involvement of works councils in manpower regulation have compelled employers to engage in more careful and long-term manpower planning and to deploy the core labour force flexibly in both functional and numerical terms (Streeck 1987). But more recent developments suggest that German employers too, are seeking greater numerical and wages flexibility. Although attempts to attain this have so far remained isolated cases they are now seen as the beginning of a more pervasive future trend (Sengenberger 1984: 331f). ...

A last important issue to be settled is whether the emergence of a paradigm change is compatible with the capitalist organization of production and, if so, how it fits into Marxian theorisation of the labour process. Kern and Schumann point out that the new industrial strategy is an employer initiative, aimed at adjusting the production process to their changed market strategies, and that the reorganization of work is not a response to worker unrest or demands nor is it based on humanitarian impulses. Thus a non-Taylorist mode of worker deployment is not an end in itself but is a consequence of a different mode of capital utilisation. The new automated technology demands very high rates of capital investment, and the return on that investment is more assured if it is complemented by greater investment in labour. Thus, flexible specialisation is regarded as a capitalist rationalisation strategy which happens to yield considerable benefits also for labour. It tries to increase industrial efficiency through, and not against, worker competence (*Handlungskapazität*). Often the reorganisation of work is not consciously planned but evolves, after periods of trial and error, as a consequence of other changes in production (Drexel 1984: 108).

The new mode of labour utilisation does, however, constitute a break in capitalist thinking. Labour has long been thought of as a factor disruptive of production, to be substituted as far as possible by machines and restricted and controlled as much as possible. This has been a central tenet of the Braverman thesis on the labour process in capitalist society. The new strategy, in contrast, implies that labour is a valuable resource and that worker skill and initiative are productive forces which should be fully utilised (Kern and Schumann 1984: 149). ... As Drexel (1985: 123) points out, the new attitude to labour deployment implies not *just* a broader utilization of existing labour power but also its greater unfolding and development. The new mode of labour utilization does not represent a one-sided gain by capital but one which has been achieved by developing worker potential to a higher degree. The worker receives a pay-off in terms of higher skill level, greater autonomy and increased satisfaction and material reward. Granted, development of worker potential remains strictly within the limits set by the capitalist enterprise, and the unfolding of the full potential of labour is prevented by the remaining contradictions between the interests of capital and labour. ...

Achieving domination (*Herrschaftsabsicherung*) is no longer considered such an important goal by German management. This is the case, partly, because automatic control of production processes secures sufficient worker effort. But it is also true that workers are no longer regarded as system opponents. They are viewed as people who are willing to make compromises because their own interests are becoming more closely tied in with those of their employer (Kern and Schumann 1984: 152). But, at the same time, management has become more dependent on the goodwill of workers to keep the new, highly complex and vulnerable apparatus in operation. This is not to say that management control of workers has become unimportant but merely that it no longer takes the old form. As has been pointed out by many of Braverman's critics, subsumption of labour does not necessarily occur by close task control in the labour process. But this relaxation of control in the labour process ... is a peculiarly German phenomenon.

To sum up this section, flexible specialization in Germany is seen to have the following characteristic features. It is, as yet, only an emergent trend.

Taylorism has not been completely abandoned, but fundamental organizational innovation is very much on the agenda; technology is held to play a crucial role in the process of change, and a management committed to, and capable of instigating, far-reaching technological innovation is an integral part of the transformation process; the labour market situation has made available a sizeable pool of skilled polyvalent labour to operationalise the new strategy; the system of industrial relations facilitates relatively smooth technological change and the attainment of functional flexibility; the new 'professional' worker, although sharing some features with the craft worker of old, is not identical to him; the benefits of the new industrial strategy for workers need to be generalized by political means beyond the core industries; the strategy of flexible specialisation is an integral part of capitalist rationalisation but it signifies an important change in capital's attitude to labour deployment which has more positive consequences for labour than the old Taylorist concept. ...

Flexible specialisation in Britain?

... Where the strategy of 'flexible specialisation' is adopted the British version differs from the German one in several ways. It is rarely conceived of as a comprehensive industrial strategy in which the use of complex new technological systems is integrated with the creation of greater skill resources and the broader deployment of skilled labour on the one side, and a new 'industrial relations' approach, evoking worker commitment and cooperation, on the other. An attempt to adopt such a comprehensive strategy in the British context meets with too many impediments and tends to become unstuck in the pursuit of one or several of its constituent elements. Consequently it is usually the case that the strategy is embraced only partially and is combined with elements of the old Taylorist model of labour deployment into a hybrid type. Alternatively, the pursuit of functional flexibility culminates in a contest between management and labour over the elimination or retention of union control over labour deployment. A preoccupation with industrial relations moves to the centre of the field, and the attempt to realise a comprehensive new manufacturing policy becomes jeopardised.

What then are the impediments in the British industrial context which hinder the successful realisation of the new industrial strategy in a consistent form? One important constituent element of the new model is the reorganisation of the productive apparatus, replacing old special-purpose machinery with new automated equipment of a highly complex type. The degree of flexibility permitted by the new technology increases with the technical sophistication of the equipment and with the degree of integration of individual technical devices into a comprehensive system. Such a reorganization of production requires a management committed to technological innovation, confident to forge ahead, and competent both to acquire the right type of equipment and to put it into operation and maintain it without too much disruption of the productive process. Such energetic technological innovation requires not only the commitment of considerable financial resources but also a high level of technical expertise among management and support staff at all levels. Neither precondition typically exists in British industrial organisations. ...

Although the high level of unemployment in Britain makes available a large pool of labour, this labour is, on the whole, not of the right type to restructure work organisation in line with the new production concepts. Due to the decline of the apprenticeship system, skilled labour has been declining in relative terms. In the engineering industry, for example, where skilled labour has traditionally been most prevalent, the number of craftsmen undergoing training has halved between 1978 and 1984 (*Skills Bulletin,* 1, 1987: 11). Moreover, the traditional skilled worker does not possess the polyvalency which ensures flexible deployment. In those cases where management is committed to operating the new technology with skilled, polyvalent labour — for maintenance such labour is becoming a *sine qua non* — they have had both to invest resources in initial and further or re-training *and* to overcome union resistance to the elimination of demarcation between crafts. ...

All this is not to say that functional flexibility is rarely sought or obtained by British management. The recent IMS study (1986: 8) of this problem found that nine out of ten manufacturing firms in their sample had been seeking to increase functional flexibility of their workforces since 1980. Daniel (1987: 168f) established that management had a greater commitment to flexibility in worker deployment and that establishments using microelectronic technology were twice as likely as those not using it to have taken steps to promote it. But 34 per cent of all works managers still felt constrained in their freedom to distribute tasks between different categories of workers. The impediments to the realisation of flexible labour deployment are such that success is often only limited or of short-term duration. ...

It has already been indicated that 'industrial relations' issues represent an impediment to the attainment of work restructuring in the direction of greater functional flexibility. The new forms of work organisation, it was shown in the German context, require that workers act more autonomously and adopt a greater amount of responsibility for the smooth and continuous functioning of the complex productive apparatus. This exercise of responsible autonomy on the part of workers presupposes that management trusts them to use this autonomy in the interest of the enterprise. A strategy of 'responsible autonomy' assumes that management feels fairly secure and confident about the existing balance of control in the enterprise and is not constantly locked into a contest for control. It also presupposes that workers identify to a large degree with management goals and accept a part of the responsibility for the accomplishment of these goals.

In the British industrial relations context, with its long tradition of 'minimal involvement' and adversarial pursuit of sectional interests, such a climate of mutual trust and co-operation cannot easily develop. Many studies have shown that British management does not and cannot feel confident and relaxed about the existing balance of control. In many instances management has shown itself intent on exploiting labour's current weakness and changing the balance of control in management's favour (IMS 1986). Instead of seeing the elimination of demarcation as one necessary step in the larger strategy of creating a polyvalent, flexible and more responsible labour force it often becomes a goal in its own right and degenerates into a contest of strength between management and labour. ...

The foregoing argument has made it clear that although a new market strategy and a quest for the more flexible organization of production are also a lively concern of British management there are formidable impediments in the way of realising a comprehensive and consistent industrial strategy. There exist difficulties about creating the necessary technological foundations. But the more formidable problems appear to be those of achieving a new approach to management–labour relations and a non-Taylorist practice of labour deployment. The example of Britain shows, contrary to the claims of Piore and Sabel (1984), that countries without a pervasive craft ethos will not necessarily remain wedded to the old model of industrial organization. Instead managements in such countries are more likely to develop a hybrid strategy, combining a changed market orientation with a high-tech version of production along the old Taylorist lines. Although greater functional flexibility of labour and upskilling is practised, the pursuit of numerical flexibility and of the greater casualisation of the labour force appears to be the more widely adopted alternative. Although numerical flexibility can successfully cope with uncertainties in demand of a quantitative type it is doubtful whether a casualised labour force can handle other aspects of market uncertainty, such as frequent product changes or product diversification, and the demand for customised high-quality goods.

Conclusion

A quest for 'flexible specialisation' has been characteristic of both German and British management during the 1980s. But the attempts to adjust the organisation of production to new and changing market demands have taken different forms in the two societies, and the industrial strategies devised possess different degrees of logical consistency and/or comprehensiveness. ... Whereas in Germany the new strategy is very much technology-led and -inspired, in Britain the impetus has come more strongly from the relaxation of constraints previously exerted by labour market conditions and the industrial relations system. ...

German employers, able to draw on a large pool of skilled, polyvalent labour and union cooperation for functional flexibility, have further reinforced and extended functional flexibility. British managements, in contrast, possessing none of these advantages, have made only limited moves in the direction of greater functional flexibility. They have, instead, significantly increased their recourse to numerical flexibility and the concomitant expansion of a peripheral labour force. The German strategy has been consistent with the restructuring of work along non-Taylorist lines and the upskilling of the labour force, albeit only in some industries. The

British attempt to gain greater flexibility, in contrast, typically has not been linked to the broader and fuller use of worker capacity. The emphasis has been more on destroying old forms of utilising skill rather than creating new ones. Consequently, the British approach has had ambiguous consequences for skilled labour — some upskilling but the loss of union control over labour deployment. It has had only negative effects for semi- and unskilled labour. For them the Taylorist thrust of work organisation has intensified and employment conditions have significantly deteriorated.

Management efforts to regain control, in order to secure greater workplace discipline, complete the Fordist/Taylorist model. German management have adopted a consistent strategy of flexible specialisation which, on balance, constitutes a progressive move from the point of view of labour. Moreover, it is likely to achieve the successful realisation of the new market strategy. High quality and product diversity can only be obtained with skilled, polyvalent and responsible labour. Whether the British alternative of a high-tech version of Fordism will be able to cope with the new market demands must be regarded as doubtful.

References

Braverman, H. (1974) *Labour and Monopoly Capital,* New York, Monthly Review Press.

Daniel, W. (1987) *Workplace Industrial Relations and Technical Change,* London, Frances Pinter.

Drexel, I. (1985) 'Neue Produktionsstrukturen auf Italienisch?', *Soziale Welt*, vol.2, pp.106–27.

Düll, K. (1985) 'Gesellschaftliche Modernisierungspolitik durch "neue Produktions-konzepte"?', *WSI Mitteilungen*, vol.3, pp.141–5.

Friedman, A. (1977) *Industry and Labour. Class Struggle at Work and Monopoly Capitalism,* London, Macmillan.

Institute of Manpower Studies (IMS) (1986) *Changing Working Patterns*, a report for the National Economic Development Office in association with the Department of Employment, London, IMS.

Jürgens, U., Dohse, K. and Malsch, T. (1986) 'New Production Concepts in West German Car Plants', in Tolliday, S. and Zeitlin, J. (eds) *The Automobile Industry and its Workers*, Cambridge, Polity Press.

Kern, H. and Schumann, M. (1984a) 'Neue Produktionskonzepte haben Chancen', *Soziale Welt*, vol.35, nos.1–2, pp.146–58.

Kern, H. and Schumann, M. (1984b) *Das Ende der Arbeitsteilung? Rationalisierung in der industriellen Produktion*, Munich, Verlag C.H. Beck.

Littler, C. (1982) *The Development of the Labour Process in Capitalist Societies,* London, Heinemann.

Mooser, J. (1984) *Arbeiterleben in Deutschland 1900–1970*, Frankfurt, Suhrkamp.

Piore, M.J. and Sabel, C. (1984) *The Second Industrial Divide*, New York, Basic Books.

Sabel, C. (1982) *Work and Politics*, Cambridge, Cambridge University Press.

Sengenberger, W. (1984) 'West German employment policy: restoring worker competition', *Industrial Relations*, vol.23, no.3, pp.323–43.

Streeck, W. (1987) 'The uncertainties of management in the management of uncertainty: employers, labour relations and industrial adjustment in the 1980s', *Work, Employment and Society*, vol.1, no.3, pp.281–309.

Wood, S. and Kelly, J. (1982) 'Taylorism, responsible autonomy and management strategy', in Wood, S. (ed.) *The Degradation of Work? Skill, Deskilling and the Labour Process*, London, Hutchinson.

Wood, S. (1982) *The Degradation of Work? Skill, Deskilling and the Labour Process,* London, Hutchinson.

CHAPTER 7 WORK DESIGN AND CORPORATE STRATEGIES

Graeme Salaman

CONTENTS

1   INTRODUCTION

This chapter explores the way in which work and workers are controlled and directed within the industrial organizations characteristic of modern capitalist societies. Its subject matter is not all types of work, for much is not considered here: work done in the home for example, or work in small organizations, or professional work.

My exploration of work control strategies will be primarily through a consideration of two questions: how is modern factory work structured or designed, and why is it structured in these ways? This focus on work structures takes place within the broader context of an analysis of the emergence of large-scale bureaucratic work-places within modern industrial economies.

Such an analysis requires movement across time: an understanding of how work is structured and controlled now, in the present, requires some knowledge of how industrial organizations developed historically. And any informed assessment of how work is likely to be structured and controlled in the future requires an understanding of the dynamics, possibilities and contradictions that characterize the organization of work in modern industry. We shall find that, to some limited but important extent, the form of work, and the basic philosophy lying behind the design of work, through time vary; and we shall describe these variations, some of which are now very evident. But underlying the variation we can discern a constant pattern: an oscillation between two contradictory pressures producing two distinct approaches to work design — two poles between which there is movement, as each position resolves the problem of the other but then reaches its own limitations.

These two poles are: tight management control, producing alienation and resentment (and poor quality) on the workers' part; and delegated control, even a degree of workers' autonomy, producing better quality work, but introducing the possibility of decreased management authority. These alternative approaches to work design have been described by Friedman (1977) as *direct control* and *responsible autonomy.*

I will argue that within modern capitalism, in order to ensure cost control (and thus achieve competitiveness), and to achieve those levels of profitability that are necessary to satisfy shareholders, management find it necessary to direct, supervise and control both the worker and his or her work. The development of modern industry has, in part, been characterized by attempts by management to wrest this control from the workforce without damaging levels of production. Strategies of control of work have an impact on skill levels and on worker attitudes and behaviour, and thus on the quality and quantity of production. Different approaches to work design place emphasis on one or other of two opposing principles: they either attempt to reduce skill to a minimum as part of a strategy of maximum control over the content, pace, quantity and quality of work, with all the consequences for worker withdrawal and antagonism; or they attempt to engage and exploit a proportion of the willingness, intelligence and creativity of workers through various means, including a more relaxed approach to job design, with enhanced discretion. But this may clash with management's need, ultimately, to retain firm control over the direction, quantity and cost of labour.

This chapter is organized as follows:

Section 2 offers an account of the emergence of large scale bureaucratic workplaces within modern capitalism and identifies their distinguishing characteristics and organizing principles. This is done, first, in order to locate the design and control of work within the organizational context which supplies the constraints and requirements that frame its design and make it necessary; and secondly, in order to identify the imperatives which still inform the organization and design of work, and which will continue to do so.

Section 3 addresses the design of work within such organizations, and plots, historically, the gradual emergence of the approach to work known as Taylorism (or Scientific Management) and, later, as Fordism.

Section 4 attempts to account for various approaches to work design. It offers two forms of explanation: that work is structured directly by the pressures of the market within capitalism, i.e. by the need to cut costs and retain control; and that work is determined by the technology that is employed in the work process.

Section 5 argues that variations in the ways in which work is designed and controlled can be seen to centre round two objectives, namely the achievement of control and of consent. It considers the significance of these values to modern management and seeks to account for the historical movement between the two objectives. Finally, this section considers the direction and implications of future and current strategies of work control.

2   THE EMERGENCE OF INDUSTRIAL BUREAUCRACY

Although it is true that the characteristic features of the work organizations of the industrial revolution emerged slowly, unevenly and sporadically, it is possible to identify the key features of these organizations which represented a series of fundamental innovations.

First, work became organized around profit, and as a consequence labour was bought and sold, measured and used just like any other commodity. The subordination of production to profit also became the principle which guided the design of work, the structuring of organizations and the nature of the employment contract.

Domestic manufacture of matchboxes in the nineteenth century

Associated with the dominance of this principle was the concentration of large numbers of workers in factories and thus the need to organize and manage the workforce, as well as to ensure that workers behaved in ways which supported management structures and management aims. This organization of the workforce — in ways which were intended to assist the achievement of profitability — became the responsibility and interest of the manager/entrepreneur. The use of large numbers of workers was not in itself new. But, as long as these had been dispersed under the 'putting out' system, the way workers behaved and used their time was not of immediate interest to the entrepreneur.

Once they were gathered together in factories, however, all this changed. First, how they worked, and how much material or time they wasted, became of vital concern to the entrepreneur for it was no longer 'their' time or material they were wasting. This required devoting attention to what employers saw as the moral aspects of employment. Secondly, once workers were concentrated it became possible and advantageous to organize (design, subdivide) their work to achieve a division of labour which allowed more productive use of power and machinery and space to generate increased output. This required the development of management and organization: divided work must be designed, coordinated and integrated. Once work was divided, each contributor to the process became interdependent with every other. One absence, and the entire process might be halted. The flow of work required a disciplined and reliable workforce.

Thus two major objectives of the new activity of management within the factory system were (a) the achievement of control and discipline, and (b) the development of management structures. The achievement of discipline and reliability had implications for recruitment and training and for the 'management of meaning': i.e. the attempt by management and external agencies to define the moral context of work and employment in terms which supported what management wanted of workers and management's rights to make these demands.

Recruitment, for example, was not simply a problem of numbers, but of attitude. Commentators noted the aversion of workers to entering the new large enterprises with their strict rules. In consequence, paupers and convicts were often forcibly recruited, especially pauper apprentices. 'Is it surprising' asks Foucault, 'that prisons resemble factories, schools, barracks, hospitals which all resemble prison?' (Foucault, 1977, p.228).

The concern of the early entrepreneurs to encourage appropriate 'responsible' attitudes and moralities — the preoccupation with self-control and abstinences in various forms: sexual morals, 'licentiousness', religious attitudes, thrift, bad language etc. — was on the one hand an attempt to destroy pre-industrial habits and moralities, and on the other hand an attempt to inculcate attitudes of compliance towards the values of factory life: obedience, regularity, punctuality, 'respect' for property. 'A man who has no care for the morrow, and who lives for the passing moment, cannot bring his mind to indulge the severe discipline, and to make the patient and toilsome exertions which are required to form a good mechanic' (quoted in Pollard, 1965, p.196). Thus, from the beginning, management realized that the control and direction of work and workers required a form of moral control:

> The worker who left the background of his domestic workshop or peasant holding for the factory, entered a new culture as well as a new sense of direction. It was not only that 'the new economic order needed ... part humans: soulless, depersonalised, disembodied, who could become members, or little wheels rather of complex mechanism'. It was also that men who were non-accumulative, non-acquisitive, accustomed to work for subsistence, not for maximisation of income, had to be made obedient in such a way as to react precisely to the stimuli provided.
> (Pollard, 1965, p.254)

The development of the factory system not only entailed managing this moral dimension, it also required the management of active surveillance to ensure compliance with the new requirements of factory work: a surveillance which was both required and made possible by the concentration of workers. The factory allowed the entrepreneurs or their agents to achieve greater levels of output through organizational structures. However, the introduction of fragmented, specialized work allied to machinery introduced a new problem for the entrepreneur: the problem of control, and coordination. This problem was solved by the development of management as a specialist activity: to manage and

A nineteenth-century factory: artillery manufacture at Woolwich, 1862

coordinate the divided work of shopfloor employees, and to supply
specialist management activities. In short, these objectives were
achieved through bureaucratic organizational structures, for it was not
possible to run a large-scale organization, with a division of labour
among shop-floor workers who were now directly employed, on the
same basis as the earlier pre-modern forms of organization were run.
The new business organizations were 'transformed from chaotic and ad
hoc factories to rationalized, well ordered manufacturing settings'
(Goldman and van Houten, 1980, p.108). These organizations can be
seen as bureaucratic in the sense that attention was given to ensuring
the achievement of regular, standardized, orderly, predictable
behaviour. This was achieved by a variety of means, rules, and
procedures (often written), clearly specified and demarcated jobs and
responsibilities, administrative hierarchies run by formal authority
deployed by office-holders (managers) selected by clear criteria,
involved in well-defined career routes.

Whereas initially the entrepreneurs' agents were likely to see their
positions as resources to be exploited, a *manager's* job gradually became
distinguished from its incumbent and salaries were regularized and
formalized. Similarly, as factories grew in size, rules and procedures,
ways of working and systems of operation became formalized, covering
not only disciplinary matters but the organization of work and the firm.
And these became the responsibility not of workers, but of their
managers. Also, as the division of work developed and became more
specialized and differentiated (see the next section), management was
required to develop coordinating and integrating functions. 'Specifically
bureaucratic mechanisms, notably the detailed division of labour,

formalized hierarchy, and the isolation of technical knowledge from workers, proved the most successful means of effecting both social control and efficiency' (Goldman and van Houten, 1980, p.113). This conscious erosion of what under the putting-out system, had been effectively workers' control over their work is one of the distinctive characteristics of modern industrial organizations.

To summarize then, the management of work within capitalism progressively took place within large bureaucratic work structures where workers were concentrated and directly employed by the entrepreneur, who was now the employer. Within these organizations, labour was bought, sold and deployed as a commodity to achieve profit, and work was organized around two managerial requirements: (a) to achieve control and direction and to locate these as aspects of management's responsibilities; and (b) to ensure that workers developed appropriate, reliable attitudes towards their work, tools, products and employers.

In the next section we shall consider how these twin goals of control and consent were achieved by various approaches to work design.

3 WORK DESIGN AND THE RISE OF MODERN INDUSTRY

3.1 THE EARLY INDUSTRIAL PERIOD

In the early stages of the development of capitalism, entrepreneurs/ employers were relatively little interested in transforming or controlling the process of work, so long as the traditional structures of job organization delivered to them products that they could sell for a profit. Although work was now done for the capitalist employer, this made little difference to its organization and conditions, as we note below. Marx called this stage of the development of work in capitalism the *formal subordination* of labour. 'Lacking the means to increase the productivity of labour on a technological basis, economies could only be achieved through such methods as increasing the length of the working day. A shift towards the *real subordination* of labour could only be ensured by a development of the productive forces, and introducing and using machinery, science, and the expanded scale of production associated with large-scale industry.' (Thompson, 1983, p.42.)

During the early stages of the Industrial Revolution there was no one single theory of work design and organization. Initially, a variety of approaches are apparent, though, as we shall see, work changed over time in certain identifiable directions. The main reason for this was that in the early industrial period many employers were not responsible for

The gang boss: re-paving the Strand, 1851

managing workers or their work. Job design and organizational structures were thus not the responsibility of the employer. 'Capitalism in its early stages expands, and to some extent operates, not so much by directly subordinating large bodies of workers to employers, but by subcontracting exploitation and management.' (Hobsbawm, 1968, p.297.) Thus for many workers the immediate employer was a subcontractor. The main employer provided capital and raw materials and handled the sale and distribution of the finished goods.

Within internal contract systems, work design (such as it was) and discipline were the responsibility of the subcontractor, or gang boss. Littler (1982, p.66) identifies three forms of internal work contract: (a) those based on family relations and familial control; (b) those based on a master craftsman and craft control; and (c) those based on a gang boss with gang control. These types occurred within different industries. The system of internal contract had many advantages for employers. Essentially it solved their problems of management and work control by allowing them to delegate these to intermediaries. And it allowed flexibility in the numbers of staff employed (an objective that lies behind current management interest in forms of subcontract). Not all nineteenth-century work was organized on this basis however. In some cases entrepreneurs controlled work directly as employer and manager. In others, control was achieved by means of traditional foremanship.

Littler has argued that the distribution of these types of work control among British industries depends on three key aspects of the relationship between capital and labour, which themselves derive from decisions about products and production processes within the context of the availability of necessary skills. The three dimensions are:

1   The extent of pre-planning or pre-conceptualization of the
    production process;

2   The extent of employer dependence on 'skill' and workers' abilities
    generally;

3   The extent of employer dependence on pre-existing forms of group
    or cultural solidarity and subordination. (Littler, 1982, p.69.)

This list is important for the focus of the present chapter. It is the first of
many attempts to identify the determinants of job design. We shall find
that many of the ingredients of Littler's list occur in other lists. Note
how Littler's list not only combines two key elements — management
priorities (of planning, etc.) balanced by management dependence on
employees' skills — it also argues a relationship between them, with
managers seeking to achieve control and coordination of work
(predictability) and workers seeking to retain skill (a degree of
autonomy). The result of the interplay of these two opposed forces
generates a pattern of work control. This interplay will figure in many
other approaches.

3.2   LARGE-SCALE INDUSTRY

The 'Great depression' of the late nineteenth century saw the gradual
and uneven emergence of new work forms. Falling prices and profits led
employers initially to adopt two inter-related strategies: (a) to reduce
labour costs and (b) to use labour more extensively — i.e. to employ
more workers or get existing employees to work more hours. But soon a
different solution emerged, one which was to mark the beginning of a
radically new approach to jobs. This was to use labour more intensively
— i.e. to achieve more productive use of a given quantity of labour. This
development was closely allied to the decline of internal contract
structures which had in any case by now reached the limits of their
potential. As noted in Section 2, the new drive for more productive
(intensive) use of labour meant that management now took an interest
in the closely designed control of work, within the context of direct
employment. The close connections between these three key
dimensions of work — job design, control structures and aspects of the
employment relationship — was forged for the first time.

Late Victorian employers were aware that they could no longer rely on
sub-contractors to arrange the supply, discipline and organization of
work, that these matters must now fall within their responsibility, and
that they must be so ordered as to make employees more productive
than previously. Nevertheless these employers were at a loss. 'In the
entrepreneurial firm, although the need for control was great, the
mechanisms for achieving it were very unsophisticated, and the system
of control tended to be informal and unstructured. The personal power
and authority of the capitalist constituted the primary mechanism for
control.' (Edwards, 1979, p.25.) In the first place, there was no available
model of how to set up an industrial organization: the structure within

which employees appointed as managers must take decisions about, and manage, shop floor staff. The emergence of management as a function required the development of a model of management organization. This was something new. Existing models of organization frequently assumed that management must remain coterminous with ownership in order for management staff to identify with the goals of the organization. The development of a bureaucratic approach to industrial organization as outlined in Section 2, and such as occurred in the railways, Navy, or Naval dockyards, only slowly emerged as the preferred solution to the inherent problem of these early organizations: namely, the deep-seated distrust of managers and agents. The initial solution — to establish self-contained profit-based systems within the organization (sub-contract structures) — was replaced by the development of explicit structures of closely-defined jobs surrounded by rules with explicit regulation and monitoring: in other words, bureaucracy. In the next phase the principles of bureaucracy were applied to the design and organization of shop floor work, for this was the second difficulty faced by the Victorian employer.

During the last two decades of the nineteenth century and up to the First World War, work redesign occurred in a number of industrial organizations, albeit hesitantly and without any guiding principles save two: (a) the development of a new approach to supervision, whereby the gang boss was replaced by a number of more specialized and regulated functions, with many traditional areas of authority removed, and (b) a new payment system whereby the employer took responsibility for payments to workers, and thus for instituting some system of work measurement. Both these developments increased bureaucratic control: specification of duties, regulation of behaviour, the setting of standards, measurement and monitoring. One obvious implication of management's taking responsibility for work measurement and payment was that it facilitated management's concern to manipulate the relationship to its advantage: to identify productive and less productive workers and processes, and to be able to gauge the results of changes in work design, technology or organization. However, although these developments laid the ground for changes in work design, these were not to occur until somewhat later.

With respect to factors impinging on job content, Marx argued that the emergence of the last stage of changes in work forms — large-scale industry (mid- to late nineteenth century) — saw the increasing use of machinery to cheapen labour and enlarge surplus value for the employer. Marx argued that machinery in the factory allows for the intensification of effort and the 'deskilling' of work. This is an important and influential argument which was signposted in Chapter 5 and to which we shall return. Note that it contains two key elements, interrelated in this case, which can nevertheless, be separated: (a) machinery can be used to cheapen and deskill labour and (b) this process may result in increased profit margins. The use of machinery to

Women machinists in a Hong Kong factory

deskill and therefore lower labour costs has been one major way of increasing profit margins. However, it may not be the only way in which profitability is enhanced. If there are other possible strategies related to work design which also have this effect, the long term tendency in job design might be less unilinear, more differentiated. Nevertheless Marx here clearly identified a major and very common possibility, the managerial attractions of which include an implication of great significance: redesigning jobs through deskilling in order to change the type of people who could do the work. Managers are then free to change their policy on *allocation* of categories of workers to jobs: resulting frequently in the replacement of expensive employees with cheaper ones, a move that frequently was — and is — associated with the replacement of skilled workers with less-skilled ones, of men with women.

During and immediately after the First World War, British employers began to apply principles of work rationalization which derived from Frederick Taylor's principles of Scientific Management (already introduced briefly in Chapter 5). Because of the importance of Scientific Management, we shall now consider its principles and their development in some detail.Although these principles were often contested, and made slow and very uneven progress, some industries proved more susceptible to them than others. And although the content and application of Taylorism within the UK differed from that in the USA, by the 1930s Taylorite ideas were widely disseminated and applied within the UK, even if not all cases could be seen as full-blown applications (see Littler, 1982, pp.138–45, and Littler and Salaman, 1984, pp.13–14).

3.3   TAYLORISM

As Gill has noted, all manufacturing systems contain three separate
activities: (a) the transformation of work pieces (e.g. turning a piece of
wood into a chair leg); (b) the transfer of work pieces between workers
and operations; and (c) the co-ordination and control of these two
processes so that enough pieces of wood are available to operatives, the
finished pieces flow smoothly through assembly, etc. Each and all of
these process can be conducted mechanically or manually (Gill, 1985).
The history of the transformation of work within modern capitalism, a
process which is not and never will be complete, has involved the
mechanization of each of these stages. The first major approach to work
rationalization — Scientific Management, based as we have seen on the
work of Frederick Taylor — focused on the *first* stage: the operatives'
work on the work-piece.

Taylor's thinking developed from earlier ideas: Gilbreth's work of the
late nineteenth century and the writings of Ure and Babbage, noted and
used by Marx, which stressed the value of a separation of management
design and control (management functions) from the work of execution
(shopfloor work). The nature and consequences of a detailed division of
labour for productivity had of course been noted earlier by Adam
Smith.

In essence, Taylorism advocates the detailed application of the division
of labour to work tasks and the achievement of a new and more
thorough form of control over work. Management not only takes
responsibility for the sub-division of work, but, as a result of doing so,
is able to expropriate any decision-making elements which were
traditionally a constituent element of a job requiring skill (incorporating
skill into a job means giving it a degree of decision-making autonomy).

ACTIVITY 1   You should now read **Reading A, 'Understanding Taylorism'**, by Craig
Littler, which you will find at the end of this chapter.

As you read, make sure you understand the following concepts which
are used by Littler and explained in the Reading:

1   the 'dynamic of deskilling';
2   the 'division of management' or 'functional management';
3   'rational-legal authority' in Weber's theory of bureaucracy;
4   the 'wage-effort' bargain.

If you are not sure, go back, find the phrase and read the relevant
paragraph again.

This Reading raises a number of points highly germane to the theme of
this chapter. First, it identifies the key principles of Taylorism. Note
how these are organized around five principles of the application of the

division of labour which 'constitute a dynamic of deskilling'; four principles for achieving control over work performance; plus a view of the employment relationship which defines this in terms of 'minimum interaction'.

An important feature of this article is its attention to the nature of the relationship between the approach of Taylorism and the development of modern bureaucracy. We have noted that many of the late nineteenth century changes in British industrial organizations involved a gradual move towards regulation, specialization, formalization and so on, which we have described as bureaucratic tendencies, or forms of organizational rationalization. Yet how do these rationalizing tendencies on the organizational and job design fronts interrelate?

This issue constitutes the second major theme of Littler's article. The reference to Weber and the five overarching beliefs about rational–legal authority at the beginning of this section is to Max Weber's conceptualization of the key features of bureaucracy (an ideal type). He argued that bureaucracy depends upon the establishment of support for societal authority based not simply on tradition, or the personal charisma of a leader, but upon, as Littler puts it: 'belief in a set of abstract, impersonal rules applicable to everyone' (Littler, 1978, p.193). This is fundamental to the possibility of bureaucracy, the key elements of which are contained in the table (Table 2) in the Reading. Note that while some of these bureaucratic elements concern the organization of control, two refer to aspects of how staff are employed. Using these criteria, Littler argues that there is an overlap between the two approaches, and that it is possible to see Taylorism as the application of bureaucratic criteria on the shop floor, with the qualification that unlike conventional bureaucratization of office-based organizations, Taylorism involves the bureaucratization of control, but not of employment (Littler, 1978, p.193).

The third section, 'Taylorism in its historical context' rehearses a broadly similar argument to that offered earlier in this chapter. Towards the end of this section there is an interesting point which will recur in the argument of this chapter: that Taylorism represents a particular strategy which contrasts with that of the 'Human Relations' school. This approach, which relates directly to the second of the two approaches to work design discussed at the beginning of this chapter, will be considered more thoroughly later.

Finally, the article addresses the implications of Taylorism for the 'wage-effort bargain'. This expression describes the arrangements between every worker and his or her employer, whereby the employer buys time and effort from the worker in exchange for wages. This relationship contains an opposition of interest as each party benefits from increasing the contribution of the other party and decreasing his or her own. In this section, Littler argues that Taylorism impacts on the wage-effort exchange by obscuring the standards by which workers might judge, and consequently limit, their input of effort, and by assisting management control over the determination of effort-levels. Littler's final point should also be noted: that Taylorism has a continuing influence.

3.4 FROM TAYLORISM TO FORDISM

Taylorism was followed by a development which acknowledged the principles of Scientific Management but also moved on from the mechanization and rationalization of work on the work piece or object to mechanization of the flow of these objects between operatives. This is called Fordism, and, as you will recall from Chapter 5, it derives from Henry Ford who initiated it. We must separate this restricted sense of Fordism as a strategy for the management and design of work from, firstly, the idea of Fordist industries as in some way dominant in an economy, and secondly, from the more general use of the expression noted in the Introduction to this book, which sees it as an indication of a stage in the development, not just of work and industry, but of society: Fordism as an acknowledgement that '… mass production meant mass consumption, a new system of the reproduction of labour power, a new politics of labour control and management, a new aesthetics and psychology, in short a new kind of rationalized, modernist, and populist democratic society' (Harvey, 1989, p.126).

For our purposes, the term will be limited to Fordism as an approach to work design and industrial organization. As such, it consists of standardized products, a high degree of mechanization, and flowline production, all on a broad basis of Taylorized work processes. These elements occur within, and depend upon, high volume production and sales: mass production and mass sales. The mechanization which accompanied Fordism represented a development over basic Taylorite mechanization in that machines were capable of continuous operation at high speeds, and were set up by a separate cadre of specialized workers. But, while this was important as a necessary precondition of Fordism it was not, as Chapter 5 pointed out, of its essence. That lies in the development and application of the flow line principle: work pieces flowing mechanically, often on a conveyor line, past stationary Taylorized operatives. The value of this to an employer who is concerned about the design of work to achieve profit and the manipulation of the wage-effort bargain, is that it allows management to control the pace of work. The results of the Fordist approach were remarkable: chassis assembly before the assembly line took 12.5 hours. On the assembly line it took 2 hours 40 minutes (Flink, 1975, p.77).

Ford's use of Taylorite job fragmentation and deskilling was not new. But he expanded these tendencies to new extremes. One interesting consequence of this was that Ford found that despite increased control of the pacing of work, enhanced control of the worker at work was insufficient to achieve adequate control of the workforce. Absenteeism and turnover were high, while workers took every opportunity to withdraw or reduce their part of the wage effort bargain. Fordism here

'On the assembly line...'

encountered a classic paradox of work design within capitalism: that
maximizing management control and management exploitation of
production cuts costs and increases productivity, but it also destroys the
basis of commitment, willingness and intelligence upon which all
industrial work is based, even the deskilled high-volume work of
Fordism. Thus, in terms of management objectives at work *vis-à-vis* the
workforce, the paradox is that success breeds failure. This is vividly
caught in the description of assembly-line work by one of the
employees interviewed by Hew Beynon in *Working For Ford.*

> Working in a car plant involves coming to terms with the assembly
> line. 'The line never stops', you are told. Why not? ' … don't ask. It
> *never* stops'. The assembly plant itself is huge and on two levels,
> with the paint shop on the one floor and the trim and final
> assembly departments below. The car shell is painted in the paint
> shop and passed by lift and conveyor to the first station of the trim
> assembly department. From this point the body shell is carried up
> and down the 500-yard length of the plant until it is finally driven
> off, tested, and stored in the car park.

Few men see the cars being driven off the line. While an assembly worker is always dealing with a moving car it is never moving under its own steam. The line — or 'the track' as some managers who have been 'stateside' refer to it — stands two feet above the floor level and moves the cars monotonously, easily along. Walking along the floor of the plant as a stranger you are deafened by the whine of the compressed air spanners, you step gingerly between and upon the knots of connecting air pipes which writhe like snakes in your path, and you stare at the moving cars, on either side. This is the world of the operator. In and out of the cars, up and over the line, check the line speed and the model mix. Your mind restlessly alert, because there's no guarantee that the next car will be the same as the last, that a Thames van won't suddenly appear. But still a blank — you keep trying to blot out what's happening. 'When I'm here my mind's a blank. I *make* it go blank.' They all say that. They all tell the story about the man who left Ford to work in a sweet-factory where he had to divide up the reds from the blues, but left because he couldn't take the decision-making. Or the country lad who couldn't believe that he had to work on *every* car: 'Oh no. I've done my car. That one down there. A green one it was.' If you stand on the catwalk at the end of the plant you can look down over the whole assembly floor. Few people do, for to stand there and look at the endless, perpetual tedium of it all is to be threatened by the overwhelming insanity of it. The sheer audacious madness of a system based upon men like those wishing their lives away. I was never able, even remotely, to come to terms with the line. Mind you, I never worked on it. But that's another story.
(Beynon, 1984, p.119)

Ford, as you may well recall, sought to counter the mindless character of assembly-line work by developing a series of social initiatives among workers outside the workplace, in order to encourage the appropriate attitudes, generate legitimacy and achieve worker identification with the company. However, while acknowledging the value of these worker attitudes, Ford sought to achieve them outside the design of work. Others as we shall see sought to design work in ways which encouraged and trapped worker commitment and energy.

3.5   ALTERNATIVE FORMS OF WORK DESIGN

It is important to emphasize that Taylorism, and later Fordism, never constituted the only forms of modern work organization. We have also noted that these approaches were themselves fragmentary and incomplete in their application. They were particularly prevalent in car assembly which was seen as a paradigm case of modern work forms — representing the factory of the future — but which in fact represented something of a special case, for Taylorism and Fordism were applied unevenly across industries and sectors.

Nevertheless, within the car industry Taylorism was very pervasive. By the early 1950s a study of the experience of work among car workers found six major characteristics of mass production work: mechanical pacing; repetitiveness; minimal skill requirements; no choice of tools or methods; minute sub-division of tasks; and little requirement for mental attention. These characteristics, the study argued, were associated with higher than usual absenteeism rates (Walker and Guest, 1952).

In 1955, a study was conducted by Davis *et al.* into the principles for job design within American industry. Its conclusions are represented below in Table 7.1. These findings identify the priorities of management with respect to job design in the industrial sector, in America in the mid 1950s. Note that the highest priority is given to reducing the time necessary to perform the operation; the lowest priorities are attached to flexibility, supervision, safety.

Table 7.1   Major considerations in choice of particular methods for performing operations (based on 24 operations)

Major considerations ranked in order of weighted aggregate rating	Total number of times mentioned in order of importance from high to low					Weighted aggregate rating
	5	4	3	2	1	
Minimizing time required to perform operation	14	4	1	-	-	89
Obtaining highest quality possible	4	6	1	3	-	53
Minimizing skill requirements of operation	1	3	4	3	4	39
Utilization of equipment or tools presently on hand	1	4	2	-	-	27
Minimizing floor-space requirements	2	2	1	1	-	23
Achieving specialization of skills	-	1	4	1	1	19
Minimizing learning time or training	-	-	4	-	1	13
Minimizing materials handling costs	1	-	-	2	1	10
Equalizing and developing full work load for workcrew members	-	1	1	1	-	9
Providing operator satisfaction	-	1	1	1	-	9
Minimizing equipment in tool costs	-	1	-	1	1	7
Controlling materials used in operation	-	-	1	2	-	7
Providing maximum production flexibility	-	1	1	-	-	7
Simplifying supervision of operation	-	-	-	-	3	3
Providing maximum safety in operation	-	-	-	1	1	3

Source: Davis *et al.*, 1972, p.71

Yet alongside the spread of Taylorism/Fordism there existed other approaches to work design which in many respects represented alternatives or even opposites. These arose for a number of reasons. First, the implementation of Taylorite principles of work design was expensive, and it was always clear that such expenditure could only be justified when the volume of throughput was sufficient to enable the process of fragmentation of jobs to be pushed to its limit. Fordism depends on high volumes of production allied to standardized products for consumption in mass markets. Without the appropriate volume of production, the process of task differentiation will cease at a level short of that assumed in classic Fordism. For this reason, the spread of mass,

Fordist forms of production was historically limited to 25 per cent by value of industrial production in the USA (Lund, quoted in Littler, 1985, p.19). (Note that these figures refer to manufacturing industry. Taylorism/Fordism was not seen as applicable to the service industries.)

In other cases shop floor resistance allowed workers to persuade managers to hold back from the imposition of Taylorite principles. And sometimes it was employers themselves who were resistant on moral, religious or humanitarian grounds, or indeed even for the practical reason that Taylorism was simply inefficient. This seems, *prima facie* a strange argument in the light of the claimed benefits — for example, of Fordism on car assembly lines. Nevertheless it echoes a concern voiced by Ford himself, and noted earlier, that although Fordism supplied tight control over the process of production, it not only fails to achieve a similar level of control over the work force, but it actively undermines such control by subjecting workers to an objectionable form of production discipline. It thus achieves certain forms of control (over work speeds for example) but may sacrifice others (over quality, and over workforce attitudes and commitment). Thus some managers soon sensed the possibility that individualizing the worker, destroying forms of worker social organization (work groups), and subjecting workers to oppressive forms of work control and speeds of work flow, might have explosive implications for worker behaviour, specifically for the possibility of attracting workers' creativity and goodwill.

Unlike Taylor, for whom this was a matter of total indifference, Henry Ford, as we have seen, sought to engage the commitment and participation of the worker through out-of-work activities. Ford himself wrote: 'Machines alone do not give us mass production. Mass production is achieved by both machines and men. And while we have gone a long way toward perfecting our mechanical operations, we have not successfully written into our equations whatever complex factors represent Man, the human element' (Ford, quoted in Littler and Salaman, 1984, p.91). Other approaches to work design sought to maintain or generate workforce involvement and to tap their creativity through the design of work itself. That is, they identified and sought to address what they saw as the conflict between design principles which enforced increased production at the cost of worker commitment, and the need for any production system to be based, in the medium to long term, on the achievement of worker involvement and goodwill.

For example, Davis *et al.* (1972) on the basis of their survey of job design practices, concluded that current job design practices are consistent with Scientific Management — minimizing the dependence of the organization on the individual and maximizing the contribution of the individual to the organization:

> By adhering to the very narrow and limited criteria of minimizing immediate cost or maximizing immediate productivity, it [Scientific Management] designs jobs based entirely on the principles of specialization, repetitiveness, low skill content and

minimum impact of the worker on the production process. Modern management then frequently spends large sums of money and prodigious efforts on many programmes that attempt to:

1   counteract the effects of job designs;

2   provide satisfactions, necessarily outside the job, which the job cannot provide; and

3   build up the satisfaction and importance of the individual which the job has diminished.

(Davis *et al.*, 1972, p.81)

In the face of the increasingly obvious problems of Taylorism/Fordism, companies in the post-war period began to experiment with alternative approaches to job design in order to overcome the 'human' problems that had arisen. Two major principles were used: job enlargement (increased range of activities) and job enrichment (increased authority).

An early example of these developments in the UK was at ICI. By the late 1960s, ICI managers were aware of the negative implications of existing work arrangements — namely over-staffing and inflexibility. Systems of control and fragmentation had led to restrictive practices and had located decisions remotely from where they were implemented. A process of job appraisal led to significant job redesign, by enrichment and enlargement. The results, from the company's point of view, were positive: reduced labour costs, more effective use of supervision, improved machine utilization and apparent improvement in worker morale (Roeber, 1975).

An alternative approach to job design came together under what was known as the Quality of Working Life Movement (QWLM). This movement drew on a number of sources, one of which was early British work on what was called the 'human factor' which stressed that people working *with* machines did not work *like* machines. This work was based in turn upon the discovery of 'fatigue' among munitions workers during the First World War. Research had shown that increasing the number of working hours did not lead to increased output: '... any reduction in hours cut the incidents of accidents, absenteeism and scrap; a drop in daily hours from twelve to ten increased net daily output; a further reduction from ten to eight, with a six day-week produced similar though less marked results ... ' (Rose, 1988, p.68). These findings, which flew in the face of received wisdom, were supported by later arguments about the social character of workers' work attitudes and behaviour. In the following section, the theoretical underpinnings of this approach will be more fully developed. In essence the QWLM argued that Taylorism/Fordism solved some production problems but generated others: rigidity, bureaucracy, worker dissatisfaction, poor quality work, distrust between worker and manager. The solution was an approach to work design which ran directly counter to these principles and thus avoided these difficulties while developing commitment, flexibility and creativity. QWLM asserts a number of key principles (see Littler, 1985, p.21).

1   The principle of closure — that is, the scope of the job should include all the tasks necessary to complete a product or process. Theoretically, the predicted result is that work acquires an intrinsic meaning and people can feel a sense of achievement.

2   The incorporation of control and monitoring tasks. Jobs should be designed so that an army of inspectors is not required. The individual worker, or the work team, assumes responsibility for quality and reliability.

3   Task variety — that is, an increase in the range of tasks. This implies a principle of comprehensiveness, which means that workers should understand the general principle of a range of tasks so that job rotation is possible.

4   Self-regulation of the speed of work and some choice over work methods and work sequence.

5   A job structure that permits some social interaction and perhaps cooperation among workers.

This last point — that work should be a source of social relationships and thus a focus for some sense of belonging, of group membership, and even ultimately of personal identity — derives largely from the 'Human Relations' movement. This approach based on the famous studies undertaken by the Western Electric Company at the Hawthorne Works in Chicago from the 1920s to the early 1940s, concluded that work behaviour (levels of output, standards of quality, etc.) and work attitudes (satisfaction, frustration, tolerance of supervision etc.) were strongly influenced by social relationships at work, especially in the work group. Thus, 'social man' was 'discovered' to supplant, or rival, the economic man of Taylorism. Human Relations argued that:

> within work-based social relationships or groups, ... behaviour, particularly productivity or co-operativeness with management, was thought to be shaped and constrained by the worker's role and status in a group. Other informal sets of relationships might spring up within the formal organizations as a whole, modifying or overriding the official social structure of the factory, which was based on purely technical criteria such as the division of labour. (Rose, 1988, p.104)

This approach to work design also drew upon the work of researchers from the Tavistock Institute, who identified the advantages in terms of output and morale of self-managing work groups with a degree of autonomy. For example, mechanization of coal mining had resulted in the elimination of the traditional role of a miner with responsibility for a variety of tasks and with little or no supervision; what developed instead were specialized work roles, with different activities allocated to different shifts of miners, associated with different wage rates. This

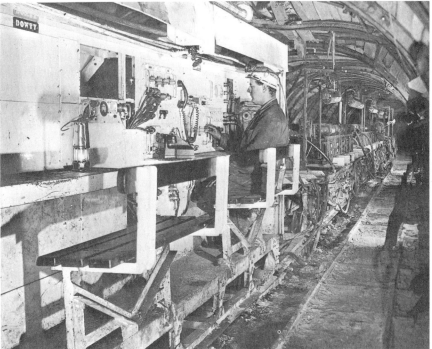

Traditional and longwall mining

differentiation resulted in constant disagreements about pay rates, poor
relations between shifts and a huge growth in management activity. In
some cases, however, working conditions had encouraged the
development of a form of work organization which displayed output
and morale advantages over the specialized, Taylorized approach.

> These composite shortwalls were worked by multi-skilled groups
> on a common pay scheme which were responsible for the whole
> coal-mining cycle on any shift. They were self-selecting and
> leaderless groups, had over 40 members, and made their own task
> and shift allocations. The level and continuity of their production
> were significantly better than on comparable longwalls and
> absenteeism was markedly lower.
> (Buchanan, 1989, p.84)

The Tavistock work, which has been used to argue that technology does
not determine the nature and organization of work roles (see below), has
also been used to generate principles by which jobs may be designed to
achieve greater efficiency for worker and organization. These principles,
which concern job content and the importance and nature of work
groupings, were initially confined to the work experiments of far-
sighted radical or humanistic employers: for example, the installation of
job enrichment in the Endicott plant of IBM in 1944; job enlargement in
the Eindhoven plant of Philips in the 1960s, as well as in their
Australian and Scottish factories; the use of autonomous working
groups in Volvo and Saab. In the first instance they were far from
widespread. A debacle at the Lordstown plant of General Motors,
however, encouraged greater interest in work forms which might avoid
the disastrous consequences of the advanced form of Taylorism initially
implemented there. As Buchanan explains:

> The [Lordstown] plant was designed to produce one hundred
> vehicles an hour with a single operation cycle time as low as
> twenty seconds. This was publicised as the 'pattern of vehicle
> production of the future'. By January 1972, incomplete and
> damaged cars were being made faster than they could be repaired.
> By February 1982 the Union of Auto Workers had lodged over
> 5,000 grievances about work standards, job losses and 'speed up'
> in the plant. Management complained about sabotage and neglect.
> Cars were being made with broken windscreens and mirrors, cut
> upholstery, keys broken in locks and washers in carburettors.
> Welding machines were mysteriously reprogrammed to weld
> bodies in the wrong places, and some cars left the line with all
> their doors locked. The workers' grievances were not resolved, and
> the result was a strike which lasted a month, affected 7,800
> workers in the plant and a further 8,800 other workers indirectly,
> cost the company an estimated $160 million in lost production,
> and cost the workers around $11 million in lost wages.
> (Buchanan, 1989, p.86)

The result was a new level of public identification of, and management concern about, the human factors of production: so-called 'blue-collar blues'. General Motors altered the work design at Lordstown and began to show interest in worker motivation, and in forms of organization which encouraged and tapped worker involvement and creativity rather than destroying them. These principles have recently attracted considerable interest. It is argued that with customers increasingly concerned about quality, reliability, speed of delivery and product variety, workers' attitudes and behaviour become crucial to corporate success: 'A deskilled, unmotivated, uncommitted and inflexible workforce is not competitive when such careful attention to costs, quality and delivery schedules is fundamental to capturing and retaining changing and unpredictable markets' (Buchanan, 1989, p.93).

4 THEORIES OF WORK DESIGN

How can we account for these variations in work design? Are they the result of technology applied to work? Or the requirements of modern capitalism as these impact on the firm? Is there any scope for managers to choose how work is designed? In the following sections these questions will be explored and the various explanations assessed.

4.1 TECHNOLOGY AND WORK

Job content is closely linked to technology; and technology has powerful influence on job content. But some authors have gone further and argued that technology *determines* job content. That is, any work technology, or machine, once designed and installed, has direct determinant influence over job content and skill levels. After all, if work involves the activation of a mechanical operation on a work object, which is itself mechanically transferred from one work station to the next, the dominance of technology over job content would seem to be very great, if not total. The essence of the argument is that technology requires that certain tasks be performed, and this in turn determines jobs, organizational structures and attitudes and behaviour.

Various writers have argued that job content is determined by technology. These include Kerr *et al.* (1973) and Bell (1974), who see technology as having a major influence over all aspects of society. Also Blauner (1964) has suggested that four types of work technology can be distinguished: craft, machine-tending, assembly-line and continuous-process, and that these types (of which the continuous-process would become the dominant) produced different reactions among workers because of the jobs with which each type was associated. Woodward (1970) has argued that key aspects of work organization were determined by technology — for example, that technological complexity was related to longer lines of command. Sayles (1958) has argued that the modern factory is a 'social system erected by the technological process' (Sayles, 1958, p.93) and that degrees of work conflict were determined by production technology.

These views certainly have a degree of validity. For example, under Taylorism there is indeed a close relationship between the capacities and requirements of the work machine and the job of those who 'attend' the machine. It may indeed seem as if the job and its associated skill level is determined by the technology, and thus beyond choice, and beyond critique. In the early stages of the development of factories, for example, a commentator wrote that, 'The principle of the factory is ... to substitute mechanical science for hand skill, and the partition of a process into its essential constituents ....Skilled labour gets progressively superseded, and will eventually be replaced by mere overlookers of machines' (Ure quoted in Berg, 1985, p.67).

Despite the close connection between work technology and work content it is also important to explore this relationship in terms of the ways in which technology is produced and applied. If technology is to be seen as causally determinant, it becomes equally important to explore the factors that in turn determine the nature of technology. Yet while technology theorists are eager to explore the connections between technology and job design, they are far less interested in analysing the development of technology, seeing it, if it occurs at all in their analysis, as the neutral and inevitable development of technical/scientific advance. Blauner, for example, identifies three factors shaping technical advance: the state of mechanical and scientific processes, the nature of the product, and economic and engineering resources in particular firms (see Thompson, 1983, p.21). Social issues involved in technological development are, according to this approach, conceived along the lines noted by Ford in the remarks quoted earlier about the need to identify and ameliorate the social problems implied by a particular work technology.

ACTIVITY 2   Before reading further, consider whether, in your view, technological factors *are* the main determinants of work design.

It is certainly the case that, within any given industry where the same products are produced by the same production process, the content of jobs and the structures of interrelated jobs have much in common. However, this similarity can be overstated. International and comparative studies by, for example, Dore (1973) of Japanese and British factories using the same technology, Gallie (1983) of British and French oil refineries, and, more recently, by Lane of the same countries, all show that technology alone is not sufficient to account for differences in the allocation of tasks to jobs, in qualifications of workers and in skill levels. Furthermore, while any given level of similarity of jobs stems from equipment design similarities (for, given a determination to produce a product commercially, a firm will have little choice but to use available production processes and associated technology which are in turn connected to specific combinations of labour force skills) it is a mistake to regard this situation as one of technological determinism. Although a firm's managers may regard the selection of production process and technology as external and constraining, the development of these processes and technologies is not autonomous or independent, nor is it separate from the purposes for which it is used within organizations.

The constraining effect of technology lies mainly in the development costs attached to devising and setting up new work technologies and processes. 'Where the fragmentation of jobs around a new machine has occurred historically, then the cost of developing some alternative technology may be considerable. Moreover, the technical choice involving a Taylorite configuration of labour may result in a short-term productivity gain which could eliminate any competitors pursuing a longer-term strategy under market conditions' (Littler and Salaman, 1984, p.92). In addition, the constraints of technology follow from management choice in other areas which then impinge heavily on technological factors. If production technology constitutes a constraint on employers, this does not imply that the development of technology is an independent force: ' ... all social arrangements are the outcome of choices, which are shaped by the aims and objectives of those making binding decisions ... The structure of jobs is not automatically determined but is the outcome of specific decisions selected from a range of options by employers' (Garnsey et al., 1985, p.46). Factors influencing these management choices would include the basic production process, the economic environment (levels of demand, degrees of competition), industrial structure (how many competitors, the size of margins) employment regulations, institutional constraints (education and training) (Garnsey et al., 1985, p.48) and conceptions of work and of workers held by managers (Argyris, 1972).

An understanding of the choice and impact of work technologies on job content must therefore be part of a more general analysis of the forces and priorities which shape control strategies. Within this, one major aspect of decisions about work technologies is how they will impact on work skills. This question is often the fundamental issue lying behind choice of technology. However, numerous writers have argued that technologies can be developed and selected with quite different consequences for skill levels: while some replace skills, others can be used to enhance them: the choice between these two options is not pre-determined. Indeed, a major issue in any understanding of the effects of technology on work must be the socially-determined nature of work technologies, and especially the ways in which managements select technologies and use these to effect their purposes, including the control and deskilling of work.

4.2   THE LABOUR PROCESS APPROACH

The expression 'labour process approach' refers to an approach to the understanding of job design which stems largely from the work of Marx, as represented through the more recent work of Braverman (1974).

Braverman's analysis of the nature and development of work under capitalism locates these firmly and causally within an analysis of the requirements of capitalism for work organizations and thus management. The keystone of Braverman's analysis of work is the insistence that work design under capitalism reflects not the dictates of technology but the central imperatives of capitalist accumulation. His analysis of work starts from an historical unity of conception (deciding what to do and how to do it) and execution (doing it). Braverman plots the progressive dislocation of these two aspects of work as management first expropriates conception and then the allocation of this back to the workforce, but in a fragmented and differentiated form. There are thus two crucially interrelated features of work design under capitalism: management's expropriation of the control of work, by which the management function itself is constituted; and the activities of this management function in achieving and implementing control of the workforce through the systematic and progressive sub-division of work. This entails the disintegration of work into its elements which is allocated to discrete jobs, thus cheapening labour, enhancing productivity and guaranteeing effective capitalist control of the labour process by eroding skills which could form the basis of resistance to management.

Braverman's view of tendencies in job design is thus essentially and fundamentally class-based. The design of work, and the dynamics which drive the development of work design, stem from the pressures for capital accumulation as these impinge on management. These dynamics, when mediated by management through increased managerial control over deskilled and 'rationalized' work, performed by workers who have no other means of earning a livelihood save by selling their labour power to capital, produce the experiences and relations that construct and reproduce class formations.

Braverman sees Taylorism as representing perfectly 'the specifically capitalist mode of management' since it demands (and justifies) increased managerial control as crafts are destroyed and work fragmented and deskilled. Braverman regards Taylorism as 'nothing more than the outlook of the capitalist with regard to the conditions of production' (1974, p.86). This is because it enormously enhances managerial control through job design and associated technology (e.g. the assembly line in Fordism), and allows expropriation of skill through time-and-motion study. Braverman identifies three key principles in Taylorism: the separation of execution from conception; the achievement of management control of work-based knowledge; and the replacement of worker skill by management dominated science and technology. This in turn is achieved through three developments. First, under capitalism, workers' labour must be brought under the control of the employer in order to maximize profit; secondly, this control must be attained in the most efficient way possible so as to reduce costs and time; and thirdly, this is obtained through the design of work within a differentiated division of labour.

ACTIVITY 3   Why would it be in the capitalist's interest to 'deskill' work?

A crucial element of Braverman's view of Taylorism as inherently central to capitalist requirements of work is the need for the employer to deskill employees' work. This necessity springs from a number of implications of skill itself. First, skill involves power and control. It involves control because the basis of a work decision is the knowledge, skill and experience of the worker, and as long as these reside with the worker, management must accept the workers' decision (for example about how a job should be done, how long it should take, etc.). It implies power because, as long as the skilled worker has an asset (knowledge, expertise) on which the work process depends, the worker is able to negotiate better terms. Therefore, argues Braverman, there is a built-in and inevitable need, fully developed in Taylorism, for managers to seek progressively to reduce the skill levels of jobs and to appropriate the decision-making aspects of skill as a part of management planning, design and coordinating functions: 'all possible brain work should be removed from the shop and centred in the planning or lay-out department' (Taylor, quoted in Braverman, 1974, p.113). This process was supported by the development of work technologies which allowed more developed mechanization and deskilling, the skill now residing in the process or the machine rather than in the operative.

Braverman's approach thus represents an ambitious attempt to relate aspects of the economy — the imperative for capital accumulation under capitalism — to the design and thus to the experience of work; and it sees the necessary and inevitable features of work under capitalism as reflecting directly these pressures. It therefore represents an important contribution to the topic of this chapter: the exploration of the connections between external, market forces and the design of work, seeing the design of work not only as the product of class relations, but also as reproducing class differences through work experiences.

Before assessing this thesis, however, it is important to note that this approach has two implications for aspects of job content. First, in this approach, technology used at the workplace is not a neutral force. The development of Scientific Management was closely associated with the development of science and technology and this relationship between work rationalization and new technology continues. Economic factors arising from the imperatives of capital thus underlie the process of scientific development. Secondly, Braverman regards any attempts to adjust work design in favour of enhanced variety, enrichment etc. as cosmetic and manipulative at best, aimed at accustoming the worker to the capitalist mode and form of production, but unable to interrupt the inevitable long-term trend towards deskilling and enhanced managerial control.

Braverman's thesis is, however, open to a number of criticisms. First, Braverman exaggerates the actual extent of deskilling. We noted earlier that Scientific Management, while important, has never constituted the only approach to work design. Moreover, Taylorism was always more complex and varied than Braverman suggests, and its spread and development were frequently opposed and resisted. More recent studies of the impact of Information Technology (IT) on work have failed to support the deskilling thesis. Jones, for example, argues on the basis of research into engineering skills that:

> ... the evidence ... further contradicts even modified theses about general and inherent tendencies to deskill because of 'laws' of capitalist exploitation and accumulation. Even in a very small sample, mainly from one sector of engineering, there was sufficient variation among enterprises to confirm the decisiveness of product and labour markets, organizational structures and trade union positions as independent influences on the forms of skill deployment. There is nothing 'inherent' in the hardware of NC (Numerical Control) or its concept that would allow for the deskilling and control and surveillance assumed by ... theorists of the labour process.
> (Jones, 1982, p.198)

Thus is it doubtful that deskilling is the major tendency in work design, for it appears that other, reskilling tendencies, may also occur.

In addition to this, Braverman's emphasis on management's interest in deskilling is excessive. He assumes that management must always seek to achieve deskilling and that they will always be successful. Yet it is doubtful that management actually develop and seek to implement coherent, planned work design strategies. Braverman's approach suggests a conception of management as always aware of what their strategy needs to be: somehow they know and seek to achieve exactly what is necessary for the continuing success of the companies they manage and this entails constant deskilling. This conception of management is simplistic in its lack of attention to management ideologies, optimistic in its view of management competence, and monolithic in its view of management as a single, homogeneous category. In summary, Braverman greatly exaggerates the possibility of management foresight, omniscience and solidarity.

Apart from these objections, even if management did want to deskill (and assuming that deskilling is the only feasible form of work design), it certainly cannot be assumed that they will be able to achieve their goals in the face of various forms of resistance from the workforce. In conclusion, while we can accept Braverman's identification of the need

Reskilling: a work experience project

to relate developments in the labour process to the imperatives of capitalist organization, his over-emphasis on an omniscient management constantly seeking to achieve deskilling is inadequate. What is required instead is an attempt to relate the forms and phases of the development of the capitalist control over the labour process to phases in the development of capitalism itself (Coombs, 1985).

ACTIVITY 4   Before starting the next section, make a list of the *main* criticisms against the Braverman thesis.

5   STRATEGIES OF CONTROL: CONSENT VS CONTROL

The analysis of work design and control strategies offered so far has identified two main variants: a Taylorite/Fordist approach which deskills and maximizes control, often through technology or the assembly line, and an alternative Human Relations approach which apparently loosens control and enlarges skill. It has already been suggested that these two approaches may be substitutes for each other, each offering management the possibility of achieving one key requirement, but each endangering another fundamental need. This section will explore this proposition. It is a significant area for study, not only because it may offer a key to understanding the history of the development of work forms, but, just as importantly, because it may allow us to undertand current and future trends.

We begin by considering two quotations. First, from Burawoy, who argues that management must achieve more than direct control of work: 'As a practical tool of increasing capitalist control, Taylorism was a failure' (Burawoy, 1979, p.278). And, secondly, Friedman's view that 'Braverman too must be criticised for confusing one particular strategy for exercising managerial authority in the capitalist labour process with managerial authority itself. Taylorian Scientific Management is not the only strategy available for exercising managerial authority, and given the reality of worker resistance, often is not the most appropriate' (Friedman, 1977, p.80). Friedman distinguishes between two polarized strategies of work design: 'direct control' which includes Taylorism and Fordism, and 'responsible autonomy' which attempts to engage the commitment and support of workers. Under direct control, management controls work through close specification of tasks and supervision and the reduction of skill. Responsible autonomy, in contrast, works through 'the maintenance of managerial authority by getting workers to identify with the competitive aims of the enterprise so that they will act "responsibly" with a minimum of supervision' (Friedman, 1977, p.48). Here workers are encouraged to identify with managerial goals by being allocated some responsibility; paradoxically management gains control by losing it. Movement between these two poles is determined by the degree of worker resistance and competitive market pressures. It is clear that responsible autonomy is more appropriate where workers have managed to retain skill, and that direct control is appropriate with a weakened or unorganized workforce and a production process organized around high-volume production, long product runs and mass markets.

Other writers have contributed importantly to this analysis of managerial work strategies by noting that management approaches to job design must be seen as part of larger strategies of control which incorporate factors other than simple work design: namely, structural control and the design of the employment relationship. Using these dimensions of overall control, Edwards (1979) argues that management within capitalism involves two elements: coordination of divided functions, and the achievement of authority whereby the desired work behaviour is obtained. In early capitalism, managerial control was achieved simply by the employer/entrepreneur directly and personally overseeing and directing all operations. This form of control was limited by size; it soon encountered the need to develop structures of control which could cope with larger and more complex work organizations. (In fact, as noted earlier, it is misleading to talk of *one* form of control in early capitalism; if there are variations in work control strategies within capitalism they are not historically specific but may well coexist during the same period.)

Edwards argues that simple control was replaced by various experiments which coalesced into *structural* forms of control — i.e. control achieved through organization. The first of these was technical, whereby work was controlled by machinery and the assembly line. The next was bureaucratic, whereby workers were controlled by rules and procedures and the detailed specification of work content and method. Edwards' classification is weakened by its insistence on sequential historical periodization, each form giving way to the next in a step-by-step unilinear unfolding. Further, Thompson argues that control of work within capitalism involves three elements: ' ... the mechanisms by which employers direct work tasks; the procedures whereby they supervise and evaluate performance in production; and the apparatus of discipline and reward' (Thompson, 1983, p.122.) Nevertheless it remains useful here as an example of an approach which clearly sees each approach to work design as a conscious management attempt to resolve the problems of the previous approach and to address the particular requirements of the current stage of capitalist development. It is also of value in its insistence that strategies towards work design must be located within the context of management strategies on other dimensions of control, namely organizational structuring and the design of the employment relationship. The last of these is particularly pertinent to issues discussed in Chapter 6, since it lies behind management's use of labour-market segmentation strategies — for example, distinguishing core from periphery workers, or primary from secondary terms of employment.

5.1 STRATEGIES OF CONTROL: MANAGEMENT CHOICE, ITS DETERMINANTS AND LIMITS

We have identified two polarized work design strategies. Is there any evidence that managers actually make choices between these two? And if they do, what determines the direction of the choice?

Child notes 'The concept of strategy implies a rational consideration of alternatives and the articulation of coherent rationales for decisions' (Child, 1985, p.108). In these rather demanding terms it cannot be said that managers often have explicit strategies for job design. Management planning of job design is frequently characterized by vacillation, factionalism, short-termism and randomness. Management rationality is negotiated and ad hoc. With respect to work issues,

> ... much management policy-making and execution is piecemeal, uncoordinated and empiricist .... Detailed planning and implementation of a strategic character is also problematic in British firms (although no doubt it is attempted) because the means and conditions of 'strategic' goal achievement can simultaneously shade over into becoming demanding objectives themselves. (Jones and Rose, 1985, p.98)

But while management's freedom and ability to select job design strategies are constrained, not least by the historically-given set of organizational, institutional and attitudinal structures which support existing arrangements and which are difficult to change, there are still areas of discretion left to management. 'Employers pursue strategies aimed at achieving their objectives and priorities, selecting options within these areas of discretion.' (Garnsey, *et al.* 1985, p.50.)

However, none of this means that the approach under consideration is without considerable value; only that a number of qualifications about the limits of the concept must be borne in mind in this case. First, it is important not to use or accept too limited and focused a view of management strategy on job design, nor to see, for example, Friedman's distinction between 'direct control' and 'responsible autonomy' approaches to job design as necessarily implying that these are conscious and explicit choices, or as implying that management is necessarily explicitly concerned with issues of job design. They are probably more concerned with production targets, marketing, cost reduction, distribution etc. Nonetheless, these preoccupations will have implications for what is expected and required from employees' work, and so will have consequences for job design. All management strategies will represent some sort of attempt to ensure organizational survival, which, within a modern capitalist economy, means achieving accumulation or improving levels of profitable growth — usually increasing market share and improving margins through cost control. These strategies may in themselves contain no direct reference to job design issues (although other strategies on Human Resource Management may refer to new developments in job design: team working, Total Quality Management, flexibility etc.). But whether business strategies contain explicit reference to job design and job control issues or not, they in fact hold definite implications for job design, as Child argues in the following passage:

> ... investment in new technology is reportedly undertaken to meet targets such as improving the consistency of product quality, reducing inventory, or increasing the flexibility of plant. The appreciation of the production process held by the managers who approve the investment may not even include a clear conception of how the labour process is organised and controlled. Senior managers, particularly in larger organisations, often exhibit good understanding only of the work of a relatively small group of colleagues and subordinates, such that a 'psychological boundary' exists between them and the labour process (Fidler, 1981). At this elevated hierarchical level managers tend to deal in terms of statistical abstractions such as throughput volume, wastage rates, stock levels, delivery performance, unit costs, budget variance, and employment costs. Managerial policies on new technology need not therefore articulate explicit statements about the organisation of the labour process. Nonetheless, they effectively amount to strategies towards the labour process if the choice of a particular

technology imposes certain constraints on its operation and manning, and if the strategic expectations attached to the new technology also impose constraints on labour process design. Moreover, management will influence the route by which these strategic intentions are operationalised, by selecting those specialists and subordinates who are to act as work organisation designers. Each of these, be they production engineers, industrial engineers, systems analysts, craft-trained line managers or social scientists, will have their own relatively specific orientation towards the organisation and control of the labour process.

Managerial strategies therefore establish corporate parameters for the labour process which are unlikely to be inconsequential even when there is attenuation between policy and implementation. Purcell (1983) makes a comparable point in arguing that, within the modern large enterprise, managements have established corporate systems of centralised planning and financial control which have significant implications for the location of and control over bargaining about incomes and employment. The process whereby managerial intentions feed through to the workplace is therefore regarded as one in which managerial strategies play the role of 'steering devices' that have 'knock-on effects', to use terms suggested by Grieco (1983). This still allows for the fact that in different industrial sectors the extent to which strategies are formulated centrally or locally, unilaterally or bilaterally, can vary considerably. This perspective is also compatible with a recognition that the strategies may sometimes be unspecific and poorly understood, that they may be subject to reinterpretation and opposition by functional and junior managers, and that they may encounter worker resistance both informally in the workplace and through trade union action. Even in the absence of such opposition, the translation of policies and strategic decisions to the organisation of the labour process will require detailed working out by lower levels of management, by specialists (who might include external consultants) and possibly by shopfloor and office workers themselves.
(Child, 1985, pp.111–12)

ACTIVITY 5   What, according to Child, are the implicit consequences that managerial strategies have for job design?

If corporate strategies contain implications for job design even when they do not directly address job design or work control issues, then is it possible to identify the factors that relate to, or even determine, variations in the way that jobs are designed? We have seen that while mechanistic explanations in terms of technology or the requirements of capitalism are inadequate, explanations in terms of management strategy must recognize the complexity and opacity of such strategies.

Does this mean that ultimately we can predict nothing, but must rely on empirically investigating the post-hoc links between capitalist requirements and a particular approach to job design in every instance? We would argue that, in fact causal patterns are apparent.

Coombs seeks to locate work strategies within the context of an analysis of available sources of competitive and cost advantage, and specifically in terms of the possibility of technologically-driven advantage. He argues that tendencies in job structuring are triggered by the stage of development of technological innovations, and the extent to which these provide declining levels of benefit, thus encouraging the search for more radical, innovative solutions. He further argues that during a technological upswing, when the development of a regime of mechanization is in its initial phase, the efficiency of some production processes will be susceptible to considerable improvement as a result of the permissive character of the technical change (Coombs, 1985). Thus considerable improvements in performance can be achieved relatively easily without much attention to work design efficiency. But during a downswing, when 'performance improvement in some production processes is proving hard to achieve using the old technological paradigms', performance enhancement from technology becomes less possible. This sparks a search for possibilities for change through work redesign, organizational restructuring, changes in employment and so on.

Kelly, on the other hand, focuses more on developments in product and labour markets in explaining the choice of control strategy. He argues that, in seeking to understand the relationship between capitalism and the design of work, it is not enough to focus on the *extraction* of surplus value (i.e. the need to reduce costs to enhance profit); rather, attention must also be given to the *realization* of surplus value:

> ... we need to consider the full circuit of industrial capital as the starting point for analyses of changes in the division of labour; purchase of labour power; extraction of surplus value within the labour process; realization of surplus value within product markets. There is no sound theoretical reason for privileging one moment in this circuit — the labour–capital relation within the labour process — if our objective is to account for changes (or variations) in the division of labour.
> (Kelly, 1985, p.32)

Goods must be sold , as well as made, and management's concern to ensure sales is not only as important as concern for production, it has implications for job design. Kelly addresses a key issue: why is it that some organizations are able and willing to go against the more prevalent trend (i.e. prevalent in the early 1980s) of detailed and repetitive division of labour that is Taylorism? This question goes to the heart of the subject matter of this chapter — how far work forms in capitalism are determined and constrained, or are open to choice, and, if open to choice, what determines the possibility and direction of that choice?

Kelly notes that much labour process analysis assumes an inevitable antagonism between management and labour which is, in fact, less important to management than the anarchic competitive relations between firms competing for shares or markets. He argues that the full process of production and sales involves a series of contradictions or management dilemmas at different stages of the process: 'Firms try to match the qualifications and attitudes of workers to their particular labour process; they endeavour to organise the labour process in such a way that it efficiently and effectively produces the desired commodities for the firm's chosen product markets' (Kelly, 1985, p.33).

But things change — product and labour markets change, and these changes will immediately raise questions about the appropriateness of the labour process for new workers and new products for new customers. Kelly seeks to illuminate our understanding of the issues through a consideration of the electrical engineering industry. Within this industry a problem emerged: efforts to expand market share through enlarging product range caused a threat to labour productivity, and efforts to support productivity with long production runs (the high volume solution) of a restricted product range threatened market share. Productivity was also threatened by full employment: disgruntled workers could leave and find work elsewhere.

According to Kelly, these conditions produced three responses: a reduction of product range; allocation of products to specialized plants; and job redesign. For example, job redesign took the form of job enlargement, the reduction or elimination of the assembly line and its replacement with individual work stations. These changes have produced reported increases in productivity of 10–20 percent. But Kelly points out that, since the changes were associated with financial incentive schemes and with more direct supervisor control, these increases may be explicable in terms of classic, Taylorite mechanisms.

The changes in job design within the electrical industry represent a move away from Taylorism in terms of *job content*, but still remain within the Taylorite mechanisms with respect to the *context* of work. Yet these changes were not in themselves forced by any management priority to control and cheapen work. They were, rather, outcomes of the need to resolve wider, strategic contradictions between length and number of assembly lines and product range.

5.2   STRATEGIES OF CONTROL: THE IMPLICATIONS OF CHOICE

We have argued that management pursue strategies which either directly or indirectly have implications for job design, organizational structuring and the structuring of the employment relationship, which in turn have fundamental implications for societal divisions. The design of work has implications for the distribution of many of the experiences and resources which constitute the determinants of class. Choices about skill levels, levels of surveillance, wage rates etc., determine the forms of differentiated work experience which underlie classes. But we have seen that choices of job design also produce variations in job design and experience within the category of jobs which are defined as working-class jobs. These variations determine divisions within this category on gender or race or regional grounds.

Job design strategies will affect the content of work and employment experiences, and how these may be differentiated. They could also influence where employment and production occur. Essentially, management strategies towards job design not only determine work experience in terms of job content, degree of autonomy, pay levels, degree of security etc., but also have important implications for decisions about the allocation of workers to jobs and about the location of jobs, regionally, nationally and globally. These two dimensions, namely allocation and location, interconnect significantly. Once an allocation decision is taken about the sorts of workers ideally required (skill levels, degree of unionization, work attitudes, cost of employment), this has implications for decisions about where to locate.

While it is empirically a simplification (as we have seen from discussion in the previous chapter) to describe labour markets as segmented into primary and secondary, it is the case that this 'ideal type' classification is helpful in understanding employer strategies: for we find that market and industrial variables relate closely to firms' propensity to design jobs and employment in terms of primary or secondary conditions. Primary employment industries tend to use modern technology, face predictable demand, have some capacity to control their markets, and are characterized by strong collective bargaining. Secondary employment firms and industries tend to lack these characteristics (see Garnsey *et al.* 1985, p.53).

The segmentation of labour markets as a consequence of employers' strategies has consequences for external social divisions. Existing societal and institutional factors serve to structure and segment the supply of labour — the division of labour within the household, the socialization of children into specific work attitudes and expectations, exposure to education etc. — and these experiences affect the degree of vulnerability of workers. Vulnerable workers are most likely to end up in jobs which could be characterized as belonging to secondary labour market conditions.

These workers are not only less able to pick and choose among jobs while being more dependent on jobs with poor conditions, they are also less able to exert political influence, through collective bargaining for example. They cannot easily negotiate better conditions. Thus, as discussed in Chapter 6, migrant workers and women are particularly likely to take employment in the secondary sector, and this creates further vulnerability and disadvantage for them.

The important point about labour market segmentation is the suggestion that management strategies and choices lie behind the creation of dual

Cleaners at Heathrow airport

labour markets — the supply of jobs — and, furthermore, that these strategies reproduce and support the disadvantages they exploit. These strategies of labour market segmentation may reflect the competitive realities of the industry or sector as these have built up over time; for if all companies in large-scale retail, for example, use low-wage, part-time, disadvantaged workers, then the cost of breaking with this precedent is considerable.

Secondly, are these management strategies likely to work in terms of management objectives? We have argued against a simplistic, somewhat conspiratorial conception of an omniscient management artfully designing jobs as part of a grand design, largely because management is not as competent as this, nor as far-sighted nor as efficient. Nevertheless, we have also argued that the variation in work design (Scientific Management on the one hand, enriched and enlarged Quality of Working Life Movement type jobs on the other) reflects management's awareness of the failings of Scientific Management. This implies a purposeful conception of management and strategy. And, indeed, the very expression *strategy* does suggest a view of action that is designed to achieve a consequence and is therefore measureable in terms of its outcomes. Management is under pressure, even if indirectly, to achieve forms of job design which support the achievement of corporate strategies which in turn ensure competitive survival. We can thus see the process whereby managements experience competitive pressures to which they react by constructing strategies of which job design strategies may be an implicit or explicit element, as the working-out of a class dynamic. 'Class dynamic' refers to the process whereby managers identify and respond to pressures in the organizational environment —

i.e. pressures emanating from a market economy, by pursuing objectives such as increasing turnover, cutting costs, gaining market share — which require for their implementation strategies of job design and of employment which create the experiences that sociologists define as class experience and structures.

These are class strategies not simply in the sense that these forces generate responses (the design of jobs, the distribution of reward, decisions to sack, or close down) which represent the bases of class experience, but in the more general sense that the pressure on management to design jobs to achieve their management objectives in itself represents a class dynamic. The pressures to reduce costs and increase margins, to increase market share at the expense of competitors by whatever means are ultimately divisive: neither the benefits, nor the costs are equally distributed. Those who have only their labour to sell may be in a weak position to benefit from corporate success, and it is they who may suffer most and first.

But there is a final twist to these class implications of job design strategies, and one which reflects the class dynamic from which they arise, and with which they engage. This concerns the question of how far the various control strategies are likely to achieve their purposes. Can work design formulas be found which escape the paradox that every success breeds its ultimate failure, or the dilemma of excessive control, or lost control?

Hyman has argued that the essence of strategy is determined, not by the requirements of capitalism as such, but by the contradiction involved in satisfying these requirements. Thus it is impossible simultaneously to satisfy all the pressures and requirements impacting on firms, and in particular to resolve the contradiction noted in this chapter, involving the dilemma between ensuring the most profitable organization of work and achieving or regaining the commitment of staff. Managerial strategies of work control cannot transcend this dilemma; they simply adopt a particular position, a position which cannot prove satisfactory in the long run.

Hyman notes that the ' ... function of labour control involves both the direction, surveillance and discipline of subordinates whose enthusiastic commitment to corporate objectives cannot be taken for granted and the mobilisation of the discretion, initiative and diligence which coercive supervision, far from removing is likely to destroy' (Hyman, 1987, p.41). The value of discretion etc. to the employer is obvious with skilled workers; but it is also important in the case of formally semi- or unskilled workers where a considerable element of 'tacit' skills remains — i.e. skills which are not recognized but which lie behind the ability to perform allocated tasks.

In recent years there have been a number of developments in the design of work: not just job enrichment and enlargement, but quality circles, cell- and team-working, Just-In-Time programmes, culture-change programmes, the move to Service Level Agreements and competitive tendering within local authorities, and others. Since the area of work design is a profitable market for consultants and management writers it is particularly important to separate out the prescriptive element from actual developments on the ground. Undoubtedly these do not match in scope, permanence or effect the claims often made for them. Nevertheless the evidence is that changes are occurring in work design. Do these represent a qualitative change from the traditional pattern?

Interestingly, current developments can be organized almost exactly in terms of the classification offered in this chapter. They do not seem to have escaped the dilemmas outlined above. On the one hand, many of the changes involve attempts to enlarge or enhance job content, as with enpowerment (enrichment) or flexible, team- or cellular-working. These involve altering traditional job boundaries so that the jobs associated with the production of a discrete element of the total product — for example, making the doors for a commercial aircraft — are allocated not to a number of individual work roles, but to a team. But, as we have noted, enlarged discretion endangers management's ultimate control over the speed, quantity and quality of work.

There are two possible solutions to this problem, both of which are associated with the move to team-working. One is to locate control not in the work process, as in the assembly line, but in relations between workers, so that each team, by virtue of being dependent on other assemblies from other teams, puts pressure on its colleagues to maintain the flow of materials and assemblies. Just-in-time and service level agreements between departments, and the concept of internal customers, are all variants on this theme of socializing control: i.e. making workers control each other, often through the notion that workers are each other's customers. This is particularly significant since it is a further example of management's concern to disguise control while achieving it. The emphasis on customers as a source of pressure on workers offers the advantage that control is seen as no longer emanating from managers — those who set the rules — but from the requirements of production for profit within markets.

The other solution lies in the management of meaning. The messages may differ from the Victorian entrepreneurs' strictures on thrift, loose morals, drink and time-keeping, but the control strategy is essentially the same: change behaviour and achieve commitment by bombarding staff with instruction and exhortation defining the necessary attitude and behaviour, then enforce the message through selection, training, appraisal, assessment, possibly through the use of psychometric tests and elaborate assessment methods.

But few managements rely entirely on the success of such programmes. They don't need to do so because modern Information Technology systems allow detailed surveillance of all aspects of workers' work, as it occurs. A cashier's mistakes on an electronic till, a bank receptionist's success rates with new customers, the number of times a phone rings before it is answered by a telephonist, wastage levels, work speeds, errors, these can all be captured instantaneously. The techniques of control and meaning management may have changed but the basic mechanisms remain, as do the contradictions which inform them.

Summary and conclusion

This chapter has explored the nature and determinants of modern job design strategies. It has attempted to identify the major dynamics which inform the design of work, to show how these originate in certain requirements of a modern industrial economy and to consider how they are enforced by management. A crucial element of the argument has been the identification of two opposed tendencies — two poles — between which control strategies tend to swing, since any position on which it rests is, ultimately, untenable. Current developments in job design will not escape from this modernist dilemma.

REFERENCES

Argyris, C. (1972) *The Applicability of Organizational Sociology,* Cambridge, Cambridge University Press.

Bell, D. (1974) *The Coming of Post-Industrial Society,* London, Heinmann.

Berg, M. (1985) *The Age of Manufactures,* London, Fontana.

Beynon, H. (1984) *Working for Ford*, Harmondsworth, Penguin.

Blauner, R. (1964) *Alienation and Freedom,* Chicago, Chicago University Press.

Braverman, H. (1974) *Labour and Monopoly Capital,* New York, Monthly Review Press.

Buchanan, D. (1989) 'Principles and practices in job design', in Sissons, K. (ed.) *Personnel Management in Britain,* Oxford, Basil Blackwell.

Burawoy, M. (1979), *Manufacturing Consent,* Chicago, Chicago University Press.

Child, J. (1985) 'Managerial strategies, new technology and the labour process' in Knights, D. *et al.* (eds) (1985).

Coombs, R. (1985) 'Automation, management strategies and labour-process change' in Knights, D. *et al.,* (eds) (1985).

Davis, L.E., Canter, R. and Hoffman, J. (1972), 'Current work design criteria', in Davis, L. and Taylor, J.C. (ed.) *Design of Jobs,* Harmondsworth, Penguin.

Dore, R. (1973) *British Factory — Japanese Factory,* London, Allen and Unwin.

Edwards, R. (1979) *Contested Terrain,* London, Heinemann.

Fidler, J. (1981) *The British Business Elite,* London, Routledge and Keegan Paul.

Flink, J.J. (1975) *The Car Culture,* Boston, M.I.T. Press.

Friedman, A. (1977) *Industry and Labour,* London, Macmillan.

Foucault, M. (1977) *Discipline and Punish,* London, Allen Lane.

Gallie, D. (1983) *Social Inequality and Class Radicalism in France and Britain,* Cambridge, Cambridge University Press.

Garnsey, E. *et al.* (1985) 'Labour market structures and work-force divisions' in Deem, R. and Salaman, G. (eds) *Work, Culture and Society,* Milton Keynes, Open University Press.

Gill, C. (1985) *Work, Unemployment and the New Technology,* Cambridge, Polity Press.

Goldman, P. and van Houten, D.R. (1980), 'Bureaucracy and domination: managerial strategies in turn-of-the-century American industry', in Dunkerley, D. and Salaman, G. (eds) *The International Yearbook of Organization Studies,* London, Routledge and Kegan Paul.

Grieco, M. (1983) 'Contribution to discussion. Conference on organization and control of the labour process', Owens Park, Manchester.

Harvey, D. (1989) *The Condition of Postmodernity,* Oxford, Basil Blackwell.

Hobsbawm, E.J. (1968) *Labouring Men,* London, Weidenfeld and Nicholson.

Hyman, R. (1987) 'Strategy or structure: capital, labour and control', *Work, Employment and Society,* vol.1, pp.25–56.

Jones, B. (1982) 'Destruction or redistribution of engineering skills?', in Wood, S. (ed.) *The Degradation of Work?* London, Hutchinson.

Jones, B. and Rose, M. (1985) 'Managerial strategy and trade union responses at establishment level' in Knights, D. *et al.* (eds) (1985).

Kelly, J.E. (1985) 'Managements redesign of work: labour process, labour markets and product markets' in Knights, D. *et al.* (eds) (1985).

Kerr, C. *et al.* (1973) *Industrialism and Industrial Man,* Harmondsworth, Penguin Books.

Knights, D. *et al.* (eds) (1985) *Job Redesign: Critical Perspectives on the Labour Process,* Aldershot, Gower.

Littler, C.R. (1978) 'Understanding Taylorism', *British Journal of Sociology,* vol. 29, no.2, pp.185–202.

Littler, C.R. (1982), *The Development of the Labour Process in Capitalist Societies,* London, Heinemann.

Littler, C.R. and Salaman, G. (1984) *Class at Work,* London, Batsford.

Littler, C.R. (1985) 'Taylorism, Fordism and job design', in Knights, D. *et al.* (eds) (1985).

Pollard, S. (1965) *The Genesis of Modern Management,* London, Edward Arnold.

Purcell, J. (1983) 'The management of industrial relations in the modern corporation', *British Journal of Industrial Relations,* vol. 21, pp.1–16.

Roeber, J. (1975) *Social Change at Work,* London, Duckworth.

Rose, M. (1988) *Industrial Behaviour: Research and Control,* Harmondsworth, Penguin.

Sayles, C.R. (1958), *Behaviour of Industrial Work Groups,* New York, John Wiley.

Thompson, P. (1983) *The Nature of Work,* London, Macmillan.

Walker, C.R. and Guest, R.H. (1952) *The Man on the Assembly Line,* Cambridge, Mass., Harvard University Press.

Wood, S. and Kelly, J. (1982) 'Taylorism, responsible autonomy and management strategy' in Wood, S. (ed.) *The Degradation of Work?* London, Hutchinson.

Woodward, J. (1970) *Industrial Organization: Behaviour and Control,* Oxford, Oxford University Press.

READING A   UNDERSTANDING TAYLORISM

Craig Littler

The Principles of Taylorism

Taylorism grew out of the systematic management movement in the USA in the 1880/90s. Like some of the other early management reformers, only with a greater intensity, Taylor believed in the original sin and the original stupidity of the worker. According to Taylor ' ... the natural instinct and tendency of men is to take it easy, which may be called "natural soldiering"'. Moreover, any man phlegmatic enough to do manual work was too stupid to develop the best way, the 'scientific way' of doing a job. Thus the role of the workman was a passive one: they should ' ... do what they are told to do promptly and without asking questions or making suggestions'. It is interesting to contrast this view of original sin and original stupidity with the Confucian view of original virtue.

If we look at Taylorism as a form of work organization, then we can proceed to analyse it in terms of three general categories: the division of labour, the structure of control over task performance, and the implicit employment relationship.

Bearing in mind practice as well as theory, then it is clear that Taylorism involves systematic analysis of the labour process and the division of labour, followed by their decomposition in accordance with several principles. The systematic analysis of work (Taylor's First Principle) was in order to develop a 'science of work'. And this systematic job analysis forms the basis for the calculation of production costs, the establishment of standard times for every task, and the associated incentive payment system.

The decomposition is based on the following principles:

1   *A general principle of maximum fragmentation.* This prescribes that after analysis of work into its simplest constituent elements, management should seek to limit an individual 'job' to a single task as far as possible.

2   *The divorce of planning and doing* (Taylor's Fourth Principle). This principle in particular is based on the idea that the worker is too stupid to understand his own job.

3   *The divorce of 'direct' and 'indirect' labour.* ... progressively suppressing that part of the worker's activity which consists of preparing and organizing the work in his own way.

This principle is given little theoretical attention but is very significant on the shop-floor. It is an essential component of more intensified work. Indeed it is the Taylorian equivalent of Babbage's principle. All preparation and servicing tasks are stripped away to be performed by unskilled, and cheaper, workers as far as possible.

Source: Littler, C.R. (1978) 'Understanding Taylorism', *British Journal of Sociology*, vol.29, no.2, pp.185–202.

4   *Minimization of skill requirements and job-learning time.*

5   *Reduction of material handling to a minimum.*

These five principles constitute a dynamic of deskilling. Taylor had generated a system of taking labour (i.e. job roles) apart. It was a system remarkably similar to that envisaged by Babbage 50 years earlier. The major difference is that Babbage did not construct a corresponding principle to the divorce of planning and doing.

It must not be thought that Taylorism was the only cause of an increasing division of labour. Taylorism was *both* a consequence and a cause of deskilling and the corresponding co-ordination problems.

Babbage had no clear idea of the problems of, and the means of, re-co-ordination of the fragmented job roles. Systematic management grew out of the intensified problems of the integration of the new division of labour. These had been created by larger factories, more specialized machines and job roles pre-Taylor, and the failure of the internal contract system under changed conditions.

The second major aspect of Taylorism then is the new structure of control, of integration, which it offered. This had a number of aspects:

1   *The principle of task control (Taylor's Third Principle).*

This element has been obscured by the circumlocutory way in which Taylor described it. He talked about 'bringing the science and workmen together'. What it means in practice is a 'planning department' which plans and co-ordinates the entire manufacturing process:

> The work of every workman is fully planned out by the management at least one day in advance, and each man receives in most cases complete written instructions, describing in detail the task which he is to accomplish, as well as the means to be used in doing the work. ... This task specifies not only what is to be done but how it is to be done and the exact time allowed for doing it.
> (Taylor, 1964, p.39)

This is how 'science' and the workman are brought together. A crucial aspect of this 'bringing together' is the prescribing of uniform practices and operating procedures; in other words, standardization. This represents an historical shift towards a more total control, a new level of control, over the labour process.

In relation to supervision, standardization renders 'the production process more open to understanding'. ... In other words, it is an important step towards increasing 'observability' of a subordinate's task performance by reducing the problems arising from the incongruence of superior/subordinate skills. In practice the idea of a planning department with its conglomeration of functions envisaged by Taylor at the apex of the organization was rarely realized.

Complete task control could not be achieved simply by a planning department and standardization. Other mechanisms were necessary.

2   Functional organization

This principle is usually lost sight of because it was rarely put directly into practice. Even the early acolytes had reservations about functional fore-manship. Nevertheless, functional organization should be noted for several reasons.

Functional organization is important as a prescription because it represents the idea of a *division of management:* a movement away from a single hierarchy (Taylor calls this the 'military plan'). For Taylor the role of the foreman and gang-boss was too wide, too powerful, and not clearly circumscribed. It needed to be subdivided and deskilled as much as the roles of the workmen:

> Functional management consists in so dividing the work of manage-ment that each man from the assistant superintendent down shall have as few functions as possible to perform. If practicable the work of each man in the management should be confined to the perform-ance of a single leading function.
> (Taylor, 1964, p.99)

Thus Taylor advocated dividing the shop-floor foremen into four (setting-up boss, speed boss, quality inspector, and repair boss), and placing them under the control of the planning department. Foremen like workers became subject to the rule of clerks.

Braverman, and many other writers, use the following quote to illustrate the Taylorian attack on craft autonomy:

> all possible brain work should be removed from the shop and centred in the planning or laying-out department. ...
> (Braverman, 1974, p.113)

But nobody completes this quotation. Let us do so:

> ... leaving for the *foreman* and *gang-bosses* work strictly executive in nature.
> (Taylor, 1964, pp.98–9)

And this statement occurs in the midst of a long section analysing the need to sub-divide *managerial* roles.

The implication I want to draw is that Taylorism and functional organiza-tion had an historical significance in relation to 'over-powerful' foremen and internal contractors as much as to craft deskilling.

Secondly, functional organization is significant because it was taken seri-ously by non-Western societies: Russia, and China to a lesser extent. Indeed Brugger seeks to characterize Taylorism *in terms of* this principle.

The argument is simple: a major problem for large, complex organizations is 'integration' of conflicting instructions. There are two basic ways this can be achieved — technologically or ideologically. If we cross-relate this distinction to the structure of command, then we get the following possi-bilities:

Table 1

Command Structure	Type of Integration	
	Technological	Ideological
Staff-line	Modern, Western, Industrial Organization	Chinese Organization during the early 1960s
Functional	Taylor Model	Some Chinese experiments

(Adapted from Brugger, 1976, Fig. 14, p. 275)

The value of this perspective is that it locates these particular Taylorite ideas within a frame of possibilities, and suggests what happened to the Taylorian model in practice — namely a shift to staff/line organization. Taylor's prized 'planning department' became a series of departments clipped onto the side of the existing command structure.

3   Time study and the creation of a monitoring system

The institutionalization of time study represents the creation of a *separated* monitoring system over subordinate activities. The time study and scheduling system depends upon the workers filling in job-cards and/or time sheets. These written communications constitute a flow-back of information to the planning departments, and enables them to determine effort-levels and compare performance. The point to be emphasized is that this flow of information largely bypasses the foremen, bypasses, that is, the existing command structure.

The reduced 'observability' in large, complex organizations because of increased physical separation and reduced congruence of superior/subordinate skills had to be solved by some means. This was even more imperative if the dynamic of deskilling was to continue.

What I am arguing further is that as we move from specialization to fragmentation of labour it creates different types of problems which must be solved at the level of the structure of control.

4   Incentive payment system

The significance of this element of Taylorism has been much over-rated and misunderstood. I will attempt to understand the real significance of incentive payment systems below.

Some of the mechanisms of control advocated by Taylor and institutionalized in various forms, constitute not only control over task performance, but means towards perpetuation of that control. For example, the concentration of 'brainwork' in the planning departments represented a transfer of knowledge: Taylorism 'tends to gather up and transfer to the management all the traditional knowledge, the judgement and skill of the workers'. And, we might add, a transfer of knowledge from the internal contractors, gang-bosses and traditional foremen.

Secondly, though Taylor never developed any systematic ideas on training, the move towards job roles incorporating minimal training time was a crucial step towards shifting control of training to the employer. It reduced the potential power base for job control.

The third aspect of Taylorism relates to the employment relation. It is this which enables us to clearly relate Taylorite work organization to bureaucracy.

The employment relation embodied in Taylorism has been best brought out by L.E.Davis:

> ... there is minimal connection between the individual and the organization in terms of skill, training, involvement and the complexity of his contribution, in return for maximum flexibility and independence on the part of the organisation in using its manpower. In other words the organisation strives for maximum interchangeability of personnel (with minimum training) to reduce its dependence on the availability, ability, or motivation of individuals. (Davis, 1966, p.302)

Davis calls this relation the 'minimum interaction model'.

Nelson discovers that Taylorism has little to say about the 'labour problem', i.e. the problem of *social* integration. In brief his argument is that Taylorism presents itself as an answer to the problem of solidarity when in fact it was an answer to the problem of system integration. This argument falls down because Nelson discovers an *omission* within Taylorite ideas of work organization which in many ways represents part of its *contribution* to capitalist organization. As Friedmann points out Taylorism succeeded 'not *in spite of* but just *because of* its omissions' (Friedmann, 1955, p.65).

Taylor himself may not have fully realized the relational implication of his ideas, but this does not matter. Minimum interaction continues to be the cultural reality in many Western organisations.

The Relationship of Taylorism to Bureaucracy

It is common to see Taylorism as part of a wider 'rationalization movement', or as one type of a formal or classical theory of administration. However, little attempt is made to relate Taylorism to the Weberian concept of bureaucracy. This failure to do so has led to serious consequences. The major effect has been to leave Taylorism isolated from the main body of sociological theory. It is something to throw bricks at but never to use as a tool of analysis.

In order to relate Taylorism to the concept of bureaucracy it is necessary to make a fundamental distinction within the Weberian model.

If we summarize the five overarching beliefs about rational-legal authority as a belief in a set of abstract, impersonal rules applicable to everyone, then the remaining elements of the ideal type can be divided into two categories: those that describe the officials' relationship to the organization (or the 'employment relationship'), and those that are largely concerned with the structure of control. This results in the following picture:

Table 2

Structure of control	The employment relationship
1 Continuous organization and bound by rules.	1 Separation from means of production and administration
2 Hierarchy	2 Non-appropriation of office
3 Systematic division of labour, with the necessary and delimited powers	
4 Work performance is governed by rules, which may be either technical or legal. (Plus specialized training)	
5 Written records and communications	
6 Unified control system, i.e. monocratic	3 Formally free labour
	4 Appointment on basis of contract
	5 Selection based on technical or professional qualification
	6 Career system based on either (a) seniority or (b) merit
	7 Fixed, money salaries and pension rights
	8 Full-time commitment, i.e. sole or primary occupation

Note: The elements above the line are characteristic of Taylorism, whereas those below are not.

If we examine Taylorism in the above context, then it is clear that Taylorism represents *the bureaucratization of the structure of control, but not the employment relationship.* Taylorism does not involve, nor imply, a career system ... , nor fixed salaries ... . Instead it involves what we have called the minimum interaction relation between individual and organization. ...

The central significance of a career structure within an organization has been suggested by many writers. Career structures and career motivation are a major, definitive characteristic of 'bureaucratic' organization. And this element should be used to distinguish between different types of rational-legal work organization. Thus the major characteristic of Taylorite work organization is the lack of any notion of a career system. It is this which distinguishes it from other available models of organization at the turn of the century; for example those based on the public service organizations such as police, railways and post office.

Taylorism in its Historical Context

It is not possible to really understand Taylorism without grasping the historical context, not just in macro terms, but in terms of the specifics of work organization pre-Taylor. It is the strength of Braverman's analysis that he looks at Taylorism in this light, but his analysis is vitiated by an historical romanticism.

Braverman's basic understanding of Taylorism revolves around the idea of the craft system. It is the transfer of knowledge from the crafts, and its monopolization by management which Braverman sees as the essence of Taylorism. This monopoly, under the name of 'science', is used to control each step of the labour process until the craftsman is no more than an 'animated tool of management'. In sum, the historical change is from the craft system to Taylorism, such that Taylorism had the effect of degrading the crafts.

This is an historical confusion. By the turn of the century in the USA, and by the inter-war period in Britain, job knowledge was not, in general, locked into the craft system, nor was the locus of planning concentrated in manual job roles. Failure to consider the institutionalization of Taylorism leads to a misleading telescoping of history.

This type of romanticism concerning craft control within US industry at the turn of the century has been strongly attacked by Jean Monds, who encapsulates the misleading vision of the 'good old days' with the title 'The Lost Paradise of Craft Autonomy: with F.W.Taylor as Serpent'. In fact Monds is attacking the work of Montgomery and Katherine Stone, but Braverman's arguments are partly based on their work, and represent a similar vein.

Monds' argument is straightforward. Job control by various craft groups was limited in the USA, and many of the practices of job control had been destroyed *before* Taylor arrived on the scene. Secondly, conflicts and exploitation between skilled and unskilled mar the image of paradise.

If we leave behind the craft romanticism of Braverman and Montgomery, then it is necessary to think of an historical shift not from a simple craft system to Taylorism, but from forms of *sub-contract* to Taylorism. Up to the 1870s in Britain the traditional managerial system in many industries was based on some form of internal contractor, who in large part ran the shop-floor. These varied from

> a small number of substantial sub-contractors as in mining, or large numbers of skilled workers as sub-contractors each employing only a few child or unskilled assistants.
> (Pollard, 1968, p.59)

Moreover by the 1870s and 80s the craft element had often been drained from the contracted work-group, leaving an ugly husk of piece-mastership and exploitation.

If we appreciate this fragmented structure of the nineteenth-century work-organization, we are less likely to focus on a limited segment of workers — the craft aristocracy — and thus ignore the system of social relations which are involved. We are less likely either to bathe the early period of capitalism (which after all was the period that Marx was writing about) with a roseate hue.

This is not to say that the transition was a simple shift from internal contract to Taylorism, any more than from the craft system to Taylorism.

There is not space here to detail the historical changes, but in many industries the role of the internal contractor was inherited by powerful, directly-employed foremen. The picture shifts from a top-hatted sub-contractor to a bowler-hatted foreman. It was not until the inter-war period in Britain that the heirs of a modified Taylorism drastically reduced the foreman's area of discretion.

It is important to question the conventional version of Taylorism, which has it that Taylor knew nothing of, nor about, work-groups and their significance for the organization. According to the accepted version Taylor was a 'machine and money' man with his mind fixed upon the individual.

This is nonsense. Taylor knew all about work-groups. He knew about solidary work-groups. He knew about their significance in regulating output; he called it 'systematic soldiering' because he did not like it. 'Human relations' represents the 'discovery' of that which Taylorism had been concerned to destroy — work-group solidarity.

But there is a further point. It is not just a question of Taylor versus the workers (this is the predominant image in Braverman). The Taylorites were concerned to destroy the traditional relationship between the foremen and the workers, between the internal contractor and the workers. The point is that pre-Taylor, pre-systematic management, the distinction between formal and informal work groups was not always clear cut.

From this perspective, 'human relations' represents a different managerial tactic in relation to work groups. The Taylorite tactic is to try and break the power of the work teams and work groups by pressure, and by appeal to individual ambition: to atomize the workforce. This is the dynamic reality behind 'technological integration'. Human relations represents an alternative approach; it represents a pale suggestion of 'ideological integration', of ideological control. The latter as a dynamic process is best expressed by Brugger in relation to Chinese experience.

The Chinese approach:

> ... seeks to focus loyalty not only upon the formal organisation, but upon levels both higher and lower than the organisation. At the lower level ... *to infuse existing levels of group solidarity with commitment to the same values as the formal organisation.* At the higher levels, it seeks *not* to extend the focus of loyalty through a hierarchy of formal organisation, but to focus it upon a particular symbol cluster which is the source of legitimacy not only of different levels of formal organisation but also of informal groupings.
> (Brugger, 1976, p.268)

Thus, discussion of Taylorism in terms of whether it represents too individualistic an understanding of the social realities of work organization is to doubly misunderstand Taylorism, and the historical path which it represents.

Wage/Effort Exchange

The purpose of this section is to look at Taylorism from a rather different perspective — that of wage/effort exchanges. This approach is complementary to more general ideas on the structure of control and the processes of the division of labour.

An entire literature has built up around payment systems since the 1890s. It has frequently dominated managerial discussions of work organizations, and Taylorism itself has become ensnared in this form of interpretation, such that the notion of incentive wages is still seen as the predominant element in Taylorism. This is a mistake. Rather than allow the literature and concepts of payment systems to swamp sociological analysis, it is necessary to do the reverse: to penetrate payment systems with precise analytic tools.

Let us start by attempting to deflate the fundamental distinction within payment system literature: that between time-wages and piece-wages. It is necessary to recognize the common basis of all types of wages:

> But in the practice of industry, whether a man be employed on a time-wage or on piece-wage, both the time occupied and work done are, as a rule, taken into account ... time-wage very often has a piece basis, and piece-wage has in practically all cases a time-basis. (Schloss, 1898, p.13)

In other words, time-wages are usually based on mutual expectations about the quantum of work. For example, many foremen and sub-contractors in the latter part of the nineteenth century would set production quotas. Similarly, piece-work involves implicit assumptions of earning so much *per day*, or per week. Thus, as Behrend argues, every employment contract involves both a wage-rate bargain and an effort-bargain.

Thus, the sociological significance of Taylorism in relation to wage/effort exchange does *not* lie in a simple shift to piece-work. Indeed Taylor himself argued that his system of management could be applied *under any payment system,* and that a variety of payment systems can be used in the same factory depending on circumstances.

Given this, then a crucial question in relation to payment systems relates to effort determination: how do workers decide what effort to put into their work?

There are three broad answers: (a) custom and practice, or (b) based on formal standards, or (c) a conflictual tension between the two. It is this distinction, rather than the usual classification, which is sociologically and historically important in relation to payment-systems.

Using the above distinction it is possible to construct the following classification of wage/effort exchange systems:

Table 3

Informal Standards of effort		Formal Standards of effort	
		Unilaterally determined	Bilaterally determined
Piece-work or time-wage		e.g. the Taylorite system	e.g. standard price lists

This classification brings out the crucial aspect of Taylorism in this regard. And indeed Taylor saw his system in this way:

> ... this whole system rests upon an accurate and scientific study of unit times, which is by far the most important element in scientific management.
> (Taylor, 1964, p.58)

In addition, the above classification overlaps with a second distinction. It is possible to distinguish between wage/effort exchange systems in terms of their 'transparency'. Some payment systems, such as simple piece-work, make the relation of effort to earnings transparent; (both supervisors and workers are fully aware of the effort bargain involved for each task) whilst other systems completely obscure the effort/wage relationship.

The relevance of the notion of 'transparency' to the Taylorite payment schemes is that they attempted to make the wage/effort relationship *more* opaque than simple piece-work, in order to provide a built-in rate cutting factor. The way that this was done is as follows: instead of just mapping the output rate onto a wage scale, a third intermediary scale is introduced, namely an 'effort scale'. This is usually derived from some output target or 'standard job-time'. And this effort scale provides an apparent arithmetic rationale for the wage scale, and obscures the relationship between the output rate and the wage scale.

Hobsbawm argues that during the nineteenth century there was a slow withering of the customary, traditional ideas concerning labour effort. This occurred through a collective learning process; a collective re-orientation to the market system. However, it is not just a question of the slow assimilation of the 'rules of the game'. A traditional, normative basis to levels of work effort must be socially constituted. In this case standard effort-levels are built into the occupation or skill. *Therefore, if job-roles are fractured during an accelerating division of labour, an increasing number of workers are thrust into positions for which there are no customary standards.* It is this which constituted a major part of the 'labour problem' at the end of the nineteenth century.

Thus Taylorism represents the historical switchover from traditional effort-norms to the creation of new social mechanisms for constituting effort standards. However, at this point in the argument we encounter another paradox.

Baldamus and other writers have emphasized that time-study rests on pre-existing notions of wage/effort relationships and of the level of effort in a particular work situation:

> Whether one is successful or not in finding the 'required' standard times depends decisively upon the discovery of the preconceived, habitually maintained standards of normal exertion in any type of operation. The true purpose of scientific objectivity in the practice of work-measurement is precisely the opposite of what it claims to be in theory. ... The true purpose ... is to guess as consistently as possible the purely subjective element of effort standards, and subsequently to adjust rates of pay in accordance with them.
> (Baldamus, 1961, p.46)

How can a time-study practitioner discover pre-existing notions of effort-levels where there are none? If work-study was a managerial solution to the widespread *lack* of traditional effort-norms, how can it be based on 'prevailing notions of the right level of effort'?

The answer is that most research on the operation of work-study is based on ongoing systems, where the work-study practitioner is concerned with minor method or product changes. However, in a situation of more radical job-changes, a situation of fragmentation and associated technological change, the work-study man is a more active participant in establishing the standard effort/levels than some writers would have us believe. For example, in the 1920s and 1930s in Britain many factories established assembly and sub-assembly lines for the first time, fragmenting many jobs in the process. And the deskilled workers, often women, brought to the bench ignorance and often credulousness about 'the right level of effort'.

A distinction introduced by Baldamus enables the argument concerning the relationship of bureaucracy to Taylorism to be completed. This is the distinction between *effort stability* and *effort intensity* controls. Effort stability mechanisms shift 'effort' about, so that it is stabilized between people and over time. Effort now comes in neat packets, and all the 'packets' dance to the same rhythm.

It is not only necessary to iron out effort, but also to boost it up. This is the aim of effort-intensity controls. They are not necessarily *separate* from effort-stability controls in practice. Some means of control (e.g. training, incentive schemes) can have a dual function. However, this distinction enables us to understand the different significance of two aspects of the Taylorian work-study process. Rate-setting, that is establishing a rate for a job, is primarily a matter of effort-intensity control. It is at this point that any 'speed-up' effect is inserted into the task situation; whilst once established, incentive schemes are primarily a matter of *stabilizing* effort, of effort routinization.

It is important to note that stabilizing effort ensures calculability and predictability within the organization. For Weber, bureaucratic organization ensured a high degree of calculability, *but when we look at the bureaucratization of the structure of control in industrial organizations, then what Taylorism adds to the Weberian elements* (work study, monitoring system, incentive payment system) *is concerned with the processes of determining and fixing effort-levels.*

Thus, the bureaucratization of control in industrial organizations, as opposed to state administration, necessarily involves some controls over effort stability and intensity.

Summary and Conclusions

If sociology is to understand the changes in the forms of work organization from the late nineteenth century to the present, then it is necessary to penetrate the clichés about Taylorism. In particular it is necessary to avoid construing Taylorism as an abstracted ideas-system, and to avoid the 'Ambrit fallacy'. Thus we have analysed Taylorism in terms of the division of labour, the structure of control over task-performance, and the implicit minimum interaction employment relationship.

Further, Taylorism represents a form of organization devoid of any notion of a career-structure for the majority, unlike other forms of organizational model available at the turn of the century, such as the railways and post office. Therefore Taylorism can be defined as the bureaucratization of the structure of control, but *not* the employment relationship.

Historically, Taylorism should be understood as the modern structure of control, the lineaments of the new factory system, replacing the systems of internal contract which were forms of indirect employment and control. It is largely a misinterpretation, based on historical compression, to see Taylorism as the rabid destroyer of the craft system. What underlies both Taylorism and the bureaucratic model is the notion of *direct employment,* of an unmediated employment relationship.

In industrial organizations, calculability essentially involves processes of determining and fixing effort-levels. Thus, Taylorism also represents the historical shift to the creation of new social mechanisms for constituting effort-standards within an accelerated dynamic of deskilling. It is this rather than incentive wages which is the crucial element in Taylorism in relation to wage/effort exchange.

It should be clear that the purpose of 'Understanding Taylorism' is not only to analyse past forms of work organization, but to grasp the present. Taylorism has a continuing influence West and East. A sociological focus on the ideological level has obscured the ramifying impact of Taylorism. Only if we comprehend the structure of control of the labour process can there be any hope of moving beyond a neo-Taylorism, whatever the political umbrella.

References

Baldamus, W. (1961) *Efficiency and Effort,* London, Tavistock.

Braverman, H. (1974) *Labour and Monopoly*, New York, Monthly Review.

Brugger, W. (1976) *Democracy and Organization in the Chinese Industrial Enterprise, 1948–53,* Cambridge, Cambridge University Press.

Davis, L.E. (1966) 'The design of jobs', in Davis, L.E. and Taylor, J.C. *Design of Jobs,* Harmondsworth, Penguin.

Friedmann, G. (1955) *Industrial Society,* New York, The Free Press.

Pollard, S. (1968) *The Genesis of Modern Management,* Harmondsworth, Penguin.

Schloss, D.F. (1898) *Methods of Industrial Remuneration,* London, Williams and Norgate.

Taylor, F.W. (1964) *Scientific Management,* London, Harper and Row.

CHAPTER 8 POWER, CONFLICT AND CONTROL AT WORK

Diane Watson

CONTENTS

1   INTRODUCTION

In this chapter we shall be exploring some aspects of work behaviour and work experience. The kinds of work people do (or are prevented from doing) in society have a significant impact on the level of material rewards they receive. Some work, such as domestic work within the private world of the family, goes largely unpaid, whilst different forms of paid work are rewarded with different amounts of income and prestige. Furthermore, the nature of the work people do plays a crucial role in their experience of the world and the ways in which they are perceived and evaluated by themselves and by others. Work therefore is not only about material rewards and status. It is also about individual experience of 'self' and identity. The type of work we do is one of the major means by which we are located in the broader social structure, and it has implications for experience far beyond the immediate work environment.

Chapters 5, 6 and 7 of this book have explored the rise of factory production, the horizontal and vertical structuring of work at the level of the national and international economies (labour segmentation and the new international division of labour), and the vertical and horizontal structuring of tasks in the design of factory work (Taylorism, Fordism, work design and the labour process). Clearly, the structuring of occupations and issues of work design have an impact on individual work experience and locate individuals within structures of power and control at work. In this chapter we shall be exploring these power aspects of work relationships, the conflicts which arise at work, and questions of 'control'.

One of the values of sociological analysis is that, in its focus on large-scale patterning and structure, it directs our attention towards some of the ways in which the actions of individuals are constrained by the nature of the structures of which they are a part. Such analysis has highlighted the major inequalities of power existing between different social classes or different dominant groups, and has alerted us to some of the ways in which power is used to further and maintain existing advantage. However, one of the dangers associated with this type of structural analysis is a tendency to underestimate the role of human motivation and intention in the working-out of social processes. Individuals are not passive recipients of an all-embracing, determining social structure. On the contrary, *in the most constrained of circumstances individuals will act resourcefully to exercise whatever control they can over their situation*. In this context, therefore, the operation of power and control is not merely a one-way, top-down process. It is a two-way, dialectical process where even the relatively powerless have some scope to control their lives, and where every exercise of power is likely to bring forth a number of responses involving accommodation and resistance. The perspective adopted here is one which sees social life as a vast network of individuals and groups; a network within which there is a multiplicity of conflicts, in which the 'powerless' exercise power and in which everybody seeks 'control' in some way. This is absolutely not to say that society is composed of elements which are equally matched and which are competing on an 'even field'. However, it is to say such things as: power can be exerted from 'the bottom upwards' as well as from the top down; conflict at work is not just between managers and managed or employees and employed but can exist between worker and customer, and worker and worker; control is sought by all social actors in playing out their roles in life, however humble those roles might be.

In this chapter we shall examine these issues by:

- Exploring the concept of power and drawing out its relationship to conflict and control.

- Looking specifically at processes of power and conflict between men and women in the social and sexual division of labour by focusing on the occupation of midwifery and its relationship to the male medical profession.

- Examining the dynamics of work relations between employers and employees within the technical division of labour in work organizations. In particular, the relationship between conflict and cooperation will be explored and *individual* and *collective* responses to processes of power and control examined.

- Looking at the way in which individual identity is bound up with the work people do and the ways in which individuals act to control situations to 'give themselves space' and to retain their dignity. This will be done by means of the experiences of a restaurant waiter — here representing the growing service sector of the modern economy.

2   POWER AND THE DIVISION OF LABOUR

2.1   THE CONCEPT OF POWER

Power is a concept over which there has been much debate and disagreement, especially because part of its meaning derives from the theoretical perspective within which it is used. (See *Penguin Dictionary of Sociology:* POWER.) Some approaches — American *functionalist* sociology, for example (see *Penguin Dictionary of Sociology:* FUNCTIONALISM) — would see power as shared between groups and as playing a positive social function in enabling individuals and groups to work together in the pursuit of common goals. However, it has been more common in sociology for power to be conceived of as involving issues of control and coercion, where some groups use power to gain advantage over others in *competition* for scarce and valued resources. Weber's definition of power, for example, stresses that power is about 'the probability that a person in a social relationship will be able to carry out his or her own will in the pursuit of goals of action, regardless of resistance' (*Penguin Dictionary of Sociology:* POWER). This is a more negative view of power involving coercion and a 'contest of wills' (Rueschemeyer, 1986, p.12). In this view, power involves choice and intention by one (controlling) party and the possibility of resistance and conflict by those controlled.

One recognized difficulty with this definition is that, in its focus on behaviour and decision-making, it tends not to engage with the more covert aspects of power in non-decision making. So, for example, if we were to observe a given set of union–management negotiations over pay, hours or benefits, we might be able to see relatively clearly those occasions when one party has used power to gain advantage over the other. But what we will *not* be able to see is the way in which power operates to keep issues off the negotiating agenda. If one party has power to control which issues are legitimate items for discussion and decision-making, then it is, in effect, using its power to suppress the discussion of issues which might challenge existing arrangements. If management are able to control the agenda for discussion in such a way that unions are not able to raise issues that would question management's right to control, manage or structure the work in a particular kind of way, then they are using power, but in a less clearly observable manner. Furthermore, power may involve the capacity to shape the wants, expectations and 'taken-for-granted' understandings of individuals. For example, through the subtle control and manipulation of advertising and media images, individuals may be unaware of the operation of those processes of power over their experience and 'may "voluntarily" do what another wants, without any sense of coercion' (Pringle, 1988, p.50). Again, these processes are far less open to observation and investigation.

Finally, other forms of sociological analysis, such as some variants of Marxist sociology, would see power as an element of structural relationships which exists independently of the wills and intentions of the individuals concerned. Power therefore arises out of the mode of production of a given society and involves conflict between social classes, as opposed to conflict between individuals and social groups.

Whatever the starting point, it is clear that the operation of power in society has to do with some groups having the capacity to affect others with a view to gaining an advantage over them. This capacity often involves conflict and overt attempts at control. How, then, does it happen that some groups occupy more advantaged positions in the work environment than others? To pursue this further let us return briefly to the concept of the *division of labour*.

2.2 THE DIVISION OF LABOUR

One of the characteristic features of modern, industrialized societies is an advanced and complex social division of labour, a feature which is relevant to the operation of power, conflict and control in the work environment (see *Penguin Dictionary of Sociology:* DIVISION OF

LABOUR). All societies, whether simple or complex, display some kind of specialization of tasks and, in simple societies, these are usually organized around differences such as those of age or sex. This is not to say that sex or age *determine* the tasks undertaken. Even in societies where the level of economic development or social and cultural complexity are similar, there would appear to be a wide variation in the nature of the tasks undertaken by men, women and different age groups, and in the nature of the social relations which exist between them. As Rueschemeyer has observed of the division of labour, 'even in its most elementary forms it is more than a biological phenomenon: it is a human creation and particularly social in character' (1986, p.2). Consequently, the overall division and specialization of work tasks within society as a whole (*the social division of labour*), within a specific production process (*the technical division of labour*) or between men and women (*the sexual division of labour*), are the products of the intentions and actions of individuals as they go about organizing their lives, and the lives of others, within the constraints imposed by the nature of the economic and social framework in which they operate. Furthermore, this process of dividing, allocating and organizing specialized tasks, and the differential access to scarce and valued resources associated with it, clearly involves relationships of power and control. Some individuals and groups occupy more advantaged positions in the overall division of labour and can, in turn, make use of that advantage to shape the future division of labour with the aim of advancing and supporting their interests further. In short, the division of labour is created out of the operation of power, and power, in turn, arises from the division of labour.

While there is no doubt that increasing specialization and social division of work tasks underlie the move from simple to more complex structures, there is strong debate about the *consequences* of an advanced division of labour for both the society and the individuals concerned. In relation to the wider social division of labour, some classic writers (Comte, Spencer and Durkheim, for example) observed that increasing specialization at the level of society brought with it fundamental changes in the nature of societal integration itself. This involved both increased levels of conflict and increased cooperation and interdependence (Cuff and Payne, 1979, p.27). The increasing specialization of tasks within society brings with it the potential for increased integration as different groups depend upon one another for the different and complementary skills and products which they provide. At the same time, however, the potential for conflict is increased, as some work comes to be more highly regarded and rewarded, and some groups take on the role of coordinating and controlling the work of other groups. These developments involve the *acquisition of differential levels of power and create the potential for conflict in the control and coordination process.*

As the eighteenth century writer Adam Smith (1723–90) noted, massive increases in the productivity of the workforce were made possible by the subdivision of work into small, specialized, repetitive tasks which involved little skill and judgment on the part of the workers involved (see Book 1 (Hall and Gieben, 1992), Chapter 3). With the growth of capitalist, industrialized, factory production, this advanced specialization took place in the context of *control* by owners and managers concerned with making profit on the goods produced. Consequently, relationships of power and inequality have become embedded in the production process and have an impact on the way in which work is experienced by the individuals involved.

Whilst a complex division of labour forms the basis of much of modern industrial production, and has indeed resulted in vast increases in output and productivity, the process has not been without negative and unintended consequences. As Book 1 (Hall and Gieben, 1992), Chapter 3 outlines, Smith himself was aware of the effect of the division of labour on the human experience of factory work, and on relationships of power and control within the work environment and beyond. And Durkheim (1858–1917) also recognized that sectional interests, and a preoccupation with differential material rewards, could give rise to a 'normlessness' and purposelessness which he conceptualized as the pathological condition of *anomie* (see *Penguin Dictionary of Sociology:* ANOMIE). The effect of these developments for the individual were also elaborated by Marx (1818–83) in his concepts of *alienation* (see *Penguin Dictionary of Sociology:* ALIENATION) and *exploitation*, which describe how individuals are prevented from fulfilling their true natures at work. According to Marx, this became especially problematic under capitalism where, in effect, human labour becomes a commodity to be purchased and organized by employers and managers in the pursuit of profit. Furthermore, Marx, like Smith, Comte, Spencer and Durkheim, saw that the influence of the division of labour extended far beyond the production process to affect the fundamental nature of the wider social structure itself.

Although there appears to be broad agreement that 'structured inequality in society grows directly out of the division of labour' (Rueschemeyer, 1986, p.31), writers have differed markedly in identifying the most significant social divisions. For example, Marx focused on the two mutually dependent but antagonistic classes (bourgeoisie and proletariat) which he saw as arising from their different relationships to the means of production within the capitalist structure. Durkheim emphasized the role of occupational specialization in the differential values placed upon the varied tasks carried out by different occupational groups in a society, whether capitalist or not. And Weber (1864–1920) highlighted the ways in which different status groups, formed around characteristics such as ethnicity, property and educational qualifications, use their differential access to power to protect and further their own advantage in the competition for scarce and valued resources, whilst at the same time closing off avenues to other groups who are less advantaged and deemed outsiders (Murphy, 1988, pp.8–9).

Whereas the above eighteenth- and nineteenth-century writers tended to focus on processes of specialization within technical and economic processes, more recent analyses of the division of labour have widened the concept to include the sexual division of labour (Rueschemeyer, 1986, p.3). When looking at the division of tasks between men and women at the level of society, within the occupational structure, within the production process or within the home and family, there is a clear demarcation between the types of activity generally allocated to males and those allocated to females. How these differences in the division of labour occur is open to debate and much disagreement. However, the concept of patriarchy has proved useful in demonstrating the dominance of men over women, both within the family and wider social arrangements, irrespective of the specific nature of the society involved. It is another dimension along which to explore the nature of the division of labour and the operation of conflict, power and control in the work environment, and it is to this that I shall turn in the next section of this chapter.

Summary

- The division of labour is essentially social in nature and does not automatically arise from biological differences such as those of age or sex.

- An advanced and complex division of labour has the potential to increase social integration through increased interdependence. At the same time it has the capacity to increase conflict as different groups use power and advantage to protect and defend their own interests *vis-à-vis* other groups.

- The concept has been used in three broadly different ways: to refer to the social division of labour at the level of the wider society; to refer to the technical division of labour within the production process; to refer to the sexual division of labour between men and women in society.

- Increased division of labour brings with it a number of significant consequences: increased production and productivity; problems in the conditions of work and work experience; and structured inequality along the lines of classes, occupational and status groupings.

2.3   OCCUPATIONS AND ORGANIZATIONS

When we ask individuals about the type of work they do, they are likely to respond either in terms of their *occupation* or in terms of the kind of formal *organization* in which they undertake their work. So, for example, a person might say that he or she is a teacher, a lorry driver, a secretary, a window cleaner, a trade union officer or a traffic warden. Or they might even say that they don't work because they 'stay at home' or are 'just a housewife'! On the other hand, they might answer by saying that they work for a particular company, the local council, a named trade union, the civil service, or in a hospital, a bank or a factory. Or they might answer 'I work for myself' — meaning that they are self employed or in business — or 'I am out of work' because at the time they are unemployed.

Historically, sociologists have analysed work from both an occupational and an organizational perspective. From an occupational perspective, the focus would be upon those significant and distinctive patterns which develop as people carry out a particular type of work activity on a regular and persistent basis. From an organizational perspective, the emphasis is upon 'the ways in which some people conceive of and design work tasks in the light of certain ends and then recruit, pay, coordinate and control the efforts of other people, who do not necessarily share those ends, to fulfil work tasks' (Watson, 1987, p.166). Clearly, in modern, complex, industrialized societies much occupational work takes place within the context of organizations (doctors within hospitals, for example) and the organizational context rather than the occupation itself may assume more importance. Where sociologists have made most of the occupational focus, however, has been where, for some reason, the work is seen to be particularly distinctive or peculiar, or is of particularly high status. The work of embalmers, police officers, traffic wardens and refuse workers would be examples of the former, and professions such as medicine and law examples of the latter. In examining the operation of power, conflict and control at work, it is perhaps not surprising that considerable attention has been given to the experience of work within the technical division of labour in large, complex work organizations. (For a perspective on why this has been so, see Chapter 7, which discusses Taylorist and Fordist principles as they have been applied to the labour process.) We shall return to work organizations later on in this chapter. For now, I would like to examine the operation of processes of power in the context of the *occupational division of labour*, using as an example the sexual division of labour in the historical development of the medical profession.

3   CONTROL STRATEGIES

3.1   OCCUPATIONAL CONTROL STRATEGIES

In examining the occupational division of labour I want to focus on the ideas of Max Weber since they can help us to understand the ways in which the members of some social groups, such as high status medical practitioners, take action to maximize their own opportunities for access to scarce rewards whilst at the same time restricting or closing off access to other groups who are defined as outsiders. This process of *social closure* (see *Penguin Dictionary of Sociology:* SOCIAL CLOSURE) was used by Weber to refer to 'the process of subordination whereby one group monopolizes advantages by closing off opportunities to another group of outsiders beneath it which it defines as inferior and ineligible' (Murphy, 1988, p.8). In defining competitors as outsiders, dominant groups use manifestly obvious characteristics such as property, race, language, gender, religion, educational credentials or occupation to subordinate others. Whilst Weber and Marx would agree that the ownership of property, in the form of the means of production, is the foundation upon which the class structure is laid, Weber differed from Marx in that he saw property as the basis of but one form of social closure used by a minority group to exert power over others. Weber conceptualized relationships founded on property and social class as being similar to other forms of monopolization of opportunities by dominant groups, although he argued that in all cases the process involved the operation of power and domination. As tasks become more specialized some tasks become defined as more important than others and differential status and rewards are attached to them. Weber's theory of monopolization and social closure is clearly a theory of power and domination because groups and classes are only in a position to monopolize opportunities to gain advantage if they have the *power* to do so (Murphy, 1988, p.9).

Building on the above analysis we may see that *gender* and *occupation* are two dimensions along which we may explore processes of social closure, which also take us into debates about the social and sexual division of labour and the operation of power, conflict and control in the work environment. As is discussed in Book 1 (Hall and Gieben, 1992), Chapter 4, some authors have argued that the pre-industrial family was both *patriarchal* and *gynocentric,* where women were subject to male control in the family but where their productive and domestic skills were seen as vital to the success of families and the survival of societies. With industrialization, male control within the private world of the family was broken down and women came more under the control of male employers within the public world of paid work and employment. At the same time, the commercialization of the economy meant a decline in the importance of the family as an economic institution, a consequent decline in the value of women and a loss of many of their traditional skills including, for example, the practice of herbal medicine. I shall take up this issue of the role of women in medicine by means of the first reading associated with this chapter. This is a short extract from Anne Witz's essay, 'Patriarchy and the labour market: occupational control strategies and the medical division of labour'. By examining the respective roles of men and women in the medical profession, both historically and contemporaneously, we should be better able to see the ways in which Weber's ideas about power and domination operate in actuality.

In the full essay, Witz elaborates on Weberian closure theory by building on the work of Parkin (1974; 1979) and applying the analysis to gender inequality and discrimination in the medical profession. Parkin has identified two related strategies involved in social closure, both of which are used by groups as a means to enhance their own position at the expense of others. The first is the process of *exclusion,* which involves the operation of power in a downward direction. Privileged groups attempt to exclude other groups from access to valued resources by defining them as inferior or ineligible, and closing off opportunities to them. An illustration would be the past exclusion in the USA of black workers from white trade unions as a means whereby white workers sustained their own privileges. The second strategy is defined as *usurpation.* This is where attempts are made by less privileged groups to exert power in an upward direction in order to gain access to resources from which they have traditionally been excluded by more privileged groups. An example would be where black workers in the USA struggled for the right to become union members, thereby obtaining access to the benefits previously monopolized by their white competitors. This whole process is made more complex by the fact that some groups employ strategies of *dual closure.* Using the trade union example, trade union members may act to exclude potential competitors from membership by defining them as ineligibles, whilst at the same time engaging in usurpatory strategies against employers —for example, strikes — in order to increase their group's share of resources.

Although acknowledging that some groups are systematically disadvantaged in terms of power, it may still be argued that strategies of exclusion and usurpation involve the exercise of power and control in both a downward and upward direction. Different groups are not evenly matched, but there is still scope for groups to take action to attempt to shift the balance of power and improve their access to scarce and valued resources. In addition, it may be argued that power is also exerted horizontally as well as vertically. To illustrate this, Witz shows how, in the occupational field, strategies of *demarcation* may be employed. Whilst closure strategies of exclusion and usurpation involve 'occupational control over the sphere of an occupational group's own labour', demarcation involves 'those aspects of control that extend beyond the sphere of control of its own labour and touch upon related labour or occupations' (Witz, 1986. p.16).

Witz uses an historical perspective to explore the professionalization of medicine since the sixteenth century. Before the passing of the 1858 Medical Act, women had been widely and actively involved in the practice of medicine and were dominant over men in some branches. This took place domestically, in the context of marriage and family relations, and more publicly 'in something approaching professional practice, both as licensed and unlicensed practitioners' (Witz, 1986, p.20). In their domestic practice women acquired their skills primarily from their mothers and, if literate, from medical books written in English (not Latin), by women, for a female audience. In their professional practice, women acquired skills and knowledge informally from husbands and other male relatives and used these within the context of the family and close neighbourhood. Women's access to medical knowledge was, consequently, largely dependent upon their relations with men, and, Witz argues, patriarchal structures therefore surrounded women's medical practice in the sixteenth century and were the context in which medical practice became more formal, public and professionalized. During this process of professionalization, female domestic practice was perceived as a threat by male practitioners operating within the guild system, and the exclusion of women from organized medical practice was gradually reinforced through licensing mechanisms and restricted access to the guild system. The significance of the Medical Act of 1858 was that whilst, on paper, it did not bar women with proper qualifications from medical practice they were *effectively* excluded because they were denied access to universities and medical schools, which now provided the only route to medical knowledge recognized by the medical profession.

Witz uses this case of the professionalization of medicine to illustrate the way in which processes of professional closure were put into operation by men, with the consequence that women were gradually excluded from medical practice and men acquired the organizational means of occupational control. However, power was not exerted downwards only, as 'medical men were met with countervailing strategic responses from aspiring medical women' (Witz, 1990, p.679), and women did continue to practise their skills domestically and professionally well into the eighteenth century. Nevertheless, in the long term, women did become a 'class of ineligibles who were unable to practise legitimately' (Witz, 1986, p.17) and men were able to regulate the supply of labour to the occupation.

In short, men were able to exclude women from becoming doctors in the organization of the medical profession through *strategies of closure*. In addition, through *strategies of demarcation*, they were also able to use their power beyond the sphere of control of their own labour in order to influence those other related and adjacent branches of medical practice not incorporated into the mainstream of medicine. Midwifery is a case in point.

ACTIVITY 1   You should now read **Reading A, 'Patriarchy and the labour market'**, by Anne Witz, which you will find at the end of this chapter. As you read, make a note of your responses to the following questions:

- What patriarchal strategies of demarcation does Witz outline?
- What factors were relevant in preventing female midwives from obtaining a better medical education?
- Why was 'organization' seen to be crucial in this process? Which groups were most powerful in influencing the development of the midwifery occupation?
- What was the relationship between male medical practitioners and female knowledge of midwifery? What strategies of demarcation are particularly relevant to this issue?

- Do you see evidence in the reading of midwives engaging in strategies of occupational closure? Were these strategies successful?
- What wider relevance do you think these historical discussions of midwifery may have to the study of power, conflict and control at work?

In the essay from which Reading A is extracted, Witz examines the operation of occupational control strategies in the medical division of labour. In so doing she identifies the ways in which male control over women's work in the medical field is intimately linked to patriarchal structures within the home and family. The historical framework in which medical skills were acquired by women is shown by Witz to be linked to patriarchal forms of dominance in the family and illustrates some of the ways in which 'patriarchal power has been utilised as a resource in struggles around the division of labour, as well as how the exercise of this power has materially affected the position of both men and women' (Witz, 1986, p.15). The sexual division of labour manifests relationships of power and subordination which, in some part, reflect the relations of dominance and subordination which exist in family relationships. Work tasks become segregated along the male–female divide, and power is mobilized to restrict access to work with high status and correspondingly high rewards. This is illustrated by the female midwifery occupation, about which Witz argues that the male

Typical birth scene (fifteenth century). For centuries childbirth was conducted exclusively by women.

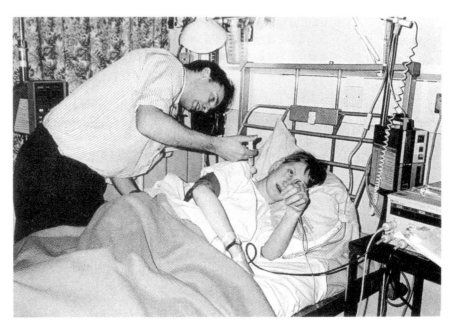

Preparing for birth in a modern hospital

medical profession has employed demarcation strategies of 'pre-emptive de-skilling', 'pre-emptive incorporation' and 'pre-emptive closure' to structure the medical division of labour in its favour. Male medical practitioners have proceeded to 'cream off' more complicated aspects of midwifery into obstetrics, leaving midwives to handle only those aspects related to 'normal' labour (pre-emptive de-skilling). Male practitioners have also taken into their sphere of competence new techniques, such as the use of surgical instruments, before they can be fully adopted by the other group (pre-emptive incorporation). And they adopted strategies to ensure that midwives were unable to organize themselves on the same terms as the male practitioners, thereby undermining the ability of related occupations, such as radiography and nursing, to adopt strategies of closure themselves (pre-emptive closure).

This analysis of occupational control strategies in the medical division of labour is a useful illustration of the ways in which existing structural conditions, such as patriarchal forms of home and workplace organization, have implications for the operation of power, conflict and control in work situations. In this particular instance we have chosen to explore the differential status and prestige allocated to certain occupational groups within the social division of labour and have, in addition, combined this with an exploration of some aspects of the sexual division of labour. The study of the role of women in medicine serves as one illustration of the extent to which male power is used in the furtherance of male interests. But it is also an illustration of some of the ways in which subordinate groups take action to control their own situation as they respond to the actions of others and attempt to exert countervailing power and control in an upward direction. Women in medicine did not passively allow men to monopolize the best of work and rewards in medicine without attempting to resist and organize. And in these attempts they were acting to exert control over processes and outcomes in ways that involved conflict and frustration.

At this point you might find it helpful to reflect on the relevance of this discussion of occupational roles in the medical profession to aspects of your own experience. Consider the following:

- From your own experience of the medical profession, either as a worker or as a patient, have you observed clear differences in the types of activity undertaken by men and women, and any differences of status and prestige associated with those tasks?

- Can you apply the general principles which emerge from Witz's article to other types of professional work? Law and accountancy come to mind. Can you think of others?

- What do you think is the value of the historical perspective used by Witz in helping us understand and explain why work becomes 'gendered' in this way?

Summary

I began this chapter by arguing that the concepts of power and the division of labour are central to our understanding of conflict and control at work. This is because, within every division of labour, there is an asymmetry of power which has consequences for the experiences of individuals and groups concerned. I argued that the concept of a division of labour has been used in different ways to refer to the social, sexual and technical divisions of labour, and that one organizing principle along which work in society has been organized has been occupational and professional specialization. Occupational and professional specialization manifests distinct patterns of employment associated with men and women which we may hope to understand better by employing the notion of the sexual division of labour. My use of the midwifery example was intended to illustrate both of these aspects of the division of labour.

I now want to turn the discussion away from the broader social division of labour to examine work relations between employers and employees at the point of production in the individual workplace. Here we shall be examining the technical division of labour within the context of large scale, formal organizations involved in capitalist, industrial production. In this way I shall be building on the ideas introduced in the earlier chapters of this book.

3.2   ORGANIZATIONAL CONTROL STRATEGIES

Not all formal organizations are concerned with industrial production. Indeed, if we were to pursue the medical case study further we would see that 'specialisation and complexly organised division of labour in the practice of medicine are closely associated with the advent of the large and technically well-equipped hospital' (Rueschemeyer, 1986, p.128). The power of the medical profession in modern society is derived not only from their monopoly of specialized medical knowledge, but also from their organizational control of other health practitioners in the modern hospital. By taking on the more complex and better-paid tasks, and delegating to others the more routine aspects of medical practice, medical practitioners have retained power and control within the organizational context of the hospital.

What is common to all modern work organizations is that they are *formally designed* by owners and managers to achieve certain ends. Management make decisions about what tasks should be done, by whom, with what technology, and in what organizational structures. The fact that some people are organized and controlled by others sets the framework for conflict, resistance and accommodation because 'any kind of organization where some people control others has an undercurrent of struggle over how things will be done' (Collins, 1982, p.61). Individuals and groups will attempt to change the social organization of the workplace for their own benefit, and contest the goals set by those with different interests from themselves.

In work relations at the point of production there is, at the most basic and fundamental level, a relationship of 'structured antagonism' between employer and worker which arises 'in all work organizations in which workers' ability to work is deployed in the creation of a surplus which goes to another group' (Edwards, 1986, p.5). Under competitive capitalism, formally free labour becomes a 'commodity' bought and sold on the market. However, what the employer actually purchases is the individual worker's capacity for work (labour power) and not the actual work done (the labour). It is in the organization of the labour process that the workers' capacity to work is translated into actual work done and where conflict occurs over the ways in which this is to be achieved. In entering the employment relationship workers surrender a considerable degree of personal autonomy and agree to subject themselves to being 'used' by others in pursuit of particular ends. Employers, on the other hand, are faced with the problem that they cannot simply achieve their aims through control and coercion. They need the cooperation and compliance of the workers involved. Consequently, although the employment relationship involves management and workforce in a battle of *conflicting interests*, it also ties them into a relationship of *mutual dependency,* where employees rely on the employer for their livelihoods and managers need to ensure the workers' continued willingness to work. To this extent, the issue is not one of 'control versus resistance' but of a recognition that work relationships 'involve co-operation, adaptation and accommodation as well as conflict. And these things are not separate but are produced together.' (Edwards, 1986, p.5.)

ACTIVITY 3   To explore these processes of control and resistance, adaptation and accommodation, you should now read **Reading B, 'Shop-floor culture'**, by A. Pollert. As you read, make a few notes on the following:

- What different forms of control and discipline of the work force are referred to?
- What evidence of personal work experience and responses to control and discipline can you find?

Because Pollert's research work was conducted using 'participant observation' (see *Penguin Dictionary of Sociology*: PARTICIPANT OBSERVATION), the author was placed in an excellent position to convey a graphic description of the ways in which this particular work environment was experienced and individual personal meanings constructed. However, this is but a short extract which, of necessity, has had to omit many of the colourful personal quotations which occur in the full text. In spite of this, it is a useful illustration of the range and variety of techniques and structures, both explicit and implicit, used in the control and discipline of the workforce in a specific economic location and factory environment.

In Reading B, it is likely that you will have noted the tight discipline imposed on the labour process by means of systems of job evaluation, work study and grading, personal supervision in the context of the work hierarchy, and clearly-stated rules and regulations. Note too the more subtle elements of control referred to in the discussion of 'Discipline and sexual politics'. Here we have the suggestion that compliance may be secured through 'an ideology of femininity' (Thompson, 1983, p.152), where even such apparently straightforward occurrences as sexual banter and pranks can become 'a language of discipline' with 'class control being mediated by patriarchal control' in the work environment. What this highlights is the point made by Bradley that labour should not be taken as a genderless category 'because women are both viewed differently and used differently by employers and managers' (1986, p.71). When dealing with women workers, managers employ different control strategies, use technology differently and develop different hierarchical and authority relations. Women's expectations of their work will be influenced by the availability of other work in the job market. For example, the fact that women may seem relatively content with the worst-paid, least-desirable factory jobs may reflect the fact that these jobs are still better paid and more desirable than the general run of cleaning jobs and shop work available to women. Furthermore, with regard to labour turnover, Pollert (1981, p.104) has suggested that high levels of female turnover must be related to the acceptance amongst women that work is but a temporary interlude between school and marriage and a family, and as such is secondary to the needs of the family and the needs of male workers. An understanding of the ways in which women respond to the operation of power and control at work is therefore clearly relevant to their experiences outside of the organizational division of labour.

Finally, in the section 'Holiday camp or prison?', Pollert suggests that those 'who are most successfully controlled and manipulated are, by definition, the least conscious of how it happens'. The women on the shop floor had little information about the reasons why things were as they were, or how changes came about in the order of things. Consequently, they were inclined to articulate their understanding of control issues in terms of personal and individual factors, rather than structures of work and management, and to respond 'at the symbolic

Factory worker

level of shop floor culture' rather than at the practical level of 'shop floor organization'. Pollert suggests therefore that control is exerted over the women workers, albeit indirectly, through their acceptance of the existing framework of work relations and their lack of power to propose or implement alternatives. In this context, the notion of *alienation* alerts us to processes which give rise to individual experiences of powerlessness and discontent in the face of large-scale, impersonal and fragmented work processes.

However, in the context of the workers' 'general powerlessness over the labour process' and the detailed constraints over their working lives, there is, in this extract, evidence of creative individual and group responses aimed at exerting informal controls over their 'alienated relations of production'. These 'creative attempts' to make something of the conditions of work involve such things as reading whilst working, listening to 'muzac', day-dreaming, 'switching-off', establishing friendship patterns, casual companionship interactions and sexual joking and horseplay. Systems of control imposed by the nature of the work technology, and the need to undertake certain tasks, are not passively experienced but are actively mediated by individuals as they produce rituals and strategies for resistance and accommodation.

As Reading B illustrates, employers have historically made use of a range of methods to exert control over and gain the compliance of the workforce. You may recall from your reading of Chapters 5 and 7 that one basic means of exerting management control was through the discipline of factory production, together with the detailed application of Taylorist and Fordist principles of work organization to work tasks within the factory. It has been argued, by Braverman (1974) in particular, that the work tasks of employees have followed a universal trend towards de-skilling and fragmentation. More widely, it has been suggested that workers are subjected to regulation by their overall position in the labour market, by assembly-line technology, by structures of supervision, by complex rules and regulations, by institutionalized collective bargaining and by monetary incentives such as piece-work and bonus schemes. These frameworks of control have the potential for generating negative and damaging feelings of deprivation and de-humanization, and for creating an overall atmosphere of what Fox (1974) has termed 'low trust' relationships. Moreover, they confront management, in turn, with the renewed problem of how to engender commitment and involvement in the tasks undertaken.

In Reading B we saw some of the dehumanizing and alienating consequences for individuals of working with a particular assembly-line technology. Reading C will explore more fully these experiences of being 'controlled by the line'. Machines and technology cannot in themselves control people. However, the requirements of working with machines to achieve certain pre-set goals are such that, for the workers involved, it can come to feel as if they are being controlled by the technology.

'Controlled by the line'

ACTIVITY 4   Now read **Reading C, 'The dictatorship of production'**, by Ruth
Cavendish. This is another participant observation study.

As you read, note how Cavendish reflects on the way in which the
workers are 'appendages' to the line, slotting in 'like cogs in a wheel'
with very little scope to 'oppose the organization of the work'. Note too
how she suggests that the experience of working with this particular
type of technology pervades the whole of one's life, physically and
mentally, whether in the work environment or not, and changes the
very way in which *time* itself is actually experienced.

An interesting notion to reflect on here is that of 'time-discipline',
which plays a central part in Foucault's conception of 'disciplinary
power'. Foucault argued that the eighteenth century saw a shift away
from 'sovereign power' based on fear, terror and physical torture,
towards a form of power 'which achieves its strategic effects through its
disciplinary character' (Clegg, 1989, p.153). 'Disciplinary power', as
Foucault calls it, first developed in institutions such as monasteries and
prisons, but soon became widely disseminated through other
institutions such as schools and, eventually, the capitalist factory, where
its practices fitted well with the needs of early capitalist
industrialization. 'Disciplinary power works exactly through the
construction of routine' (Clegg, 1989, p.167) and, in time, the
'chronology of the world was transformed, often in one generation, from

one of Holy days, local feasts and the unremitting but seasonably variable rhythms of agricultural production into one based on the rhythms of the industrial machine, overseer, and the clock of factory discipline applied to factory "hands"' (Clegg, 1989, p.175). Unlike sovereign power, which required only a distant, ceremonial reminder of its presence, disciplinary power was at the very centre of life, controlling the very framework of time, rhythm and action. These concepts of time-discipline and disciplinary power are relevant to the whole of organization in modern societies but are especially germane when examining forms of work which are particularly regimented in their technology and work relations.

It is also worth reminding ourselves that, by comparison with other kinds of work, only a minority of workers are, or ever have been, employed to work on assembly lines. However, this is not to say that work in other contexts may not be experienced in ways similar to those described by Cavendish. For example, the systems and procedures associated with desks and typewriters, filing cabinets, ladders and stools, may equally well be experienced as constraining, debilitating and frustrating, as the following extract (derived from yet another participant observation study) suggests:

> In the case of a small or medium-sized office, filing is one of many tasks, and frequently affords the opportunity to inject a little of one's own personality into the system; but in the case of the large, complex organization such as the one where I now found myself, the division of labour is such that filing becomes a total occupation, and time-and-motion experts have rigidly excluded the possibility of personalizing the system. From the employer's point of view, the latter situation is ideal for the employment of temporary staff, since the work is standardized and requires no special knowledge, nor any idea of how the firm works as a whole.
>
> In the small office, even though it means spending some time in getting to know the complexities of the firm as a total system, and in finding out who its personnel are, at least the clerk may ultimately gain a conception of how her work fits into the whole. In the case under study, however, I am tempted to use the term 'alienation' to describe a situation where the worker was but a cog in a wheel, performing a standardized task and lacking any understanding of how that task meshed with the rest of the organization.
>
> Thus, with minimal understanding of the filing system, and no idea whatsoever of the nature or functioning of the company, I struggled to master the process of filing into bays. ... It would be hard to overstate the dreadful conditions of the work — dirt, splinters, laddered tights, aching backs and feet — all were part and parcel of this tedious occupation.
> (McNally, 1979, p.163)

Although Braverman (see above) and others see such de-skilling as part of a universal trend, their arguments have been both criticized and refined. For the purposes of this discussion, it is enough to note that management's attempts to develop control structures have not been straightforwardly *imposed* on a passive workforce, but have been *contested* by workers in the negotiation of order and control in the employment relationship. How then are we to understand these processes of control and negotiation? One way forward is through the notions of the *effort bargain* (Baldamus, 1961) and the *implicit contract* (Watson, 1987).

The concept of the 'effort bargain' is a useful way of making connections between global theorizing about those fundamental conflicts of interests which exist in the employment relationship of 'structured antagonism', and the local, concrete behaviour of groups and individuals which actually takes place at the point of production. The notion of 'effort bargain' is particularly associated with the work of Baldamus (1961), who noted that the employment contract cannot be fully specified in advance of the work being carried out, but has to be negotiated and re-negotiated in the context of actually carrying out the work. While it is possible to negotiate rates of pay and hours of work in advance, it is not possible to negotiate on matters relating to how much work should be done, or in what specific ways. The employer cannot know in advance of every eventuality or fully control the way in which workers conduct their work. Consequently, the employment contract in this broader sense of 'effort bargain' is, to a very large extent, imprecise and open-ended with much of the commitment remaining implicit — the 'implicit contract'. And it is this which introduces uncertainty and indeterminacy into the employment relationship and into the striking of bargains over effort. Because the employment contract is implied, and not fixed or stable, 'two major factors tend to threaten its stability — the push towards increased efficiency on the part of the employer and the tendency towards collective action and challenge on the part of the employee' (Watson, 1987, p.101). And recognizing this inherent tension focuses attention upon the scope for variation which exists in any given work context and on the actions of managers and workers in attempting to shift the balance of the bargain in their favour.

Employees' strategies

We have considered briefly some of the more obvious technical and organizational means which employers use in their attempts to exert control over the workforce, and examined some personal responses and experiences. Let us now turn to some of the *strategies* used by employees to exert their own control in the employment relationship.

There is an initial tendency when thinking about questioning power, conflict and control at work to focus on overt forms of conflict, such as personal disagreements between individuals, or organized forms of conflict such as strikes. As the above discussion of power suggests, it is easier to isolate and examine the behavioural aspects of *overt* power and leave unexamined *hidden* or *covert* forms. For that reason I now want to examine some of the less obvious forms of industrial conflict as well as the more commonplace ones. What needs to be clarified at the outset is that sociological analysis is not primarily concerned with those conflicts which relate to personalities and friendship patterns in the work environment. These may be intrinsically interesting, and of relevance to psychological study, but they are not the prime focus for sociologists, who are concerned with structured relationships at the level of society and the organization.

Within work organizations conflicts between employer and employees may be manifested in a number of ways. Kerr has summarized these as follows:

> The strike is the most common and most visible expression. But conflict with the employer may also take the form of peaceful bargaining and grievance handling, of boycotts, of political action, of restriction of output, of sabotage, of absenteeism, or of personnel turnover. Several of these forms, such as sabotage, restriction of output, absenteeism, and turnover, may take place on an individual as well as on an organised basis and constitute alternatives to collective action.
> (Kerr, 1964, p.171)

There is a large body of research in industrial sociology which has examined the influence of technology, workplace organization and informal structures on individuals at work (see Edwards, 1986). Individuals do not necessarily have much choice over the type of work they do and do not necessarily take very kindly to the imposition of methods of tight control on their behaviour at work. Studies such as Roy's 'Banana time: job satisfaction and informal interaction' (1960), Beynon's *Working for Ford* (1984), Cavendish's *Women on the Line* (1982), or Gabriel's *Working Lives in Catering* (1988) are but some examples which give a feel for what it is like for individuals who do work which involves little or no intrinsic satisfaction.

Some studies have focused on the ways in which individuals walk out of a job, and have examined levels of labour turnover as a useful indicator of conflict and dissatisfaction with a given organization or type of employment. Others have examined levels of absenteeism and accidents in an attempt to make connections between boredom and dissatisfaction at work and the individual's personal responses to it. Leaving the job, going absent or allowing oneself to be drawn along in a mechanical way by the task are clearly examples of direct and individual responses to the work relationship. Other responses, such as group rituals and fooling around, sabotage, pilfering and fiddling also involve the operation of group norms in the work environment. Roy's 'Banana Time' and Pollert's 'Shop-floor culture' (Reading B) offer graphic examples of how a group of workers collude to produce patterns of interaction which make the boredom of work more manageable and enjoyable. Taylor and Walton's study (1971) of industrial sabotage suggests that destructive physical sabotage can represent attempts by individuals and groups to reduce boredom and frustration, facilitate the work process and exert control over the work environment. Ditton's study (1977) of fiddling amongst bread salesmen, and Mars and Nicod's study (1984) of fiddling and pilfering amongst hotel waiters, indicate that these forms of theft not only serve as a means of expressing individual and group control over the work environment, but also serve management's interests by providing individualistic forms of expression as opposed to collectivist forms of organization. As Zeitlin has said in 'A little larceny can do a lot for employee morale':

> Theft serves as a safety valve for employee frustration. It permits management to avoid the responsibility and cost of job enrichment or salary increases at a relatively low amount of money per man per year. Uncontrolled theft can be disastrous for any business concern but controlled theft can be useful. Employee theft, used as a motivational tool, can be an economic benefit to an organization, if management find it too costly to meet its traditional responsibility to pay a living wage'.
> (Zeitlin, 1985, p.276)

One strategy for exerting control at work is by means of group agreements which arise amongst workers paid on incentive schemes to restrict their output to agreed levels. The benefits to workers of output restrictions and group-controlled fiddles have been well documented and include the protection of piece-work rates from management interference and control, the stabilization of earnings levels, the promoting of work group solidarity and the capacity to allow workers some leisure at work once the allocated tasks have been completed (see Edwards, 1989, p.188). Furthermore, as the quotation above suggests, management are often a party to these forms of work group control. They come to regard them as accepted ways of getting the work done, reducing the levels of external supervision required and encouraging a sense that workers are in control of their own situation (Edwards, 1989, p.193).

Generally speaking, the ability of individuals to take action to defend themselves against attempts to change the balance of the implicit contract or effort bargain is limited. Alongside the forms of action discussed above, groups of individuals who occupy similar positions in the organizational division of labour will tend to come together and mobilize themselves around common interests, seeking *collective forms of representation* to defend and further their interests *vis-à-vis* other groups in the employment structure. The strike is perhaps the most visible form of collective response to the existence of conflict and control at work. Strikes are often regarded as mere 'tips of the iceberg' when it comes to analysing industrial conflict and are generally seen to be weapons of the last resort when it comes to making adjustments in the effort bargain. However, sociological study suggests that the analysis of strike behaviour can be misleading if it concentrates only on the strike itself without giving due attention to the dynamics of relations which preceded this overt manifestation of power and conflict.

Overall, what this discussion serves to highlight is that aspects of work behaviour such as sabotage, strikes, pilfering or absenteeism are not automatic and generalized responses to individual experiences of frustration at work, but can vary according to the specific nature of work relations in any given work situation. Along with other individual and collective expressions of control over the work environment, they serve to illustrate that the operation of power, conflict and control at work is not a one-way process. Power and control are also exerted by those in subordinate positions and those who, at first sight, appear to occupy a powerless position.

Any consideration of organizational control strategies in the technical division of labour is not complete without addressing the role of *institutions*, such as trade unions and personnel and industrial relations management structures, in the handling of conflict and control in the employment relationship. In spite of very obvious differences between their roles, trade unions and industrial relations management structures both play a part in *institutionalizing* the conflicts of interest which exist within the employment relationship and which emerge from the negotiations around the effort bargain. Formalized institutions such as trade unions and management structures have developed to handle these conflicting interests and to channel power and conflict within organizations. The success, or otherwise, of these more formalized structures will shape, in part, the extent to which power and conflict are expressed in informal shop-floor culture or explicit shop-floor organization, in collective organization or individualized responses, or in constructive or destructive responses on the part of employees at work.

Furthermore, it must be recognized that trade unions and management institutions are composed of individuals, whose day-to-day work is crucially involved in the management of conflict and discontent, and that these individuals have a central role to play in the operation of power, conflict and control at work. For example, in my book *Managers of Discontent* (Watson, 1988) I explored, through an analysis of personal accounts, some dimensions of the part played by full-time trade union officers and industrial relations managers in the control and manipulation of conflict in work situations. 'Managers of discontent' is a term that was first used by C. Wright Mills in his study of American labour leaders. In *The New Men of Power* (1948), Mills examined the role played by senior, full-time trade union officers in managing the fundamental, and endemic, conflicts of interest which arise from the employment relationship. According to Mills,

Even as the labor leader rebels he holds back rebellion. He
organizes discontent and then he sits on it, exploiting it in order to
maintain a continuous organization. The union leader is a manager
of discontent. He makes regular what might otherwise be
disruptive, ... is a regulator of disgruntlement and ebullience ...
[and] an agent in the institutional channelling of animosity.
(Mills, 1948, p.9)

A meeting of union officials and management

In my own research I extended the term 'managers of discontent' to
include the occupation of industrial relations manager. Whilst union
leader and industrial relations manager belong to institutions with quite
different rationales and, on the face of it, appear to be on opposite sides
of the structural conflict of interest referred to above, there are
similarities in their roles and location within the employment structure.
Both are formally employed to handle the problems and conflicts
arising out of the employment of labour in modern society, and both are
involved in the use of power to control the shifting balance of the effort
bargain. The following extract from my book illustrates this point:

> Their daily experiences in their work, and their relationships with
> other parties to industrial relations processes, had confirmed
> officers' and managers' views that there was a *fundamental
> conflict of interest* between employer and employee and that this
> was reflected in the nature of industrial relations work. For
> example, officers and managers alike stressed that, as one said, 'the
> very nature of industrial relations is conflict'.
> (Watson, 1988, p.165)

Union officers and managers both agreed that a central part of their role
was to make conflict bearable and to find ways of 'using conflict

productively'. Officers spoke of looking for ways to 'compromise', 'dissipate' or 'narrow' conflict, and managers of finding ways to 'water conflict down', 'reconcile views' and 'search for a common approach', making use of the energy generated by conflict in beneficial ways. What my research indicated was that the conflicts and tensions inherent in the system are manifested in the *work experience* of those who occupy roles outside the industrial relations system and have implications for their personal experiences of power and conflict at work. In turn, these individuals use their power, and the power derived from their institutions, to control the work environment and shape it in favour of their own group's interests. This issue of personal experience, and the location of the individual in control structures, takes us to the final part of the chapter, which will deal with *personal control strategies*.

3.3   PERSONAL CONTROL STRATEGIES

In this final section of this chapter I want to explore further the extent to which the kind of work people do has an impact on their personal identity, dignity and sense of worth. As I suggested at the beginning, the type of work we do has implications for our sense of 'self', our feelings of identity, our sense of worth in the eyes of others, and our feeling of security and location in relation to other groups in society. This occupational factor in our sense of personal identity has been stressed by Everett Hughes in his studies of 'humble' and 'proud' occupations, and explored through his concept of 'dirty work'. Hughes argued that every occupation has within it elements of 'dirty work':

> It is hard to imagine an occupation in which one does not appear, in certain repeated contingencies, to be practically compelled to play a role of which he thinks he ought to be a little ashamed. In so far as an occupation carries with it a self-conception, a notion of personal dignity, it is likely that at some point one will feel he is having to do something that is *infra-dignitatem* ['beneath one's dignity'].
> (Hughes, 1958, p.50)

Consequently, every member of an occupation has some concern to control and minimize those elements of his or her work which are likely to bring about feelings of revulsion, disapproval or fear amongst people not intimately involved in the day-to-day problems of carrying out such work. High status occupations, such as medicine, are able to do this by delegating 'dirty work' to those of lower status whilst at the same time surrounding their own work with a mystique of superiority, honour and altruism. Other groups are less successful in getting the support and understanding they desire from the public and may find that it becomes necessary for them to find ways of adjusting to the social stigma associated with their work. Some occupations fare worse than others on this issue but what is common to all is that status and prestige cannot be taken for granted. This situation creates tensions and insecurities for people in the work situation which may be exacerbated if they are faced with negative images held by others about what they do for a living. This is particularly problematic when we bear in mind that work is one of the major sources of identity and status in modern societies.

These problems of image and identity are especially difficult for people who work in service occupations, such as taxi drivers, porters, bar staff and waiters. It is to the work of the restaurant waiter that I shall turn to examine some of the processes of power which operate in the work situation to shift the boundaries of control between waiter and customer. In a culture which stresses independence and self expression it is particularly problematic for individuals (especially men!) to place themselves in a position where they must take orders from others. Whilst some people clearly have no choice but to take on this type of work they do not necessarily do so with ease. Consequently, to support their feelings of dignity and self worth they have to find ways of asserting themselves in relation to clients and customers. In the extreme, every kind of service occupation has customers who are awkward and unpleasant and who are dealt with in subtle ways that ensure that the feelings of the service worker are not unduly threatened. However, even in the ordinary and mundane circumstances of daily work, service workers will also find ways of retaining control and power in the work environment.

A good example of this is provided by Reading D, 'The politics of service', by G. Mars and M. Nicod. This is an extract from a book written from a research project designed by Mars, and carried out by Nicod, who worked as a waiter for almost two years in the restaurants of five British hotels. As the authors argue, it is not possible to learn about the inside of the world of waiters just by walking into restaurants. What is necessary is for the researchers to adopt the approach of the anthropologist and to 'live among the people they are studying and to participate as far as possible in their day-to-day life' (Mars and Nicod, 1984, p.2). The reasoning behind this is that, if the researcher were to question the worker, many aspects of his or her experience would be so taken for granted that even the most sensitive of informants would not think to report them. It was therefore through the process of participant observation that the perceptions of Nicod were developed.

In this reading you will find that the author uses the concepts 'boundary-open' and 'boundary-closed' to refer to customer types. At an earlier point, the authors defined these as follows: 'boundary-open' types as those with whom the waiter may relate in an open, relaxed, light hearted, joking and semi-informal way; in contrast, 'boundary-closed' types require that the service staff 'subordinate' themselves by adopting 'the non-person role'. Relationships with this type of customer are consequently constrained and formal, requiring the waiter to be seen to act within clearly prescribed limits, observing the official role that 'the customer is always right'. 'Boundary-openness brings a decline in ritual activity; boundary-closure supports it.' (Mars and Nicod, 1984, p.73.)

Waiter and customers

ACTIVITY 5   You should now read **Reading D, 'The politics of service'**, by G.Mars and M. Nicod. As you read, note your responses to the following questions:

- What is meant by 'getting the jump on the customer'?
- In what ways does the waiter attempt to assert control?
- Do the activities of the waiter involve cooperation as well as conflict?
- What strategies can waiters adopt if the customers place them under pressure?

In Reading D we are given some insight into the work experiences of waiters and some understanding of the *personal control strategies* they adopt to exert power, in a relatively powerless environment, in order to retain dignity in the face of public definitions of their inferior position. The particular research method adopted seems especially valuable in helping the researcher and the reader to 'get inside the experience' of the waiter and see the world, albeit temporarily, from their perspective. What this extract illustrates is that, even in positions of subordination, individuals will take control of their situation and find ways of wresting some of the power from other, more powerful participants.

4   CONCLUSION

In this chapter we have explored various dimensions of the operation of power, conflict and control at work. How power, conflict and control are defined depends, in part, on the theoretical perspective which is brought to bear in a given situation. However, the chapter has ranged over some of the *occupational, organizational* and *personal control strategies* which are adopted by groups and individuals in the pursuit of power and advantage in the social, technical and sexual divisions of labour. The concept of the division of labour has proved fruitful in highlighting the *asymmetry of power* which exists between advantaged and subordinate groups at all levels, and a variety of control strategies have been explored to evaluate the extent to which power and control operate upwards in the hierarchy as well as downwards. It is interesting to note that conflict and integration, and conflict and cooperation, are integral elements of the social, sexual and technical divisions of labour. And even in the case of individual control strategies, efforts are directed by the individuals concerned towards a consistency of experience which involves the management of conflicting perceptions about their identity and dignity. In exploring these issues we have made use of a variety of research approaches but especially those aimed at gaining understanding of those personal meanings which are attributed by individuals to their experiences of power, conflict and control in their working lives.

REFERENCES

Abercrombie, N., Hill, S. and Turner, B.S. (eds) (1988) *The Penguin Dictionary of Sociology*, 2nd edn, Harmondsworth, Penguin.

Baldamus, W. (1961) *Efficiency and Effort*, London, Tavistock.

Beynon, H. (1984) *Working For Ford*, Harmondsworth, Penguin.

Bradley, H. (1986) 'Technological change, management strategies, and the development of gender-based job segregation in the labour process', in Knights, D. and Willmott, H. (eds) *Gender and the Labour Process*, Aldershot, Gower.

Braverman, H. (1974) *Labor and Monopoly Capitalism*, New York, Monthly Review Press.

Cavendish. R. (1982) *Women on the Line*, London, Routledge.

Clegg, S. (1989) *Frameworks of Power*, London, Sage.

Collins, R. (1982) *Sociological Insight*, New York, Oxford University Press.

Cuff, E.C. and Payne, G.C.F. (eds) (1979) *Perspectives in Sociology*, London, Allen and Unwin.

Ditton, J. (1977) *Part-time Crime*, London, Macmillan.

Edwards, P.K. (1986) *Conflict at Work*, Oxford, Blackwell.

Edwards, P.K. (1989) 'Patterns of conflict and accommodation' in Gallie, D. (ed.) *Employment in Britain*, Oxford, Blackwell.

Fox, A. (1974) *Beyond Contract: Work, Power and Trust Relations*, London, Faber.

Gabriel, Y. (1988) *Working Lives in Catering*, London, Routledge.

Hall, S. and Gieben, B. (eds) (1992) *Formations of Modernity*, Cambridge, Polity Press.

Hughes, E.C. (1958) *Men and their Work*, New York, Free Press.

Kerr, C. (1964) *Labor and Management in Industrial Society*, New York, Doubleday.

Mars, G. and Nicod, M. (1984) *The World of Waiters*, London, Allen and Unwin.

McNally, F. (1979) *Women for Hire,* London, Macmillan.

Mills, C. Wright (1948) *The New Men of Power: America's Labor Leaders*, New York, Harcourt Brace.

Murphy, R. (1988) *Social Closure*, Oxford, Oxford University Press.

Parkin, F. (ed.) (1974) *The Social Analysis of Class Structures*, London, Tavistock.

Parkin, F. (1979) *Marxism and Class Theory: A Bourgeois Critique*, London, Tavistock.

Penguin Dictionary of Sociology: see Abercrombie *et al.* (1988).

Pollert, A. (1981) *Girls, Wives, Factory Lives*, London, Macmillan.

Pringle, R.C. (1988) *Secretaries Talk*, London, Verso.

Roy, D. (1960) 'Banana time: job satisfaction and informal interaction', in *Human Organization*, vol.18, pp.156–68.

Rueschemeyer, D. (1986) *Power and the Division of Labour*, Cambridge, Polity Press.

Taylor, I. and Walton, P. (1971) 'Industrial sabotage: motives and meanings', in Cohen, S. (ed.) *Images of Defiance*, Harmondsworth, Penguin.

Thompson, P. (1983) *The Nature of Work*, London, Macmillan.

Watson, T.J. (1987) *Sociology, Work and Industry*, London, Routledge.

Watson, D.H. (1988) *Managers of Discontent*, London, Routledge.

Witz, A. (1986) 'Patriarchy and the labour market: occupational control strategies and the medical division of labour', in Knights, D. and Willmott, H. (eds), *Gender and the Labour Process,* Aldershot, Gower.

Witz, A. (1990) 'Patriarchy and professions: the general politics of occupational closure', *Sociology*, vol. 24, no. 4, pp.675–90.

Zeitlin, L.R. (1985) 'A little larceny can do a lot for employee morale', in Littler, C.R. (ed.) *The Experience of Work*, Aldershot, Gower.

PATRIARCHY AND THE LABOUR MARKET

Anne Witz

... I argue here that one way in which patriarchal power has been utilised as a resource in struggles around the sexual division of labour has been in the form of strategies of closure and demarcation pursued within the context of occupational control strategies, and that workplace or occupational organisations have provided the institutional means whereby patriarchal power has been mobilised and patriarchal control maintained within the labour market. ...

The patriarchal structuring of professional dominance and subordination: midwifery and the male medical profession

Some aspects of patriarchal strategies of demarcation are demonstrated most vividly by examining the relationship between female midwifery practice and male medical practice. First, there were attempts by members of the medical profession to renegotiate boundaries between midwifery and medical practice by fragmenting midwifery and incorporating certain aspects of midwifery into 'obstetrics' and by ensuring that midwives were restricted to the sphere of *normal* labour, seeking medical assistance for abnormal labour. These may be described as patriarchal strategies of *pre-emptive de-skilling*: the midwife's sphere of competence was narrowed and strictly bounded as aspects of midwifery practice were expropriated and placed within the exclusive sphere of competence of medical doctors. Second, a patriarchal strategy of *pre-emptive incorporation* was pursued in relation to the use of surgical instruments in childbirth, particularly the use of short forceps, and midwives were never able to incorporate these tasks within their own sphere of competence. Finally, strategies of *pre-emptive closure* ensured that midwives were unsuccessful in their attempts to organise on the same terms as physicians, surgeons and apothecaries despite attempts to do so in the seventeenth century.

Physicians and midwives: a case of pre-emptive closure

Midwives were unsuccessful in their early attempts to organise and were therefore unable to construct the organisational means of professionalisation, despite attempts to do so in the seventeenth century.

> The danger which threatened midwives by the exclusion of women from the scientific training available to men did not pass unnoticed by the leading members of the Profession.
> (Clark, 1919)

In 1616 midwives of the City of London petitioned the King for a Charter and for incorporation into a society so that:

Source: Witz, A. (1986) 'Patriarchy and the labour market: occupational control strategies and the medical division of labour', in Knights, D. and Willmott, H. (eds) *Gender and the Labour Process*, Aldershot, Gower, pp.15, 27–32.

> ... the skill of the most skilfullest in that profession should be bettered, and none allowed but such as are meete ['suitable']: which cannot be performed unless the said midwives be incorporated into a societye.
> (cited in Donnison, 1977, p.13)

They also petitioned for lectures on anatomy, for regulations and for better education (Clark, 1964, p.236). The petition was received favourably by the King, but was then forwarded to the College of Physicians for comment, who immediately drew up a set of counter-proposals which, if they had been implemented, would have placed the powers of examination and instruction in the hands of the College. Most crucially, they appeared to have objected to the fact that it was *women* who were attempting to organise:

> The College recognised that many abuses arose from the unskilfulness of ignorant midwives; but it thought the plan of making them into an incorporated society to govern themselves new, unheard of and without example in any commonwealth.
> (Clark, 1964)

This, together with the fact that the College of Physicians had the power successfully to pre-empt branches of medical practice such as apothecaries from organising autonomously, meant that the midwives' movement to organise was stalled for the time being. In 1634, once more without success, another move to incorporate midwives was made.

In the latter half of the seventeenth century Mrs Cellier once again demanded the opportunity for midwives to receive better medical education and improve their skills (Aveling, 1872). In 1687 Mrs Cellier appealed to James II to unite midwives into a corporation by Royal Charter:

> ... it is humbly proposed, that your Majesty will be graciously pleased to unite the whole number of skilful midwives, now practising within the limits of the weekly bills of mortality, into a corporation, under the government of a certain number of the most able and matron-like women among them, subject to the visitation of such person or persons, as your Majesty shall appoint; and such Rules of their good government, instruction, direction and administration as are hereunto annexed.
> (Aveling, 1872; Clark, 1919)

Mrs Cellier recognised the necessity for organisation if the interests of midwives were to be represented and their status as a profession secured. The King agreed to her request but nothing was done.

London midwives appeared to be aware of the need to organise midwifery practitioners and ensure some form of protection against the encroachments of medical men. They also perceived the need for the more systematic training in midwifery skills, and to construct some organisational means of distinguishing between skilful and unskilful midwives, in much the same manner as medical men were doing in their guilds and college.

Obstetricians and midwives: pre-emptive de-skilling and pre-emptive incorporation

By the end of the seventeenth century midwifery still remained a predominantly female occupation, but the crucial point to note here is that whilst women continued to *practice* midwifery, *they had failed to organise*. It was in the eighteenth century that male practice in midwifery grew unabated:

> As the century wore on so the decline of the midwife continued — a cumulative process accelerated by the interested propaganda of a section of the medical profession, and, in particular, of younger men anxious to capture the midwifery which gave the entrée to general practice.
> (Donnison, 1977, p.37)

Patriarchal strategies of pre-emptive de-skilling occurred as medical men engaged in a gradual process of expropriation of midwifery knowledge and skills and accumulated their knowledge of midwifery largely by observing the practices of midwives themselves. Dr. Willoughby, a famous seventeenth century man-midwife, makes constant reference in his writings to midwives whose practice he had observed (Aveling, 1872). As part of their strategy of de-skilling and narrowing the midwife's sphere of competence, medical men repeatedly inveighed against any intervention by midwives in the process of childbirth, thus attempting to reduce the role of midwife to that of an *attendant*. At the same time, it was the use of instruments in difficult deliveries that provided the lynchpin for the medical men's parallel strategy of pre-emptive incorporation, and the monopoly gained by surgeons over the use of instruments proved of considerable advantage in pre-empting midwives from incorporating the use of instruments into their own sphere of competence.

Demarcation strategies pursued by medical men in relation to midwives reached their zenith in the last quarter of the nineteenth century during the protracted debate around proposals for midwife registration. This debate was essentially about the status of midwives, the precise nature of their sphere of competence and, most crucially, the terms of their subordination to the medical profession. Important disagreements emerged *within* the ranks of the medical profession during the course of this debate, which may be interpreted as discussion about which demarcation strategy to push through to its logical conclusion; that of pre-emptive incorporation or of pre-emptive de-skilling.

Sections of the medical profession who opposed the registration of midwives advocated the virtual abolition of midwives and were effectively arguing for the complete incorporation of midwifery skills within the sphere of competence of the medical profession; the physician's sphere of competence would be extended to incorporate not only abnormal but also normal labour. The patriarchal structuring of the medical division of labour is revealed in the abolitionists' argument that women should be restricted to a subservient role in the provision of health services and, accordingly, that the role of midwife should be replaced by that of the 'obstetric nurse' who 'under the charge and supervision of a medical man, carries out that portion of attendance which is more suitable to a mere woman, the changing of sheets and the attending of the patient, and attentions of that kind' (Select Committee on Midwife Registration, 1892). Abolitionists were arguing for a strategy of incorporation that would not simply de-skill midwives by creaming off certain of their obstetric skills, but would incorporate all aspects of midwifery practice, not just the use of instruments, within the sphere of the medical profession.

The advocates of the de-skilling strategy, the most prominent of whom were members of the Obstetrical Society formed in 1858, were medical men concerned to *control* and *limit* the practice of midwifery by restricting the midwife's sphere of competence to that of normal labour and subordinating them to the medical profession. The de-skilling strategy involved the devolution of certain midwifery tasks onto midwives, who would operate within a strictly bounded sphere of competence and control. The advocates of the de-skilling strategy, because they did not advocate placing the midwife directly under the supervision of a doctor, had to ensure that the midwife did not transgress the occupational boundary between midwife and doctor. To this end, the Obstetrical Society took a lead in advocating the education and registration of midwives, as they sought to ensure that the midwife did not gain sufficient medical education to transgress occupational boundaries by dealing with medical matters surrounding abnormal labour. Midwives were to be educated 'to know their own ignorance' (Select Committee, 1892). The Obstetrical Society's scheme for midwife registration also proposed that midwives' licences were to be renewed annually by the General Medical Council, who were also to have the power to strike off women who attended abnormal labours and did not seek medical assistance.

Midwives themselves were equally divided over the terms on which they wished to see the registration of midwives. Two midwives' organizations, the Female Medical Society and the Obstetrical Association of Midwives, advocated registration as a method of achieving professional closure that would produce and reproduce high-status and well qualified midwives with a licence that would give them equal status to male medical practitioners and extend their sphere of competence to include abnormal as well as normal labour (Donnison, 1977; Select Committee, 1892). These organisations also proposed that there should be *two* classes of midwives, a subordinate class for the less qualified and a superior one for the highly skilled midwife with a more extensive medical education. The implication of this demand was that middle-class midwives wished to use some of the same means of occupational closure as medical men. However, they would have had to defeat the interests of male medical practitioners of their own class, who sought to preserve their professional dominance by means of patriarchal subordination. This poses an interesting and cross-cutting set of class and patriarchal dimensions in structuring the medical division of labour.

The sexual composition of occupations that have been subject to processes of pre-emptive de-skilling, pre-emptive incorporation and pre-emptive closure may therefore be seen to be of key importance in patterns of domination and subordination in medicine; the medical profession sought to subordinate and control the female practice of midwifery by means of patriarchal strategies of demarcation.

References

Aveling, J. (1872) *English Midwives: Their History and Prospects,* London, Churchill.

Clark, A. (1919) *Working Life of Women in the Seventeenth Century,* London, George Routledge.

Clark, G. (1964–72) *A History of the Royal College of Physicians in London,* vols. 1–3, Oxford, Clarendon.

Donnison, J. (1977) *Midwives and Medical Men,* London, Heinemann.

Select Committee on Midwife Registration (1892) P.P. XIV, Evidence.

READING B SHOP-FLOOR CULTURE

A.Pollert

Rules

Churchmans, like any other factory, imposed discipline at several levels. There was the tight hold over the labour process, as described in job evaluation, grading and work study. Then there was personal supervision in the presence of chargehands, foremen and supervisors. And there were rules — the written rules of the rule book, and visual reminders stuck up on notices. ...

While they were not unreasonable or heavily repressive in themselves, like all rules imposed from above they were reminders of the workers' subordination to discipline. Bending or breaking them, like at school, were not so much rational objectives as symbols of autonomy and self-assertion.

It was in the context of their *general* powerlessness over the labour process, together with these minute constraints over 'how they went', that the women created their own shop-floor culture. ... So women replaced the rule book, as far as possible, without conscious, deliberate organisation, with an informal code of resistance to being turned into machines, to boredom, to the humiliation of being ordered around. ... Whatever forms of escape, distraction or entertainment they adopted, tobacco still rushed

Source: Pollert, A. (1981*) Girls, Wives, Factory Lives*, London, Macmillan, pp.129–57.

through their fingers, into the endless packets and cartons, which the machines rattled on. But at least it made life tolerable:

CHERRY   No, it's not too bad in here, seeing that I knows most of them. It's not so strict in here. I expected a factory to be a real dark place, hardly any lights, real strict. It's daylight in here; I think that's why I likes it, because I expected it to be worse than it was.

Or, as Willis put it, 'working class culture … is not generally one of celebration and mastery. It is basically one of compromise and settlement: *a creative attempt to make the best of hard and brutalising conditions.*' (Willis, 1978, p.107.)

Bringing in their own world

These 'creative attempts' were largely about surviving the mind-destroying boredom. 'Cutting off' or separating the 'inner self' from what is objectively happening on the 'outside' is one of the sorry 'skills' we are forced into, in an existence dominated by alienated relations of production. It is otherwise known as 'wishing one's life away'. Some girls actually prided themselves in the art of switching off, pitying those who were bad at it, and thinking themselves lucky to be working at all. …

In some departments … it was hard to block out the world, especially while concentrating on watching the little red light go on or off on the automatic scales, and deftly adding or picking out a few drams of tobacco. Yet some Grade 1 weighers … had so perfected their robotic dexterity that their minds somehow found room to function in other directions, like looking at magazines or photographs on their laps while their hands managed half a second's freedom from the tobacco to flick a page or pass the picture across to a work-mate. There were even some who accomplished the amazing feat of reading a novel secretly. Such wonders of the human brain were constant reminders of the endless resourcefulness inspired by the struggle against rotting away.

Of course, there was some day-dreaming going on: mostly it was about home; women with children worried about what time they would pick them up, whether they would be late or not, whether they could catch the usual bus and fit in the shopping, what to cook for tea. Or, with younger girls, it was naturally about escape:

RAQUEL   I don't really think about anything unless I'm going out and then I think about what I'm going to wear.

Twice a day there was a reprieve from the grey sameness of a working day: Muzac. (It was impossible not to be reminded of [Aldous Huxley's] *Brave New World* or [George Orwell's] *Nineteen Eighty-four.*) Too bad that it had to be a deafening blare to be audible. But it was still keenly looked forward to:

VAL	It's the best part of the day when the records come on.
STELLA	12 o'clock! Jimmy Young! They missed him twice last week!

But the one great refuge from work was in each other:

JENNY	You've just got to be friends with everyone. Like you might be doing your weighing on a machine, like its terrible, isn't it, if someone's not talking to you. But if you're talking to them and friends with them, it's all right.

Friendship was important at all sorts of levels, from casual mates to close intimacy. In the quieter departments, such as the stripping room and the hand-packing room, talking in low voices between pairs created a soft atmosphere of personal life, strangely incongruous with the speed and intensity of work. Close couples were especially important, particularly among older women, who distinguished them clearly from looser relationships. ...

EMY	The best thing ever happened to me was I made true friends with Ida.
IDA	Yes, that's the best thing.

But looser companionship was very important for stimulating discussion — where noise permitted. Conversations on the shop-floor explored controversial themes such as sex, marriage and abortion — mainly among the younger girls — and child-rearing, psychology, the 'nature–nurture' problem, health and the Welfare State among older women. Significantly these were all part of the women's world of home and the important business of caring for life. The split between their deep involvement in these issues and their detachment from their immediate activity again highlighted not only the nature of their alienated work but also where their priorities and consciousness lay. ...

Discipline and sexual politics

... Men, especially young men, were a rarity. So girls took every opportunity to flirt, giggle, tease, whenever they could. But the men they were in most frequent contact with were their supervisors. And this was the catch. For sexual banter and pranks became something more than a laugh — it became the language of discipline:

STEVEN	You see, I believe in a friendly basis. I believe in saying, 'You help me and I'll help you.' But the environment of the girls has changed. This permissive society — now these girls are changing with it. Well I'm afraid they're not so mature, not so reliable as they used to be. That makes our job harder.

The peculiar struggle over rules between male supervisors and girls was a complex, tense balance between confrontation and collaboration: complex, because class control was mediated by patriarchal control, and neither side of the relationship could separate them; tense, because if either side went too far in the sexy word-play, if the girls' flirtations turned to disrespect or the chargehand's sexist cajolery went too far, the rules of the game could snap. As we shall see, supervision was a much more subtle exercise than it had been twenty years earlier. For, in addition to the swing to a more diplomatic approach, management had to contend with the fact that girls and women had become more confident at work. Since the Second World War there was full employment, and an enormous demand for women workers — and the war itself had proved women's capacity. ...

Not only were they subjected to the discipline of work and of factory rules, on top of this, as women, they were exposed to constant sexist patronisation, not just from the chargehands and foremen, but from any men that worked around them: 'Hey gorgeous', 'Do us a favour, love', 'Come here, sexy' — all are familiar addresses for most women. Supervision was sexually oppressive, the manner usually cajoling, laced with intimate innuendo, and provocative jokes, hands placed on girls' shoulders as they worked, imposition mixed with flattery. To survive with some pride, without melting into blushes or falling through the floor, the girls had to keep on their toes, have a ready answer, fight back. They were forced into a defensive–aggressive strategy — but always on the men's terms. They had to collude. And in this they also colluded with the language of control. ...

Calculation and manipulation were part of factory politics. Steven had each individual and each 'crew' measured up. The girls likewise knew their strength and how far they could go. The Number 7 crew were a particularly bold and 'defiant' lot, and if a chargehand interfered when they thought it was none of his business they just shouted at him to 'Get off', or 'Leave us alone' (always half-joking). He would reply, 'Now don't be cocky' — but they would all laugh. It was all part of the game. Some genuinely liked him: 'He's as good as gold — don't tell him, mind, or he'll get big-headed.' Others more cynically thought him 'soft', 'pliable', 'you can do what you want with him'. Others sensed their weakness with him, thought him 'a two-faced bastard' and kept quiet.

Because girls derived some enjoyment from these skirmishes, it was a successful way of keeping them in line. Their use of female sex appeal as a way of getting round their supervisors, or retaliating against authority, was always a double-edged weapon, which in the long term hurt them and nobody else. For if they won momentary victories of self-assertion, it was only by colluding with the conventional male attitudes towards the female as sex object, and laid them open to sexist advances whether they liked it or not. ...

The ultimate perniciousness of femininity as a weapon of shop-floor resistance was its individualism and competitiveness. It worked only on the isolated occasion. Because it took the sting out of conflicts, its very success detracted from developing collective, organised strategies of struggle, which left the individual and the group helpless if it came to the crunch. ...

Holiday camp or prison?

... In spite of constant references by supervisors to the 'more relaxed atmosphere' of discipline, the 'holiday-camp atmosphere' and 'free-and-easy managers', the older women who remembered the crudely authoritarian days of the factory still expressed uneasiness about the present, nostalgia about the past. ...

They had partly assimilated the managerial 'human-relations' ideology that things were better than before. It fitted in with the dominant world-view of industry as a happy partnership between capital and labour, and everyone, from the company to the media, was telling them they were getting a better deal, more freedom and security than before. Even 'women's liberation' was no longer just an idea for bra-burning cranks. Yet daily experience told them otherwise. They recalled the comparative flexibility of doing their jobs before 'job assessment' and grading, and knew that they now worked far harder. They knew in every nerve and muscle the exhaustion of being tied to a machine rate or a grade. While they were told it was 'a holiday camp' by the supervisors, some, like Stella, likened it to a prison. And as for their improved status as workers, they were told to be 'responsible', but they had no control. As women, they had to contend with a more sophisticated but no less powerful system of discipline and patriarchal control than before.

What did they really believe, then? They knew that they were workers, and bosses were bosses. They knew who had money and power. And, in spite of their collusion, they knew too well their disadvantages regarding men, both in the factory and in the family. Then why did they not work out a coherent explanation of how they were controlled and manipulated now, and why it was more subtly oppressive than before?

The answer lies in the connection between ideology, experience and fragmentary consciousness, for those who are most successfully controlled and manipulated are, by definition, the least conscious of how it happens. If the women knew they had less freedom than before ... they could not point to any one event or change and say: 'That was when things began going wrong.' For the whole skill of successful worker incorporation into the employers' strategy and ideology is the smooth, invisible operation. This is not 'conspiracy' theory. Things just 'happened' to the women: new agreements between company and union, job assessment, grading, new machines, factory reorganisations, new supervisors, new treatment — they all 'happened'. It was part of the structure of industrial relations. They were cut off so entirely from their union that they knew nothing of the details of negotiation which had led to these changes. Lacking this experience, they could articulate the effects but could not map out a causal chain of reasons. Their lack of a coherent picture of what was happening, their piecemeal experience of 'unfair grading' here and 'having to be blue-eyed' there meant no links were made between the two. Control issues remained individual, personalised. Consciousness remained fragmentary. This was not because nobody had stood up and delivered a lecture on the theory of 'Scientific Management', 'The Human Relations Approach',

'Patriarchy and Incorporation'. It was because they had little concrete experience of organisation and personal involvement in collective struggle. This was why resistance to control remained at the symbolic level of shop-floor *culture* without shop-floor *organisation*. It was a step forward; but on its own it posed no threat.

References

Willis, P. (1978) *Learning to Labour: How Working Class Kids get Working Class Jobs,* London, Saxon House.

READING C   THE DICTATORSHIP OF PRODUCTION

Ruth Cavendish

Speed up

Most of the women agreed that the pace of work had become faster over the years. The light was flashing quicker, more trays had to be done, but there was less work to be done on each UMO ['unidentified mechanical object'][1] . They also claimed that the conveyor belt itself moved faster, and jobs which used to be done by two people had gradually been turned into one-person jobs. ...

Control of the line

The women ran the line, but we were also just appendages to it. Its discipline was imposed automatically through the light, the conveyor belt and the bonus system. We just slotted in like cogs in a wheel. Every movement we made and every second of our time was controlled by the line; the chargehands and supervisors didn't even have to tell us when to get on. They just made people like Josey obey if they wouldn't buckle under. You couldn't really oppose the organisation of the work because it operated mechanically. The only things you could challenge were the petty rules, or management's attempts to speed up the work. The bonus system and the line speed even led the women to discipline each other; getting 'up the wall' put out the person behind and we had informal arrangements to help avoid that. But these also ensured that we made up the right number of UMOs, so the supervisors' job was really done for them. ...

Doing time

It is impossible to put over in writing the speed of the line, the pace of work, and the fiddliness of the jobs we had to repeat all day long, as tray followed tray down the line. We were physically geared up, straining to get it done as fast as we could, and the atmosphere was frantic. Everything

[1]This deliberately vague term was coined by the author in order to disguise the identity of the motor components factory that she worked in.

Source: Cavendish, R. (1982*) Women on the Line*, London, Routledge and Kegan Paul, pp.98–124.

was rushed — work, breaks, drinking tea, reading the paper. We were so speedy that we rushed at everything, and the breaks were very short compared to the work time. At lunchtime we rushed to clock, ran to the canteen, or out shopping, and ran back again. There was no time to slow down or do anything at 'normal' pace. It took me hours to relax after work and stop feeling the line whirr through me. Until then I turned everything into mechanical operations to be done as fast as possible.

Working on the line changed the way you experienced time altogether. The minutes and hours went very slowly, but the days passed very quickly once they were over, and the weeks rushed by. Some days were even slower than others, and everyone agreed whether the morning was fast or slow, and whether the afternoon was faster or slower than the morning. We joked about how we were wishing our lives away, wishing it was 'going home time' or Friday afternoon. ...

The day seemed very long; 10 in the morning was like 2 in the afternoon had been to me before. The afternoon (that is, after 12.45), was called 'the evening'. By 2.30 you could see your way to the end of the evening, and after the last break at 3.10 there was only another hour to go. The stretches of nearly two hours without a rest were very exhausting, and the breaks seemed far too few. ...

Sometimes 7.30 to 9.10 seemed like several days in itself, and I would redivide it up by starting on my sandwiches (hidden under the torque checking machine) at 8 a.m. I would look at the clock when we'd already been working for ages, and find it was only 8.05, or, on very bad days, 7.50 — more than another whole hour to go to the first break. Then I redivided the time into half hours, and ten-minute periods to get through, and worked out how many UMOs I'd have done in ten minutes, twenty minutes and half an hour; then I thought about everyone from my previous life and whether they would have got up yet and when they would be leaving for work. It was the same every day after lunch — you'd have been working for what seemed like days and days, but it was only 1.20 and there was more than an hour to go to the next break. ...

Even though the hours went so slowly, I couldn't remember everything that happened in the day. It seemed so long and so much had happened: discussions, breakdowns, small dramas, a union meeting perhaps. When you looked back on the week it seemed very long and eventful, yet I couldn't remember whether a particular incident happened this week or last. All the days were the same, but we made them significant by their small dramas. Unless I wrote down what happened in the evening, Monday, Tuesday and Wednesday were all jumbled together in my mind by the end of the week. ...

Some of the older women trundled on all day, not particularly put out by the boredom. Anyway, there was nothing you could do about it. Arlene was deep in memories, and Alice sang hymns to herself. Grace always found something to laugh about, and Daphne watched everything that went on. Anna was absorbed in counting how many UMOs we got through and whether there were more or less than yesterday. But we younger ones were always moaning about how long the day was. We tried to rush to the loo in work-time to add a couple of extra minutes to the break. We were overjoyed if a light was missed or there was a breakdown. We had our tea prepared and the paper open on the right page so we wouldn't waste a split second of the break when the siren went. But we were so tensed up, we didn't relax at all. I tried to get to the middle page of the *Guardian* by lunchtime, just leaving the business news and television programmes for the afternoon. Then I scrounged other people's papers, or women's magazines and was enthralled by love stories that I'd normally sneer at. ...

The work limited what you could do in your spare time, and completely determined the rest of your life. This was why Rosemary didn't like having too many friends, because of the time it took visiting them, and why most of the women thought it was no life for a youngster. It was easy to see the pressures forcing you into marriage, with stability, routine and no surprises; you could relax together in front of the box in the evening, and have a regular shopping, cleaning and going-out routine. The women who shared bedsits, like Rosemary and Doreen, and Ann and Eileen, had such an organised domestic life that they would appear almost middle-aged in comparison with students of the same age.

The work changed my life completely. It was impossible to go on seeing all my friends, even those I was particularly close to, because physically I just wasn't up to it. I never went to visit them during the week — they had to come to me because I would have to go to bed so early. I always resisted going out for a meal and the cinema because of time, money and tiredness.

Physical survival

The speed of the line affected your whole body. Constant physical pressure for eight hours left you tensed up. We all felt the same. I don't know whether assembly line workers suffer from stress diseases more than other types of worker, but it wouldn't surprise me. Arlene had recently started seeing 'a butterfly' in front of her eyes and the doctor said she had high blood pressure. Many women were taking Valium and Librium for 'nerve trouble'. They all looked older than their age — pale, tired and drawn. They thought I was about eight years younger than I was and I thought them ten years older. Even the 20-year-olds had deep lines round their eyes.

Everyone complained about being 'jaded'. Getting up at 6.30, and working virtually non-stop from 7.30 knocked you out; you had to go to bed early not only to recover but also to be able to get up so early again. If you were off for a day, it was generally acknowledged you'd 'slept in' because you were too exhausted. You needed to take a day off now and then just to catch up on sleep. I used to think it was a waste of time to take a day off work just to sleep until I found you really needed to. Some of the women 'slept in' regularly, about once every two weeks, so the absenteeism rate must have been quite high.

My diary was full of days when I was 'bursting inside', 'gone over my physical limit', 'whirring', or had 'pains in the chest and felt faint'. It must be bad for the heart to push yourself so hard, and work at a pace much faster than is normal for the body.

It certainly took years off their lives. Apart from looking worn out, they thought fifty was old and didn't expect to live much after sixty or retirement age. That was realistic statistically, given that manual workers have a much lower life expectancy than professional workers. The two labourers who died while I was there were just under sixty, and three other men were said to have dropped dead from heart attacks on the shopfloor during the past year. On my last day, one of the progress chasers, in his mid-forties, had a heart attack. Alice thought the fact it was only men who dropped dead at work proved that 'we women are much stronger'. But the older women did look really haggard and some had difficulty keeping up with the speed. ...

The struggle to keep going at such a basic physical level came as a shock to me; I hadn't anticipated what a strain the work would be and resented having to spend so much of my time out of work just recovering. Sleeping and eating became a much more central part of life. The other women were accustomed to it, but that made little difference — the work still took an enormous physical toll.

READING D   THE POLITICS OF SERVICE

G.Mars and M. Nicod

> In this game, you've always got to be one step ahead. If you let the customer get the upper hand, before you know where you are he'll be treading all over you — and then it'll be too late to do anything about it.
> (Hotel waiter)

It might be assumed that a waiter cannot easily choose what line of treatment he receives from those he serves. Certainly it might be thought difficult for a waiter to influence the customers when he is so obviously of lower status than they are. But waiters can seize and hold the initiative by skilful manipulation and by using subtle aggression. This is what Whyte referred to in his Chicago restaurant study, as 'getting the jump on the customer':

> The first question to ask when we look at the customer relationship is: 'does the waitress get the jump on the customer, or does the customer get the jump on the waitress?' The skilled waitress tackles the customer with confidence and without hesitation. The relationship is handled politely but firmly, and there is never any question as to who is in charge.
> (Whyte, 1946, pp.132–3)

Source: Mars, G. and Nicod, M. (1984) *The World of Waiters*, London, Allen & Unwin, pp.65, 79-88.

The waiter tries to get the jump

Although the customer is more likely to have the advantage over the waiter than vice versa, we find that the waiter, however passive his role may appear, will himself have some control. Usually both parties in a service encounter are sufficiently attuned to each other's role to avoid open confusion. The maintenance of this surface of agreement, this veneer of harmony or working consensus depends on each party feeling obliged to pay lip service to a crude overall definition of the situation. But people define situations in different ways. Thus, between waiter and customer in boundary-open transactions, a reciprocal show of affection, cordiality and good-will towards the other is maintained. In a boundary-closed trans-action, on the other hand, the waiter takes on the role of service specialist, anxious not to become too involved with the personal problems of his client, while the customer responds, from a standpoint of social distance, with a show of respect for the competence and integrity of the waiter performing his role.

Boundary-breaking devices

When there is a clear understanding that those being served share some, but not all, of the defining features of a boundary-open transaction, the waiter's ability to seize the initiative will often depend upon whether he can break down the remnants of the boundary dividing the server from the served. One waitress, when serving a family with a young child, for instance, would often adopt the following strategy. As soon as the family were seated and waiting to give their order, she would approach their table and then deliberately knock over the child's drink. In doing this, she would make it appear to be the child's fault. She would then take the initiative in sorting out the mêlée this caused, and at the same time put the whole family under an obligation to her. 'Don't worry, he's only a baby — I can easily get him another.' It is difficult for those of higher status to maintain formality and social distance when there is such an imbalance of obligation owed by them to those of lower status. This strategy had a further advantage for the waitress because she could arrange this switch in initiative without causing any loss of face on her customers' part, since it is generally agreed that children are irresponsible, not fully socialised and apt to cause accidents. ...

The printing of menus in French, a feature in nearly all higher level hotels, tends to shift the initiative to the waiter. His advantage arises because of uncertainty that its use causes a surprisingly high percentage of cus-tomers. One indeed cannot help but feel that this mystification is being deliberately fostered by many hotels as part of the English obsession with maintaining and enhancing social distance. Two American tourists com-plained in our second high-level London hotel because, after travelling for two months in Europe, they had looked forward to their arrival in England where people spoke their own language: 'But what do we find when we get here? ... A menu written in French just like the rest of the Continent!'

When a waiter comes across customers who obviously stumble over the French terms for food, he has increased flexibility in shifting the transaction to either the boundary-open or the boundary-closed mode. He can, that is to say, adopt the role either of friendly adviser or of relatively distant service specialist.

Some strategies, particularly in lower prestige restaurants, are especially designed to deritualise the waiter's performance. For example, some waiters swear in public to good effect: 'Oh bugger, I've dropped the bloody peas.' (In this case, words which caused one waiter to lose his job, were used here to accelerate intimacy between those served and those who serve. Much depends on the way the words are used to convey a particular meaning.) Others use slang, colloquialisms, expletives and familiar forms of address; or perhaps crack jokes, grin, or make light-hearted remarks designed to reduce the possibility of boundary-closure. ...

Taken together, devices of this kind provide a basis for the co-operative activity that follows. They are not, of course, part of the organisation's official strategy, but the impression the waiter is giving typically is not inconsistent with it. However, other strategies, if not kept a secret from the customer, *would* contradict and discredit the impression officially being fostered. Customers can be treated respectfully, face-to-face, then ridiculed, gossiped about, caricatured, cursed and criticised when the waiters are backstage: here, too, plans may be worked out for 'selling' things, 'touting' for tips or employing 'angles' against them.

Touting for tips takes several forms. For example, the waiter can provide larger portions, extra items, coffee with cream instead of milk, or special items normally in short supply, such as melba toast, or petits fours. This is often preceded by a phrase such as 'Would you like any extra ..., sir?' to make the customer aware that such treatment is provided as a special favour. It also means that the waiter may delay commitment or extricate himself from the situation, should the customer's response be inappropriate. ...

Operating outside the boundary

In the final analysis, though, the waiter must always show a proper concern for the trust placed in him by the people he serves: if a customer demonstrates complete faith in the waiter's judgement, nothing should be done that may destroy or damage this trust. For instance, if a waiter is asked to recommend something on the menu, he should suggest a wide range of dishes, not merely the most expensive ones. And the price of what the customer orders should make no difference to the service he receives. Similarly, the wine waiter in our second high-level London hotel thought that it was wrong to fill people's glasses to the brim. Quite apart from the fact that the wine's bouquet could not be fully appreciated, it made people drink faster and order more than they really wanted.

Whatever the waiter does, then, to ensure that he has control of the situation, it must always lie within the accepted limits of the service relationship. A waiter may advise, suggest, influence, persuade, badger, or cajole — but he must never *appear* to dictate from inside the boundary. Indeed, particularly in higher status hotels, a waiter may find it easier to control transactions from outside the boundary. Here the parties engaged in the transactions maintain the spirit of those consummating a coldly bargained agreement, not exchanging favours. Thus in such higher status hotels — whose staff can be categorised as being 'craft-oriented' — a waiter will take particular pride in the skills he uses to manipulate customers from the outside; and it is here that the service specialist is supreme.

Nonetheless, in boundary-closed transactions, the subordinate nature of personal service means that a waiter frequently feels a resentment that must remain unarticulated. While not wishing to render customer satisfaction impossible, a waiter may use his service skills to cheat or insult the customer, or at least cause some indefinable disquiet. To do this he must use strategies that combine subtle aggression with what should be able to pass for good professional conduct. One waiter we knew had developed a particularly effective method of inducing dissonance — especially when directed at the socially insecure. He would repeat all the orders offered by the customer in French but would do so with an emphasised accent at each repetition. He was able thereby to suggest that the hapless customer was obviously unused to expensive eating-out because he could not even pronounce the names of the dishes correctly!

Before he can engage in this kind of aggression, a waiter must first establish visibly that he is acting within the prescribed limits of his official role and that, on the surface at least, he accepts certain moral obligations. Thus, some customers prefer him not to intrude or come too close because they can never be sure to whom he will convey their secrets. Knowing this, the waiter may lower his voice as he enters their presence, throwing himself, as it were, into the role of being seen but not heard. In doing so, he appeals to those he serves to treat him as if he were not present; as someone who can be relied on to keep their secrets and not betray their trust. In our high-level London hotels, the waiters frequently dropped their voices to a whisper whenever they entered a customer's presence. ...

A second distancing technique the waiter can employ is to make use of politely formal terms, such as 'sir', 'madam', 'Mr. X', or 'Mrs X', whenever he addresses customers directly. Behind their backs he may refer to them by bare surname, first name, nickname, or some title which relegates them to an abstract category: for example, 'pig', 'peasant', 'snob', 'regular'. If the waiter wishes to maintain some dignity while making clear the disrespect he really feels, he may adopt a slighting pronunciation, say, an exaggerated emphasis upon the 'sir' or 'madam'. Given that customers are treated relatively well to their faces, they cannot isolate discourtesy implied by the tone of voice, mannerisms, innuendoes, or *double entendres* that the waiter may use to heap abuse or familiarity upon them. Nor can customers, by implication, effectively bring an official complaint against a waiter without more substantial evidence than mere subtle discourtesy.

We have suggested two standard ways in which waiters keep their distance — by lowering their voices and through politely formal terms of address. So long as the line is sustained, the waiter can then freely use his special knowledge and experience to derogate the customer's dignity with impunity. Because of the mass of rules and (often spurious) expertise surrounding dining out and social etiquette, as the specialist the waiter is ultimately always in a stronger position than those he serves. A good example of this occurred in our second London hotel when a customer complained that the brandy he had been given was not Rémy-Martin as he had ordered, but a less expensive one. By taking the glass back and returning impassively with it a little later, the waiter managed to create the impression that the brandy *might* have been changed for the kind which the customer had ordered. On the other hand it might not. In fact, it was the same glass of brandy and the customer had been deceived, but it would take a particularly confident customer to send it back a second time. ...

Perhaps the cruellest treatment that waiters can mete out is when a customer makes a complaint or orders something, and this is formally acknowledged, but then he receives something he did not really bargain for. Thus whenever someone ordered lobster bisque in our first London hotel, he was frequently taken by surprise to find the brandy poured into the soup and lit. Those who did not know better would wait several minutes until the flames subsided. Depending upon whether he wanted to 'give the customer a hard time', the waiter might intervene and show him how to dip his spoon into the soup and not get burnt. ...

[The] waiter [might get] the jump by an elaborate display of craft expertise. The same result may be achieved by reversing the strategy: by putting on an equally conspicuous display of incompetence, presented as a willingness to go to extremes, in order to meet customers' expectations which are inappropriate. One waitress explains:

> I remember one family coming in that looked right out of place, not frozen steak types, frozen faces, though. Son in his mid-twenties, mother and sister, I should think. He had tiny little feet with very highly polished shoes. I couldn't help noticing because he didn't once look at me while he was ordering, kept swinging his foot up and down and watching that. They got on to the wine list, which had one or two reasonable ones — nothing special — and after a big discussion he asked me for a bottle of Mateus Rosé, 'well-chilled'. We kept a couple in the fridge door, so I brought one of those through. Wouldn't do at all: 'I said "chilled", not cooled.' I looked as sorry as I could, went back to the bar and got the big iron bucket we used for tipping the slops into. I filled it up with all the ice I could find — great big blocks — stuck the bottle on top and brought the whole lot back into the restaurant. I had to lift it over people's heads, so they all noticed. I put it on a spare table — they were small and very close together — and said, 'That should be chilled in about a quarter of an hour, sir. Would you like your starter now?' He tipped me about 20 per cent of the bill.
> (Waitress, Steak house)

The same informant provided us with a downmarket example of maintaining — or retrieving — dignity by conveying disrespect for the customer in such a way that it provides no clear ground for complaint.

Sometimes a party of half-a-dozen would come in and you could tell before they'd even sat down that they'd want the cheapest meal we did. But they'd spend ages eating all the rolls, drinking water and pretending to discuss it. Then, 'Miss! We'd like to order now, please', and a hand pulling at your sleeve if you were hovering too close. I'd usually have the order written down already, or pretend to, so I could look straight at them while they went round the table: 'I *think* I'll have the plaice and French fries'; 'Yes, that'll do me — I'm not very hungry'; 'Well, I won't be difficult.' Then I'd look at my pad and nod: 'Six fish and chips — right away, sir.'

Finally, if a customer chooses to put the waiter under pressure, he may be mistreated or 'taught a lesson' to his face. Where the waiter is abused by those he serves, he may well decide that the relationship has 'blown' and cannot be restored. In such circumstances he may aim to cause humiliation or discomfort — at least to the extent that a real transition takes place in relative power, standing and authority. When a customer complained loudly in our second London hotel that he had been brought a plate of scallops when he had ordered mussels, the waiter knew that he had made no mistake, but gave him the opportunity to choose again. The customer then asked for a lobster or prawn salad but did not specify which. The waiter, choosing to cause him the maximum possible inconvenience and expense, ordered the dressed lobster, the most expensive on the menu, which took twenty to thirty minutes to prepare (the prawn salad at a third of the price would have taken five minutes). Customer complaints can usually be coped with: the aim is to contain them. When they are delivered loudly, and are therefore made public, however, containment ceases to be an option.

References

Whyte, W.F. (1946) *Human Relations in the Restaurant Industry*, New York, McGraw Hill.

ACKNOWLEDGEMENTS

Grateful acknowledgement is made to the following sources for permission to reproduce material in this book:

CHAPTER 1: *Text:* *Reading A:* Therborn, G., extracts from 'The rule of capital and theories of democracy', in *New Left Review*, vol. 103, 1977; *Reading B:* Konrad, G., extracts from *Anti Politics*, Quartet Books, London 1984 and Harcourt Brace Jovanovich, NY; *Reading C:* Bobbio, N. *The Future of Democracy*, pp.37–9, Polity Press, 1987; *Reading D:* Sadurski, W. 'Populism and the constitution', *Polityka*, 8 Sept., 1990. Permission to reproduce translation granted by *Polityka*, Warsaw, Poland. *Illustrations: pp.16, 17, 19, 29:* Mansell Collection; *pp.24,37:* Popperfoto; *p.33:* Paul Lowe/Network; *p.45:* Justin Leighton/Network; *p.48:* Richard Kalvar/Magnum.

CHAPTER 2: *Text:* *Reading A:* Alber, J. 'Continuities and changes in the idea of the welfare state', *Politics and Society*, pp.415–67, vol.16, no.4, 1988, Butterworth, Heinemann, Mass.; *Readings B and D:* Pierson, C., 'Social democracy and the coming of the Keynesian welfare state'; 'The welfare state as "the crisis of crisis management": Offe', *Beyond the Welfare State*, Polity Press, 1991; *Reading C:* Miliband, R. © Ralph Miliband 1989. Reprinted from *Divided Societies* by Ralph Miliband (1989) by permission of Oxford University Press. *Tables:* *Tables 2.1, 2.3, 2.4, 2.6:* Rose, R. 'The growth in central government departments, 1849–1982', 'Public employment as a percentage of national employment, 1951–80', 'Changes in employment in major functional programmes, 1951–80', 'Changes in the scale of major public programmes in the UK', from *Big Government*, pp.132, 136, 157, 193, Sage Publications Ltd, 1984; *Table 2.2:* Berger, J. 'Public expenditure in fifteen OECD countries', from 'Market and state in advanced capitalist societies', in Martinelli, A. and Smelser, N. *Economy and Society*, © International Sociological Association, Sage Publications Ltd, 1990; *Table 2.5:* Tilly, C., 'Military expenditure as a percentage of state budgets 1850–1975', *Coercion Capital and European States*, Basil Blackwell Inc., 1990. © Charles Tilly 1990; *Tables 2.8, 2.9:* Kennedy, P., 'War expenditure and total mobilised forces, 1914–19', 'Armaments production of the powers, 1940–43', *The Rise and Fall of the Great Powers*, Alfred A. Knopf Inc. 1987; *Table 2.11:* from Goldthorpe, J. *Order and Conflict in Contemporary Capitalism*, Table 3.1, reprinted by permission of Oxford University Press. *Illustrations:* *p.80:* One of a set of promotional photographs distributed by the firm of Krupp in 1892. From a copy held in Chicago University Library; *p.82:* Culver Pictures; *p.83:* Reproduced from *Women in Wartime: The Role of Women's Magazines 1939–1945*, Jane Waller and Michael Vaughan-Rees, Macdonald Optima, 1987; *p.88:* Freedom Press; *p.100:* Popperfoto; *p.107:* From David Harvey, *The Condition of Postmodernity*, 1989, Basil Blackwell; *p.110:* Associated Press/Martin Cleaver. *Figures:* *Figure 2.3:* Kingdom, P., 'Pressure groups and policy communities', *Government and Politics in the UK*, p.421, Polity Press, 1991; *p.126:* Offe, C., Keane, J., figure illustrating structure of welfare capitalism taken from *Contradictions of the Welfare State*, Hutchinson, 1984.

CHAPTER 3: *Text:* *Reading B:* Melucci, A. *Nomads of the Present*, pp.70–3 (extracts), Hutchinson Radius, 1989; *Reading C:* Rucht, D., 'The strategies and action repertoires of new movements', in Dalton, R., Kuechler, M. (eds) *Challenging the Political Order*, Polity Press, 1990; *Reading D:* McCarthy, J., Zald, M. *Social Movements in an Organizational Society*, pp.21–5 (extracts), Transaction Books, 1987; *Reading E:* Kitschelt, H., 'Political opportunity structures and political protest', *British Journal of Political Science*, Cambridge University Press, vol.16, 1986; *Reading F:* Szabó, M., 'Sozale Bewegungen, Mobilisierung und Demokratisierung in Ungarn', in Deppe, R. Dubiel, H., Rödel, U. (eds) *Demokratischer Umbruch in Osteuropa*, Suhrkamp Verlag 1991 (translated by Alan Scott for the Open University). *Illustrations:* *p.134:* Otto Griebel *Die Internationale* (1929) 125x185 cm. Sächsische Landesbibliothek Abt. Deutsche Photothek Richter; *p.135:* Curt Querner *Demonstration* (1930) 87x66 cm. Staatliche Museen zu Berlin, National-Galerie; *p.138:* Justin Leighton/Network; *p.144:* Raissa Page/Format; *p.149:* Melanie Friend/Format; *p.157:* Greenpeace/James.

CHAPTER 4: *Text:* *Reading B:* Turner, B.S., 'Outline of a theory of citizenship', *Sociology*, vol. 24, no. 2, May 1990. Reproduced by permission of the author and the British Sociological Association; *Reading E:* Marshall, T.H., 'Citizen and social class', in *Citizenship and Social Class and Other Essays*, 1950, Cambridge University Press; *Reading F:* Pateman, C., *The Disorder of Women*, 1989, Polity Press. *Illustrations:* *pp.184, 186, 191:* Mary Evans Picture Library; *p.188:* Punch; *p.193:* Communist Party of Great Britain Picture Library; *p.195:* Associated Newspapers Ltd; *p.200:* LSE Information Office.

INDEX